25.00

INTERNATIONAL STUDIES

THE MIDDLE EAST IN
CHINA'S FOREIGN POLICY 1949–1977

INTERNATIONAL STUDIES

Published for the Centre for International Studies,
London School of Economics and Political Science

The Centre for International Studies at the London School of
Economics and Political Science was established in 1967 with the aid
of a grant from the Ford Foundation. Its aim is to promote research
and advanced training on a multi-disciplinary basis in the general field
of international studies.

   To this end the Centre sponsors research projects and seminars and
endeavours to secure the publication of manuscripts arising out of
them.

Whilst the Editorial Board accepts responsibility for recommending
the inclusion of a volume in the series, the author is alone responsible
for the views and opinions expressed.

ALSO IN THIS SERIES

THE MIDDLE EAST IN
CHINA'S FOREIGN POLICY
1949–1977

YITZHAK SHICHOR
Executive Director, the Harry S. Truman Research Institute, and
Lecturer, Department of East Asian Studies at the
Hebrew University of Jerusalem

CAMBRIDGE UNIVERSITY PRESS

CAMBRIDGE

LONDON · NEW YORK · MELBOURNE

Published by the Syndics of the Cambridge University Press
The Pitt Building, Trumpington Street, Cambridge CB2 1RP
Bentley House, 200 Euston Road, London NW1 2DB
32 East 57th Street, New York, NY 10022, USA
296 Beaconsfield Parade, Middle Park, Melbourne 3206, Australia

© Cambridge University Press 1979

First published 1979

Printed in Great Britain by
Western Printing Services Ltd, Bristol

Library of Congress Cataloguing in Publication Data
Shichor, Yitzhak.
The Middle East in China's foreign policy, 1949–1977.
(International studies)
Bibliography: p.
Includes index.
1. Near East – Foreign relations – China. 2. China –
Foreign relations – Near East. I. Title.
DS63.2.C5S52   327.51′056   78-58801
ISBN 0 521 22214 1

TO MY FATHER

CONTENTS

TABLES

ABBREVIATIONS

AAPSO	Afro-Asian People's Solidarity Organisation
CB	*Current Background*, published by US Consulate General, Hong Kong
CCP	Chinese Communist Party
CPPCC	Chinese People's Political Consultative Conference
CPSU	Communist Party of the Soviet Union
ECMM	*Extracts from China's Mainland Magazines*, published by US Consulate General, Hong Kong
JMJP	*Jen-min jih-pao (People's Daily)*
JPRS	*Joint Publication Research Service*
NCNA	New China News Agency
NPC	National People's Congress
OPEC	Oil Producing and Exporting Countries
PDFLP	People's Democratic Front for the Liberation of Palestine
PDRY	People's Democratic Republic of Yemen
PFLOAG	People's Front for the Liberation of the Occupied Arabian Gulf
PFLP	People's Front for the Liberation of Palestine
PLO	Palestine Liberation Organisation
PR	*Peking Review*
PRC	People's Republic of China
SCCS	*Shih-chieh chih-shih (World Knowledge)*
SCMM	*Selections from China's Mainland Magazines*, published by US Consulate General, Hong Kong
SCMP	*Survey of China Mainland Press*, published by US Consulate General, Hong Kong
SWB/FE	*Summary of World Broadcasts, the Far East*, BBC
SWB/ME	*Summary of World Broadcasts, the Middle East*, BBC
UAR	United Arab Republic

Note on the transliteration

Chinese has been transliterated according to the Wade–Giles system; Arabic has been romanised according to the University of London's *Bulletin of the School of Oriental and African Studies*, except when another form is more familiar such as Nasser (instead of Nāṣir), Kassem (instead of Qāsim), or Yasser Arafat (instead of Yāsir ʿArāfāt).

PREFACE

In the past decade or so great progress has been made in the study of China's foreign policy and international behaviour. Yet, whereas Peking's policy in Asia, Africa and even Latin America, has been extensively treated, the role of the Middle East in its foreign policy has not received adequate attention. One reason for this, I believe, has been that China's performance in the Middle East since the 1950s has not secured for it any influence comparable to that of other powers. While these powers have been able to establish definite zones of influence and some presence in the Middle East, China is still considered an outsider in the area. By implication, therefore, it has been assumed that the Middle East has always played a marginal role in China's calculations.

This study attempts to correct this view by providing a comprehensive analysis of China's Middle East policy. It concerns not so much China's relations with the Middle East (though, necessarily, these will be discussed as well) as the role of the Middle East in China's world outlook. The main argument is that, although the Chinese, for many objective and subjective reasons, which will be dealt with later on, have been unable or unwilling to increase their influence and presence in the Middle East, they have never lost sight of its importance in their strategy and foreign policy considerations.

The term 'Middle East' used in this study does not correspond exactly to the Chinese usage. In fact, the Chinese themselves do not have a precise definition of this term. Sometimes they use *Chin-tung* (Near East) and sometimes *Chung-tung* (Middle East), or even both together – *Chung-chin-tung* (Middle and Near East). As they have explained, these ambiguous terms were created by the Europeans, for whom the Far East included the countries bordering the Pacific; the Near East included the countries of South Europe, Northeast Africa and Southwest Asia, where the three continents meet; and the Middle East comprised the countries between the Far East and the Near East.[1] As in

many other fields in the early 1950s, the Chinese adopted the
Soviet definition which was not altogether different from the
European one: the Middle East included Iran and Afghanistan,
and the Near East Turkey, Syria, the Lebanon, Iraq, Israel,
Trans-Jordan, Saudi Arabia, the Yemen and South Arabia, Cyprus
and also Egypt and the Sudan.[2]

Nonetheless, the ambiguity remained. Sometimes the Chinese
regarded Iraq as part of the Middle East and Egypt and the
Sudan as part of Africa. Indeed, the publishers of a book on Near
and Middle East countries specifically noted that Egypt and the
Sudan had been excluded as being part of Africa.[3]

Officially, the Chinese usually adopted the term 'West Asia'
(or even 'Southwest Asia'). Middle Eastern affairs were handled
in China's Foreign Ministry either by the Department of West
Asia and Africa (1956–64 and 1969–72) or, even more specifically,
by the Department of West Asia and North Africa (1964–9 and
since 1972), which covered the 'Middle East' exclusively.

As far as the management of China's foreign relations is concerned, combining the Middle East with Africa, let alone North
Africa, was logical as well as convenient, not only because of
their many common characteristics but also because Egypt,
which was the first country in the area to establish full diplomatic
relations with the People's Republic of China (PRC), provided
the Chinese with an essential link between the Middle East and
Africa and a base of operations in both. Accordingly, Chinese
diplomats in the Middle East, as well as those in charge of Middle
Eastern affairs in the Foreign Ministry, were replaced until
recently more often by Africa-trained personnel (and *vice versa*)
than by diplomats with Asian experience. However, as far as
China's strategic outlook is concerned, there is little doubt that
the Chinese perceived the Middle East from their own particular
vantage point, much more as 'West' Asia and with definite implications for China's security problems. This has been particularly
true of those periods when the Chinese have been especially
sensitive to possible encirclement, as in the early 1950s and since
the early 1970s, and is reflected in the background and experience
of China's diplomats.

This work deals with China's policy in the area bordered by
Turkey in the north, Iran in the east, South Arabia in the south,
and Egypt in the west, not including North Africa and the Sudan.
For mere convenience this whole area is referred to as 'the Middle
East'.

This study is the outcome of several years of research in Israel and London, and is based on a Ph.D. thesis submitted to the University of London. In pursuing this research, and my interest in China in general, I have been encouraged and looked after by Professor Harold Z. Schiffrin and Professor Ellis Joffe of the Hebrew University of Jerusalem. During my stay in London I benefited greatly by the continuous and stimulating advice of Michael B. Yahuda of the London School of Economics and Political Science, as well as by the comments of Michael Leifer and John Gittings. I am deeply grateful to all of them. I also feel deeply indebted to the following foundations which kindly provided me with generous financial support, without which this study would not have been completed: the Kadoorie Family Fund for Chinese Studies (a project of the Fund for Higher Education in Israel); the Lady Davis Fellowship Trust and the Leonard Davis Institute for International Relations, the Hebrew University of Jerusalem. In revising the original study and preparing its final draft, I enjoyed the facilities and resources of the Hebrew University's Harry S. Truman Research Institute.

Last, but not least, I owe this study to the patient understanding and co-operation of my wife and children who allowed me, despite the difficulties, to devote myself to research. First and foremost, it has been done at *their* expense.

Jerusalem   Yitzhak Shichor
December 1977

INTRODUCTION

One of the basic assumptions of this study is that the Chinese
have always been concerned with developments in the Middle
East not merely as an important centre of international activity
in its own right but primarily as a part of the general historical
development of the world which affected and involved China's
own interests. The Chinese communists' interest in the Middle
East, which had long preceded the actual establishment of relations, has been closely associated with their perception of the
world situation. In Mao Tse-tung's view the world has been under-
going significant changes since World War II. The traditional
'old-colonialist' powers, such as Germany, Italy, Britain and
France, began to decline, having been forced to abandon their
overseas possessions. Instead, two antagonistic great powers
emerged, the United States and the Soviet Union which aimed at
overcoming each other. Both realised that this would not be
possible before gaining control over the vast area lying between
them, to which Mao referred in 1946 as the 'intermediate zone'.
The competition between the superpowers (the First World) over
the intermediate zone (the Second and Third Worlds), according
to Mao, has been the essence of post-war international relations.

In the late 1940s and 1950s, while the Soviets were on the
defensive, it was the United States which started its 'aggressive'
expansion in an attempt to 'fill the gap' created by the withdrawal of the traditional powers. In the 1960s, the post-Stalin
Soviet revisionist leadership, instead of concentrating on driving
the Americans out of the intermediate zone, began to expand and
compete with the United States over the control of this area. In
the 1970s, after the United States had been forced to retreat
under the pressure of the national liberation movements in Asia,
Africa and Latin America, it was the Soviet Union which was
gaining ground in an attempt to 'fill the gap'. For the Chinese,
who consider themselves part of the Third World, the superpowers' contest over the intermediate zone has always been a

source of anxiety. In their view, control of this area by a hostile power would not only precipitate a third world war but also, and not less important from Peking's standpoint, seriously endanger the survival of the PRC. This theory, which intertwined the fate of the world with that of China, provided the common ground and interests on which China has been conducting its foreign policy in the Second and Third Worlds.

China's Middle East policy reflected these considerations and particularly its sensitivity to external threats. Apparently, the Chinese have always believed that the Middle East, though far from China's borders, was nevertheless a crucial link in any attempt to encircle China and threaten the Chinese communist regime. Actually, Peking conceived of the Middle East as much more than merely a link. Because of its rich oil resources and its strategic location at the crossroads of Asia, Africa and Europe, the Chinese sometimes regarded this area as one of the main keys for the control of the intermediate zone. At times they even thought that the final outcome of the struggle between the United States and the Soviet Union would be determined in this region.

China's fundamental and consistent interest in the Middle East has been, therefore, not only to obtain diplomatic recognition and political support but, above all, to prevent the domination of the Middle East by a hostile power – be it Germany, the United States or the Soviet Union. In the Middle East Peking concentrated on urging the local governments and national liberation movements to resist foreign intervention and drive the superpowers out of the area.

This has been the 'principal contradiction'. The Chinese hardly seem to recognise the existence of any problem in the Middle East (or anywhere else in the Third World) which has not been created or sustained by foreign intervention to legitimise its persistence. Peking's interest in internal or inter-Arab issues was primarily governed and motivated by international considerations, i.e., in the light of the 'principal contradiction'. Peking reiterated that local problems should be settled by the local peoples alone and that no Middle East problem could be settled thoroughly before outside intervention, which had caused or sustained it, was liquidated. Obviously, the Chinese were primarily interested in the withdrawal of foreign powers rather than in the settlement of Middle East problems.

These Chinese attitudes have never changed but China's policy has undergone several changes since 1949. This does not mean that the Chinese merely adapted themselves to the changing circumstances in the Middle East. Rather, at any given time these changes reflected China's over-all analysis of the world situation and its relations with the superpowers. As the Chinese have said, the centre of world contradictions was not fixed and immutable but shifted with the changes in the international struggles and the revolutionary situation. Obviously, China's position and policy in the Middle East were also affected by local, as well as domestic, developments, but China's basic attitudes to the region were governed by a more general appraisal of the global situation, apparently made by Mao Tse-tung himself.

Thus, China's policy in the Middle East corresponded to fundamental perceptions of international affairs. When they believed that the world situation was becoming tense because of increased attempts by one superpower or both to intervene in the intermediate zone, the Chinese awareness of the importance of the Middle East and its relevance to China's security would increase; they would also intensify their demands of Middle East governments or national liberation movements to join their side and firmly resist the 'enemy'. Simultaneously, the Chinese would become less tolerant and more critical of local phenomena which, in their view, could undermine such resistance and which, in periods of relaxation, they would usually overlook (for example, persecution of Arab communists, inter-Arab rivalries, neutralism and non-alignment, and so on). All these were regarded as secondary matters which should await the settlement of the principal struggle – that with foreign intervention. China's intolerance, militancy and interference, followed by disappointments, might, during a period of tension, result in mutual Sino-Arab suspicions leading to cool, sometimes deteriorating, relations.

On the other hand, when they believed the powers were on the retreat, ready to relinquish some use of force, at least for the time being, the Chinese tended to lose interest in the Middle East; they would also become more tolerant of, or, more likely, indifferent to, internal or inter-Arab affairs.

This study is built chronologically around such a tension–relaxation sequence. The shifts in China's Middle East policy have been so closely connected with Peking's perception of the world situation and international developments that I have found the chronological, rather than the thematic, method of presentation more suitable in providing a faithful picture of China's Middle East policy.

In the early 1950s, when the Chinese believed they were threatened by a Western offensive, they were also concerned about Western attempts to draw Middle Eastern countries into a ring of military pacts surrounding China and the socialist camp. Adopting a more rigid international behaviour, which corresponded with the rather revolutionary mood at home, China regarded most, if not all, of the Middle East governments as lackeys of imperialism and its Middle East policy was governed by mistrust and reservations.

In the mid-1950s, following the cease-fire in Korea and Indochina, the world situation seemed much more relaxed and the domestic scene stabilised. By then, Peking had already realised that some Middle Eastern governments, notwithstanding their 'backward' political nature, were capable of contributing to the struggle against imperialism, and were also prepared to recognise the PRC. Initial relations were established and the Chinese forgot their previous reservations, though only temporarily.

In the late 1950s, however, the Chinese were once again alarmed to perceive a new Western offensive. The fact that this offensive centred on the Middle East, with threats to Syria, hostility to the Iraqi revolution and landings in the Lebanon and Jordan, further convinced Peking that this region was a key battlefield for control of the intermediate zone. China's reaction was to urge the Arabs to overcome their secondary contradictions in order to unite internally (including the communists) as well as externally, both among themselves and together with the Soviet Union and the socialist camp in order to adopt firm and uncompromising opposition to the West. These demands and evaluations, undoubtedly influenced also by the extremes of the Great Leap Forward, were denied not only by the Arabs but also by the Soviets, leading to a serious deterioration in Sino-Arab (and Sino-Soviet) relations. Consequently, in the early 1960s China lost much of its previous interest in the Middle East, not only because of the disagreements with the Arabs but primarily because of a new Chinese analysis of a relaxed world situation, growing interest in Africa, and the domestic retrenchment and recovery following the debacle of the Great Leap Forward.

In the mid-1960s, facing the combined hostility of both the United States and the Soviet Union, Peking responded in an unprecedented effort to win and mobilise Asian, African, and particularly Middle Eastern, governments against the two superpowers, using a variety of political and economic appeals. As in the late 1950s, these efforts failed completely, causing China more setbacks and disappointments, and by the late 1960s, as the Cultural Revolution was sweeping across China, Peking once more lost interest in the Middle East and Sino-Arab relations continued to deteriorate.

From 1969 to 1971, China's foreign policy was governed by the growing Soviet military threat along its northern borders. The Chinese, apparently under the influence of Lin Piao, concentrated their attention on Asia, actually rejecting American attempts at reconciliation. The Middle East still remained beyond the realm of China's immediate interests and, although formal relations with Arab governments were restored, the Chinese also resumed, and even gave preference to, their support for local national liberation movements.

Following the downfall of Lin Piao in the summer of 1971, Mao's and Chou En-lai's imprints were felt again in China's analysis of the world situation and in its international behaviour. Publicly, Peking became less concerned with the immediate Soviet threat to China and more with Moscow's increased attempts to control Europe, the Middle East, Africa and Asia, aiming at encircling China also from the south and securing their rear for an eventual attack. On the other hand, convinced that the United States was on the decline and no longer endangering them, the Chinese normalised relations with Washington and even began to approve of its anti-Soviet policies. This political investment paid huge dividends as the PRC was universally recognised and admitted to the United Nations. In the Middle East, which they now regarded as a main focus in the struggle between the super-powers, the Chinese preferred to stabilise relations with established governments, which in their view provided firmer opposition to the superpowers, particularly the USSR, rather than to cultivate revolutionary groups.

It seems, therefore, that the Middle East was far from marginal in China's world outlook and foreign policy considerations. Its achievements in the Middle East were, however, rather limited, at least until recently. The PRC gained its first foothold in the Middle East more than twenty years ago, in the mid-1950s. At that time China, which had been an outcast in the world community and rejected by the United Nations, was offered full diplomatic relations by only two Middle Eastern countries, Egypt and Syria. Since then, and particularly since the early 1970s,

China's international position has improved tremendously. Maintaining diplomatic, economic and cultural relations with most of the Middle Eastern countries and, furthermore, being a member of the Security Council, China has acquired an unprecedented potential capacity for playing a more effective role in Middle Eastern affairs.

Yet today, despite the most extensive Chinese network of foreign relations, China's real influence in and on the Middle East is probably as small as it was in the mid-1950s. This shortcoming can be attributed to several objective and, even more important, subjective factors. Among the objective factors the most important are:

One, the traditional and historical distance. Although there had been cultural, commercial and diplomatic links between the Chinese imperial dynasties and the Arabs, dating back to the second century B.C., several hundred years before Islam emerged, the Arabs were always on the periphery of the Chinese world order. These scanty traditional relations could in no way provide a sufficient basis, despite the Chinese communists' attempts, for renewing, improving or forming new relations between the PRC and the Arab countries. This also applies to the Islamic community which has existed in China since the T'ang Dynasty. The ten or so million Muslims of some dozen nationalities (less than 2 per cent of the total population) which remained in the PRC were too weak and detached from the main Islamic centres to have been able to bridge the cultural and ideological gap between Chinese communism and the Arabs. In fact, the existence of a Muslim minority in the PRC could, and sometimes did, have an adverse effect on Sino-Arab relations.

Two, the completely different cultural background and political belief systems, especially the image of China's commitment to radical, revolutionary and militant communism. Apart from vague anti-imperialist postures, there is very little in common between the Arabs and the Chinese. The Arabs' fundamental hostility to communism and communists, particularly Chinese, derived from religion as well as from nationalism, had not only delayed the establishment of relations with China but later also kept these relations at a distance, sometimes leading to serious deterioration. Although Maoist doctrines and some of China's achievements were outwardly admired by the Arabs, particularly the so-called radicals, they were basically rejected as unsuitable for conditions in the Middle East. The Arabs' suspicions of China made it difficult for the Chinese to operate in the Middle East, particularly under the watchful eyes of the Arab bourgeois–military regimes.

Three, China's limited capabilities. Whereas the Arab countries were still able to accord the PRC diplomatic recognition and establish diplomatic relations with it, there was almost nothing China could offer the Arabs in political, economic and military terms. Consequently, there was not even one field in which the Arabs were in any way dependent on the Chinese. As a result, China never had a leverage on the Arab governments and could never exert significant pressure on them.

Four, the influence and presence of the superpowers in the Middle East. Unlike in some parts of Africa, where the Chinese were able to step into a political vacuum created by the reluctance of the great powers to become involved, the Chinese found no room in the Middle East for such penetration. Parts of the Middle East which had been under Western influence were, and to some extent still are, basically hostile to the PRC. In other parts, where the Soviets had become predominant, the Chinese managed to establish correct diplomatic, economic and cultural relations. However, as the Sino-Soviet conflict unfolded, it damaged the Chinese position in the Middle East, rather than Moscow's. The erosion of the Soviet presence since the early 1970s, although hardly attributed to Chinese policy, can be regarded as its initial success in the area.

In addition to these objective circumstances there were also some very important subjective considerations which limited China's performance in the Middle East. Although the Chinese undoubtedly sought influence in the Middle East as elsewhere, their methods and aims were completely different from those of the other powers. Fundamentally, the Chinese needed Arab support not so much to enhance China's position in the Middle East, but more negatively, against the two superpowers. Unlike these powers, China never showed any interest in territorial expansion or in building overseas bases. Consequently, means for such a venture (navy, strategic air force, extensive aid programme) were never developed.

In principle, the Chinese tried to avoid military or even political involvement in matters which had no direct bearing on China's national security. China's foreign policy as well as revolutionary strategy always stressed self-reliance, meaning that Third World countries and national liberation movements should count primarily on their own resources in resisting foreign domination and intervention. China's support, whenever and wherever required by the Arabs, was generally restricted to rhetoric and symbolic material aid.

Finally, since the struggle against imperialism and social-imperialism has become the central theme of China's foreign policy, Peking tried to avoid any identification with the super-powers and refused to take part in any international or United Nations' initiative which invoked the United States and the Soviet Union. This was particularly evident in the case of the Middle East, where the Chinese consistently declined to use their new potential as members of the United Nations and the Security Council in settling its problems.

China's peculiar methods and aims in the Middle East and its primary concern with the superpowers were not always fully understood and sometimes deliberately distorted. The Arabs, who had experienced colonial rule and foreign, both Western and Eastern, intervention for many years, interpreted China's Middle East policy in those terms and did not seem to understand China's different approach. For a long time the Chinese were portrayed as a disruptive, subversive, dangerous and irresponsible element in the Middle East. Allegedly they supported 'radical' and 'left wing' Marxists secretly or openly, seeking to overthrow the national–bourgeois governments of the Middle East and promote a socialist revolution.

There is not much evidence to substantiate these allegations. Usually the Chinese stepped in to defend Arab communism, to condemn the Arab leaders, or to support local national liberation movements, only in the context of opposition to foreign intervention and only at times when they perceived imminent 'aggression' in the Middle East or elsewhere, occasions which required firm resistance. Considering the distance between China and the Middle East, China's limited economic, military and transportation capabilities, the lack of common background and traditional relations between Chinese communism and Arab communism and all the other limiting factors mentioned above, Chinese subversion in the Middle East has never been a serious threat. Since its foundation, China's main concern in the Middle East has always been with imperialism, social-imperialism, or both.

1 : CHINA'S ENCOUNTER WITH THE MIDDLE EAST

The beginning of China's active policy in the Middle East is generally linked to the Bandung Conference (April 1955), at which Chinese and Arab leaders met for the first time. This meeting led to cultural, economic and eventually diplomatic relations between Peking and several Arab countries. Yet the origins of the Chinese communists' Middle Eastern policy can be traced back to the early 1940s, long before the Bandung Conference or even the establishment of the PRC.

The origins of China's Middle Eastern policy

It was during World War II that Mao and his colleagues became fully aware of the strategic importance of the Middle East. In 1941–2 they first realised that the control of this area by hostile powers could determine the fate of the world, as well as the survival of the Chinese communist movement and China's future as a national and independent entity. Seemingly isolated from the rest of the world in Yenan's caves and preoccupied with the Japanese and the Kuomintang (KMT), Mao and the Chinese Communist Party (CCP) leaders, nonetheless, observed the international situation very carefully.

In the spring of 1941, and then the summer and autumn of 1942, some anxiety about German control of the Middle East could be detected in Chinese communist publications. With the collapse of the Allied offensive in the Balkans in April–May 1941, the whole of southern Europe fell to the Germans. The next target was the Middle East. Syria, then under a French Mandate, had already submitted to the Vichy Government which had been collaborating with Germany. Then, in early April, a pro-German clique, headed by Rashīd ʿAlī al-Kaylānī, seized power from the pro-British government in Iraq. Prospects of German occupation of the Middle East suddenly became very real.

To the Chinese in Yenan, these developments were ominous and irritating. The CCP had previously predicted (and, in fact, expected) that because of the lull on the European front Allied efforts would be channelled to the Far East, thus easing Japanese pressure on China; instead, not only did the Middle East become the main theatre of war, but an Axis victory there would imply yet a further threat to China. German control over the Middle East, with its oil fields and strategic crossroads, could lead to the collapse of Britain and its colonies and thereby divert Axis efforts towards the Pacific. The restlessness which accompanied the deteriorating situation in the Middle East is reflected in Chinese communist organs, which made extensive use of news agency dispatches, as well as editorials and commentaries.[1]

In one of them, Ch'iao Kuan-hua, then New China News Agency (NCNA) political commentator and journalist and later China's Foreign Minister (November 1974 to December 1976), analysed the situation in the Middle East. In his view, the region was becoming the crucial microcosm of the World War. He expressed concern about possible German plans to use Syria as a base in an imminent attempt to come to Iraq's rescue against British forces and simultaneously to attack Egypt. Although the article had been written at a time when the Soviet–German Pact was still in force, it was somewhat sympathetic to the Allies, expressing relief about the United States' decision to come to their aid in the Middle East.[2]

A day after this article was published, an editorial (attributed to Mao Tse-tung) appeared in Yenan's *Chieh-fang jih-pao* (*Liberation Daily*). Although much more in tune with the official Soviet stand against Britain and the United States, it nevertheless explicitly pointed to the undesirable effects of events in the Middle East on China (something only implied in Ch'iao Kuan-hua's article), namely, the danger of Germany progressing through the Middle East to the Far East and joining forces with Japan.[3]

By August, however, the situation in the Middle East had changed. The German advance had been arrested: a pro-British government was re-established in Iraq in June 1941; British and Free French troops occupied Syria in mid-July; in late August Britain and the Soviet Union seized control of Iran; the North African front was also stabilised. Although the Chinese communists attributed these successes mainly to the transfer of German troops to the Russian front and did not consider them a decisive turn in the war, they were, nevertheless, satisfied and relieved. The German setback in the Middle East meant for them that the land and sea supply routes (particularly the Persian Gulf) would continue to be used by the British and Americans, and that the German drive towards the Far East and the Baku oil fields had been cut off.[4]

The Germans, however, renewed their *Drang nach Osten* in yet another pincer movement in the summer of 1942. In June they reached al-'Alamayn, only 80 km west of Alexandria. At the same time their second offensive against the Soviet Union was launched in an attempt to reach the Baku oil fields and thus block the Soviets' Iranian supply route. Mao and the CCP leadership were fully aware of the implications of both German campaigns on the situation in the Far East:

Hitler launched an offensive of unprecedented fury on Stalingrad and the Caucasus. He endeavoured to capture these two objectives at great speed for the twofold purpose of cutting the Volga and seizing Baku, intending subsequently to drive against Moscow to the north and break through to the Persian Gulf in the south; at the same time he directed the Japanese fascists to mass their troops in Manchuria in preparation for an attack on Siberia after the fall of Stalingrad. Hitler vainly hoped to weaken the Soviet Union to such an extent that he would be able to release the main forces of the German army from the Soviet theatre of war for dealing with an Anglo-American attack on the western front, and *for seizing the resources of the Near East and effecting a junction with the Japanese*; at the same time this would allow the main forces of the Japanese to be released from the north and, with their rear secure, to move west against China and south against Britain and the United States.[5] [Italics added.]

This was written before the full extent of the victories of al-'Alamayn and Stalingrad became known. By late 1942, both offensives had been repelled. In an interview Mao gave to foreign and Chinese reporters in June 1944 he stated that the turning point in the war had been the Allied initiative begun at the end of 1942 in North Africa and the Pacific, and later continued with the opening of the second front in Europe.[6]

Thus by 1941–2 Mao had realised that the outcome of the war would be determined in key areas, such as the Middle East, which lay between the major antagonistic powers of the time. This realisation foreshadowed his 1946 'intermediate zone' theory.

Analysing the new international situation following World War II, Mao observed that the main contradiction in the post-war world lay not between Moscow and Washington but between US-led Western imperialism and the Asian, African, Latin American and even some capitalist countries. Mao was convinced that an American attack on the Soviet Union and the socialist camp was inconceivable so long as the United States did not have complete control over this vast intermediate zone. He, therefore, predicted that in the coming years the United States would direct most, if not all, its efforts towards the domination of the intermediate zone, rather than elsewhere.[7] Lu Ting-yi, then Director of the Department of Information of the CCP, elaborated:

The United States is far away from the Soviet Union with a large area lying between. In this neutral area, there are capitalist countries, colonial and semi-colonial countries of three continents, Europe, Asia, and Africa. In addition to other conditions, it is very difficult for the United States to attack the Soviet Union... We cannot say that the American imperialists do not want to attack the Soviet Union; but the American imperialists cannot attack the Soviet Union before they have succeeded in oppressing and putting under their control the American people and all capitalist, colonial and semi-colonial countries. To oppress and put under their control these countries is impossible. Therefore, the contradiction between the United States and the Soviet Union, though it is one of the basic contradictions, is not an imminent one, not a dominant one in the present political situation.[8]

Mao's intermediate zone theory was to become the cornerstone of China's Middle Eastern policy. In the late 1940s and early 1950s Mao believed that the United States and its 'lackeys' had indeed launched an offensive against the intermediate zone in general and China in particular. As was the case in the early 1940s, these perceived threats made the Chinese more aware of the crucial importance of the Middle East and more concerned about the 'strategic link' between hostile powers' involvement there and the security of the recently founded PRC. Therefore, while being preoccupied with the American build-up in the Far East, the Chinese were also watching 'imperialist intervention' and attempts to create an 'aggressive bloc' in the Middle East:

The U.S.A. is trying to set up an aggressive Middle Eastern bloc by dragging in Pakistan ... the U.S. war-makers for a long time have been trying to drag Pakistan into planned U.S. Middle East and South-East Asian aggressive blocs and to convert Pakistan into an important war base for the U.S.A. in this region... The U.S.A. is also urging Pakistan to conclude an alliance with a member of the Atlantic Alliance, Turkey, to sow discord between Pakistan and other Moslem states, to put pressure on those Arab states reluctant to join the U.S. aggressive organisation... The U.S.A. is sparing no effort to use Pakistan to link its aggressive power in the Middle East with that in South East Asia. It wants to form a U.S. aggressive 'bloc' extending from the Middle East to the Far East to menace peace-lovers in Asia to a greater extent... The people of China are clearly following the activities by the U.S.A. and Pakistan for a military alliance. Both eastern and western parts of Pakistan are close to the south-western borders of China.[9]

Several months later the Chinese coined the term 'military crescent'. They regarded this 'military crescent', which allegedly stretched from Japan to the Middle East and included South Korea, the Ryukyus, Formosa, Indochina, Pakistan, Persia and Turkey, as a direct act of hostility not against the Soviet Union and Eastern Europe but against China, and even more so against the countries of the 'crescent' themselves.[10]

Peking's Middle East policy had been based on the assumption that, although a common enemy faced both China and the Middle East, at any given time the latter was much more exposed and vulnerable. For this reason the Chinese urged the peoples and governments of the Middle East in the early 1950s not to participate in American military pacts and encouraged what they called the 'national liberation movement' in that area to drive away any imperialist presence (both military and economic).[11] This has remained China's fundamental strategic interest in the Middle East, though the policies adopted to accomplish it have varied considerably over the years.

In the early 1950s, China's Middle Eastern policy tended to be inflexible and dogmatic. This was the combined outcome of the domestic, regional and global situations. At home, the recent revolutionary experience as well as the militancy which accompanied the enforcement of CCP rule over the entire Chinese mainland made the Chinese suspicious and tenacious with regard to the outside world. They were further disturbed by the submissive attitude of the Middle Eastern countries and their lack of firm resistance to Western encroachments. But, above all, it was the perception of potential threats to their security, not to mention the war in Korea and Indochina, that put the Chinese on the alert.

Peking's world seemed to have been rigidly divided into two camps: that of the 'enemies' included the United States and its 'lackey' governments in Western Europe and Latin America; that of the 'friends' included three categories in strict order: first, the Soviet Union; then, fraternal socialist countries in Asia (North Korea, Vietnam, Mongolia) and Eastern Europe; finally, the people's anti-imperialist movements in Asia (Malaya, the Philippines, Burma, Indonesia, etc.), the Middle East (mainly in Iran and Egypt) and Africa, as well as the workers in the capitalist countries.[12] 'These two camps', the Chinese stressed, 'include all the world's nations, all the world's countries, all classes, strata and parties'.[13] Already in the early 1940s, again under circumstances of international tension, Mao expressed this view of the 'two camps':

In the international situation of the 1940s and 1950s, the heroes and brave fellows, whoever they may be, in the colonies and semi-colonies, must either line up on the imperialist front and become part of the forces of world counter-revolution, or line up on the anti-imperialist front and become part of world revolution. They must do one or the other, for there is no third way.[14]

Theoretically, this rigidly dichotomised world outlook applied to the Middle East also: Peking regarded the people's 'liberation movements' as the most effective force which could undermine imperialist positions in the Middle East and thereby promote China's fundamental interest in that region. The Middle East became a centre of resistance to imperialism, second at that time only to Southeast Asia: 'the victory of the Iranian people's struggle against imperialism and the blow against the war plans of the aggressive imperialist bloc is not a small matter ... The Egyptian people's struggle against imperialism is ... a first step to victory, a blow against imperialism, and is also serious enough.'[15] Both struggles, referring to Iran's nationalisation of the oil industry and Egypt's abrogation of the 1936 Anglo-Egyptian Treaty, and in fact any other act against imperialism in the Middle East, were ultimately attributed by the Chinese to the people's 'pressure' on the governments concerned. All Middle Eastern governments were apparently considered subservient to the West. In practice, however, despite this rather revolutionary orientation, China's attitude towards the main actors on the Middle East scene was more pragmatic, flexible and ambivalent.

Although the Chinese condemned 'Western imperialism' in general, they have always distinguished carefully between secondary enemies, who were less dangerous and with whom temporary alliances could be sought, and the principal enemy, against whom the struggle should concentrate. The awareness of these distinctions and the exploitation of 'contradictions' among the enemy camp constituted one of the basic elements of China's Middle Eastern policy from the early 1940s on. At that time, the Germans and Japanese were the principal enemies, a situation that justified a united front with the Allies. After World War II, the United States became the principal enemy, trying to expand in the intermediate zone at the expense of the former colonial powers:

England's far-flung dependencies and colonies – Canada, South [Africa], Australia, Atlantic Islands, Middle East, Palestine and Arabia, Egypt and Mediterranean and finally India, Burma and elsewhere – are all scenes of American imperialistic attacks on England under the American imperialist policy of world domination. In certain places, these clashes have already become or are brewing up armed struggles.[16]

Thus as early as the 1940s the Chinese observed that the Middle East had been subject to a fierce contest. Britain and France were trying to secure the remnants of their traditional spheres of influence, while the Americans now tried to increase their control. The fact that Britain had been the main colonial power in the Middle East did not lead the Chinese astray:

British imperialism is a dying beast which cannot stand up to a struggle. In their struggle against Britain the peoples of Egypt and the Middle East should not harbour any illusions about U.S. imperialism. America is the imperialist Power that is now aiming at replacing Britain in aggression against the Middle East. There are obvious contradictions between U.S. and British imperialism in their fight to dominate the Middle East. To the peoples of the Middle East the former is the more vicious enemy. But if they harbour any illusions about America, this will bring painful and bitter consequences in its train.[17]

Similar flexibility characterised China's attitude towards Middle Eastern governments. Apparently, the Chinese maintained that these governments were collaborating with Western imperialism and belonged, therefore, to the forces of counter-revolution. Yet, as we have seen, when the Chinese distinguished between 'enemies' and 'friends' they entirely ignored the governments of the Middle East (as well as those of Asia and Africa) in their classification. In other words, despite their insistence that non-alignment was impossible, the Chinese could not, and perhaps did not want to, commit themselves to identifying Afro-Asian governments as either revolutionary or counter-revolutionary.

China's ambivalence stemmed from the realisation that the Western grip on the Middle East was particularly strong because, as Peking put it, this area (with the exception of Egypt) was, following World War I, the last region to have become entangled with modern imperialism.

Therefore, the most important method of imperialism to dominate the Middle East was not through direct colonial rule but rather through buying over rulers, grooming and backing up puppets, and concluding special treaties indirectly with rulers. We know that the rulers of these countries all represent feudal and tribal rotten elements of the upper classes who accept imperialist support and [financial] contribution.[18]

After World War II, old-style British and French imperialism was replaced by a new-style American imperialism which, by pretending to defend the independence of the Middle Eastern nations, deceived them and gained control over the most important functions of their governments.[19] As a result, Middle Eastern governments were considered independent only in the formal sense and still remained 'oppressed nations' (*ya-p'o min-tsu*) or 'dependent countries' (*fu-shu kuo-chia*). It was precisely for this reason that the Chinese expected these governments, sooner or later, to launch a struggle against the West. Indeed, in the early 1950s the Chinese detected initial signs of such resistance. Whereas some governments were definitely pro-Western, like Turkey,[20] or a type of 'direct puppet, like Trans-Jordan', others represented the type of 'the opportunists, shifting and veering in the middle of the road of opposing imperialism, like Iran and Egypt'.[21] Thus, although in theory the Chinese rejected the existence of a 'third road' in international politics, in practice they acknowledged its existence.

China's analysis of the international and Middle Eastern situations was unacceptable to the Soviets, despite Peking's insistence that its foreign policy was 'precisely the same as the Soviet Union's foreign policy',[22] and that 'the Chinese people take the same positions as those of the Soviet Union and fully support the Middle East people in their struggle against imperialism'.[23] In the first place, the Soviets rejected Mao's intermediate zone theory. For them, the fundamental contradiction in the world still involved the United States and the Soviet Union directly; the Middle East, Asia, let alone Africa – far from being the decisive and primary arena in the socialist–imperialist struggle, as the Chinese maintained – played a supplementary and secondary role at best. Moreover, whereas the Chinese detected rivalries and contradictions within the Western camp, and distinguished between principal and secondary enemies, the Soviets still regarded 'imperialism' as a homogeneous phenomenon.

Implicitly, the Chinese were also more flexible and, indeed, optimistic about the role of Middle Eastern governments in the anti-imperialist front. They believed that the main problem in the Middle East was not the political nature of governments but outside interference and control. This, in their view, was the ultimate source of all the evils in the Middle East (and elsewhere). Unless foreign intervention was eradicated first, no 'socialist' revolution would stand any chance of success. Class struggle under the existing Middle Eastern circumstances was immature and even harmful to the national liberation struggle, which was much more important and urgent.[24]

The Soviets, on the other hand, tended to judge Arab regimes, especially Egypt, not according to their international orientation but rather according to their domestic politics.[25] From this angle, all Middle Eastern governments, without exception, were categorised as 'enemies' which could in no way contribute to the struggle against imperialism. Consequently, Moscow was more oriented towards an internal political transformation of the 'reactionary' and 'bourgeois' Middle Eastern governments, to be carried out through a revolution led by local communist parties.

China was far less interested in the Middle Eastern communists, not only because of the lack of previous relations, but mainly because of the priority given to national liberation. In this context, the 'people' has always been regarded as the dominant factor, rather than the communist party. Unlike the Soviets, who conceived of the 'people' in a stricter sense,[26] the Chinese used the term in its broadest meaning:

The key to victory in the movement of the peoples of Egypt and the Middle East for independence and sovereignty lies in rallying and uniting the broad masses of people within their respective countries and in joining up with other peace-loving peoples throughout the world in resolute struggle against both British and U.S. imperialism. In this struggle against imperialism the masses are the foundation which must be relied upon.[27]

Referring to Egypt, the Chinese noted that '*all classes* have raised their level of national consciousness' and were ready 'to throw out the foreign aggressors'.[28] [Italics added.]

This does not mean that communist parties were totally ignored. Occasionally, the Chinese paid tribute to the local communists but only in the context of 'national liberation', and never mentioning revolution:

In Egypt, the Sudan, Iran, Iraq, Syria, the Lebanon, Israel and other countries, although the working class is not so large in number, yet they had already begun to awaken, begun to organise, united all around the communist parties, and began to play a leading role in the national independence and liberation movement.[29]

In telegrams sent to the congresses of the Young Communist League and the Communist Party of Israel the Chinese expressed respect 'for their heroic struggle against imperialist colonial war and enslavement', and wished them 'victory in the struggle for national independence, democracy and liberty'.[30] In the same way, when Peking mentioned the Iranian communist Tudeh (People's) Party, it was done only in the context of the anti-imperialist struggle.[31]

Finally, Peking's more tolerant approach towards the Arabs also stemmed from the limited proportions of China's Muslim problem, compared with that of the Soviet Union. Whereas the Soviets feared that any improvement in their relations with the Middle Eastern governments would stimulate nationalist and irredentist sentiments among the Muslim (and Jewish) nationalities of the Soviet Union,[32] Peking approached the Middle East free of such prejudice. As a result, the Chinese were much quicker than the Soviets in exploiting Islam for improving relations with the Muslim countries and regarded it as an asset rather than an embarrassment.

When the communists came to power there were in China about ten million Muslims divided among no fewer than ten different ethnic groups, such as Uighur, Hui, Kazakh, Tatar, etc.[33] Although representing less than 2 per cent of the entire population, their significance was far greater internally as well as externally than their numbers seemed to warrant. Correctly manipulated, the religious affiliation of China's Muslims with Islamic countries such as Pakistan, Afghanistan and Indonesia, not to mention the Arab countries, could, in Peking's view, contribute towards the achievement of some of China's foreign policy aims.

Initially Peking was slow to perceive the relevance of Chinese Muslims to its foreign policy. Muslims were primarily regarded as an internal issue, and indeed, in the first years of the Chinese communist regime, Peking could not conceal the maltreatment of Chinese Muslims; several Muslim insurrections were ruthlessly suppressed and their leaders executed.[34]

This could hardly have won China many friends, particularly among the Arab countries where, to make things worse, Muslim refugees who had fled from China were gathering. Thus, in 1950, the 'Turkestani community' in Cairo complained to King Ibn Sa'ud that the occupation of Sinkiang had been followed by chaos and a general attack on the Muslim inhabitants.[35] Again, in 1951, in response to a wave of trials and executions of Chinese Muslims, 'Turkestani circles' in Cairo and Karachi were said to have accused the Chinese communists of suppressing the 'independence movement', closing Muslim schools, appointing new imams who had been taught communist doctrine, forcing women to unveil, and so on.[36]

Although undoubtedly betraying real concern about the fate of China's Muslims and reflecting basically anti-communist Arab feelings, these reports must also be interpreted in light of the situation in the Far East, and primarily the Korean War. Both South Korea and Taiwan tried to exploit the Chinese oppression of Muslims, as well as feelings of Islamic solidarity, to their own advantage.[37] Not surprisingly, Washington, too, believed that a Middle Eastern Islamic pact including Turkey, Pakistan and Egypt, apart from defending the Middle East, could have an 'enormous impact' on Muslims in the Soviet Union and China and possibly help to create a fifth column in these countries.[38]

It was perhaps to counter the wave of allegations of late March and early April 1951, but probably even more in response to the abstention of many Muslim countries in early February, when China had been condemned as an aggressor by the United Nations, that Peking began to exploit the Muslim issue to win the sympathy of the Muslim and Middle Eastern countries. The Chinese emphasised that, in fact, it was the Muslim peoples of the Middle East and North Africa who had been oppressed by imperialism; since China was fighting imperialism they, therefore, all shared common interests and should be part of one united front. The victory of the peoples of the Middle East, the Chinese said, 'is indivisible from the victory of the Chinese people in their fight against American aggression and for aid in Korea',[39] and 'Moslems in China cannot sit idly by and see Moslems oppressed. We should oppose U.S. imperialism in unison with all Moslem countries and oppressed nationalities.'[40]

From then on Muslim communities in China, as well as prominent Chinese personalities from religious, academic and political circles, were mobilised to serve China's Middle Eastern policy.[41] In order to enable the revolutionary theories of Mao Tse-tung 'to be universally made known to the peoples of the Middle East and North Africa', the Chinese began translating several important Chinese communist documents into Arabic.[42]

Peking also began to demonstrate that never had the condition of China's Muslims been better than under communist rule. In a speech delivered by Burhān, then Chairman of the Preparatory Committee of the China Islamic Association, at a reception in honour of the Muslim delegates from various countries to the Peace Conference of the Asian and the Pacific Regions on

18 October 1952, he said: 'China has about ten million Moslems of ten nationalities . . . The establishment of the People's Republic of China . . . marked a milestone in the history of China's nationalities of Moslem faith and other nationalities. National discrimination and oppression are gone, and a new, happy life has unfolded before them.'[43] Burhān himself was later to play an important role in Sino-Arab relations.

In sum, Peking seems to have been much more aware than the Soviet Union of the common interests the Middle Eastern national–bourgeois governments shared with the socialist camp, on the one hand, and of the 'contradictions' between them and the West, on the other. In consequence the Chinese, long before the Soviets implicitly regarded some of the Middle Eastern governments as potential, and at times actual, partners in the anti-imperialist front.

Informal governmental relations

Although the Chinese paid considerable attention to the Middle East as early as the early 1950s, formal relations between the PRC and the countries of the region barely existed before the Bandung Conference. No department in China's Foreign Ministry dealt exclusively with Middle Eastern affairs. Apparently, the Middle East fell within the area of responsibility of the Department of Asian Affairs, whose Director, Ch'en Chia-k'ang, was later to become China's first ambassador to Egypt. When this department was divided early in 1955, the Middle East, along with the Indian sub-continent and non-communist Southeast Asia, was assigned to the Second Department of Asian Affairs.[44]

China's 'relations' with the Middle East in the first half of the 1950s were restricted mainly to the informal 'people's' diplomacy. Since most, if not all, Middle Eastern governments adopted a somewhat negative attitude towards the PRC, Peking could only establish contacts with leftist and oppositionary personalities, some of whom were in exile. Even economic transactions with the Arab countries (mainly Egypt) were made only with private 'industrial and commercial interests'.

Despite their reservations and suspicions of the Middle East bourgeois–nationalist, not to mention feudal–reactionary, governments there were indications in those years that the Chinese were willing to establish all kinds of formal relations with them. However, China's willingness met with a reluctant and, in fact, negative response. The best example is the case of Israel, with which the Chinese held preliminary but futile negotiations.

Explorations with Israel

On 9 January 1950 Israel became the first Middle Eastern government to recognise the PRC. The Israeli Foreign Minister sent Chou En-lai the following cable:

I have the honour to inform Your Excellency that the Government of Israel has decided to recognise your Government as the de-jure Government of China. Gladly avail myself of this opportunity to express to Your Excellency my Government's sincere hopes for the prosperity of the Chinese nation as well as my own best wishes.[45]

There was no indication in the recognition cable of any intention to establish diplomatic relations with China. Chou En-lai's reply cable did not mention this possibility either.[46] Nevertheless, the Chinese apparently believed that Israel had implicitly expressed the wish to establish full diplomatic relations with China,[47] and they kept repeating their conviction while holding negotiations with Israel until early 1955.[48]

China's interest in Israel in the early 1950s derived mainly from pragmatic considerations. Even before the PRC was proclaimed, Mao and China's communist leadership had expressed their readiness to establish diplomatic relations with any government provided it would sever relations with the Chinese nationalists and adopt a friendly attitude towards the PRC.[49] Israel never had relations with the KMT and the recognition was undoubtedly considered a friendly act.

Israel's affiliation with the United States, of which the Chinese have always been aware, did not bother Peking too much for several reasons. Firstly, while continuing to foment anti-American attitudes among the Middle Eastern governments (as well as everywhere else), the Chinese never regarded such attitudes as a prerequisite for establishing diplomatic relations. China maintained diplomatic relations with states which clearly fell within the American sphere of influence and which, unlike Israel, even joined American military pacts not only in Europe but in Asia as well (Pakistan, for instance). Secondly, the Chinese, following the Soviets, regarded Israel as a country which had succeeded in gaining independence from Western colonial rule after a bitter national liberation war. By late 1949 Moscow had reappraised its attitude towards Israel; China, on the contrary, began adopting a

much more flexible approach towards national–bourgeois governments, Israel included.

But the main reason for China's repeated attempts to start a
dialogue with Israel was China's quest for recognition, diplomatic
relations and political support (primarily in the United Nations).
This quest became even more urgent following the Korean War
and China's growing isolation in the international arena.

From April 1950 to August 1955 no foreign government recognised the PRC; on the other hand, there were six countries which
had recognised China as early as 1950 but did not establish
diplomatic relations. These were Britain, Ceylon, Norway, Israel,
Afghanistan and the Netherlands.[50] One of China's main foreign
policy aims during that period was to set up normal relations with
those countries so as to expand China's network of diplomatic
representation. Indeed, relations with the three European countries were established in 1954; as for the Asian ones, the Chinese
later admitted: 'During the past five years we have exerted efforts
for the establishment of normal diplomatic relations with Asian
countries that had recognised our Government, promoted friendly
relations and developed trade with them.'[51] Although China
developed trade and friendly relations primarily with Ceylon and
Afghanistan, Israel was also part of the general effort.

Following its exchange of cables with Israel, Peking made
several attempts to contact Israeli diplomats, mainly in Moscow.
In June 1950 the Chinese chargé d'affaires visited the Israeli
Legation in Moscow and, according to a report sent to Jerusalem
on 20 June had asked, on instructions of his Government, whether
Israel was planning to send a diplomatic mission to China. No
clear answer could have been given to him on the spot, and he
asked to be informed as soon as the Israeli Government's reply
should arrive.[52]

The fact that the Chinese initiative took place in Moscow was
of particular significance as the Chinese ambassador to the USSR,
Wang Chia-hsiang, was also China's senior Vice Minister of
Foreign Affairs. It seems that China's dialogues with Israel, either
in Moscow or elsewhere, were co-ordinated with the Soviets and
even China's attitude towards Israel reflected, until the mid-1950s,
the ups and downs of Soviet–Israeli relations. The Chinese probably found it appropriate to consult Moscow as far as their
relations with Israel were concerned because the Soviet Union
had been the first government which accorded Israel a *de-jure*
recognition, and maintained diplomatic relations – except for a

few months in 1953. Moreover, Peking held Moscow responsible for the 1947 United Nations Partition Resolution on the basis of which the State of Israel was proclaimed:

The Soviet Union, loyal to the defence of weak and small nations, did not accept the imperialist oppressive policy and proposed to establish in Palestine one Jewish–Arab independent and democratic state; if this plan could not be realised, then two independent-democratic states should be established – one state for the Jewish people and the other state for the Arab people. On the basis of the Soviet proposal the United Nations formulated the Palestine Partition Plan, and on 29 November 1947 the United Nations General Assembly passed the Palestine Partition Resolution.[53]

The timing of China's initiative in Moscow is more difficult to explain. Perhaps the Chinese (and the Soviets) wanted to clarify their international position, bearing in mind both the Third Plenary Session of the Seventh Central Committee of the CCP, held at the beginning of June, and the forthcoming war in Korea. It is also possible that China's sudden interest was stimulated by Israel's activities in the United Nations in June. Israel, along with eight other countries, supported a proposal (which was eventually rejected) to invite the PRC to participate in the United Nations' Conference for Technical Aid to Undeveloped Countries.[54]

Despite China's marked interest in establishing normal relations, however, Israel's response was practically negative. Already at the end of January 1950 Israel's Ministry of Foreign Affairs informed its legation in Moscow that there was no intention of opening a mission in Peking and, due to financial difficulties, proposed to use Israel's legation in Moscow for diplomatic communication with China. At the end of June the legation was informed that 'the Government had decided in principle to establish diplomatic relations with People's China, but nothing should be done in this direction until the situation in the Far East becomes clear'.[55]

Apart from avoiding diplomatic relations, Israel's attitude towards China remained quite friendly. When the question of Peking's representation in the United Nations was voted on for the first time, on 19 September 1950, Israel supported the resolution to oust the delegates of the Republic of China (Taiwan) and to admit those of the PRC. Almost a fortnight later the Israeli minister attended a National Day reception at the Chinese Embassy in Moscow. Peking's awareness of Israel's stand in the United Nations was reflected in the long speech made by China's special representative, Wu Hsiu-ch'üan, in the Security Council on 28 November 1950. He named Israel among the sixteen countries which voted and 'warmly' (*je-lieh*) supported the efforts to admit China to the United Nations.[56]

This 'cat and mouse' process was interrupted – but not stopped – by the United Nations debates on the Korean War from January 1951. While China favoured a proposal to convene a seven-nation conference to solve the Korean problem, Israel put forward a Truce Proposal which Peking interpreted as intended to allow the United States time to reorganise its forces and to bury the issue in endless discussion. Nevertheless, the Chinese were careful not to reproach Israel directly: on 9 January 1951 NCNA released a TASS dispatch under the title of 'Malik Attacks Israeli Delegate's Truce Proposal'. Only later that year did the Chinese say that the cease-fire proposal that had been produced conformed to the demands of the United States and was 'based on Israel's proposal'.[57]

Indeed, on 1 February 1951 Israel, together with another 43 countries, voted to condemn China as an aggressor in Korea, but Peking was careful not to blame those governments which had already taken steps in favour of China, and tried to rationalise its defeat: 'Even those countries which voted for the calumnious resolution do not wholeheartedly support America's disastrous adventure. It was under unprecedented pressure – open threat and covert enticement – that they passed the U.S. resolution.'[58]

If Peking did not consider Israel's vote for the condemnation resolution (as well as for the embargo resolution of 18 May 1951), as an obstacle to the continuation of the dialogue, neither did Jerusalem. At the beginning of October the Israeli Foreign Minister sent greetings for China's National Day to Chou En-lai, saying: 'I have the honour to convey to your excellency and Government and people of the Chinese People's Republic congratulations and best wishes in my own name and that of the Government and people of Israel on the anniversary of the foundation of the Chinese People's Republic.'[59] And, moreover, on 6 November 1951, and again on 25 October 1952, Israel voted *against* the American resolution to postpone the debate on Peking's representation in the United Nations.

Despite these gestures, in late 1952 and during the first quarter of 1953, China's attitude towards Israel became hostile. There was little in Sino-Israeli relations to justify this hostility. Apparently, it was China's reflected reaction to the deterioration of relations between Israel and the Soviet bloc. This deterioration started with the Slansky trial in Prague,[60] continued with the alleged 'doctors' plot' in Moscow,[61] and culminated in an explosion near the Soviet Mission in Tel Aviv, following which Moscow severed diplomatic relations with Israel.

It was under these circumstances that the Chinese published, for the first time, several strongly-worded original as well as translated articles attacking Zionism in general, and Israel in particular.[62] Zionists, they said, 'had tried to establish a bourgeois republic in Palestine in order to take government and rule into their own hands ... but although nominally dominated by the Zionists, in reality, as everybody knows, the ruling of this nation rests in the hands of the American imperialists'.[63] Israel was regarded as 'an outpost of the "American Democracy" in the Near and Middle East', and 'as the most reliable aggressive base in the Middle East, except for Turkey'. Peking, furthermore, charged that

the first Israeli Government under the leadership of MAPAI [Israel Workers' Party] headed by Ben-Gurion was extremely opposed to the Soviet Union, communism, peace and the people. In the international arena they did not cease from fabricating reactionary propaganda, urging generations of Jewish people living in the Soviet Union and many in the People's Democratic countries 'to return to the homeland' (i.e., to destroy the unity among the peoples of the Soviet Union and the People's Democratic countries), or through secret means and dirty tricks they seduced them 'to serve Israel' (i.e., to become engaged in spying activities).[64]

It is hard to determine whether it was intended as a retaliation against China (or all the communist bloc), but when the proposal to postpone the debate on China's representation was put to the vote at the United Nations General Assembly on 15 September 1953 Israel for the first time abstained, thereby setting up a pattern which was followed with few exceptions until 1965.

Nevertheless, in late 1953, possibly because the Soviet Union had resumed diplomatic relations with Israel, Peking attempted a fresh start in its dialogue with Israel. Several meetings between Chinese and Israeli officials, mostly at the Chinese initiative, took place in Moscow, Helsinki and even in London.[65] The most fruitful dialogue started in January 1954 in Rangoon, Burma, between the Chinese ambassador, Yao Chung-ming, and Israel's minister, David Hacohen. In their first conversation the Chinese ambassador officially informed the Israeli minister that the Government of China had welcomed the establishment of an Israeli mission in Burma and expressed willingness to have trade relations with Israel.[66] Although he did not mention diplomatic relations it seems that ultimately this is exactly what he meant. As Chou En-lai explained later, China's policy was 'to promote business relations ... so as to improve mutual contacts and understanding and create favourable conditions for the establishment of normal relations'.[67]

As a next step in this direction Jerusalem proposed to send a trade delegation to China and the matter was passed in February 1954 to Peking. Until late June there was no reply, but Yao Chung-ming assured David Hacohen of China's interest in establishing trade *and* diplomatic relations with Israel,[68] saying that it was Chou En-lai himself who had to make the decision.[69] Indeed, when Chou En-lai passed through Rangoon on his way from Geneva, he met David Hacohen at a reception on 29 June 1954 and promised to take care of the proposed visit of the Israeli delegation to China after his return.[70] On 14 September 1954 Israel received an official Chinese invitation to send a delegation to negotiate trade as well as other questions regarding 'the two friendly countries'.[71] Again, it seems that Sino-Israeli negotiations in Rangoon were held with the complete approval and even encouragement of the Soviets.[72]

There is little doubt that the Chinese interpreted their dialogue with Israel optimistically. On 23 September 1954 Chou En-lai stated at the First Session of the First National People's Congress that 'contacts are being made with a view to establishing normal (*cheng-ch'ang*) relations between China ... and Israel'.[73] In his speech the Chinese premier chose to overlook Israel's vote in the United Nations three days earlier *for* the resolution to postpone the debate on the China issue; Israel immediately made it known that the vote had been a result of a misunderstanding and, in a note passed to China's ambassador in Rangoon on 23 September, claimed that it had been made contrary to orders. At the time, this explanation seemed fully acceptable to both the Chinese ambassador and his Government.[74]

A week later, the Israeli premier again sent Chou En-lai a message of greetings on the occasion of China's National Day.[75] Yet in November, when the Government of Israel finally decided to send the delegation to China, its members were instructed to confine the talks to trade alone, not to raise the question of diplomatic relations, and to give an affirmative but non-conclusive answer if the Chinese should do so.[76]

From 28 January to 21 February 1955, an Israeli delegation, including representatives of trade and industry, as well as the

Director of the Asia Department in Israel's Foreign Ministry, visited China. During the visit the Chinese expressed more than once their friendliness and respect for Israel and the Jewish people, and reiterated their willingness to develop trade relations. As had been anticipated, diplomatic relations were also discussed. Both Chang Han-fu, China's Vice Foreign Minister, and the Director of the Department of Asian Affairs in China's Foreign Ministry, with whom lengthy talks were held, showed obvious interest in establishing full diplomatic relations with Israel. They even went as far as to offer Israel a compound in Peking for an embassy as compensation for Jewish property confiscated in Shanghai.[77] Again, there is evidence that the whole visit had been approved by the Soviets.[78]

Yet, despite the warm welcome extended to the delegation, its visit was hardly mentioned by NCNA or China's communication media.[79] By early 1955 and even late 1954 the Chinese were much more careful in their overt attitude towards Israel than they had been in September 1954,[80] and for good reasons: in the meantime preparations for the Afro-Asian Conference were in full swing and Peking definitely knew that under the pressure of the Arab countries Israel had not been invited.

As will be shown later, the success of the Bandung Conference became a cardinal objective of China's foreign policy at that time. Considering Israel's reluctance to establish diplomatic relations with the PRC, Peking did not find it too difficult to comply with the Arab demands, particularly after initial progress had been registered in Sino-Arab relations.

Reservations about the Arabs

Unlike Israel, none of the other Middle Eastern governments extended diplomatic recognition to the PRC before mid-1956. After the establishment of the PRC Egypt, as well as other Arab governments, continued to regard the Nationalist Government in Taiwan as the only legal representative of the Chinese people. This view was reinforced when the Political Committee of the Arab League decided on 20 August 1950 to recognise Nationalist China.[81] No wonder, therefore, that as a member of the Security Council Egypt voted on 13 January 1950 against the Soviet proposal to exclude Taiwan's delegate from the Security Council on the ground that he did not represent China. Peking, for its part, immediately branded Egypt a 'lackey of American imperialism'.[82]

Later, however, Egypt began to abstain in the United Nations votes on issues concerning China both directly and indirectly. On 27 June 1950 Egypt abstained when the Security Council asked member states to aid South Korea in repelling the North Korean attack.[83] Although they were not yet involved in the war, the Chinese considered this vote a test of the degree of freedom from American influence of Security Council members. Indeed, Egypt's abstention instantly triggered an angry American reaction as well as indirect threats of retaliation.[84] These threats were probably effective because in December Egypt's Acting Foreign Minister told journalists that the Egyptian delegation to the United Nations had been instructed to support United States policy against Communist China, since the issue no longer was the war in Korea but the open conflict between communism and democracy.[85]

Nevertheless, despite US pressure, from June 1950 to the end of that year Egypt abstained in four other votes concerning China in both the Security Council and the General Assembly.[86] Moreover, rumours of imminent Egyptian recognition of China had been circulating since May,[87] and on 11–12 December 1950 the Egyptian Parliament was engaged in a long debate about a proposal calling the Government to improve relations with the socialist bloc, including 'Egyptian recognition of the Chinese Communist regime'.[88]

Peking's appreciation of Egypt's stand was reflected in Chou En-lai's proposal of 17 January 1951, submitted to the First Committee of the United Nations, to convene a seven-nation conference to solve the Korean and other Far Eastern problems. The seven countries he named were China, the Soviet Union, the United States, Britain, France, India and Egypt.[89] The Chinese selected Egypt not only 'as the biggest among the Arab countries' or because 'China wished that there would be one country to represent the Arab bloc',[90] but also because 'Egypt is the leader of Africa, is one of the non-permanent member states of the Security Council, and since it had not supported the plan of aggression in Korea raised by U.S. imperialism, it is not a lackey of U.S. imperialism'.[91]

Thus within a year the Chinese had reversed their attitude to Egypt and, furthermore, had begun to acknowledge its leading role in the Middle East as well as in Africa. Cairo was flattered by Chou En-lai's proposal. Egypt's Acting Foreign Minister, Muḥammad Ṣalāḥ al-Dīn, declared: 'This choice is an evidence of honour to Egypt's international position and her sound policy towards the problems of the Far East.'[92]

Even before Chou En-lai's proposal became known, and certainly afterwards, the Egyptian press generally disapproved of the American intention to condemn the PRC in the United Nations as an aggressor in Korea. Among the reasons given for the disapproval were Egypt's neutrality, the prospects of establishing relations with China and America's support and friendship for Israel.[93]

Peking also began to pay attention to the role played by other Arab countries within the United Nations, particularly after the Fifth General Assembly had condemned China, on 1 February 1951, as an aggressor in Korea: an overwhelming majority of forty-four countries voted for the condemnation (among them Iran, Iraq, the Lebanon and Turkey); seven opposed it (including the Soviet bloc, Burma and India); and among the nine that abstained there were four Arab countries (Egypt, Saudi Arabia, Syria and the Yemen) and another three Asian Muslim countries (Pakistan, Afghanistan, Indonesia). Commenting on the resolution the Chinese concluded: 'Some growing number of nations, especially the Asian and Arab countries, have broken away from the voting machine controlled by the U.S. imperialists and expressed dissatisfaction with America's aggressive policy.'[94] A *People's Daily* editorial quoted the Egyptian delegate as saying: 'The untimely U.S. [*sic*] resolution seriously undermines and probably shuts off the remaining hope of a peaceful solution [in Korea].'[95]

In 1951 the Chinese perceived other signs of an 'anti-imperialist awakening' among the peoples and governments of the Middle East. One example was Iran. In April Peking praised the Persian Government which – 'in response to the demand of the people', to be sure – had passed an act for the nationalisation of the oil industry; it had 'vacillated and wavered' for a time but finally decided on immediate enforcement of the nationalisation and announced the dissolution of the Anglo-Iranian Oil Company.[96] However, towards the end of the year, the Chinese attitude changed: indeed, the Persian Government had 'followed the struggle movement of the Persian people' for oil nationalisation, but it had become clear that the real requests of the people had been ignored.[97] Finally, early in 1952 the *People's Daily* came to the conclusion that the 'Iranian ruling bloc' was collaborating with US imperialism while 'suppressing the people's progressive forces'.[98]

Another example was Egypt. In October 1951 the Chinese praised the Egyptian Government's abrogation of the Anglo-Egyptian Treaty of 1936 and the Sudan agreements of 1889 as 'perfectly justified and reasonable', and in keeping with Egypt's demand for full independence and sovereignty; the Egyptian people, Peking said, had expressed their support for this step.[99] In the same manner the Chinese noted, not without satisfaction, that 'with the support of the Egyptian people, the Government of Egypt has rejected the proposal of the four countries', referring to the attempts by the United States, Britain, France and Turkey to create a Middle East Command.[100]

Bearing in mind Egypt's steps towards greater independence, the Chinese considered the 23 July 1952 *coup d'état* as a setback. Following several days of 'wait and see' Peking seemed to have adopted the official Soviet attitude. The Egyptian *coup d'état* was interpreted as no more than a change of government similar to other political upheavals that had taken place in Egypt, Syria, and Iraq, all without exception attributed by the Chinese to direct Anglo-American interference and contest for power. This *coup*, however, caused more anxiety in Peking since it had allegedly been engineered not by England (like the previous ones) but by the United States.[101]

This was one of the earliest examples of China's interest in 'backward' governments, provided they demonstrated anti-imperialist tendencies. The Chinese appreciated Egypt's *ancien régime*, which though under tight British control, could still have challenged England. On the other hand they denounced the new military clique as totally in favour of, and subservient to, US imperialism, in addition to being a 'fascist military dictatorship' suppressing the people. The contrast between past and present regimes was made quite clear, leaving no doubt about China's preference:

The Egyptian Government declaration in October 1951 on the abrogation of the 1936 Anglo-Egyptian Treaty was the first important victory of the Egyptian people's patriotic movement... Around 1951, when Egypt declared the abrogation of this Treaty, the Egyptian people had already started a very resolute struggle against the British aggressors, and, moreover, proceeded with an armed struggle. Now, the Naguib dictatorial regime, with the support of imperialism...hinders the Egyptian people's movement fighting for independence and freedom.[102]

For their part, Egypt's Free Officers, at least in the first year and a half of their rule, adopted a more negative stance towards the PRC, compared with that of the pre-July 1952 Egyptian Government. Thus, in their first UN vote on the China issue after assuming power, Egypt's new military leaders abandoned the former abstention pattern and, together with Iraq, Iran, the Lebanon and Turkey, supported, on 25 October 1952, the United States-sponsored resolution to postpone consideration of any proposal to exclude Taiwan from the United Nations (Syria, the Yemen, and Saudi Arabia continued to abstain).

During 1953, however, both Peking and the Arabs, especially Egypt, gradually and carefully began to reconsider their mutual attitudes. The Indian Government played an important part in stimulating Arab, and particularly Egyptian, interest in relations with China. Panikkar, India's ambassador to Egypt and to other Arab countries and formerly India's ambassador to the PRC, tried to persuade officials in the Arab capitals to which he was accredited that they should adopt a more 'realistic' attitude towards Peking.[103]

From early 1954, both China and Egypt abandoned their mutual rigid antipathy in favour of a more flexible approach. The Chinese, indeed, continued to criticise Nasser and the Egyptian Government:

In the Middle East there are some countries that in recent years came to exercise fascist military rule, proclaimed the Communist Party illegal, dissolved several political parties, deprived the people of their democratic rights, all these measures can only illustrate the weak and fragile basis of their rule. Certainly, the development of the revolutionary movement of some Middle Eastern countries is not even; there are revolutionary movements in several countries that are still placed on a comparatively low level.[104]

This attitude was maintained right up to the eve of the Bandung Conference: 'Nasser's regime continued to carry out a suppressive policy against the people... After obtaining the country's supreme power, Nasser made mass arrests of the Muslim Brethren Association and other politically alien elements.'[105] Peking seemed to have misinterpreted and misunderstood many Egyptian measures throughout 1954, including the Suez Canal Evacuation Agreement with Britain, as being harmful to the interests of the people, and beneficial to 'U.S. imperialism': 'the Egyptian rulers exert pressure on the people of the country who seek peace, clarifying that they wish to remain "neutral" in the "cold war"'.[106] But, at the same time the Chinese welcomed and appreciated the

Egyptian Government's rejection in principle of any plan to create a military pact in the Middle East, and in particular, its refusal to join any such pact.[107]

Cairo also adopted an ambivalent attitude: the domestic campaign against communism continued and rumours of forthcoming Egyptian recognition of the PRC were firmly denied.[108] When Chou En-lai arrived in Cairo on 24 June 1954 on his way from Geneva to India, no Egyptian official came to greet him. In his statement the Chinese premier totally ignored the Egyptian Government, praising only the people: 'It is a pleasure to me to have the opportunity of passing through Cairo on my way to visit India. The Chinese people have consistently been sympathetic towards the struggle of the people of Egypt for independence. I wish to avail myself of this opportunity to convey my greetings to the Egyptian people.'[109] However, the next day Egypt made an attempt, acknowledged by Peking, to correct the bad impression. Ṣalāḥ Sālim, Minister for National Guidance, said on 25 June that although there was no official contact with Chou En-lai in Cairo, Egypt was grateful for his statement.[110]

Later, Peking reported on Egypt's keen interest in Chou's meeting with Nehru and quoted an Egyptian official as saying that Egypt supported any peace move and joined hands in fighting imperialism.[111] These indirect Egyptian gestures towards Peking culminated in Nasser's first public remarks on China in an interview he gave late in August 1954. While still maintaining diplomatic relations with Taiwan he nevertheless emphasised that Communist China was a fact which should be universally accepted, whereas to 'recognise a few people in Formosa and neglect Red China's millions... is a sort of an international joke'.[112] And in another interview Nasser went on to say: 'We have been following very closely the developments in the Far East and the position of Red China. We are still studying the question of recognising Red China, even though we are against Communism.'[113] Later that month, Egypt abstained in the United Nations China vote.

In the meantime, trade relations – always regarded by China as an avenue to better mutual understanding that might lead to normal relations – had already been established between China and 'industrial and commercial interests' in Egypt.[114] In early January 1953 it was reported that China had been interested in buying one million cantar (approximately 45,000 tons) of Egyptian cotton, and an agreement to this effect was signed.[115] In 1953

China bought more Egyptian cotton than in the record year of 1939, and in 1954 even more.[116]

Most of the Sino-Egyptian trade consisted of Chinese imports, which increased steadily, as can be seen in Table 1. While Sino-

Table 1. *Sino-Egyptian Trade, 1951–5 (in million US dollars)*

	1951	1952	1953	1954	1955
Chinese imports	0.9	8.9	10.4	11.4	24.5
Chinese exports	0.8	0.6	0.6	0.8	0.9

Sources: Robert Loring Allen, *Middle Eastern Economic Relations with the Soviet Union, Eastern Europe, and Mainland China* (Charlottesville, Virginia: Woodrow Wilson Department of Foreign Affairs, University of Virginia, 1958), p. 77. See also 'Amélioration des echanges commerciaux avec la Chine Communiste', *La Bourse Egyptienne*, 7 May 1954; *Le Commerce du Levant* (Beirut), 30 April 1955; *Communist China 1949–1959* (Kowloon, Hong Kong: Union Research Institute, 1961), part III, p. 29.

Egyptian relations were gathering momentum, there were initial hints that two other Arab governments were reconsidering their China policy. Thus, the Chinese quoted the British Minister to the Yemen telling journalists in August 1954 that 'the Government of the Yemen fully supports and whole-heartedly welcomes the call for recognising the People's Republic of China'.[117] And in October China participated, for the first time, in the Damascus International Fair.[118]

Later, these three governments of Egypt, Syria and the Yemen were the first in the Middle East to establish diplomatic relations with the PRC.

Impartiality on Arab–Israeli relations

China's stand on the Arab–Israeli conflict should be analysed and understood in global–strategic, and in local–tactical, terms. Whereas the strategic Chinese interpretation of the conflict has remained fundamentally consistent to this very day, attitudes towards the parties concerned have changed considerably according to the circumstances.

In global–strategic terms, the Chinese have always attributed the origins of the conflict, as well as its persistence, to foreign power intervention. These rival powers – Britain and the United States in the 1950s – incited and then supported one client-party against the other, in an attempt to sustain or increase their own influence and control in the Middle East.

Peking traced the roots of the dispute back to the contradictory promises given by Britain during World War I and afterwards to the Jews and the Arabs, concerning their national aspirations in Palestine.[119] After World War II, when its rule in Palestine became unstable, Britain tried to postpone solution of the problem and to use the United Nations to maintain its power. However, the Chinese claimed, the Soviet Union put forward the Palestine Partition Resolution, which provided for the termination of the British Mandate in Palestine, and the establishment there of a Jewish state, an Arab state and an international zone. In accordance with this resolution the Republic of Israel was proclaimed on 15 May 1948.[120]

The Arab–Israeli War which erupted immediately afterwards was regarded by the Chinese as a clear example of Anglo-American incitement: 'At the time when the establishment of the Republic of Israel was first announced, England instigated the Arab League states to attack Israel, while the United States was aiding Israel in secret.'[121] In Peking's view this was the first indication of 'Anglo-American contradictions' in the Middle East; Israel and the Arabs were thus sucked into a war which, in fact, was an Anglo-American contest for power in the area.

While 'contending' with each other the British and American imperialists were also 'colluding' to exploit the Arab–Israeli conflict in order to curb the genuine people's struggle: 'In 1948 Anglo-American imperialism plunged Egypt into the Palestine War, intending to weaken the Egyptian national liberation movement.'[122] Britain, anxious to preserve its power, diverted the increasingly violent opposition to its presence: 'In order to prevent uprising British imperialism had recourse to a vicious terrorist method ... [it] induced Egypt to participate in the war against Israel.'[123]

Arab–Israeli relations since 1948 have been interpreted by the Chinese in a similar way: after the armistice agreements had been signed, Anglo-American provocation caused frequent clashes in the border areas, leading to an unprecedented deterioration in Arab–Israeli relations.[124]

In tactical terms the Chinese originally maintained a neutral and balanced stand on the Arab–Israeli conflict, slightly inclined, until the mid-1950s, in favour of Israel. Peking held the Arab governments not less responsible than Israel for the 1948 war and for the fact that the Partition Plan's provision for an Arab state in Palestine had not been implemented: 'Places inhabited by Palestinian Arabs were part of what had been occupied by Jordan, Egypt, and Israel.'[125]

This stand was apparently based not only on the prospects of establishing diplomatic relations but also on the assumption that both Israel and the Arabs belonged, at least potentially, to the anti-imperialist camp; both have been dominated for so long by Western colonial rule, which had manufactured and sustained the conflict between them. In China's view, the principal contradiction in the Arab–Israeli conflict has been not between Jews and Arabs but between both and the West: 'War against the Jews still could not divert the Egyptian people from their [real] object of struggle.'[126]

The Chinese also distinguished clearly between the local peoples, who resisted imperialism and desired peace, and their governments, in particular the 'reactionary' Arab regimes and the Arab League, which co-operated with imperialism and promoted tension so as to consolidate their own power:

In 1948 the Anglo-American imperialists provoked a war between the Arabs and the Jews in Palestine. The Arab League, using 'Holy War' [*jihād*] as a slogan, called upon all the Arabs to participate in the war against the Jews. They attempted to use the war to divert the people's psychological hatred of the foreign colonialists and the feudalism in their own countries, and as a result to increase taxes and to build up modern troops.[127]

Israel's role in the conflict was treated much more leniently for two reasons: firstly, the Israeli Government, particularly after the renewal of diplomatic relations with Moscow, undertook not to join any Western-sponsored military–regional pact; secondly, Peking believed that there were better prospects of establishing relations with Israel, which had already recognised the PRC, than with the Arabs.

Under these circumstances the Chinese advocated an ultimate solution to the Arab–Israeli conflict along the lines of the United Nations Partition Resolution. In order to seek a lasting peace, they argued, the Arabs and the Israelis should negotiate directly without interference from foreign countries.[128] This Chinese formula remained intact throughout the later years, despite the tactical shifts in China's Palestine policy.

To sum up, when the Chinese came to Bandung to meet Arab leaders, the Middle East was far from being *terra incognita* to them. On the contrary, not only had they followed Middle Eastern events from 1950 (and in fact even earlier) with close attention but, furthermore, some of the basic orientations and attitudes characteristic of China's Middle East policy after April 1955 had already taken shape.

Apart from seeking recognition and political support, particularly on the Taiwan issue, China's main interest in the Middle East was to encourage an anti-imperialist 'struggle' which would undermine the imperialists' vital strategic and economic interests there and thereby disrupt what they thought were imperialist plans to encircle and eventually attack China.

By the mid-1950s the Chinese had already concluded that at least some Middle East governments (notably Egypt, Syria, the Yemen and also Israel) were ready to establish informal or even formal relations with China, or to support its claims with regard to Taiwan and the United Nations. Some of these governments also revealed a certain degree of opposition to Western schemes of 'aggression'. This was sufficient reason for China to ignore the bourgeois or feudal character of these governments (about which the Chinese harboured no illusions) and to seek their friendship.

At that time China definitely did not regard relations with Israel and the Arab countries as mutually exclusive. China was well aware of the Arab–Israeli conflict but attributed it, like all other political, economic and social problems in the Middle East, to imperialist instigation and interference. In China's view, the main 'contradiction' in the Middle East has been between the local countries and imperialism of all kinds. All other 'contradictions' have been secondary and, therefore, could not be settled before the main 'contradiction' was settled. This was, and still is, the basic principle of China's Middle East policy.

2 : SINO-ARAB PEACEFUL CO-EXISTENCE

China's encounter with the Middle East in the early 1950s did not produce any regular and established relationship. At that time, believing that the West was assailing Asia and Africa, the Chinese were not inclined to compromise with Middle Eastern governments, which they considered reactionary and subservient to Western imperialism. In turn, these governments, which had already opposed Chinese communism on national–religious grounds as well as under the influence of their Western mentors, became even more suspicious and hostile as a result of Peking's uncompromising international stance. However, from 1953–4 the Chinese began to perceive certain changes in the world situation: Western 'imperialist aggression' had been checked; the socialist camp had become stronger; and the Asian and African countries began to resist outside intervention. All these developments brought about a relative relaxation of international tension which enabled both China and the Arabs to reconsider and revise their respective attitudes and eventually to establish lasting relations.

China interpreted the settlement of the Korean and Indochinese problems as a major setback to the West. All over the world there were indications that the former colonial powers had been forced to retreat. The United States, which tried to expand into Asia and Africa at the expense of these powers, had to face not only their resistance but also that of the Asian and African peoples and the socialist camp.

The American advance further aggravated the 'contradictions' within the Western camp. Unlike the Soviet Union, China realised that imperialism had become less monolithic as some Western powers were beginning to drift away from American influence: 'Prior to the present incident [Egypt's nationalisation of the Suez Canal], Britain and France had taken some rather wise actions favourable to the relaxation of international tension. The Chinese Government hopes that Britain and France will deal with the Suez Canal question in the same spirit.'[1]

The new relationships within the Western camp were particularly evident in the Middle East. Britain and France, reluctant to give up their traditional spheres of influence there, disapproved of the American penetration. These contradictions, which later erupted in the Suez invasion of October 1956, gave the local peoples, in China's view, new opportunities to resist imperialism.

Indeed, the Chinese saw many signs of growing independence in the Asian and African countries, which confirmed what they had been implying, namely, that some of these countries, despite being ruled by national–bourgeois governments or even by feudal-type monarchies or aristocracies, offered (or had been ready to offer) firm opposition to Western encroachments. Again, the Middle East provided outstanding examples: apart from Iraq, no Arab country joined the Baghdad Pact which China watched with much anxiety; the Jordanian Government dismissed General Glubb, British Commander of the Arab Legion; Saudi Arabia persisted in its dispute with Britain over the Buraymi Oasis; Egypt signed the arms deal with Czechoslovakia, nationalised the Suez Canal and resisted the Anglo-French and Israeli invasion; and three Arab countries, Egypt, Syria and the Yemen, recognised the PRC and established diplomatic and other relations with Peking. Ignoring – outwardly at least – the 'reactionary' character of most Middle Eastern governments,[2] the Chinese considered them as basically hostile to Western colonialism: 'In Africa and in the Near and Middle East, the Arab countries headed by Egypt are resolutely defending their national independence, courageously resisting the activities of the imperialist aggressive bloc to violate their sovereignty and creating division among them.'[3]

The Asian–African resistance to imperialism, and the setbacks the latter suffered, in China's view altered the world's power balance. The East was becoming fundamentally stronger than the West: 'The tremendous progress which the socialist states have made in all spheres of construction testifies beyond all doubt to the superiority of the socialist system ... With this change in relative strength, the international situation is definitely tending towards relaxation.'[4]

The Chinese needed this relatively calm world situation, not only because of the opportunity to consolidate and improve China's international position but also because of domestic necessities. This link between domestic and foreign affairs was spelled out very clearly by Mao Tse-tung:

International conditions today are favourable to our accomplishing our [economic] tasks during the transition period. . . To carry out these tasks, we need a period of peaceful construction. Can we have this period of peaceful construction? Our comrades in the Ministry of Foreign Affairs, in the International Liaison Department, and in the army will have to exert themselves before we can achieve it.[5]

At the Eighth Congress of the CCP Vice Premier Ch'en Yi repeated: 'To fulfil this gigantic task ["Building China into a prosperous, strong and highly industrialised socialist state"], we must strive to create an international environment of lasting peace. It is precisely on this basis that we make our decisions on foreign policy.'[6]

China's foreign policy in the mid 1950s indeed reflected these considerations. It was at that time that Peking started the dialogue with the United States and improved bilateral relations with Europe. In their policy towards the Asian–African countries, the Chinese adopted the five principles of peaceful co-existence as the basis for conducting relations with countries of different socio-political systems. This definitely did not mean that the Chinese had abandoned the struggle against imperialism. On the contrary, all along they insisted that Western aggression and intervention in Asia, Africa and Latin America should be countered not by peaceful negotiation but by firm resistance and struggle. Therefore, China sought not only diplomatic recognition and normal bilateral relations but also tried to organise these countries, on the basis of their common opposition to imperialism, into a united front against outside intervention.

China did not regard Western intervention in the Middle East, whether it was the Baghdad Pact or the Suez invasion, as a local problem. Rather, such intervention was always regarded in the larger Asian–African context and as involving China's interests; the Anglo-French invasion was 'also a serious challenge to the 1,600 million people of Asia and Africa'; the Egyptian people's struggle was 'compatible with our interests, as well as with the interests of the oppressed people of the world, and with those of the people in Asia and Africa.'[7] This message the Chinese repeatedly tried to convey not only to the Asian–African countries but also to the New Soviet leadership. In their policy towards the Soviet Union, the Chinese claimed their right to participate in settling Asian–African problems and urged the Soviets to adopt a vigorous stand vis-à-vis the West. These considerations and premises provided the basis of China's Middle East policy in the mid-1950s.

China's evolving tactics in the Arab world

In late 1954 and early 1955, Peking started signalling the Arabs. For the first time, Arab visitors came to China at the invitation of various semi-official Chinese organisations. Whereas the visit of an Israeli delegation was deliberately played down, the Arab one received much publicity.

Simultaneously, a series of articles appeared in Chinese periodicals, describing the historical relations between China and the Arabs and expressing the hope 'that the traditional friendship between the peoples of China and the Arab world will not only be fully resumed, but will continue to grow'.[8]

A further step in this direction was taken by the Chinese at the (leftist) Conference of Asian Countries which opened in New Delhi on 6 April 1955. Although less important than the forthcoming Bandung Conference, the Delhi Conference was nonetheless used by China (whose delegation numbered forty and included such prominent Muslims as Saifudin) to introduce its new Middle East policy. Peking's interest in forming relations with the Arabs was spelled out clearly by Kuo Mo-jo, head of the delegation:

The Chinese people and the Arab states are separated by high mountains and vast oceans, but between us there has been a long-standing historical friendship. We have conducted frequent trade dealings and exchanged ideas and achievements in science and art. From the 15th century onward, contacts between us began to lessen and finally ceased almost entirely. Today, however, new and world-shaking changes are taking place. Many of the Eastern nations have rid themselves of foreign domination. The peoples of the Middle and Near East stand for peace, freedom and national independence, and co-operation with others. The Chinese delegation pays its warm respect to the delegations of Syria, the Lebanon and Jordan, and through them to the peoples of these countries. Now we are restoring our cultural and economic exchange. The Chinese people not long ago sent an exhibition working group to Syria, which was received in a friendly fashion by the people there. This marked a happy beginning in this direction.[9]

This laid the ground for the Bandung Conference, which undoubtedly narrowed the gap between China and the Arabs. Personal acquaintances produced trade, cultural and eventually diplomatic relations. Yet, in this respect, the conference's importance should not be exaggerated. Those Middle Eastern governments, such as Turkey, Iran, Iraq, the Lebanon, Jordan and Saudi Arabia, which had maintained a hostile attitude towards the PRC prior to the conference, continued to oppose Peking afterwards as well. They showed no signs of having been impressed or influenced by Chou En-lai's so-called 'brilliant performance', despite his support of the Palestine cause. As for Syria, the Yemen and, in particular, Egypt, their governments had already begun adopting a more sympathetic attitude towards the PRC in late 1954, so that the friendship they demonstrated towards the Chinese delegation in Bandung should not have come as a great surprise. Even these governments, as was proved later, were in no hurry to recognise Peking.

Economic and cultural initiatives

Already at their first meeting in Rangoon, on their way to the conference, Nasser had told Chou En-lai that he was unwilling to discuss political matters such as recognition of the PRC or an Egyptian vote for the admission of the PRC to the United Nations.[10] By that time, however, the Chinese had come to realise that winning wider diplomatic recognition and political support (especially on the Taiwan issue), which they were eagerly seeking, should not be a prerequisite for, but rather the outcome of, establishing economic and cultural relations. Chou En-lai, therefore, carefully and patiently followed Egypt's lead. As Nasser's close associates disclosed, Chou En-lai made no attempt to raise political issues in either Rangoon or Bandung.[11] Instead, he offered China's assistance in connection with two of Egypt's principal concerns: arms purchases, and the sale of cotton.

According to Muḥammad Ḥasanayn Haykal (who accompanied Nasser to Bandung) and other sources, Nasser asked Chou during their first meeting in Rangoon whether the Soviets would sell arms to Egypt. Chou promised to inquire; he later informed Nasser that Moscow had agreed.[12] There are two versions as to the role played by China in the Czechoslovak arms deal, announced in September 1955. One interpretation suggests that it was indeed Peking which triggered the deal and thus 'opened' the Middle East to Soviet penetration. The other view suggests that Peking merely helped to persuade the Kremlin to supply Nasser with arms after mutual suspicion had caused a deadlock in Soviet–Egyptian negotiations. These negotiations, of which the Chinese had been unaware, had allegedly already begun in early 1955, that is, before the Nasser–Chou meeting.[13]

Neither of these versions can be sufficiently documented and verified. Yet, whichever view be preferred, it is clear that China played some, albeit indirect, role in producing the first major arms deal between the socialist camp and a Middle Eastern country. Consequently, China became associated in Nasser's mind with arms (although he probably realised that Peking was as yet incapable of supplying home-made arms), and as a potential leverage against Moscow.

No less important than its mediation in the arms deal was China's readiness to buy Egyptian cotton. On the eve of the Bandung Conference, and even earlier, the Chinese had explored the prospects of developing trade with Arab countries.[14] These prospects were negotiated during the conference,[15] and trade delegations were subsequently exchanged. Within one year of the conference, the Chinese signed no fewer than ten trade agreements with the Arab countries, the most important being with Egypt (22 August 1955), Syria (30 November 1955) and the Lebanon (31 December 1955). Each agreement provided for most-favoured-nation treatment and for the exchange of government trade agencies,[16] but the one with Egypt was broader than any similar agreement concluded previously between China and an Asian–African country.[17]

From Cairo's point of view, these agreements were economically important, mainly because in 1955 Egypt's cotton crop (its main export) was unexpectedly large, while the world market price dropped considerably. In 1955 China imported from Egypt nothing but cotton, valued at $24.5 million (out of a total trade turnover of $25.4 million). It was referred to as 'the biggest cotton deal in Egyptian history'.[18] Indeed, in 1955, the value of China's cotton imports from Egypt was more than double that of 1954, although it represented only 8 per cent of the total value of Egypt's cotton exports. In 1956 China's share in Egypt's cotton exports fell to 6.3 per cent.[19]

As the trade balance implies, the Chinese motives in signing these agreements were less economic and more political. On the strategic level, trade was regarded as a means of detaching the Arab countries from the West and drawing them closer to the socialist bloc. The cotton agreement with Egypt thus 'enabled that country to break the yoke of the imperialist monopoly of its major agricultural product'.[20] An editorial in *Ta-kung pao* explicitly expressed the hope that trade between China and Egypt would not only further mutual friendship but have a favourable effect on the fight against colonialism as well.[21] On the tactical level, trade was exploited primarily to improve relations

with the Arab countries and prepare the ground for an eventual
diplomatic recognition of the PRC.[22] This does not mean, however, that China did not need cotton at all. For the Chinese,
cotton was an essential commodity and China has been one of the
greatest cotton-producing countries. Yet the poor quality of
Chinese cotton and the priority given to food crops, combined
with the enormous growth in consumption, made it necessary to
import cotton.[23] As the Chinese Minister of Foreign Trade put it:
'It is true that we have increased our own cotton production
substantially in recent years. But our 600 million people are
living better than ever before, and need ever greater amounts.
We are therefore willing to buy some of the cotton our friends
have for sale.'[24]

Still, China's total cotton imports amounted to only a small
percentage of its own output and, while Egypt's share in these
imports reached about 30 per cent (50 per cent in 1958), it was
only 1 to 1.5 per cent of China's own cotton production, as can be
seen in Table 2. Thus China's imports of Egyptian cotton, prob-

Table 2. *Chinese Production and Import of Cotton, 1955–7 (in
thousands of tons and in per cent)*

	China's output	China's imports		Egypt's share		
	(tons)	(tons)	(% of output)	(tons)	(% of import)	(% of output)
1955	1,518.4	82.3	5.4	23.7	28.8	1.5
1956	1,445.2	42.5	3.0	14.2	33.4	1.0
1957	1,640.0	83.5	5.0	27.4	32.8	1.6

Sources: United Nations, Food and Agriculture Organisation, *Trade Yearbook*,
vol. 1959 (Rome, 1960), p. 272; Helen Yin and Yi-chang Yin (comps.), *Economic
Statistics of Mainland China (1949–1957)* (Cambridge, Mass.: Center for East
Asian Studies, Harvard University, 1960), pp. 30–1; Nai-Ruenn Chen, *Chinese
Economic Statistics, A Handbook for Mainland China* (Edinburgh University Press,
1966), p. 408.

ably at prices above those of the world market, were governed
mainly by political considerations. For similar reasons Peking
decided to sell Egypt 60,000 tons of steel, desperately needed in
China itself for the first Five Year Plan, at prices 20 per cent
lower than those on the world market.[25]

In addition the Chinese carefully kept the balance of trade in
favour of the Arab countries, a fact never fully admitted.[26] Chiang
Ming, Deputy Minister of Foreign Trade, said on 4 September

1956 when the first year's agreement with Egypt was due to expire, that 'during the year the execution of the agreements was satisfactory. By the end of July this year, China had imported goods from Egypt amounting to £10 million, and exported to it goods worth close to £7 million.'[27] This meant a turnover of less than £17 million instead of the £20 million agreed on in August 1955, with a Chinese deficit of more than £3 million. Yet even these figures were misleading: according to Egyptian sources, exports to China in 1955 and 1956 were more than four times as large as imports.[28] Henceforth, trade was manipulated by Peking to maintain or improve political relations, as well as to indicate China's dissatisfaction: to maintain friendly relations and to win Arab support, the Chinese were ready to increase the volume of imports and pay dear for goods they did not really need. This readiness disappeared once Peking realised that the Arab governments had rejected China's interpretation of the Middle East situation, and the policies it was advocating. Political considerations were also evident in the appointment of China's 'commercial' representatives to the Middle East. Whereas the chief representatives handled trade relations, their deputies were experienced diplomats.[29]

Cultural relations and agreements, like trade, served political purposes. Throughout their exchanges with the Arabs, from Bandung on, the Chinese made extensive use of Islam; they invited Muslim leaders to China to witness the condition of China's Muslims,[30] and appointed Chinese Muslims as leaders and members of cultural delegations sent to the Middle East. These delegations and pilgrimages often remained in the Middle East for several months, visiting most of the countries in the area and meeting not only religious personalities but also high-ranking political leaders.

Worth noting is the role played by Burhān Shahīdī (Pao Erhhan), Chairman of the China Islamic Association and the holder of impressive political credentials as well.[31] He first came to Egypt in February 1956, heading a cultural delegation which toured the Middle East. Immediately afterwards he assumed the leadership of the Muslim Ḥajj (pilgrimage) mission which had already arrived in the area. He again toured the Arab countries and was received by King Saʿud of Saudi Arabia and King Ḥusayn of Jordan (both of whom maintained diplomatic relations with Taiwan), as well as by the premiers of the Lebanon, Syria and Egypt. Apparently, these meetings had political overtones. When in Syria, Burhān called on President Nāẓim al-Qudsī and 'Alī Būzū, the Minister of the Interior and Acting Foreign Minister. They exchanged opinions concerning not merely cultural links between the two countries but also the establishment of diplomatic relations.[32] In Cairo, Burhān had an interview with Amīr (Prince) al-Badr, premier of the Yemen, and with his brother.[33] Four days later, the Yemen recognised the PRC through the Chinese ambassador in Cairo.

Political consequences

Despite Peking's commercial and cultural initiatives, Sino-Arab political relations developed rather slowly until mid-1956. Realising that the key to their political progress in the Middle East was as always Egypt, the Chinese indeed concentrated their efforts on that country, hailing its 'influential role in international affairs' and 'rising international prestige'.[34] Yet Nasser was in no hurry to recognise the PRC or even to vote for its admission to the United Nations at the Tenth General Assembly in September 1955.[35] In that month the two Departments of Asian Affairs in China's Foreign Ministry, created early in 1955, probably in anticipation of a forthcoming expansion in the foreign relations network following the Bandung Conference, were reunited.[36]

China's disappointment, however, did not last long: on 16 May 1956 Egypt became the first Arab country to recognise the PRC. It seems that Nasser's decision was a rather sudden one,[37] although expected for some time. Usually, this move has been explained as an expression of Nasser's final disillusionment with the West, and particularly as a retaliation against Washington's refusal to aid Egypt. This, however, gives only a partial explanation of Nasser's recognition of the PRC. His attempts to appease the Americans having been rebuffed, Nasser had also become concerned about the sincerity of the Soviet attitude towards Egypt. He was aware of the fact that the Soviet leadership, determined to ease tension with the West, had not only begun to improve relations with Israel but also seemed to approve of an arms embargo on the Middle East.[38] According to Haykal, Nasser was worried that, if the Soviets were to join a United Nations embargo, Egypt's arms supplies would be cut off. On the other hand, China, which had helped to provide for the first arms deal, 'was not a member of the United Nations so it would not be bound by any embargo... If other sources were cut off, China would provide the loophole. So in the spring of 1956 Nasser extended diplomatic recognition to Communist China.'[39]

This account is corroborated by others. *Al-Jumhūriyya* of 22 May 1956 said: 'Jamāl 'Abd al-Nāṣir recognised China and dealt a blow to the projected Western blockade of the Arab states... People's China is the biggest producer of armaments at present and can supply the Arabs with all the war material they need.' Humphrey Trevelyan, then Britain's ambassador to Cairo, was told by Nasser that the idea of recognising the PRC had originated in Moscow. The Russians admitted that they could not oppose an arms embargo once confirmed by the United Nations. They, therefore, advised Nasser to recognise Peking in order to be able to get arms through China and thus circumvent an undesirable embargo. 'It is difficult to see any other reason for his recognition of Communist China at that moment.'[40]

Possibly Nasser's recognition of China was also intended to pressure Moscow into retreating from the idea of an arms embargo (which the Chinese detested and strongly rejected). However, all the evidence suggests that Nasser really believed that, in the event of an embargo, China could not only provide a transit channel for Soviet weapons but also an independent source of supply of conventional, and eventually of nuclear, weapons as well. To a certain extent, this accounts for the appointment of Ḥasan Rajab as Egypt's first ambassador to China. As a Major General in the Egyptian Army and Deputy War Minister, he had been in charge of armaments and war industries, and had played a central role in almost every Egyptian arms deal with both East and West.[41]

It was, of course, far beyond China's capabilities (and intentions) to supply large quantities of arms to the Middle East at that stage (or for that matter at any other time). It is however possible that, in order to win Egypt's recognition, the Chinese had made vague promises of military aid to Egypt. Thus, on the same day that Chou En-lai invited Nasser officially to visit China (18 May 1956), P'eng Teh-huai, China's Defence Minister, invited his Egyptian counterpart, 'Abd al-Ḥakīm 'Āmir, to send a government military delegation to China. Both invitations were accepted.[42] Shortly afterwards the embargo plan was abandoned and Moscow concluded a second arms deal with Egypt.

Although it is difficult to determine the precise Chinese role in the second deal, it seems that Nasser had succeeded in manipulating the Chinese, once again indirectly, into persuading Moscow to supply arms to Egypt.[43] Thus, long before the Sino-Soviet divergence was exposed, Nasser had already adopted the traditional Chinese principle of using barbarians against barbarians.

In terms of bilateral relations, Egypt's recognition of the PRC meant very little. As Chou En-lai put it:

The temporary absence of diplomatic relations between two countries is no hindrance to contacts between their governments... Before diplomatic relations were formally established between China and Egypt, visits had also been exchanged between responsible members of government departments of the two countries, and moreover the two governments had concluded cultural and trade agreements.[44]

But, in terms of China's short- and long-range foreign policy aims, the recognition could and did mean not only a major boost in prestige but also some substantial political gains.

Immediately, it meant a break in China's isolation. For more than six years after April 1950, no government had recognised the PRC (except for Nepal, on 1 August 1955) until Egypt did so, in May 1956. This act was especially significant because Egypt held a central position in the Arab world, a fact which had instant repercussions: on 4 July 1956 Syria recognised Peking, and on 21 August the Yemen followed suit. Moreover, having an embassy in Cairo, the Chinese could establish further links with North and East, as well as with sub-Saharan Africa.[45] Another tactical gain for Peking was that Egypt withdrew its recognition of Taiwan. This setback for Chiang K'ai-shek was deliberately underlined both in the NCNA reports from Cairo and in Chou En-lai's message to Nasser of 18 May 1956. Consequently, the Chinese could confidently expect Arab support for their admission to the United Nations and for the exclusion of Taiwan. Indeed, on 16 November 1956 Egypt, Syria and the Yemen opposed, for the first time, postponement of the China debate.

Strategically, these votes, let alone the act of recognition, promoted China's fundamental long-term interest in the Middle East, namely the reduction of Western predominance. Willingly or not,[46] Egypt and the other Arab countries drifted further away from the West, the inevitable outcome being increased economic, military and political relations with, and therefore dependence on, the socialist countries. China assured the Egyptians that the United States' refusal to offer them a loan would not hamper Egypt's industrialisation. The United States, Peking said, 'has forgotten that the backward countries at present have real friends and can receive sincere and unselfish support without losing their independence and freedom'.[47] Outwardly, the Chinese have always reminded the Arabs of the advantages of maintaining friendly relations with Moscow: 'In the Middle East, as elsewhere, the Soviet Union never seeks to obtain any privileges, special interest or spheres of influence.'[48]

At the same time, although they welcomed closer Soviet–Arab relations, the Chinese were suspicious of Soviet motives. As will be shown later, there is strong evidence that Peking disagreed with the Soviet gestures towards the West from the beginning of 1956, or even earlier. Having direct and official access to the authorities and the public in the Arab countries, the Chinese could not only foster firm opposition to 'colonialism' but also attempt to modify, offset, or even undermine, Soviet policies of accommodation with the West.

To take full advantage of these gains, Peking appointed Ch'en Chia-k'ang, a senior Foreign Ministry official, formerly Director of the Asia Department and Assistant Foreign Minister, as first ambassador to Egypt. He arrived in Cairo within seven weeks of the announcement of the decision to establish diplomatic relations with China (29 May 1956). Egypt was in no hurry. Its ambassador presented his credentials to Mao Tse-tung only on 17 September. A similar pattern was to be repeated several times thereafter, indicating that a presence in the Middle East was far more important to China than a presence in China was to the Arabs.

On 26 July, four days after the Chinese ambassador had presented his credentials to him, Nasser announced the nationalisation of the Suez Canal Company. It seems highly improbable that the Chinese had anything to do with the nationalisation, but their instinctive reaction was sympathetic and enthusiastic. Yet it was not until 30 July that the *People's Daily* published a relevant editorial, and only on 15 August, some three weeks after the event, was an official Chinese Government statement issued. The delay undoubtedly indicated that the Chinese were waiting to study the Soviet response. But it also betrayed, at least at the beginning, a sense of perplexity as to the possible effects of the nationalisation on the freedom of navigation.

Peking drew a clear distinction between two aspects of the problem. One, the management of the canal, regarded as an internal affair of Egypt – the only nation sovereign over the canal. And two, free navigation in the canal, which was anchored to an international obligation agreed on in 1888 and which concerned all maritime nations.[49] Still, the Chinese were puzzled. Asked on

4 August 1956 whether freedom of navigation would include ships bound for Israel, Chou En-lai replied: 'Freedom of navigation would include everybody.' When told that Egypt had prevented tankers bound for Israel from using the canal and that Nasser's promised freedom of navigation was therefore suspect in certain quarters, Chou said that that specific question should be discussed by the parties.[50] To remove any doubt China's Foreign Ministry immediately refuted the allegation that Chou En-lai was in favour of internationalisation of the canal.[51]

China regarded the nationalisation, in the words of Liu Shao-ch'i at the Eighth Party Congress, as a 'world-shaking event'.[52] It won Mao's sympathy and full appreciation as reflected in his opening address before the Party Congress on 15 September 1956: 'We firmly support the entirely lawful action of the Government of Egypt in taking back the Suez Canal Company, and resolutely oppose any attempt to encroach on the sovereignty of Egypt and start armed intervention against that country.'[53] Moreover, he announced, when the Egyptian ambassador presented his credentials, that 'the Government and people of China will do their utmost to support the heroic struggle of the Egyptian people in defending their sovereignty over the Suez canal'.[54] Similar pledges of support came from the Government, the army and other quarters in China.[55] However, apart from rhetoric China's support for Egypt was of little significance. The Chinese prepaid Egypt 20 million Swiss francs soon after its deposits had been frozen and continued to buy cotton and to provide Egypt, without payment, with large quantities of necessary goods.[56]

These gestures demonstrated the dramatic change in China's position in the Middle East between May and October 1956. Three Arab governments established diplomatic relations with Peking following trade and cultural exchanges. Not less important, Nasser's nationalisation of the Suez canal, the Arab rejection of Western-sponsored military pacts and similar 'anti-imperialist' expressions, had moved the Middle East, in China's world outlook, to the forefront of the battle against colonialism.

To adapt to this situation, a new department was created in China's Foreign Ministry: the Department of West Asia and Africa.[57] Its Director, K'o Hua, had formerly been Director of the Protocol Department and later became more closely associated with Africa than with the Middle East. Apparently it was Ho Kung-k'ai, Deputy Director of the new department from 1956 to 1963, who was in charge of Middle Eastern affairs within the

department. From 1963 to 1966 he was counsellor and chargé
d'affaires in China's embassy in Cairo. In late 1969 he was identified again as Deputy Director of the West Asia and Africa Department, and then as Director of the Africa Department.[58] In addition
to this reorganisation, Peking radio launched new transmissions
in English to Egypt and Central Africa (which began on
15 September 1956) and to Southwest Asia (which began on
18 October).[59]

Thus, when in late October Israel, Britain and France invaded
Egypt, China was far better prepared. The initial reaction to the
outbreak of war was cautious. News of the Israeli attack was first
given on 30 October, at the end of the main news bulletins. However, within the next few days, the Middle East crisis gradually
became the leading news item. In contrast to its delayed reaction
to the nationalisation of the canal, the Chinese Government this
time responded quickly, on 1 November condemning the aggression and expressing support for the Egyptian people.[60] Peking
warned that such aggression would not be tolerated and that
'a chain reaction will spring up in Asia and Africa which will put
these old imperialists in deep trouble and accelerate their destruction'.[61] The Chinese Government also felt obliged 'to lodge a
grave protest with the British and French Governments and serve
them[with] a serious warning ... [that] they would certainly be
faced with inestimably grave consequences'.[62] Finally, following
the Soviet warning, another Chinese Government statement of
7 November said: 'The Chinese Government and people cannot
stand idly by while Egypt's sovereignty and territory is [*sic*] subjected to any form of encroachment... The Chinese Government
and people, in response to the appeal of the Egyptian Government, are willing to adopt all effective measures *within our ability*,
including the supply of material aid, to support Egypt's struggle
and oppose the British and French aggression.'[63] [Italics added.]

The phrase 'within our ability' stripped this otherwise unprecedentedly firm and unequivocal statement of any operative
value. During the crisis, no commitment to specific action was
ever made by the Chinese Government, other than the decision
to offer Egypt a gift of 20 million Swiss francs in cash (about
$4.7 million). All other offers of support, undoubtedly approved
and even encouraged by the Government, were nonetheless made
unofficially and, therefore, did not commit the Government to any
action.[64] These activities encompassed the press and radio;
demonstrations; a Chinese People's Committee to Support

Egypt's Resistance against Aggression; the Sino-Egyptian Friendship Association; the accelerated manufacture of goods for export to Egypt ahead of schedule; the donation of 170,000 Swiss francs from the Chinese Red Cross; and even the alleged registration of 250,000 volunteers to help Egypt. Most of these initiatives had no more than symbolic significance.[65]

This noncommittal attitude was perhaps the most obvious indication so far of Peking's inability and unwillingness to become involved in conflicts which had no direct bearing on China's national security. Nevertheless, China's stand with regard to the Suez crisis was fully appreciated by the Arabs, even more so because its hitherto relatively flexible attitude towards Israel became, as a result of the war, more rigid.

The effects on Sino-Israeli relations

China's alienation from Israel began neither as a result of its determined preference for the Arabs, nor under their pressure. Rather, like other turns in China's Middle East policy, it concerned China's fundamental strategic outlook since it was related to a perceived attempt by foreign powers to reinstate their presence in the Middle East, with the collaboration of Israel. Until then, the Chinese apparently intended to maintain their essentially impartial attitude towards Israel and the Arab–Israeli conflict. There is no evidence to suggest that they decided, at that stage, to exploit the conflict or the Arab hostility towards Israel to their own advantage, notwithstanding the expansion of Sino-Arab relations or the Bandung Conference.

When the question of those to be invited to Bandung was discussed in December 1954 at the second meeting of the Colombo Powers at Bogor, Indonesia, the Chinese found themselves unintentionally supporting the Arab side. On 20 December the Secretary General of the Arab League submitted a note to the conference sponsors which read, among other things: 'It is known that this conference will be a regional one. It has been the policy of the Arab states not to participate in any regional conference where Israel is represented. The Arab States do not have any doubt that Israel will not be invited to this conference and [that Israel] will not participate therein.'[66]

This Arab dictate was strongly seconded by Pakistan which was, on the other hand, opposed to inviting the PRC. However, Pakistan withdrew its opposition under the pressure of India and

Burma and to avoid the undermining of Asian solidarity. 'As a consolation prize for agreeing to the inclusion of Peking, the others agreed to her demand to exclude Israel.'[67]

Apparently Peking reacted half-heartedly to this resolution:

> The Asian–African conference should not be an exclusive regional bloc. . . The five Prime Ministers declared that in seeking to convene the Asian–African conference, they were not activated by any desire for exclusiveness in respect to membership in the conference. We support this statement. Based on this statement, we consider that *the door of the conference is open to those Asian and African countries that were not invited to it*.[68] [Italics added.]

China's comments could have represented no more than lip service to the principle of universality, once Peking itself had already been invited. Yet, even if they felt genuine unease, the Chinese were in the final analysis interested first and foremost in the success of the conference and in demonstrating Asian–African 'solidarity'. To achieve these objectives, they tacitly approved of 'certain variations and minor modifications' such as the non-participation of Israel, and certainly of South Korea and Taiwan.

Furthermore, in early April 1955 China, for the first time, supported a resolution which sympathised with the Palestinians and condemned Israel. The resolution, adopted by the leftist Conference of Asian Countries in New Delhi, was much more forcefully worded than the rather moderate Bandung resolution on the same issue.[69] However, these Chinese gestures did not contradict or alter China's previous views. Kuo Mo-jo, leader of the Chinese delegation to New Delhi, still insisted that international problems including, particularly, the relations among the Middle East countries, should be solved on the basis of the Five Principles of peaceful co-existence.[70] These principles underlay China's stand on Arab–Israeli relations also at the Bandung Conference, despite Arab attempts to extort a more radical Chinese commitment.

In the first two days of the conference the Palestine issue was raised by at least seven speakers. In addition, Chou En-lai was undoubtedly further indoctrinated in his private conversations with Nasser and with Aḥmad Shuqayrī (then Deputy Secretary General of the Arab League and vice-chairman of the Syrian delegation to Bandung, who in 1964 became Chairman of the Palestine Liberation Organisation). In Bandung it was Shuqayrī who unfolded the Arab arguments on the Palestine problem, making considerable efforts to acquaint Chou En-lai with its details.[71]

Chou En-lai, however, seemed to remain uncommitted, at least in public. In his prepared speech (as distributed to the delegates on 19 April 1955) he stated briefly that 'the problem of Arab refugees of Palestine still remains to be solved'.[72] He completely ignored the problem in the speech he actually delivered, which was much milder. Moderation distinguished his comments also when the Palestine question was raised in the secret sessions of the Political Committee (consisting of the heads of delegations only) on 20 and 21 April. The debate centred on the draft resolution proposed by the Afghani delegation: 'In view of the existing tension in the Middle East caused by the situation in Palestine and of the dangers of that tension to world peace, the Asian–African Conference declares its support of the rights of the Arab people of Palestine and calls for the implementation of the United Nations resolutions on Palestine.'

Chou En-lai allegedly said that he was inclined to support this resolution except for the call to the UN, since China, not being a member of the UN, did not know the full contents of its resolutions (although all UN resolutions on Palestine had been distributed to all the delegates). He then suggested that the conference call to the UN be replaced by a 'world appeal' for the cause of the Palestine Arab refugees. He also pointed out that the problem of Palestine was essentially the outcome of foreign intervention.[73]

To draft the final resolution, a sub-committee consisting of delegates of eight countries, including the PRC, was set up. Chou En-lai used the occasion to reiterate China's fundamental interpretation that the Palestine question, like that of Formosa, would be settled only when outside factors responsible for the 'Palestine tragedy' had disappeared.[74] His interpretation was apparently rejected. The only change in the Afghani draft resolution approved by the sub-committee was an addition at the end: 'and the achievement of the peaceful settlement of the Palestine question'.

China's role in the Palestine issue at the Bandung Conference has been largely misinterpreted. It has been suggested that, in order to win their goodwill, the Chinese outdid the Arabs in their attempts to condemn Israel and uphold 'Palestinian rights' and that they urged the adoption of a more radical resolution than the one introduced by Afghanistan and supported by the Arab states.[75] This Chinese stand was said to have been especially appreciated by the Syrian delegation,[76] as well as by the former Mufti of Jerusalem, Ḥājj Amīn al-Ḥusaynī. He appeared at the

Political Committee meeting on 20 April and later joined the Yemeni delegation and, allegedly, told Chou En-lai: 'I thank you heartily for your defence of the Palestine question which was put forth in your excellent speech at the General Assembly and to the Political Committee.' Chou En-lai allegedly replied: 'We support all Arab problems in general and that of Palestine in particular as we do support the struggle of all enslaved peoples.'[77]

The Arab applause could not, however, change the fact that China's attitude on the Palestine problem throughout the conference, as well as afterwards, remained consistently uncommitted. There was no sign of Chinese encouragement to the demand that 'Palestine must be returned to the Arabs'. In fact, in its dispatches from the conference, the NCNA omitted such extremist expressions.[78] And a *People's Daily* editorial, summing up the conference, reiterated that 'the rights of the Arab people in Palestine should be respected, and the question of Palestine should be peacefully settled according to the principle of the settlement of disputes by the people themselves'.[79]

The insistence on this principle reflected China's conviction, not shared by the Arabs, that the principal contradiction in the Palestine problem has emerged not between Israel and the Arabs but between both and the Western powers. It was primarily from this perspective that the Chinese interpreted the Arab–Israeli conflict. As in the past, they blamed Britain and the United States: in order to strengthen their positions in the Middle East, they had not only instigated the conflict but later exploited the refugee problem so as to increase hostility between Israel and the Arabs, which eventually led to armed incidents. 'It was precisely in view of this kind of situation [i.e., foreign intervention] that the Asian–African Conference declared support of the rights of the Palestinian Arab people and, furthermore, of seeking the implementation of the UN resolutions in order to reach a peaceful settlement of the Palestine problem.'[80]

Thus, despite their association with the Arabs at the Bandung Conference, the Chinese still maintained that foreign 'imperialist' interference had been the ultimate cause of the Palestine problem; that the plight of the Palestinian refugees was not the fault of Israel alone but of some Arab countries as well 'because the territories which, according to the UN Partition Plan, belonged to the Palestinian Arab state had been occupied by Israel, Jordan and other countries [Egypt, which the Chinese for obvious reasons preferred not to mention]';[81] and that a possible settlement should follow the lines of the UN Partition Plan through peaceful and direct negotiations instead of the use of arms, and without outside interference.

Altogether, the Palestine issue was of minor importance to China in the context of the Bandung Conference. Only once and very briefly did Chou En-lai refer to that issue in his long report on the conference: 'In the Resolution on Other Problems,' he said, 'the Asian–African Conference supported the right of the Arab people of Palestine.'[82] This and similar vague and evasive statements have been misinterpreted as Peking's approval of the Arab arguments in the Arab–Israeli conflict.

It was China's perceived identification with the Arabs over the Palestine issue in Bandung that finally persuaded the Government of Israel to agree to establish diplomatic relations with Peking. On 29 April 1955, Daniel Lewin, Head of the Asia Division in Israel's Foreign Ministry, informed Ch'en Chia-k'ang, then Director of the Asia Department in China's Foreign Ministry, that Israel 'desires to establish full diplomatic relations with the Government of the People's Republic of China at the earliest convenient moment'. The timing of Israel's initiative was, however, unfortunate. It was inconceivable that China would have established relations with Israel so soon after the Bandung Conference, at which China, for the first time, had concluded negotiations with prominent Arab leaders. Indeed, on 21 May Ch'en replied, in a polite but noncommittal manner, that the Israeli proposal had been reported to his Government.[83] Yet this diplomatic refusal did not mean that Peking was no longer interested in relations with Israel. Such interest was signalled thereafter on several occasions.

Only two days after Ch'en Chia-k'ang sent his letter, Yao Chung-ming, China's ambassador to Burma who had joined Chou En-lai on his way home from Bandung, assured the Israeli ambassador that Chou En-lai had no intention of alienating Israel in Bandung. He said that Chou En-lai tried to evade the Palestine issue and did not mention Israel by name, but would not forestall unanimity by dissociating himself from the resolution. Furthermore, the ambassador stated that *rapprochement* between China and the Arab countries would not be accomplished at the expense of Israel, with which China still wished to maintain relations of friendship.[84] This attitude was reaffirmed at other meetings between Israeli and Chinese officials.

In July 1955 the new Israeli ambassador to Moscow arrived in

China for a visit, though private, at the invitation of the Chinese. During his visit he held meetings with the President of the Chinese People's Institute of Foreign Affairs as well as with China's Vice Foreign Minister. Both were surprisingly familiar with Israeli affairs but, when the question of diplomatic relations was raised, they replied that the time was not ripe for such relations. They added, however, that co-operation should continue in various fields and that the time would come, perhaps soon, to establish diplomatic relations.[85]

A similar message was conveyed by Yao Chung-ming at several meetings with Israel's chargé d'affaires in Rangoon between July and October 1955.[86] It seems that Israel afterwards desisted and did not renew the initiative for establishing diplomatic relations with the PRC.

China's attitude became potentially more responsive from late 1955 onwards. In several sympathetic commentaries the Chinese expressed particular satisfaction with Israel's refusal to enter regional Western-sponsored military pacts.[87] Israel's stand could hardly have been a novelty for the Chinese at that particular time. China's comments could, therefore, be interpreted as a signal to Israel. One reason for this change was China's possible disappointment with the Arabs. As we have seen above, Peking probably began to realise late in 1955 that there had been very little diplomatic progress with the Arabs since April of that year. Despite personal, trade and cultural exchanges with several Arab countries at, and after, Bandung, none had yet recognised China. Moreover, they continued to abstain in the vote on the China issue in the United Nations even in September 1955. Thus, the Chinese were still looking later that year for a diplomatic breakthrough.

The sudden improvement in Moscow's relations with Israel in mid-1956, particularly from April to July, could have been another reason for China's change of attitude. In his report on China's foreign policy presented in late June 1956 (after Egypt had already recognised the PRC), Chou En-lai declared: 'We have not let slip any opportunity to increase contacts and improve our relations with countries which have not yet established diplomatic relations with us.' At that time there were only two governments that had already recognised China but not yet established diplomatic relations with the PRC, and they were Ceylon and Israel. He continued by saying: 'We are against placing our friendly relations with certain countries on the basis of excluding other countries.'[88] This could mean that Peking did not consider its relations with the Arabs as a barrier to developing relations with Israel.

Remarks in the same spirit were repeated during the Eighth CCP Congress, held in September 1956. In his political report, Liu Shao-ch'i said: 'Our country is prepared to establish normal diplomatic relations with all of those countries which have not yet established diplomatic relations with our country. We believe that the establishment of such relations is beneficial to both sides... Our policy of peaceful co-existence based on the five principles does not exclude any country.'[89] But apparently no one in Israel monitored China's signals and there was no response. Peking had only one explanation for this: 'Owing to outside pressure, some countries are still temporarily prevented from establishing normal diplomatic relations with us. We are convinced, however, that this situation will not last long.'[90]

China's previous attitude towards the Arab–Israeli conflict also remained basically unchanged. The conflict attracted a good deal of Chinese attention in 1956:

One of the most dangerous factors in the Middle East region is the deterioration of the Arab–Israeli conflict... The Chinese people very much hope [that] together the parties concerned would be capable of achieving a peaceful settlement of the Palestine problem, with respect for and in line with the national interest standpoint of *both the Arab and the Israeli sides*, without letting the colonialists seize the opportunity to interfere in the Near East.[91] [Italics added.]

A year after Bandung, the Chinese still held the imperialists responsible not only for creating, but also for aggravating and prolonging, the antagonisms between the Arabs and Israel. It was necessary, Peking stressed, to avoid military conflict: in the absence of foreign intervention the parties concerned should negotiate and settle the Palestine question peacefully on the basis of equality, according to UN principles and the wishes of the countries of the Middle East. 'All who are interested in peace in the Middle East believe that, if efforts are made along these lines, the Palestine question can be settled peacefully.'[92]

This argument was repeated in a book, published in June 1956, in which the Chinese produced probably the most extensive account yet published in China of Israel, Zionism and the Arab–Israeli conflict.[93] The book condemned Zionism for maintaining relations with capitalist countries and with leaders like Wilhelm II, the Turkish Emperor, the Pope, Neville Chamberlain,

Mussolini and even Hitler.[94] Nonetheless, it admitted at the out-
set that 'before the Christian Era, Palestine was originally the
place where Jewish people lived together' and that there had
been an Israeli and Jewish kingdom in Palestine long before the
Arabs occupied the land.[95] After reiterating their argument that
imperialist intervention and rivalry had been the main source of
the Arab–Israeli conflict, the Chinese said: 'The people of Israel
is peace-loving . . . from their own experience in struggle [they]
fully recognise that if they want to negotiate an agreement to
settle Israel's relations with the neighbouring Arab states, the
two sides should follow the method of direct negotiation [*chih-
chien hsieh-shang*] without the interference of foreign imperialist
countries.'[96]

It is quite obvious that at that time China regarded the Arab–
Israeli conflict as an embarrassment and as one of the major
pretexts used by 'Western imperialism' to penetrate the Middle
East. The persistence of the conflict contradicted China's basic
interest in the Middle East, namely, the withdrawal of the West.
China was, therefore, sincerely in favour of a peaceful settlement
of the conflict as soon as possible. Outside interference could
lead only to war, which in turn would lead to further interference:
'Originally, the Arab–Israeli conflict, provided it remained under
the direction of a correct national policy, could have been solved
completely. However, being under the conspiracy and provocations of Anglo-American imperialism, Arab–Israeli relations will
only worsen more and more, [leading] eventually to the outbreak
of war.'[97] This was written at least half a year before war actually
broke out on 29 October 1956. Consequently, China's hitherto
rather moderate attitude towards Israel became more ambivalent,
though not yet as uncompromising as in the mid-1960s.

From late 1956, China began to regard Israel as an instrument
of Western imperialism for exerting pressure on the Arab countries and for maintaining tension in the Middle East. Even before
the Anglo-French-Israeli invasion of Egypt, the Chinese had
argued that Israel's hostilities against Jordan were a case of 'pulling the chestnuts from the fire for the Western colonialist countries, particularly Britain'.[98] Once the war started and was
followed by Anglo-French intervention, as Peking had previously
predicted, there was no reason to maintain a cautious attitude
towards Israel.[99] For the first time the Chinese named Israel as a
'tool' (*kung-chü*) of imperialist aggression,[100] and strongly condemned Israel's attack on Egypt.

What really irritated the Chinese was Israel's refusal to with-draw from Sinai and Gaza. They dismissed the suggestion that the Israeli withdrawal should be preceded by granting Israel free navigation in the Suez Canal: 'The USA has deliberately confused the pulling out of Israeli troops with the Suez Canal and Palestine question to complicate the Middle East question and to keep up tension in that area.'[101] However, six weeks later, the Chinese themselves made a similar confusion: a commentary on Peking radio denounced the United States and Britain for trying to force Egypt to grant passage through the Suez Canal to Israeli ships, without first trying to solve the question of Arab refugees in the Middle East.[102]

This led the Chinese to renew their interest in the Palestinians. A leader of a trade union delegation visiting Egypt said, for example, that the Chinese people were with the Palestinian Arabs in their struggle for human rights.[103] The joint statement repeated: 'The Chinese trade unions . . . sympathize with and support the struggle for human rights of the Arab people in Palestine.'[104]

Altogether, however, Peking interpreted Israel's role in the Suez affair as merely 'unwise' and marginal compared with the role played by Britain and France. China's analysis of the Arab–Israeli conflict remained fundamentally unchanged. In an extra-plenary session on the Middle East at the World Peace Council Meeting in Colombo, Burhān Shahīdī, one of the most important operators of China's Middle East policy, reaffirmed that, to settle the dispute, all the resolutions of the Bandung Conference and relevant resolutions adopted by the United Nations in the past must be strictly observed by *the parties concerned*.[105] In addition, China still distinguished between the Government and the people of Israel. Referring to Israel's 'armed provocation against Egypt' in October 1956, the Chinese indicated that 'the people of Israel resolutely opposed the actions of the Government of Israel which was serving as a messenger of the imperialist countries, and reso-lutely demanded improvement of relations with the Arabs'.[106]

Therefore, although the events of late 1956 and early 1957 increased Peking's suspicions of Israel, they did not lead to a com-plete Chinese rejection of relations. True, Peking no longer signalled Israel to establish diplomatic relations with the PRC (which did not necessarily mean that China had lost all interest in them).[107] But Israeli students did join a group which visited China from early April to early May 1957 at the invitation of the All-China Students' Federation. And relations were still maintained with the Israeli left: Israeli guests attended the 1 May celebrations in Peking in 1957 and, at the end of May, the Central Committee of the CCP sent its 'warm, fraternal greetings' to the Thirteenth Congress of the Communist Party of Israel.[108]

The November 1957 conference of communist leaders in Moscow was the scene of a very curious episode between Mao Tsetung and Shmuel Mikunis, Secretary General of the Communist Party of Israel. On the advice of Maurice Thorez and Palmiro Togliatti, Mikunis met Mao and asked him to influence Khrushchev to allow the rehabilitation of Jewish culture and the supply of Jewish religious necessities in the Soviet Union. Mao, having revealed some familiarity with the history of China's Jews, carried the message to Khrushchev, who changed his attitude by early 1958.[109] The Soviets, however, have not always seen eye to eye with the Chinese regarding Middle Eastern affairs.

Concealed disagreement with Moscow

As early as the mid-1950s the Middle East had begun to play a significant role in Sino-Soviet relations. A series of Western 'acts of aggression' in the Middle East between 1955 and 1959 provided China with opportunities to test Soviet policies. Gradually, Peking became aware of two modes of Soviet international behaviour. Firstly, despite their readiness to extend economic, and even military, aid to independent national–bourgeois governments, the Soviets were unwilling to exercise their own power to deter Western intervention. Moscow declined, therefore, to support genuine 'struggles against imperialist aggression' at their most critical stages. Secondly, on several occasions Moscow denied or ignored China's claimed right to participate in settling Afro-Asian problems, including those of the Middle East. Both observations led the Chinese to modify their foreign, as well as domestic, policy. Internationally, China began to identify increasingly with the peoples of Asia and Africa, advocating firm resistance to imperialism and encouraging self-reliance and persistent struggle. At home China made an unprecedented attempt to develop as quickly as possible its economic, military and nuclear capabilities (along with the purification of its society), to 'leap forward' in independence and strength.

Probably China's leaders' first opportunity to discuss Middle Eastern affairs with Soviet leaders was when a Soviet delegation, including Khrushchev, Bulganin, Mikoyan, Shepilov and others, visited China in September 1954. At that time, the West was trying to establish a new military pact in the Middle East to eventually link SEATO and NATO into one system encircling the socialist camp. The protection of the Soviet Union, the other socialist countries and China was, as Khrushchev later related, China's principal anxiety.[110] Although they probably differed on the aims of Western encroachment, the two sides apparently agreed on the proper response. The Chinese could not but fully appreciate Khrushchev's call, at that time, for a more resolute Soviet policy in Asia and the Middle East, even at some risk of a confrontation with the West.

These views were not entirely shared by 'official' Soviet foreign policy makers, represented by Foreign Minister Molotov. Being Europe-oriented, he disapproved of overstraining the limited Soviet economic and military potential by extending aid to the new Middle Eastern regimes which he still suspected. Moreover, out of conviction that the Soviet Union was weaker than the West, he precluded risking a confrontation when no direct national interest of the Soviet Union had been violated. The Chinese, who had historical reasons to dislike Molotov, did not agree with his views and supported Khrushchev's, thus interfering not only in Soviet Middle Eastern policy but also in the internal power struggle in Moscow.

It is possible that in late 1954 and early 1955 China's growing influence within the Socialist bloc and implicit approval of Khrushchev's policies enabled him to start negotiations with the Arab countries, particularly Egypt, preparing the ground for an arms deal. These negotiations had apparently lost momentum by March–April 1955, when the Soviets and Egyptians suspected each other's motives and sincerity. Allegedly, it was the Chinese who helped to break the deadlock. As we have seen, at Nasser's request they pleaded his cause in Moscow and convinced the Soviet leadership of Egypt's genuine interest in obtaining arms only from the Soviet bloc. China's intervention paved the way for the Czechoslovak arms deal but, in addition, it enhanced Khrushchev's position in the Kremlin, leading to what appeared as a firmer Soviet Middle Eastern and Asian policy.[111]

The fact that China had to convince the Soviets to adopt such a policy indicated, as early as 1955, the existence of Sino-Soviet divergence. Very soon Peking realised that the new Soviet leaders hesitated to share China's trust in the revolutionary and anti-imperialist potential of the Afro-Asian countries. They also declined to acknowledge China's claim to play a special role in Asia and Africa. This claim was based obviously on geographical and historical arguments, but even more on Peking's belief that Asian–African peoples were facing domestic and external problems similar to those of China rather than the USSR. The Chinese, therefore, regarded their own revolutionary experience rather than that of the Soviets as the only one applicable to the colonial and semi-colonial countries. China's prominence at the Bandung Conference, in which the Soviets had not been invited to participate,[112] further consolidated Chinese arguments and thereby created a crack in what was later to become a Sino-Soviet rupture.

The Twentieth Congress of the Communist Party of the Soviet Union (CPSU) in February 1956 added a few more cracks. Among other things, it increased Peking's anxiety that Moscow's determination to reach peaceful co-existence with the United States would be accomplished at the expense of assisting the peoples of Asia and Africa in the fight against imperialism. Because they regarded the Middle East as a major battleground in this fight, the Chinese carefully watched Soviet policies and attitudes towards this region. It seems that they had been disturbed even earlier by Moscow's passive reaction to Western accomplishments in the Middle East – the creation and expansion of military pacts and the deployment of troops and bases.

Soviet attempts to accommodate the West continued to irritate the Chinese. A Soviet delegation led by Khrushchev reached a common understanding with the British Government on the Middle East and particularly on the need to place an arms embargo on the area.[113] Such an 'understanding' was totally unacceptable to Peking. More than once had the Chinese stressed that the fate of the Middle East could no longer be determined in London, Paris or Washington, even with Soviet participation. 'The Middle East countries', they said, 'are capable of managing and settling their own affairs'.[114] Moreover, the Chinese were opposed in principle to any arms embargo. They regarded arms as a necessity for guarding the people's independence against imperialism, and arms deals as a legitimate and 'a normal commercial transaction between two countries' in which no one had any right to interfere.[115] Peking also rejected as inconceivable the Western demands that Egypt and seven other Arab states should maintain a military power equal to that of Israel, in spite of the fact that the Arab nations had a combined population and area many times larger than Israel's.[116] China has always considered

Western imperialism rather than Israel as the principal threat to the Middle East: any 'understanding' with the imperialists, let alone on an arms embargo, would weaken the peoples of the Middle East and thereby increase the Western presence and influence.

For these reasons Peking expected firm Soviet support for Egypt, following Nasser's nationalisation of the Suez Canal. Instead, the Chinese could barely hide their disappointment at the Soviet Union's participation in the London Conference, convened by the West to discuss the nationalisation. Chou En-lai pointed out that the conference proposed by Britain, the United States and France aimed at discussing matters concerning the sovereign rights of Egypt, and that this would be 'impermissible'.[117] The Egyptian Government's rejection of the invitation to take part in the London Conference was the first item in Peking radio's main news bulletin on 13 August, an indication of importance rarely accorded to an item of foreign news.

The Egyptian Government's refusal to attend the London conference arises from its concern to uphold its national sovereignty and dignity. This will certainly be understood and supported by all countries and people that respect Egypt's independence and sovereign rights... The canal belongs to Egypt which has every right to nationalise the Suez Canal Company, and *no country* should or has any right to interfere in this.[118] [Italics added.]

On 15 August an official Chinese Government statement further explained China's disapproval of the conference:

Many countries concerned have been excluded from the conference. The Government of the Soviet Union specifically pointed out that at least 22 other countries, *including the Chinese People's Republic*, should share the discussions connected with *the freedom of navigation through the Suez Canal*... Obviously, a conference like this [i.e., of restricted participation] has no right to make any decision on the Suez Canal, and still less has it any right to discuss any question relating to the sovereignty of Egypt... The Chinese Government holds that the exercise by Egypt of its sovereign right in nationalising the Suez Canal Company allows no interference by *any* foreign country.[119] [Italics added.]

It seems likely, therefore, that the Chinese considered Moscow's participation in the conference in spite of the absence of Egypt and China as an insult to both and as a capitulation to the West. Peking claimed to be fully entitled to join in settling the question of free navigation in the canal for two reasons. One was China's increased use of the canal, as illustrated by China's Minister of Communications, Chang Po-chün:

The Suez Canal is one of the world canals with the biggest volume of transport. It links the Mediterranean and the Red Sea, and plays a very great role in developing trade between East and West. Trade relations between the Chinese People's Republic and Egypt and other Arab countries are developing. At the same time, economic exchanges with the Western countries are increasing every year. China is a maritime country which makes wide use of the Suez Canal. With the development of national economic construction the importance of the Suez Canal to China will certainly grow with each new day. In consequence, we cannot but express great concern over the peaceful settlement of the issue.[120]

Indeed, the Suez Canal was relatively significant in China's limited volume of foreign trade. In 1955 eight Chinese-flag ships had passed through the canal. From 1955 to 1958 nearly 5.5 million tons of freight passed through the canal en route to China (about 4 per cent of all cargo shipments, making China the sixth most important destination east of the canal). For several import and export items, China's use of the canal was quite respectable. In 1958, for example, out of the total quantities of fertilisers and fabricated metals shipped through the canal, 43 per cent and 27 per cent, respectively, went to China. Forty-two per cent of all transported quantities of rice and 40 per cent of all oil seeds came from China. Seventy-four per cent of China's total tea exports and 20 per cent of its rice exports passed through the canal.[121] This was one reason why China felt entitled to participate in settling the canal issue.

Far more important, however, was the other reason, which concerned China's perception of its role in the world, particularly in Asia and Africa: 'The emancipated Chinese people fully realise their position in the world community of nations and their responsibility to defend Asian and world peace. We will never allow the imperialists to threaten and undermine at will the peace in Asia and the rest of the world.'[122] This was another reminder to Moscow of China's special position in Asia and of its contention that the centre of the struggle against imperialism was not in the West (Europe) but in the East (Asia or, to be precise, China): 'At present, the Egyptians and the peoples of other Arab countries stand on the *western* advance line of struggle against colonialism.'[123] [Italics added.]

China interpreted the Suez and other Middle Eastern events primarily in Afro-Asian terms. While emphasising the support given to Egypt by Asia, Africa and Latin America, Soviet support was hardly mentioned, if at all, and apparently referred to as 'other parts of the world' or 'elsewhere'. In his speech at the

Eighth Party Congress, Chu Teh said: 'The recent heroic move on the part of Egypt to nationalise the Suez Canal Company has been greeted with strong support by the people in Asia, Africa *and other parts of the world*, a fact which shows that the powerful tides of the widespread struggle against colonialism have continued to mount.'[124] And Mao said: 'We people who love peace in Asia, Africa, Latin America *and elsewhere* must continue to give strong support to the righteous struggle of Egypt in nationalising the Suez Canal Company.'[125] [Italics added.]

Although tacitly criticising Soviet passivity over the Suez Canal issue the Chinese definitely had neither the intention nor any interest in seeing this issue deteriorate into an armed conflict. They insisted, however, on a proper response to the West, meaning that threats should be met by counter-threats and armed intervention by armed resistance. For the Chinese it was inconceivable to offer or accept negotiations and peaceful settlement of any problem where 'imperialist aggression' had been committed:

The colonialists have brought many heavy burdens and evil consequences to the world of today. This evil system must be eliminated. The people wish to solve such questions by peaceful consultation. But this does not wholly depend on the people. It also depends on the attitude of the colonialists. Armed threats can only bring serious consequences to those who apply them. The Egyptian and the entire Arab people are not isolated. If they are forced to resist aggression, they will have widespread support.[126]

China's attempts to commit the Soviets to a more militant and resolute policy vis-à-vis the West in the Middle East failed. Following the Anglo-French-Israeli invasion of Egypt in late October 1956, the Chinese fully realised that whatever Soviet support there had been had come too late and even then was more pretended than real.

Throughout the Suez crisis the Chinese played down the Soviet role, although they did not dismiss it altogether. Outwardly, China paid its regular tribute to the Soviet stand, especially after Moscow's threat 'to use force in order to crush the aggressors and restore peace in the Middle East'. The Chinese said that the Soviet Union, 'a true friend of the people in the Middle East', was not indifferent to the situation in Egypt: 'In face of the Soviet draft resolution and warning, Britain and France are confronting not only moral restraint but a practical threat.' These actions fully proved, Peking added, that the Soviet Union was the most steadfast defender of world peace and of the freedom and independence of the Asian and African countries, as well as the most sincere and reliable friend of the Middle Eastern countries in their struggle for independence.[127]

Yet the Chinese implicitly indicated their dissatisfaction with the Soviet response to the invasion even after the warning. They regarded the Soviet's tardy contribution to a cease-fire as insufficient and irresolute:

In order to smash the intrigues of the aggressors, all people in the world who desire peace [a common Chinese allusion to the Soviet Union and the socialist countries] must *redouble* their efforts. They must continue to exert pressure on the aggressors and demand the immediate withdrawal of the Anglo-French aggressive forces from Egyptian soil so as to realise a *genuine* cease-fire in Egypt.[128] [Italics added.]

The Chinese went on to say:

The indignant protests of the people throughout the world who cherish peace and uphold justice, and particularly the people of Asian and African countries, and the just stand of the Soviet Union to resolutely safeguard peace in the Middle East have compelled the British, French and Israeli aggressors eventually to agree to a cease-fire. This powerfully demonstrates that the strength of the peace-loving people of the world who support Egypt in their just struggle is incomparably great. *Nevertheless*, the British, French and Israeli aggressive troops are *still* occupying Egyptian territory and continuing military action. The imperialists are *still* attempting to carry out their political conspiracy. To effect a *genuine* cease-fire and restore peace, it is necessary for the peace-loving people throughout the world to make continued efforts and resolutely support Egypt's struggle against aggression.[129] [Italics added.]

China's concern over the Middle East (as well as Hungary) was also indicated in the urgent meeting of the second plenum of the Eighth Central Committee between 10 and 15 November 1956. In his speech on the last day of the session, Mao referred twice to the Middle East. The communiqué said, among other things: 'Liu Shao-ch'i pointed out that all the countries in the socialist camp must firmly strengthen their unity behind the leadership of the Soviet Union in order to counter the aggression by the imperialists in the Middle East and their subversive activities against the socialist camp.'[130]

In other words, while the Chinese criticised the Soviet role in the Suez crisis (as well as in later Middle Eastern crises), they always stopped short of challenging in public Moscow's presumed leadership of the Afro-Asian anti-imperialist struggle (let alone of the socialist camp) – at least until the early 1960s. One reason could have been that China, lacking the economic and military power to support other countries, simply could not substitute for the Soviet Union as a leader; later on, however, these limitations did not prevent the Chinese from attempting to assert their leadership. The main reason was that Mao, while he was fully aware of what he believed were Soviet mistakes, had no doubt at that time that the unity of the socialist camp was vital to withstanding what he perceived as 'Western aggression'. A Chinese bid for leadership could have aggravated the 'contradictions' among the socialist countries and weakened them vis-à-vis the West. This is why the Chinese tried, until the early 1960s, to maintain the unity of the bloc at all costs by publicly aligning with Moscow's policies and attitudes, even though they disagreed with many of them. Soviet behaviour in the Middle East was only later to become an issue in the open polemic between the two.

On the one hand, the Soviets insisted that they had actively supported national liberation wars and rendered them comprehensive aid: 'It is sufficient to refer to such instances as the support for Egypt during the Suez adventure of the Anglo-French-Israeli aggressors.'[131] They also said:

At critical moments when the aggressive circles have brought the world to the brink of war, the Soviet Union, without hesitation, has thrown all its international weight, all its military might to stay the hand raised by the aggressor... This was the case in the period of the Suez crisis and it was the case during the events around Syria and Iraq in 1958.[132]

And Khrushchev later recalled: 'when we delivered our stern warning to the three aggressors ... They took us very seriously ... twenty-two hours after the delivery of our note the aggression was halted. We only had to issue our warning once – unlike the Chinese variety, which has to be repeated about a thousand times before it has any impact.'[133]

On the other hand, the Chinese, who during the crisis declared that 'the powerful pressure of the world forces of peace and the stern warning of the Soviet Union compelled the British, French and Israeli aggressors to announce a cease-fire',[134] later refuted Moscow's claim that Soviet power (particularly nuclear) had played the decisive role in defeating the Anglo-French aggression against Egypt in 1956. The defeat, Peking said, had resulted primarily from the struggle of the Egyptian people. The firm support given to them 'by the people of the world, *including* the Soviet *people, also* played an important part'.[135] [Italics added.] Following the June 1967 War in the Middle East, the Chinese tried to exploit what they called 'the Soviet betrayal' of the Arabs and again raised the Soviet role in 'checking' the Suez invasion: 'During the Suez crisis in 1956, the Soviet revisionist ruling clique, seeing that Britain and France had to withdraw their troops because of the contradictions between them and the United States, hurried forward to make political capital out of the situation by uttering a few high sounding words.'[136] In early 1973 Chou En-lai shed more light on China's arguments in a long interview with the Egyptian journalist Muḥammad Ḥasanayn Haykal. He repeated China's view that the Soviet ultimatum over the Suez war had been no more than 'an empty gun'. He then revealed that Khrushchev himself admitted to Mao, in November 1957 in Moscow, that he had known all along that the United States would in any case compel Britain and France to withdraw, so that no risk had been involved in the Soviet warning to intervene by force.[137]

While underrating Moscow's part in the Suez conflict the Chinese again reiterated the important role played by the Asian and African countries. In the final Chinese analysis the main deterrence against American intervention in the conflict, as well as the main cause of the collapse of the Anglo-French-Israeli attack, was found not in the power of the Soviet Union, which had already been committed to peaceful co-existence with the West, but in Afro-Asian solidarity.

To avoid any misunderstanding the Chinese connected the Suez crisis with the Bandung Conference, at which the Soviets, of course, had not been present:

The armed aggression by the Anglo-French invaders ... is an open challenge to the solemn resolutions of the Asian–African conference. The Asian–African countries and their people cannot allow the Anglo-French aggression to go on unchecked. As a participant in the Asian–African conference, China has the duty to carry out the resolutions of the conference by adopting all possible measures to defend peace in the Asian–African region and to oppose colonialist aggression in order to support the righteous struggle of the Egyptian people and to strike a heavy blow at the outrage of the aggressors. The paramount task now of all in the world who desire peace, *especially the people of the Asian and African countries*, is to strengthen unity, to adopt various measures that will effectively bring about the immediate cessation of the aggression by Britain, France and Israel, and force the aggressors back to where they came from.[138] [Italics added.]

Peking made it clear that 'the unity of the Asian and African countries and their resistance to aggression in any form *form the main guarantee* for the defence of independence and sovereignty and the safeguarding of peace in Asia and Africa'.[139] [Italics added.]

Summing up the Middle East events, Chou En-lai failed to mention the role of the Soviet Union. He admitted, on the other hand, that China had not realised earlier how 'powerful a force for peace' were the Asian–African countries:

The strength and role of the solidarity of Asian and African countries were demonstrated most clearly in the Egyptian event... With the support of the mass of people of Asia and Africa and all peace-loving forces of the world, the Egyptian people, by waging resolute struggle, have beaten back the colonialist aggression. They have gained initial victory in their struggle to defend their sovereignty and territorial integrity and safeguard peace in Asia and Africa. This fact has given us Asian and African peoples great encouragement. At the same time it is a great revelation to us, showing that although the Asian and African countries are not powerful in material strength, all aggression by the colonialists can be frustrated, as long as we maintain our solidarity and firmly unite with all peace-loving forces of the world and wage a resolute struggle.[140]

3 : THE STRUGGLE AGAINST IMPERIALISM

In China's analysis of the world situation, the Anglo-French military invasion of Egypt in October 1956 marked the end of a period of relative tranquillity in international affairs. But the Chinese were not so much concerned about the Anglo-French campaign itself. Although this was the first large-scale use of force by the West since the war in Korea and Indochina, Peking considered Britain and France as declining powers and the Suez episode as their desperate and anachronistic attempt to regain some of their traditional control over the Middle East. Less worried about the invasion itself, the Chinese became much more concerned about its outcome – the increased American involvement in the Middle East.

Mentally, the Chinese were fully prepared for such an eventuality. Mao had maintained all along that the United States, not Britain or France, was the principal imperialist enemy; that Asia and Africa, not the socialist camp, would provide the first and main target of imperialist 'aggression' and, therefore, the main battlefield on which to fight it; and that imperialism's expansion would only aggravate and expose its own weaknesses, or 'contradictions', thus offering better prospects for national liberation. Undoubtedly, Mao regarded the developments in the Middle East in 1957–9 as a confirmation of his theories. Consequently, his influence on China's foreign policy was felt very strongly in 1957–9. In no other period did Mao reveal so much interest in Middle Eastern affairs or talk so much about them:

An incident broke out on the Suez Canal. This is a peculiar thing. Nasser wanted to reclaim the canal and Eden dispatched troops to prevent him from taking it. . . The result is to turn the Middle East over to the U.S. The greatest contradiction [of Britain] is with the U.S., not with Nasser. The U.S. is trying to manoeuvre Britain out of the Middle East, for it harbours sinister designs of taking over the Middle East. . . Under the pretext of anti-Soviet and anti-communism, imperialism is scrambling for the Near East and the Middle East. The two camps of imperialism are fighting for colonies. . . The U.S. is ready to use its military forces to defend Taiwan. It plans to use both civil and military tactics in the Middle East. The crises they are stirring up are beneficial to us.

... The internal contradictions of imperialism in scrambling for colonies are great. We can make use of their contradictions to accomplish our ends. This is strategy.[1]

This short and straightforward analysis provided the framework of China's Middle East policy from early 1957. At that time the Chinese regarded the Eisenhower Doctrine, which had been intended to legitimise American intervention in the Middle East, as the beginning of a US-led Western offensive in Asia and Africa, concentrated in the Middle East. Mao interpreted this offensive according to his 'intermediate zone' theory, to which he referred very often in this period.[2] Indeed there had been sporadic Western attempts to undermine the unity of the socialist camp (such as the revolt in Hungary), but the socialist countries were regarded as far too strong to have been attacked directly by the West. American aggression was not directed against socialism. 'As we see it now, their attack is directed against nationalism, that is ... against Egypt, the Lebanon and other weak Middle Eastern [countries] ... they want to overthrow Nasser, destroy Iraq, subjugate Algeria, and so on.'[3]

Western concentration on the Middle East led the Chinese to conclude that the region had become extremely crucial in imperialist attempts to dominate Asia and Africa:

The present complicated and intensive struggle in the Middle East is a continuation of the fierce struggle in this area since the end of the second world war. . .

Following the second world war, there appeared in the world a number of nationalist countries, in addition to the socialist and imperialist countries. Most of the nationalist countries are following a policy of peace and neutrality. They have formed a tremendous power for peace and created great difficulties for the imperialist policy of expansion and aggression. To carry out its aggressive policy smoothly, the U.S.A. wants, first and foremost, to suppress and eliminate in the Middle East the nationalist countries adhering to peace and neutrality and the national independence movements there. The Middle East is of great significance in the American plan for aggression.

If the people of the Middle East obtain independence, it will be impossible for the imperialists to maintain their remnant colonies not only in Asia but also in Africa. Under this influence, the national independence movement of the Latin American people will also grow. It is therefore crystal clear that the U.S.A. evaluates the Middle East as a key position for it to establish a world colonial empire. . .

The conclusion of the Suez war was seen by the U.S.A. as a good opportunity for its expansion in the Middle East and Africa. Consequently it put forward the 'Eisenhower Doctrine' to 'fill the vacuum'. . . The struggle between the imperialist Powers for control of the Middle East is becoming ever sharper. This places the Middle East in the focus of the current contradictions of the imperialist bloc.[4]

In Mao's view, the situation of tension or crisis (*chin-chang chü-shih*) created by imperialism, and the continued deployment of its troops in the Middle East and elsewhere, offered many advantages to China and to the peoples concerned. On the one hand, crisis situations helped to make a clear-cut distinction between enemies and friends, to mobilise the masses – including 'middle-of-the-roaders' – and to raise the people's vigilance and determination. 'The Iraqi revolution, for example, wasn't it generated by a crisis situation?'[5] On the other hand, Western, particularly American, imperialism, in addition to its internal political and economic difficulties, had overstretched and dispersed its military bases all over the world. It thus became more and more vulnerable.[6] Furthermore, America's supersession of the other powers in the Middle East and elsewhere deepened the already existing rivalry within the imperialist camp, resulting in a lack of unity and determination. This was an opportunity to be seized.

Under these circumstances China's foreign policy, particularly in the Middle East, became more militant. It reflected primarily China's perception of the changes in the international and Middle Eastern scene from early 1957; at the same time the domestic outbreaks of radicalism following the launching of the Great Leap Forward could only reaffirm and further stimulate China's uncompromising attitude on foreign affairs.

Regarding the Middle East, China's activism was mainly rhetorical, but an attempt was also made for the first time (and apparently the last) indirectly to undermine the American presence in the region. There is by now some evidence to suggest that the Chinese bombardment of Quemoi and Matsu which started on 23 August 1958 had been motivated, at least partly, by the situation in the Middle East. Already in April 1955, at the Bandung Conference, Chou En-lai linked Taiwan and the Middle East as two fronts of the same struggle. Later, Mao very often associated these issues as the most outstanding examples of Western aggression. In 1959 he admitted: 'Three days after the United Nations called them [the Americans] to withdraw their troops [from the Middle East], we started our bombardment.'[7] The incident, he said, had been welcomed by the Arab countries: 'Because of what we've done, the American pressure on them is lighter.'[8] And in 1965 he told a visiting Palestine Liberation Organisation (PLO) delegation: 'Our artillery shelled Quemoi to engage the imperialists during the revolution in Iraq and the American landing in the Lebanon... The enemy should be engaged on all fronts.'[9]

Yet China's main efforts, as we have said, were rhetorical. Peking urged the Arab peoples to seize the opportunity and resist firmly any Western encroachment. In the face of growing imperialist intervention and aggression, the Chinese saw no room for compromise. They made it clear they could no longer tolerate what they had been able to ignore when world affairs had been relatively peaceful: the persecution of Arab communists; hostility among the Arab countries; friendly relations between the Arabs and the West; positive neutralism and non-alignment, and so on. Instead, Peking insisted that the Arab countries should implement the 'three unities':

Internal unity in the Asian and African countries, unity between the various Asian and African countries and unity between the Asian and African countries and the socialist countries are the basic guarantee for the Asian and African people in striving for and protecting national independence, and a serious barrier against the imperialists in their aggression and expansion in the Asian and African area.[10]

Co-operation with the socialist camp was undoubtedly the most important of these unities, but the Chinese themselves were not yet ready to assume the leadership of the Afro-Asian world in the fight against imperialism. In their view, this was primarily the duty of the Soviet Union. Even before the trumpeting of Soviet technological accomplishments, the Chinese had been convinced that the Soviet Union and the socialist camp were stronger than the West.[11] China, therefore, regarded the Soviet role in repelling the imperialist intervention in the Middle East as crucial. Since early 1957 Peking had urged Moscow to render the Arab countries all necessary support and to deter Western aggression by threats of retaliation.

Gradually, however, the Chinese realised that the Arabs as well as the Soviets had rejected their analysis of the world situation together with the measures they believed had been essential to resist the West. The outcome was a growing Chinese impatience with the Arab nationalists and implicit criticism of the Soviet Union, which led to strained relations with both.

Discord with the Arabs

The climax reached in Sino-Arab relations in late 1956 apparently continued in the following year when the Chinese praised Egypt's 'victory' in the Suez Canal affair. They noted that

in the rising anti-colonial struggle of the Middle East people, Egypt and Syria are playing an especially important role... Developments in the Middle East situation since the Asian–African conference effectively show that Egypt and Syria have become the core of Arab nationalism and the bulwark of the anti-colonial struggle in the Middle East.[12]

Peking also acclaimed the Egyptian people's defence of their sovereignty over the Suez Canal and their defeat of a series of imperialist conspiracies as 'a glorious model of fighting against colonialism and struggling for sovereignty and independence'.[13]

China's trade with Egypt, both exports and imports, nearly doubled in 1957 compared with the previous year. The value of China's imports from Egypt in 1957, which was more than twice the value of its exports, made China the second most important of Egypt's customers, next to the Soviet Union.[14] A new protocol for the third year of the Sino-Egyptian Trade Agreement (of August 1955) was signed in Peking towards the end of 1957. It provided for trade amounting to £26 million, just over 8 per cent more than the previous trade protocol (which had provided for £24 million of trade, or 20 per cent more than the first one).[15]

It should be noted, however, that, although both sides frequently expressed satisfaction with the execution of these agreements, their actual trading was inconsistent with the agreements' provisions. China's imports from Egypt were lower in 1956 and 1958 and much higher in 1957 than specified; exports to Egypt were always very much lower; and the total actual trade was lower than what had been agreed on.

In 1957 China became more interested in Syria, as a result of the growing tension along Syria's borders with Israel and Turkey. Peking, believing that Syria would become the next target of imperialist 'aggression', declared its support for Syria and urged the frustration of imperialist schemes. In a message to the Syrian President, Mao said: 'At a time when the U.S.A. is pushing Turkey to carry out provocations against Syria in a plot to start a war of aggression, I reiterate the firm stand of the Government and people of China to support resolutely the just struggle of the Syrian people to defend its independence and peace.'[16]

Earlier, on 26 September 1957, a Syria–China Friendship Association was founded in Damascus; four days later, a China–Syria Friendship Association under the leadership of Muḥammad Ta P'u-sheng, vice-chairman of the China Islamic Association, was launched in Peking. In October 1957, almost 16 months after Syria had recognised the PRC and a year after a Chinese ambassador had arrived in Damascus, Syria sent a chargé d'affaires, not even an ambassador, to Peking.

In the field of trade, there was in 1957 a more than six-fold increase in China's imports from Syria, against a less than 70 per cent increase in China's exports, as compared with 1956. Consequently, a huge deficit was created in China's trade balance with Syria, with imports twenty times greater than exports.

In 1957 China also revealed particular interest in Jordan, the Yemen and Oman. Peking considered Jordan as being basically hostile to the West even earlier, in 1956. This judgement seemed to have been reaffirmed when in November the Jordanian Parliament unanimously recommended the abrogation of the alliance with Britain and recognition of the PRC.[17] On 23 March 1957, according to a Middle East News Agency report, the Jordanian premier, Sulaymān al-Nābulsī, declared that the Jordanian Government intended to recognise the PRC shortly and to co-operate closely with the Chinese Government.[18] Shortly afterwards Nābulsī was forced to resign and in August Jordan established diplomatic relations with Taiwan. Thereafter, China began to encourage the Jordanian people's resistance to imperialism.

The Yemen and Oman provided China with another example of a 'people's struggle against imperialism'. After the Yemen's recognition of China in August 1956, there were no major developments in their mutual relations. China continued in 1957 to support the Yemen's claim to Aden and its opposition to Britain. Oman caught China's attention in July 1957 in the wake of Britain's attempts to suppress the local rising. As usual, Peking interpreted the insurrection as a struggle for independence and against Britain's desire to seize the oil reserves: 'We Chinese, who sympathise [with] and support all struggles against colonialism, pledge our firm support to the heroic Arabs who are fighting against British enslavement and plunder in Oman.'[19] China's sympathy and 'resolute opposition to British armed intervention' were also conveyed to Omani officials who met Ch'en Chia-k'ang, China's ambassador in Cairo, on 9 August and 21 September

1957, as well as to the Arab League in reply to a memorandum soliciting support for Oman from the Bandung countries.[20]

Altogether, Sino-Arab relations in 1957 remained friendly. Despite China's anxiety there was no armed Western intervention in the Middle East that year. Similarly, there was no substantial change in the attitude of the Arab governments to justify a change in China's policy. The next year, however, brought with it changes in both respects. Accordingly, China's Middle East policy became more militant and uncompromising.

China and the UAR: the showdown

In 1957 and 1958 Sino-Egyptian relations seemed as friendly as ever: Egypt was consistently praised by the Chinese; in early January 1958 the Egypt–China Friendship Association was formed (some 14 months after its Chinese counterpart had been created), and in April–May a long-awaited UAR military mission finally visited China.

Yet, underlying this friendship, tension was beginning to develop which led to a serious deterioration of Sino-UAR relations. This tension resulted from different interpretations of the international and Middle Eastern situation. China, whose world outlook was further radicalised by events at home (the Great Leap Forward), and by perceptions of Western offensive, became more sensitive and critical regarding the possible response of some national–bourgeois regimes. Particular attention was paid to Egypt, since in China's view the Middle East was to be the main battlefield in the new imperialist assault. Egypt was regarded not only as the leader of the Arab world but also as the pillar of Afro-Asian solidarity, as well as a base for Chinese operations in the Middle East and Africa. If Nasser deserted the anti-imperialist front in face of the West this could mean multilateral failure for the Chinese. Indeed, Nasser's actions and policy, although not affecting China directly, were regarded by the Chinese as wholly inappropriate in view of their analysis of the international situation and its implications in the Middle East. In 1957 and 1958 China disapproved, though not yet publicly, of all three levels of Nasser's policies – his internal policy; inter-Arab policy; and international policy.

Regarding Egypt's internal politics, China was particularly concerned about the lack of unity among the people as manifested by the persecution of communists. Peking insisted that communists should have fully participated, if not actually taken the lead, in the struggle against imperialism at that time of crisis:

An important condition for defeating imperialism is maintenance of the unity of all patriotic and democratic forces within a country and especially the mobilising of the revolutionary enthusiasm of the masses of workers and peasants. Many facts have shown that the broader the unity of various patriotic and democratic forces and the fuller the mobilisation of the strength of the masses of workers and peasants, the more assured is the victory of the struggle against imperialism. Any nation can place itself in an invincible position if it unites the forces of the entire people and at the same time engages in joint struggle alongside all anti-imperialist forces in the world... Communists in every country are real patriots because they have no interests of their own apart from the interests of the people. It is understandable therefore that communists in the oppressed nations are always in the forefront of national struggle.[21]

Until late 1957 China had revealed a very limited interest in the Arab communists. There have never been traditional links, or even regular communication, between the CCP and the Arab communist parties. China had practically no say, let alone influence, in Middle Eastern communist affairs. Apart from casual contacts and several Chinese attempts in 1954 to criticise Nasser's persecution of the Egyptian communists, Arab communism was largely ignored by Peking, for several reasons: the Chinese have been aware of the traditional affiliation between Arab communists and European communism, as well as of the communists' weak position vis-à-vis the Arab regimes. Moreover, the Chinese believed that the role of communists in colonial and semi-colonial countries should first be determined by the principal contradiction – that with Western imperialism rather than with local governments, however reactionary they might be. Therefore, as long as the Middle East was not threatened directly by the West, China could afford to overlook the maltreatment of local communists.

But, once the Arab countries became a major target of 'imperialist aggression', China began insisting on close cooperation between all strata of Arab society, including the communists. This pattern was already well established. Whenever the Chinese paid tribute, however casual, to Middle Eastern communists, it was always within the context of the struggle against imperialism.[22] It seems, therefore, unlikely that the Chinese harboured subversive or revolutionary intentions either behind their protests against the persecution of communists in the Middle East or in their call for communist participation in the anti-imperialist front.

Internal unity was, in China's view, a basic pre-condition in the fight against imperialism. Paradoxically, it was precisely for this reason that the Chinese had some reservations about Egypt's union with Syria in February 1958.[23] Peking anticipated that the union would mean the abolition of all political parties, particularly the Syrian Communist Party, which had been the largest and best-organised communist party in the Arab world.[24] Such fears were reflected in Chou En-lai's report to the National People's Congress on 10 February 1958:

Recently, a united Arab republic was proclaimed by Egypt and Syria. We warmly greet the founding of this new state and sincerely hope that the United Arab Republic *will rely on the patriotic and democratic forces* in Egypt and Syria to greatly encourage the Arab countries to strengthen their solidarity, smash all schemes designed to split the Arab peoples and win even greater victories in their common struggle to safeguard national independence and oppose colonialism.[25] [Italics added.]

Yet China's hopes for a united domestic front in the UAR were frustrated as Nasser continued his assault on the communists in Egypt, and even more so in Syria. Peking was still careful not to criticise Nasser in public, but there were indications of China's anxiety and resentment:

In Asia, Africa and Latin America, national independence movements are forging ahead. Though the imperialists are trying to undermine these movements by underhand means and by force, and though certain sections of the bourgeoisie in those nations are trying to restrict the growth of the people's forces which are most resolutely opposed to imperialism [i.e., the communists], facts have proved that they cannot hold back the historical advance of the people's national and democratic struggles.[26]

By early 1959, however, Nasser's anti-communist campaign had gathered momentum. The printing houses which had been founded a year earlier to print Soviet and Chinese publications in Arabic for distribution throughout the Arab countries, and which were financed by the Soviet and Chinese embassies in Cairo, were now closed. In Damascus the Government removed most Soviet and Chinese publications from news-stands.[27] It was at that time that China began to report, still without comment, on the arrests of, and hostility towards, communists in the UAR.[28]

Egypt's inter-Arab politics have also been subject to severe Chinese criticism. Peking was particularly concerned about Egypt's attempts to attain hegemony over the Arab countries, thereby undermining their independence and destroying their unity. Since early 1957 the Chinese underlined the vital need for Arab unity: 'Only by maintaining unity can the Arab states safeguard their independence. Otherwise, the Arab states will fall into the colonialist trap of divide and rule... The foremost task today of the Arab states wanting to uphold their independence is close unity.'[29] By calling for independence through unity, in contrast to 'union', Peking meant unity among independent countries, and not an imposed union whereby the independence and freedoms of one or some of the parties is lost. This was another reason why the Chinese remained suspicious towards the Egyptian–Syrian union.

But the major obstacle, in China's view, to reaching inter-Arab unity was the rift between the UAR and Kassem's Iraq. The Chinese totally disapproved of Nasser's hostility towards the Iraqi revolution but refrained from direct charges, blaming, as usual, imperialist instigation:

The imperialists are well aware that the victory of the national liberation struggles of the Asian and African peoples stems from their unity which is being strengthened from day to day. That is why the imperialists are cooking up and resorting to all sorts of despicable means to sow discord among the Asian and African peoples, incite dissension within and between their countries, seeking thus to undermine their unity so as to smite their countries one by one.[30]

This was also an indirect warning to Nasser that inter-Arab disputes were only serving the imperialists.

Finally, in the realm of international politics, the Chinese were annoyed by Nasser's growing positive neutralism which was, according to their analysis of the situation, rather negative: it meant compromise with the West, friendship with Tito whom they detested, and hostility towards the socialist countries. In the mid-1950s, when they believed that Western imperialism was still licking its Korean and Indochinese wounds, the Chinese tolerated neutralism and non-alignment in order not only to gain recognition and establish diplomatic relations but also to diminish imperialist influence and control in the Asian–African countries and to unite them. In the late 1950s, however, China had already accomplished part of its diplomatic aims and, what was more important, the world situation had changed. Neutralism, which had been tolerated in peacetime, could no longer be approved in face of persistent Western aggression. The Chinese insisted that, in order to withstand and defeat the West, firm opposition and armed struggle were imperative; since the Afro-Asian countries were too weak to carry the burden alone, they were advised to abandon their middle-of-the-road position and co-operate closely with the Soviet Union and the socialist camp.

It seems that the Chinese considered unity between the Arabs and the socialist countries as the crucial pre-condition for effective resistance to the West, even more than internal and inter-Arab unity:

Experience shows, that when the Arab people resolutely stand up against imperialism, they are able to rely on the close co-operation of the socialist camp, the extensive unity of the patriotic and democratic forces of their own countries and on co-operation on an equal basis among the Arab countries to overcome any imperialist aggression by force. *Most important among these factors is the Arab people's close co-operation with the socialist camp.* It is not only because the socialist camp is stronger than the imperialist camp but also because the support extended by the socialist camp to the people resisting aggression and its defence of peace are sincere and selfless.[31] [Italics added.]

It is possible that China began to suspect Nasser's international orientation immediately after the Anglo-French-Israeli invasion of Egypt, when Nasser agreed to the stationing of the United Nations Emergency Force on Egyptian soil. The Chinese, who interpreted the Suez invasion, and particularly the Eisenhower Doctrine which followed it, as the beginning of the new Western offensive in the Middle East, saw no room for concession and compromise, definitely not under the disguise of the United Nations: 'UN forces ... have no right to occupy one inch of Egypt's territory on behalf of the aggressive forces of Britain, France and Israel.'[32]

In the face of repeated Western encroachments on the Middle East in 1957 and 1958, China expected Egypt to lead a firm Arab opposition and strengthen relations with the socialist countries. Instead, there were indications that Egypt was tending to make accommodations with the West and to adopt anti-communist and anti-Soviet terminology, as well as policies. These indications were of particular significance because of Egypt's prominent position within the Afro-Asian bloc, and particularly in the newly-created Afro-Asian People's Solidarity Organisation (AAPSO). Indeed, the fact that the AAPSO's first conference took place in Cairo (December 1957), that its secretariat was afterwards situated in Cairo, and that its Secretary General was an Egyptian, gave Egypt the great advantage of direct supervision and influence at the expense of the communist representatives, particularly the Chinese, who played a relatively subordinate role.[33]

At the beginning, however, China's attacks were directed against neutralism in general, and Yugoslav neutralism in particular. Although Nasser was not mentioned, the Chinese were undoubtedly well aware of his close association and personal friendship with both Tito and Nehru. Thus, when the Chinese criticised Tito's two-month trip to Asia and Africa in early 1959,[34] Nasser was also offended, not only because of his friendship with Tito but also because, at his request, Tito was also representing Egypt on his voyage.[35] There is little doubt that by early 1959 the Chinese were deeply disappointed with Nasser's domestic, inter-Arab and international policies.

The real deterioration in Sino-Egyptian relations came after the abortive Egyptian-engineered Shawwāf *coup d'état* against Kassem in early March 1959. Until then, both Egypt and China cautiously avoided public protests and denunciations. Nasser's attacks were directed against communism at home and its supporters abroad, implicating the Soviet Union but not China. The Chinese concealed their grievances and made indirect accusations.

Following Shawwāf's failure, Nasser's attacks on world communism, which had definitely supported Kassem, became even more furious, but, still within the previous pattern, with no reference to China.[36] However, it was the Chinese who regarded Nasser's subversion of the new revolutionary regime in Iraq as unforgivable and, therefore, could no longer afford to remain silent. In a burst of anger Peking took the unprecedented step of attacking, in the strongest terms ever, both the UAR and Nasser personally:

President Nasser, who once won the people's respect, has recently made vicious attacks on Iraq, the Communist Parties and the Soviet Union... President Nasser's frenzied abuse against the Kassem government is already in harmony with the imperialist tune... The anti-Communist press of the UAR is currently making much noise over the slogan of 'Neither West nor East'. This is only a deliberate attempt to confuse the socialist with the imperialist countries, to confuse friends with enemies. It is tantamount to saying 'Neither enemies nor friends'. But those who want no friends will naturally not be feared by any enemy. On the contrary, this will become a step towards going over to the enemy.[37]

This was not only the CCP's view but also the Government's. In his 'Report on the Work of the Government', Chou En-lai said:

A complicated situation has arisen recently in the Arab national independence movement. Some people in power in the United Arab Republic have launched an attack on the Republic of Iraq, and then also attacked the Soviet Union, the great friend of the Arab peoples. Obviously, such actions are injurious to the cause of independence of the Arab nation.[38]

China's onslaught instantly triggered a frantic Egyptian response, which fully exploited the coinciding anti-Chinese revolt in Tibet. The Egyptian communications media (as well as those of all the Arab countries, except Iraq) openly sympathised with the Tibetan revolt,[39] and warned against similar Chinese communist intervention in Iraq. China was accused of interfering in Arab internal affairs by supporting the local communist parties and thereby undermining Arab independence, freedom and security.[40] In early June 1959 the UAR ambassador in China was recalled and the newly-appointed ambassador did not arrive until early 1960. In July and August another wave of anti-Chinese propaganda erupted in Egypt after the Chinese had been accused of inciting and fomenting the Kirkuk incidents. This, in turn, provoked further Chinese reaction, accusations and protests over the persecution of Arab communists.[41]

The repercussions of the Sino-UAR rift were also felt in the Yemen which, as of March 1958, had become part of a symbolic federation with the UAR. Initially, China's relations with the Yemen developed smoothly. In January 1958, Muḥammad al-Badr, Crown Prince, Deputy Premier, Foreign Minister and Defence Minister of the Yemen became the first Arab leader to visit China. During his visit the Chinese signed their first (and only) Treaty of Friendship with an Arab country, as well as a Treaty of Commerce and an agreement on scientific, technical and cultural co-operation.[42] China also offered the Yemen a long-term loan of $16.38 million (the largest till then to any Arab country) and undertook to build the Ṣanʿā-Ḥudayda highway and several factories. Protocols for the implementation of these agreements were signed in January 1959, though Chinese experts and technicians had arrived in the Yemen earlier.

However, in September 1959 press reports said that the Imām warned the Chinese working in the Yemen not to interfere in the country's internal affairs and to avoid contacts with its population. In November it was disclosed that twenty-five Chinese experts had been expelled.[43] This was probably an outcome of the deterioration of China's relations with the UAR. Still, Sino-Yemeni relations did not suffer greatly and there were still several hundred Chinese working in the Yemen in 1960.

The Bakdāsh affair

By the autumn of 1959 Sino-UAR relations had almost reached their breaking point. On 28 September, at China's Tenth Anniversary celebration in Peking, Khālid Bakdāsh, Secretary General of the (banned) Syrian Communist Party, made a speech in which he strongly attacked the UAR and Nasser personally. Among other things he said:

Now, comrades, the east Arab is going through a difficult time. Events have shown that the anti-communist movement openly initiated by Nasser early this year was merely the backdrop to a dangerous policy. This policy is menacing the important victory won by the Arab nations in their liberation movement over recent years. The attempt to merge Syria and Egypt, the intrigues of the ruling clique of the UAR against the Iraqi Republic, the understanding between Nasser and King Saud and King Hussein, the opening of the door to imperialist capital, and the slanders against the Soviet Union and People's China – all this shows to the people and the broadest section of the patriots of the Arab states that the bourgeois monopoly clique of Egypt are actively distorting, under an anti-Communist smoke-screen, the slogan of Arab unity and exploiting this slogan for carrying their policy based on narrow-minded and selfish class ambition. Their policy is to gather together the forces of reactionaries and imperialist agents in the Arab world, to split the national movement, to strangle democracy, to deprive the people of their elementary freedom, to seek understanding with U.S. imperialism, and to undermine the friendship with the countries of the socialist camp...
The Arab people today are subjected to a dictatorship of terror which is resorting to Fascist tactics against all patriotic and democratic forces. Hundreds of patriots, including Communists, trade unionists, democrats and youth, are now subjected to diverse forms of brutal oppression in prisons in Egypt and Syria...
Today Syria is suffering from a despotic and chaotic system never before witnessed in her modern history. Nasser wants to carry out in Iraq, Lebanon and other Arab countries what he is carrying out today in Syria, but this policy is doomed to failure.[44]

These words caused the gravest crisis in Sino-UAR relations. The UAR chargé d'affaires was ordered home immediately and the Egyptians boycotted China's anniversary celebrations both in Cairo and in Peking. In a memorandum handed to the Chinese ambassador, the Egyptian Government strongly protested against the incident, condemning it as a rude deviation from diplomatic convention, a violation of the principles of peaceful co-existence, and an interference in the internal affairs of the UAR.[45] Summing up, Nasser stated: 'We do not accept insults from anybody and we consider what happened in China as an insult. We will accept no intervention from anybody – and we consider what happened as intervention in our internal affairs.'[46]

While the UAR official protests were confined to the Bakdāsh speech itself, the Arab media, in the three weeks following the incident, unleashed a wave of bitter accusations and slanders against the Chinese communists, who were depicted as ruthless, barbarian and aggressive, both at home and abroad, the Arab world included. China was compared to Hitler's Germany and accused of attacking its neighbouring countries in search of *lebensraum* with the aim of establishing a zone of influence in the Arab world with the help of local communists. According to the Egyptian press, the Chinese wanted to turn the people of the UAR into slaves, flood their country with blood, cover it with corpses and victoriously wave the red flag above it.[47]

By 25 October the crisis had subsided. China apologised and the UAR accepted as satisfactory the Chinese explanation that Bakdāsh had been invited not by the Chinese Government but by the CCP.[48] Later, Chou En-lai allegedly told Nasser that this had been the only time that China had ever allowed itself to apologise to anybody.[49]

Yet many questions remained unresolved. Why did the Chinese invite Bakdāsh in the first place and introduce him as the Secretary General of the Syrian Communist Party, knowing, undoubtedly, that this party had been officially banned and that, furthermore, Syria was no longer an independent entity but rather an integral part of the UAR? As one Egyptian put it, this was tantamount to inviting Chiang K'ai-shek's representative to Cairo in order to attack the PRC and Mao personally in front of the Chinese communist ambassador.

Despite China's apologies, this incident cannot be brushed aside as a mere misunderstanding, as if Peking had been unaware of the consequences and could not have anticipated Egypt's fierce reaction. In fact, it is most likely that the Chinese had prior knowledge of the full content of the Bakdāsh speech and apparently did not attempt to modify it in any way or play it down. On the contrary, Peking, as if deliberately, repeated the speech in the press and radio for several days after the UAR protest. That China approved of, and identified with, the Bakdāsh speech was demonstrated in November, when an article of his was reprinted in China, repeating his charges and arguments, only in greater detail.[50]

China's rude behaviour should be analysed in view of contemporary international developments and the events in the Middle East. In early 1957, when they believed that the West was increasing its attempts to penetrate the Middle East, the Chinese became alarmed to see the anti-imperialist front splitting instead of uniting. This split occurred not only among the Arab states, engaged in internal rivalries and mutual hostility, but also among the Asian–African countries and even in the socialist camp, where disagreement between China and the Soviet Union could hardly be concealed. Giving Bakdāsh the floor should be regarded, therefore, as the culmination of China's attempts to turn the wheels back and remind Egypt, as well as Iraq and Moscow, that the main enemy was waiting not within but beyond the Arab countries.

China's attack on the UAR appeared to have been a well-calculated risk, based on a sober and realistic distinction between secondary short-term expediency, such as China's position and image in Egypt and the use of that country as a base of operation in both the Middle East and Africa, and primary long-term achievements, meaning Egypt's recognition of the PRC, its diplomatic relations with Peking, and its support of the PRC on the Taiwan and United Nations issues.

It is unreasonable to think that the Chinese would have considered the newly established, largely unknown, and still isolated Iraqi Republic as a substitute for their well-established base of operations in Egypt. In fact, all the evidence suggests that the Chinese held back from publicising their grievances against Egypt for as long as possible (until early 1959), probably to avoid losing their position. When it finally unleashed its attacks, China's position and image in the UAR had already been eroded for some time and its freedom of action restricted. As a result the Chinese had very little to lose in this tactical respect. On the other hand, they were probably quite confident of the Arabs' fundamental, long-term interest in relations with the PRC. Otherwise they would not have allowed themselves, or Bakdāsh, to attack the UAR and Nasser.

This self-confidence emanated undoubtedly from Mao himself, who realised that anti-Chinese activities were sporadic and ephemeral and, far from signalling bilateral crises, were clung to on various pretexts, such as the questions of Tibet and the Sino-Indian border.[51] Thus, Chou En-lai stated:

The imperialists, with the U.S.A. at their head, whipped up a vicious anti-Chinese wave, designed to prevent the spread of China's influence and to isolate China in international affairs. Although this scheme was joined in by the reactionaries, revisionists and their echoers in various countries and there was a hue and cry for a time, the result went contrary to their wishes. . . Solidarity and friendship of the peoples of other countries is the main stream of our relations with other countries, while anti-Chinese activities are but a backwash.[52]

These arguments were basically correct. Despite the slanders against China, the UAR continued to support the PRC in the United Nations and on the Taiwan issue, without severing diplomatic relations,[53] though complete normality was not restored for a long time.

China and Iraq: frustrated expectations

One of the main reasons for the collapse of Sino-Egyptian relations was China's criticism of Nasser's hostility towards Kassem's Iraq. For the PRC, the July 1958 revolution in Iraq was of the utmost importance, primarily from the international point of view. This does not mean that the Chinese ignored the domestic implications of the revolution – the overthrow of one of the most reactionary governments in the Middle East; the establishment of national democracy; and the decisive role played by the Iraqi communists in the revolution and particularly in its consolidation thereafter. But it seems, in retrospect, that the Chinese were not misled to believe that Kassem's regime was anything more than a military–bourgeois dictatorship, still very distant from revolutionary socialism.

Peking was mainly interested in the international significance of the Iraqi revolution and it was usually from this angle that the Chinese analysed the situation in Iraq:

The founding of the Iraqi Republic is especially significant for the Asian and African peoples, because the Faisal monarchy of Iraq was the initiator of the Baghdad Pact and a cornerstone of U.S. and British imperialist aggression in the Middle East. Now this cornerstone has fallen with a bang, and, moreover, Iraq has become an anti-imperialist forefront.

The founding of the Iraqi Republic not only helps the struggle of the Lebanese people directly, but it fundamentally alters the situation in the Middle East and greatly accelerates the process of complete destruction of the colonial forces in the Middle East and even in the world as a whole.[54]

The particular timing and nature of the revolution fit in perfectly with China's strategic set-up. It erupted in the face of growing Western pressure in the Middle East and at a time when Nasser was showing an inclination to accommodate the West. China, therefore, regarded the Iraqi revolution not only as a major blow to Western imperialism, but also as an example which might have persuaded Nasser to resume his position on the anti-imperialist front, both at home and abroad, as well as persuading Moscow to become more firmly committed against Western intervention in the Middle East.

China moved towards Iraq very quickly. Recognition was

extended on 16 July, only two days after the revolution, and within ten days diplomatic relations were established and two NCNA correspondents arrived in Baghdad. By the end of August, Ch'en Chih-fang, who had been China's ambassador to Syria from October 1956 to February 1958, was appointed ambassador to Iraq and had already arrived there. In late September the China–Iraq Friendship Association was founded in Peking with Liu Ning-yi, President of China's Federation of Trade Unions, elected as chairman. In the following months several delegations were exchanged and agreements signed, and the Chinese frequently praised the Iraqi revolution.

This sudden and enthusiastic Sino-Iraqi friendship weakened China's position in the UAR, Kassem's adversary. The Chinese could not have been unaware of the signs of a growing breach between Egypt and Iraq, but these were, at least publicly, ignored. However, following Nasser's abortive attempts to undermine the new Iraqi republic, the Chinese publicly defended Kassem. This support, the Chinese presence and activities in Iraq, and the fact that Kassem himself relied heavily in the first months of his rule on the local communists, led to a fundamental misinterpretation of Peking's role in Iraq.

Allegedly, China regarded the Iraqi revolution as the first genuine revolution in the Middle East and, moreover, as an opportunity to establish a Maoist People's Republic in the Arab world, 'to undermine the neutralists in that area and replace them with out-and-out communist regimes which could be satellites, not of Moscow, but of Peiping'.[55] It was also alleged that the Iraqi Communist Party had split into rival pro-Soviet and pro-Chinese factions, and China was accused of having manipulated and supported the 'leftist' communists, even by supplying arms, thus encouraging a communist takeover of Iraq. The Chinese, in particular Burhān Shahīdī and Ma Chien, who had spent some time in Iraq in 1959 on a cultural mission, were further accused of having actually incited, planned and organised the Mosul and Kirkuk incidents (March and July 1959), in which the communists used brutality and caused bloodshed.

Most of these allegations, which were raised by biased circles hostile to communism, to the PRC and to Kassem,[56] are groundless. There is no evidence to substantiate the allegation that China supported and directed the leftist faction within the Iraqi Communist Party, nor that Chinese had been involved in the Mosul and Kirkuk massacres. To begin with, there is no trace in the late

1950s (and, for that matter, in the 1960s as well) of any 'Chinese wing' within the Iraqi Communist Party. Secondly, there is no evidence of Chinese infiltration or influence in the Iraqi Communist Party at that time, nor at any other time.[57] China was not only too far from Iraq but also lacked the means to support and defend a 'pro-Chinese' communist regime there (there were transport problems even in initiating Sino-Iraqi trade). Furthermore, the Chinese were newcomers to Iraq and did not have previous relations either with the country or with its communists. To assume that within a few months they could have succeeded in gaining such influence over the Iraqi Communist Party, or any part of it, is to overestimate China's capabilities and underestimate the independence of the Iraqi Communist Party.

True, in the first months of the Iraqi republic, the communists enjoyed unprecedented liberty (in Middle Eastern terms) and provided one of Kassem's major sources of support. But the Chinese never considered the Iraqi revolution as anything more than a national–democratic one. They indeed appreciated Kassem's alignment with the 'democratic and patriotic forces' (i.e., the communists) but primarily as a contribution to opposing imperialism, a task which seemed to them the most urgent: 'The Communist Parties of the Asian, African and Latin American countries are becoming the core of national unity in their struggle for national independence.'[58]

China, therefore, supported Kassem not because of his socialist or communist outlook (which was superficial, at best), but because of his firm stand against imperialism. Some time later Mao said of Iraq and the UAR: 'Both are to the right of the centre, but both oppose imperialism.'[59]

Very soon it became clear that Kassem had accepted the alliance with the communists only half-heartedly and as a short-term political necessity. From mid-1959, when he felt that he no longer needed the support of the communists, who had become instead a threat to his rule, Kassem turned against them as ruthlessly as Nasser had done before him. Iraqi communists were arrested and communist literature was banned, including Mao Tse-tung's *On the Correct Handling of Contradictions Among the People*, Liu Shao-ch'i's *On the Party* and Hu Ch'iao-mu's *Thirty Years of the Chinese Communist Party*.[60]

China's enthusiasm for Kassem began to subside following his assault on the Iraqi communists. There was no public Chinese criticism since Kassem, unlike the neutralists. still retained his strong anti-imperialist posture. By late 1959, however, Sino-Iraqi relations had become lukewarm and shortly afterwards the Chinese lost interest in Kassem.

Emerging conflict with Moscow

From early 1957 to the end of 1959 the Middle East became a theatre of growing Sino-Soviet disagreements which could barely be concealed. China and the Soviet Union held different views not only on the role of the Middle Eastern communists and national–bourgeoisie, but primarily on the nature of Western aggression in the Middle East and the proper ways to deal with it.

In the past, the Chinese were far from satisfied with the Soviet response to the West. As we have seen, they knew perfectly well that the Anglo-French-Israeli invasion of Egypt in October 1956 had been repulsed as a result of American, rather than Soviet, pressure. It was precisely this development, American intervention in the Middle East, which worried the Chinese. They interpreted the Eisenhower Doctrine as the signal for an American-led offensive in the region, which required an uncompromising Soviet reaction.

In early 1957, Chou En-lai cut short his tour in Asia and hurried to Eastern Europe and the Soviet Union. His main concern was undoubtedly the crisis within the socialist bloc but, presumably, he also wanted to ensure that a firm Soviet attitude would be adopted on the Middle East question. On 18 January 1957, during his stay in Moscow, a joint Soviet–Chinese declaration was issued. Among other things it condemned the Eisenhower Doctrine and announced the readiness of the two governments to support the peoples of the Middle East to prevent 'aggression' and interference in their internal affairs.[61]

It seems, however, that the Soviets had second thoughts and perhaps found even this ambiguous commitment too far-reaching. On 11 February 1957 Moscow put forward its own Middle East proposals.[62] Placating the West, Moscow noted that it had no intention of establishing or obtaining any privileges in the Middle East and called for joint Soviet, American, British and French guarantees to the Middle Eastern countries, including a ban on arms supply. This was an obvious retreat from the joint Sino-Soviet declaration of 18 January.

Although the Chinese outwardly supported the Soviet proposal,[63] there is little doubt that they were very much annoyed.

Peking could not tolerate the idea of joint and legitimised intervention of the Western powers in the Middle East, even with the
participation of the Soviet Union. Whenever praising the Soviet
proposal, the Chinese indicated that 'the main force which will
determine the end of events in the Near and Middle East is the
countries there, not London or Washington'.[64] And, in his report
on his visit to Asia and Eastern Europe, Chou En-lai, while
expressing support for the Soviet proposal, nonetheless stressed
'the principle of non-interference by great powers in the internal
affairs of the countries in the Near and Middle East'. The affairs
of this region, he said, 'should be decided by the peoples in that
area themselves'.[65]

The Sino-Soviet differences increased in the summer of 1957
when the Chinese perceived an imminent American attack on
Syria and called for immediate action. Yet, in China's view,
Moscow's reaction was as irresolute and cautious as ever. Outwardly the Chinese endorsed all Soviet notes regarding the new
development in the Middle East, but there were again many
hints of China's dissatisfaction with the Soviet response. Commenting on these statements the *People's Daily* said that all peace-
loving countries, which showed concern for peace, should act
immediately, support the just struggle of the Syrian people and
resolutely check the US aggression against Syria.[66] A joint statement by four Chinese organisations appealed 'to all those who
cherish peace and safeguard justice, to unite still more closely
and, with the *maximum efforts and effective measures*, to stop
and smash the American conspiracy to push Turkey to attack
Syria, and to safeguard peace in the Middle East and the world
resolutely'.[67] [Italics added.]

China's implicit criticism of Soviet behaviour during the Syrian
crisis exposed a basic disagreement between the two regarding
the ways to counter Western 'aggression' in the Middle East.
This disagreement emerged primarily from a different evaluation
of the balance of power between the two camps. Peking has never
had any doubts in the long term and fundamental superiority of
the socialist camp, especially in a united front with the colonial
and semi-colonial countries. This view was greatly reinforced
following the successful Soviet launching of an intercontinental
ballistic missile and two Earth satellites. For the Chinese this
represented not so much a sudden shift in favour of the East as a
confirmation of its superiority, of which they had been confident
long before.

Peking was quick to exploit Soviet technological accomplishments in its comments on the Middle East. Washington was warned to stop its 'dangerous game' and *properly appraise* the strength of the world's anti-aggressive forces.[68] The Chinese were even more explicit:

The Soviet warning should have made the U.S.A. understand that in the era of intercontinental guided missiles, should it dare to instigate a war, it would not escape heavy blows as it did during the last two world wars... The aggressive group in the U.S.A. and its Turkish followers should recognise that times have changed. The world forces of peace are powerful enough to deal the war-makers devastating blows.[69]

China further maintained that the Western powers were fully aware that the East was more powerful. For this reason, Peking argued, the West preferred to avoid a military confrontation with the socialist camp and to concentrate its efforts not against the Soviet Union, China or Eastern Europe, but against the weaker peoples of Asia, Africa and Latin America. However, warned the Chinese, once the West was to gain control over this 'intermediate zone', it would feel strong enough to wage a major war against the socialist bloc. It was, therefore, the duty of the East to frustrate Western intervention in the Third World and thereby reduce the danger of a new world war: 'The Syrian struggle against U.S. aggression involves the question not only of Syria's interests. This is a struggle between peace and war. If the U.S. adventurist plan [to invade Syria] becomes a reality, it will be difficult to confine the armed conflict to a limited scope.'[70] The Chinese press pointed out that both world wars had started with local military action. When in Moscow in November 1957, Mao Tse-tung put it plainly:

The U.S. imperialists obstinately try to interfere in the internal affairs of other countries, including those of the socialist countries... They are particularly rabid in interfering in the internal affairs of those countries situated in the area between the U.S. and the socialist camp. The U.S. is still planning to invade independent Syria through Turkey or Israel, it is still conspiring to subvert the anti-colonialist Egyptian Government. This maniac aggressive policy of the U.S. has not only precipitated a crisis in the Middle East, but has also created the danger of a new world war.[71]

His message was crystal-clear: to avoid a new world war, Western attempts at military intervention in the Third World, and especially in the extremely important Middle East, should be prevented and stopped uncompromisingly – primarily by the Soviet Union as the powerful leader of the peace-loving countries, both socialist and nationalist.

Thus, in November 1957, despite grave doubts about Soviet

intentions of supporting Asian and African countries, including China, in their confrontation with the West, Mao nonetheless upheld the Soviet Union's leadership within the socialist camp. Allegedly, he also categorically refused to share with Moscow the burden of responsibility for national liberation movements in Asia and Africa, let alone bear it exclusively.[72]

By urging the Soviets to restrain Western 'aggression', Mao did not mean that they should intervene by armed force or become directly involved in local conflicts. According to his analysis of the balance of power, there was no need for such intervention. What was needed was firm Soviet commitments and straight-forward threats which, in Mao's view, would have been enough to deter Western 'aggression'.

Khrushchev, on the other hand, still regarded the socialist camp, despite the Soviet technological achievements, as inferior to the West. Contrary to Peking's view, he feared that firm Soviet commitments and threats to stop Western aggression by inter-vention would not prevent a new world war but rather precipitate it. On the basis of this judgement the Soviets refused to become physically involved in Middle Eastern crises or even to give a serious warning to the West; instead, Moscow declared its peace-ful intentions and readiness to renounce the use of force and always resorted to the United Nations for reaching a settlement.

The Chinese found this kind of reaction hard to accept. In their view, any manifestation of Soviet weakness would only invite further Western interference and subvert a real settlement. It seems likely, therefore, that the Chinese regarded Moscow's tolerance of the previous Western encroachments in the Middle East as an incentive to what they perceived as serious imperialist intervention and aggression in the Lebanon and Jordan in the spring and summer 1958. Western-oriented, both governments were confronted in mid-1958 by external (mainly UAR) threats and intimidation, as well as internal insurrection (particularly in the Lebanon). Following the revolution in Iraq, US and British troops came to their rescue at their request.

From the beginning, Peking regarded the Lebanese events as a domestic issue in which *no* foreign country had the right to inter-fere, and explicitly warned against using the United Nations as a cover for new imperialist aggression.[73] China urged the Soviet Union to demonstrate its power (including its nuclear potential) to deter Western aggression in the Middle East by making it an unbearable risk to the West: 'Under the historical conditions of the present age, any war unleashed by imperialism anywhere in the world will not be a localised one. It will meet with blows from the peace forces of the world.'[74]

The only 'blows' came in the form of several TASS statements denouncing 'attempts at armed interference by Western powers in the Lebanon's internal affairs' and announcing that the USSR did not intend to look with indifference on foreign intervention in any Arab country. And, although the Chinese insisted that 'the peace-loving forces of the world' would never allow the imperialists to launch an aggressive war in the Lebanon, US and British troops landed in the Lebanon and Jordan, immediately after the revolution in Iraq.

China watched the Soviet response to the invasion very carefully, reiterating Moscow's statement that the Soviet Union would not remain indifferent to aggression in a region neighbouring it and that it would have to take the necessary measures dictated by the interests and security of the Soviet Union and the preservation of world peace. Yet there was a basic disagreement between Moscow and Peking concerning the nature of those 'necessary measures'. Very soon the Chinese realised that the Soviets had no intention of taking firm action.

Nasser learnt the same lesson. When the crisis erupted he was visiting Moscow and immediately tried to mobilise Soviet help. Khrushchev, however, refused even to deliver an ultimatum to the West (as he had done during the Suez crisis) saying that the Soviet Union was 'not ready for a confrontation [with the United States]. We are not ready', he allegedly said, 'for World War Three.' The most the Soviet Union could do was to declare military manoeuvres along the Bulgarian–Turkish border, he told Nasser, 'but, I am telling you frankly, don't depend on anything more than that'.[75]

But the Chinese definitely expected more than that. On 20 July they began to apply pressure on the Soviet Union. An editorial in the *People's Daily* contained an urgent and barely concealed appeal to Moscow to take resolute action:

History has demonstrated time and again that resolute blows must be dealt to aggressors, and that peace and national independence can only be achieved by determined struggles against imperialist aggressors... If only the people of all countries take action, the aggression of the imperialists can definitely be defeated, and their war schemes stopped. 'Nothing can be saved by yielding to evil, and coddling wrong only helps the devil'... the only course left to the people of the world is to hit the aggressors on the head!

... The imperialists have always bullied the weak and been afraid of the strong. The only language they understand is that of force. Only by carrying out determined struggle can we teach these imperialist pirates a lesson...

We want peace, but we certainly are not afraid of war. If the imperialist aggressors, who have lost their senses, insist on a test of strength, then all those who refuse to be slaves must make the necessary preparations.[76]

Yet, despite their criticism, the Chinese were not yet ready to challenge directly and publicly either the leadership of the Soviet Union or Soviet behaviour in the Middle East crisis. They considered the unity of the socialist camp to be extremely important at that particular stage and, therefore, twisted in public to endorse faithfully and consistently the shifts in Moscow's position.

Thus on 21 July Peking hailed Khrushchev's proposal for a five-power summit conference in Geneva as providing a realistic path to stop aggression and preserve peace in the Middle East. But then, on 22 July, came the Anglo-American proposal to hold a summit conference within the framework of the Security Council. As this proposal was rejected (at that time) by Khrushchev, Peking also opposed it, using the opportunity to attack the United Nations and the Security Council:

Instead of the seriously composed summit conference as proposed by the Soviet Union, the British planned that the 'special meetings' would consist mainly of Security Council members. Most of the present Security Council members are American-controlled, including the Kuomintang man who represents nobody except the moribund Chiang Kai-shek and the delegate of the former Iraqi regime who represents the dead King Faysal.[77]

Unfortunately, on the same day Khrushchev changed his mind and accepted the Western proposal, framing it as a Soviet idea. After a day of embarrassed silence the Chinese welcomed Moscow's agreement to convene the summit conference within the Security Council as a major step for peace.

There is little doubt that, while outwardly approving the Soviet motion, the Chinese were deeply disturbed and implicitly disapproved of the Security Council meeting. They pointed out that the Soviet proposal had won preliminary success, but it could in no way mean that the aggressors had shown willingness to accept peace or abandon their aggressive designs. This could be achieved, Peking argued, only by maintaining vigilance and waging resolute struggle.

Indeed, on 28 July the Soviets withdrew their agreement to holding a summit meeting within the Security Council and renewed their former proposal for a five-power summit. Meanwhile, as tension was mounting both in the Middle East and in the

Taiwan Straits, Khrushchev flew to Peking for what was then described as an unscheduled emergency visit (31 July–3 August). Back from China he abandoned the entire idea of a summit conference. It has been argued that the Soviet about-face occurred under Chinese pressure or at least in order to appease Peking. But it seems unlikely that Khrushchev, who had consistently rejected China's arguments, should suddenly have changed his mind as a result of Chinese direct or indirect pressure. It is more likely that he did not regard the Chinese as entitled in any way to participate in settling Middle Eastern affairs which, he believed, they had never really understood. By now there is also enough evidence to suggest that his visit to China concerned Sino-Soviet military relations and that the Middle East and Taiwan were hardly discussed.[78]

This, however, does not mean that Sino-Soviet differences on the correct response to 'Western aggression' in the Middle East (or elsewhere) were settled. On the contrary: the Mao–Khrushchev controversy on military affairs and the fact that they did not discuss Taiwan and the Middle East could suggest that, by that time, the gap between their conceptions of war was unbridgeable. To Khrushchev, Mao's outlook on the problem of war appeared extremely 'childish' and 'hopelessly outdated', whereas Mao blamed Khrushchev for having been overcautious (in his relations with the West) and unbalanced.[79]

On the day Khrushchev left, the *People's Daily* published an editorial which could be regarded as reflecting Mao's disappointment with Khrushchev's stand. It said that peace could only be secured through struggle:

In this way, some people will not regard efforts for peace as pacifism, which paralyses the people's will to struggle and causes them to be panic-stricken in a tense situation, giving the enemies of peace a chance to make trouble. ... In order to ease international tension and maintain peace, we must not merely depend on the well-meaning wishes and unilateral efforts of the peace-loving countries and peoples. We stand for peace, but we are by no means afraid of the war provocations of imperialism. We must have firm determination and full confidence to put out the flames of imperialist aggressive war.[80]

In the following weeks the Chinese repeated their argument that talks were not enough to repel the aggressors. They accused the revisionists, explicitly the Yugoslavs and perhaps implicitly the Soviets, in their desire to solve all issues through the imperialist-manipulated United Nations, of bowing to the imperialists at the expense of the just cause of the working class and peace-loving people.[81] Unfortunately again, on the same day and apparently without Peking's knowledge, Khrushchev put forward his latest proposal to convene a special emergency session of the United Nations General Assembly to settle the Middle East problem. In the next few days the Chinese manoeuvred to support and justify this new and unexpected Soviet move, but with obvious reservations and conditions.

The Chinese Government statement of 8 August, which apparently supported the Soviet proposal, emphasised at the same time that an immediate withdrawal of the Anglo-American troops from Jordan and the Lebanon should precede any move towards a settlement. It also raised some doubts about the prospects of achieving a settlement within the United Nations: 'It is yet another test of historic significance whether an emergency special session [*sic*] of the UN General Assembly will be held in accordance with the Soviet proposal and, if held, whether it will realise the eager desire of the people of the world.'[82] To make their point crystal-clear the Chinese accompanied their statement with a strongly-worded *People's Daily* editorial which described Moscow's turning to the United Nations, and its flabby reaction to the crisis, as begging for peace instead of defending it through struggle, and as a compromise with the imperialists which would end in submission. In sharp criticism of Soviet behaviour, the editorial said that, if people indulge only in the illusion of peace and the horrors of war, actual war will fill them with panic and confusion:

The imperialists like to frighten the nervous with the choice between submission or war. Their agents frequently spread the nonsensical idea that peace can be achieved only by currying favour and compromising with the aggressors. Some soft-hearted advocates of peace even naively believe that in order to relax tension at all costs the enemy must not be provoked. They dare not denounce the war provokers, they are unwilling to trace the responsibility of war and war danger and to differentiate between right and wrong on the issue of war and peace. Some groundlessly conclude that peace can be gained only when there is no armed resistance against the attacks of the imperialists and the colonialists and when there is no bitter struggle against them. But countless historical facts have proved that the stand of these peace advocates is useless.[83]

China's efforts to commit the Soviet Union to a firm struggle against the West in the Middle East context failed completely. Henceforth, the gap between Chinese and Soviet views on global and revolutionary strategy grew ever wider.

The decline of China's interest in the Middle East

From early 1960 to mid-1963 China's relations with the Middle East were at a standstill. Diplomatic, cultural and economic exchanges were on the decline and the Chinese made no serious attempt to improve the atmosphere and regain the goodwill of the Arabs. This stagnation reflected not only the deterioration of Sino-Arab relations in the late-1950s and China's growing interest in the newly independent states of Africa but also, primarily, a new Chinese analysis of the world situation.

In 1960 the Chinese began to detect a certain degree of re-laxation in the international arena: 'It is by no means fortuitous that some of the ruling forces in the United States and other Western countries were compelled to accept some relaxation and relinquish some tension. It was the inevitable outcome of the change and development in the balance of forces in the international struggle.'[84]

China's interest in the Middle East had always been related to the Chinese perception of 'aggression' and tension in international relations. Now, following China's unpleasant experience with the Arabs, and with the changing world situation, there were clear indications that the Middle East was losing much of its importance for the Chinese. From early 1957 they had treated the Middle East as the centre of anti-imperialist struggle and as a main battlefield where the domination of the intermediate zone would be determined. In the early 1960s, however, their analysis was different: 'Africa is now both the centre of the anti-colonialist struggle and the centre for East and West to fight for the control of the intermediate zone, so that it has become the key point of world interest.'[85]

The prominence of Africa in China's world outlook harmed China's relations with the Middle East, particularly with Egypt. Between late 1958 and late 1962, China established diplomatic relations with ten African countries. Consequently, the Chinese probably believed they were no longer dependent on Egypt as their base of operation in Africa, particularly after their freedom of action had been curtailed by the Egyptian authorities. In addition, Cairo's importance as a centre of Afro-Asian activity seemed to be declining.

Partly due to Chinese pressure, the second Afro-Asian People's Solidarity Conference was held in April 1960 in Conakry, Guinea, where Egypt's influence was limited. Despite the decision that the organisation's Secretariat would stay in Cairo and that the Egyptian Yūsuf al-Sibāʿī would remain Secretary General, the role of Egypt within the organisation was permanently reduced as a result of the reorganisation of the AAPSO.[86] Soon, however, Peking came to realise that Cairo was still at the crossroads of Africa, and maintained considerable influence in Afro-Asian circles.

In fact, Sino-Egyptian relations seemed to return to a normal pattern after early 1960. On 22 January 1960, after a delay of almost eight months, a new UAR ambassador, Ṣalāḥ al-Dīn al-Ṭarāzī (a Syrian), presented his credentials in Peking. Indeed, the ramifications of the Bakdāsh affair were still being felt: Nasser increased his anti-communist campaign and articles and commentaries against China's policies and behaviour (although not in the Middle East), continued to appear in the Egyptian press.[87] But Nasser no longer seemed concerned about the likelihood of Chinese subversion in the Arab world. Asked in an interview if the possibility of Chinese volunteers joining the National Liberation Front in Algeria had been worrying him, he replied: 'I am certain that no Communist elements will, whatever happens, influence Arab nationalism in the Arab countries, including Algeria. On the contrary, the ideas of Arab nationalism will finally prevail and will always prevail.'[88] This confidence underlay Nasser's address to the United Nations General Assembly in New York in September 1960, when he called emphatically for the admission of the PRC to the United Nations.[89]

The Chinese were slower in changing their attitude towards Egypt. For example, in February 1960 Chou En-lai and Ch'en Yi were absent from the UAR National Day reception in Peking in which they had participated regularly since 1956. (They were present again for the February 1961 celebrations.) Compared with previous years, very few Chinese delegations visited Egypt. Among them was a military goodwill mission which arrived in September 1960, more than two years after a similar Egyptian mission had visited China.

Generally, the Chinese ceased their direct and public accusations against Nasser and the UAR,[90] although they still remained disillusioned about 'peaceful neutralism' and the unreliable nature of national–bourgeois leaders, Nasser included. Their analysis of the situation in the *Kung-tso t'ung-hsün* (*Bulletin of Activities*) revealed this disappointment. Without mentioning Nasser, the Chinese reiterated that 'peaceful neutralism is . . . a transitional form' and added: 'We must . . . isolate the bloc including Nehru in India and Tito in Yugoslavia and oppose American imperialism.'[91] They did, however, mention Nasser in their analysis of the situation in Africa: 'Africa itself looks like the seven powers of [China's] Warring States [403 to 221 B.C.] with its Nasser, Nkrumah, Hussein [*sic*], Sekou Touré, Bourguiba, and Abbas each with his own way of leading others. In general everyone is trying to sell his own goods.'[92]

On 28 September 1961 Nasser's way of leading Syria ended when Syria withdrew from the UAR and regained its independence. Two days later the Syrian Foreign Ministry requested China's recognition. Peking, which had tacitly disapproved of Syria's union with Egypt from the very beginning, considered the request for some ten days and finally granted recognition on 11 October. Ṣalāḥ al-Dīn al-Ṭarāzī, the Syrian who had been the UAR ambassador to the PRC, was reappointed by Damascus as the Syrian ambassador (he was replaced later, in January 1962). But the Chinese, contrary to their practice in the past, were in no hurry. Wang Ch'ung-li, formerly China's consul-general in Damascus, was appointed chargé d'affaires on 23 October 1961. Hsü Yi-hsin, the new Chinese ambassador who had previously been ambassador to Norway and Albania, was appointed only in early March 1962 and did not arrive in Damascus until late in May.

Nor were the Egyptians in any particular hurry to restore their diplomatic representation in Peking following the Syrian secession. Only in March 1962 did Cairo appoint Zakariyā al-'Adlī Imām, formerly Director of the Department of East European Affairs in the Foreign Ministry, as ambassador to China. But he did not present his credentials until 11 July, after his post had been vacant for nearly ten months.

By 1961, the lukewarm political relations, as well as China's economic difficulties, began to affect Sino-Arab trade. In 1959 and 1960, China's trade with Egypt had fallen short of the annual two-way £15 million agreed on, but China's imports still exceeded exports. In 1960, for example, Sino-Egyptian trade totalled £22.3 (instead of 30) million, with £15.5 million in imports and only £6.8 million in exports. But, in 1961 this pattern was reversed dramatically. Whereas China's exports to Egypt remained virtually the same, imports from Egypt slumped from more than £15 million in 1960 to £5 million in 1961. The main cut was in cotton imports (from 44,350 to 11,555 tons), throwing China from the position of Egypt's *second* largest cotton customer in 1959–60 to the *ninth* in rank in 1960–1.[93]

Unlike previous years, the Chinese carefully ensured a favourable trade balance from 1961 to 1964 with Egypt (as well as with the other Arab countries). Each year the total two-way Sino-Egyptian trade was about *half* of what had been agreed on. These were additional manifestations of Sino-Arab disagreements.

The existence of disagreements was further illustrated in October 1962 when war broke out along the Sino-Indian frontier. Although this war had nothing to do with the Middle East it shattered the residues of China's good image in Arab public opinion. The Arabs, particularly the Egyptians,[94] had little doubt about Peking's responsibility for the hostilities. It was not long before this conviction was turned into a fact and began to be regarded as decisive 'evidence' of Chinese aggressiveness. This attitude to a great extent governed Arab policy towards China until at least the end of the Cultural Revolution. Paradoxically, the mediatory role played by Egypt in the Sino-Indian dispute, a role basically detrimental to China's interests, nevertheless convinced the Chinese that Nasser was still a major figure to be reckoned with in the non-aligned and Afro-Asian world. This attitude, which regarded Arab and Egyptian co-operation as essential for achieving China's foreign policy ends, governed much of China's Middle East policy in the mid-1960s.

Nasser's initial reaction to the outbreak of hostilities along the Sino-Indian border was cautious. Privately, he seemed to have concurred with Nehru's view that China had chosen the road of war and violence not only to gain territories but also to humiliate India and wreck non-alignment. Later, on 12 February 1963, Nasser wrote to Tito: 'We felt without the least doubt that China had, premeditatedly or otherwise, committed a grave error... I did not conceal my opinion from China in numerous messages I exchanged in that period with Premier Chou En Lai [*sic*].'[95]

Yet of all the non-aligned and Afro-Asian leaders, Nasser was the only one acceptable to both sides. He had a long acquaintance with Nehru as well as with Chou En-lai and was, therefore, best qualified to mediate. He had to maintain neutrality, at least outwardly: 'Despite our clear view of China's policy in the problem, we avoided releasing a statement strongly condemning the aggression so that the situation might not get more involved and we might not block the road completely before every endeavour was made to find a way out of the crisis.'[96]

On 21 October 1962, following a massive Chinese attack on India, Nasser cabled Chou En-lai and offered to mediate. Within a few days both India and China agreed and on 26 October Egypt put forward its proposals.[97] However, as the Egyptians themselves admitted,[98] their proposals greatly resembled India's demands. Under these circumstances on 2 November 1962 Peking rejected the Egyptian proposals as reflecting the Indian position.[99]

Peking's rejection unleashed a wave of slanders against China in Egypt's press and radio which until then had been greatly restrained, though obviously sympathetic to India. For the first time Peking was labelled as an 'aggressor' and was openly accused of having provoked the crisis and of expansionism.[100] Simultaneously, intensive diplomatic activity between China and the Arabs, particularly Egypt, continued and culminated on 6 December 1962 with a special visit to Cairo for talks on the Sino-Indian conflict by Huang Chen, the Chinese Vice Foreign Minister. The details of his mission are unknown but it seems that, while he turned down another Egyptian proposal,[101] he was apparently trying to persuade the reluctant Egyptians to participate in the forthcoming Colombo Conference.

On 10 December 1962, the day Huang Chen left, the Colombo Conference opened in an attempt to find a settlement to the Sino-Indian conflict. Of the six participants the most active were the UAR, which pleaded the Indian cause, and Burma, which supported the Chinese. As could have been anticipated, they rejected each other's proposals and on 12 December an ambiguous compromise was reached.

Because of this ambiguity, the conference's participants visited Peking and Delhi in the following weeks, offering 'clarifications'. One who refused to go to Peking despite having been invited twice was 'Alī Ṣabrī, the Egyptian premier and representative at the conference. China's marked interest in his visit suggests that the Chinese by then considered Egypt, notwithstanding its hostile attitude, to be an influential factor in the Afro-Asian world. It was only in April 1963, when a new phase of Chinese policy in the Middle East was beginning to evolve, that 'Alī Ṣabrī finally visited China.

China's relations with Iraq were as cool and formal as those with Egypt. In April 1960 the first Iraqi ambassador to the PRC, 'Abd al-Ḥaq Fāḍil, presented his credentials – some eighteen months after the first Chinese ambassador had arrived in Baghdad.

Several Iraqi delegations visited China, including a trade union delegation which met with Mao Tse-tung on 9 May 1960, and a military delegation in September–October.[102] Several agreements were signed, while Kassem still continued his anti-communist campaign.

The Chinese also made some friendly gestures. In February 1960 the last batch of a Chinese gift of vehicles and other equipment for civil defence purposes was officially delivered to the Iraqi authorities. Commenting on this gift Baghdad radio (20 February), however, did not forget to add that the United States had granted Iraq aid on an unprecedented scale and that a US–Iraqi cultural agreement was shortly to be concluded.[103]

There is little doubt that the Chinese were annoyed by the domestic and external developments in Iraq. Yet the international circumstances, as perceived by Peking, were different and the Chinese spared their public criticism, though not entirely. In some cases they accused Kassem indirectly by reproducing, without comment, Iraqi opposition protests.[104] In other cases China's protests were more direct, for example, when 'Chinese lawyers' expressed concern about 'Iraqi patriots' (i.e., communists) sentenced to death.[105]

Sino-Iraqi relations became more complicated after Kuwait had been granted independence in mid-June 1961. Kassem's immediate reaction was to declare Kuwait an integral part of Iraq, to which Kuwait responded by inviting a British force to stay and defend the country against a possible Iraqi attack.

The Chinese found themselves in an ambivalent position. On the one hand, they tended to recognise any country which gained independence from colonialism but, on the other hand, such an act could have destroyed their already fragile relations with Iraq. Peking chose neither; instead of extending diplomatic recognition, Chou En-lai only sent congratulations to Kuwait's ruler on the attainment of independence.[106]

Peking interpreted Kuwait's independence, as many other events in the Middle East, primarily in terms of a victory over imperialism which, therefore, deserved every sympathy and support. Accordingly, the Chinese concentrated their attention in the Kuwait issue not on Iraq's claims but on the British 'armed intervention' which, from Peking's standpoint, was the real and the main problem.[107] A *People's Daily* editorial admitted that the Kuwait question was complicated and had two sides. One was the Kuwait people's demand for *liberation* from the colonial rule of imperialism and for *independence* and *freedom*; the other was the existence of different views among the Arab countries on the question of Kuwait's *sovereignty*. The Chinese left little doubt that they regarded the people of Kuwait as fully entitled to independence and freedom. Referring to the issue of sovereignty, they said that not all the Arab countries had agreed to Iraq's claim on Kuwait, but that at any rate this issue was an internal Arab affair which could and should be settled by the Arab countries through peaceful negotiation and in which imperialism had no right to interfere.[108]

Ten days later, at a reception given in Peking celebrating the third anniversary of the Republic of Iraq, the Iraqi ambassador warned against establishing any relations with Kuwait: 'Kuwait is a part of the Republic of Iraq just as Taiwan is a part of China and Goa is a part of India, and no conclusion of private pacts, formation of artificial governments or process of time can change this fact.'[109] In his reply Vice Foreign Minister Huang Chen repeated Peking's view that the main issue was foreign interference and strongly condemned the British armed 'occupation' of Kuwait. He evaded altogether the question of Kuwait's sovereignty by saying: 'The Chinese people resolutely support the proper demand of the Arab peoples: British troops must be withdrawn from Kuwait.'[110]

China's economic interest in Iraq was similarly very limited. Trade began to develop slowly in 1959 and increased until by 1962–4 it had reached about 20 per cent of China's total trade with the Middle East. Although China was one of Iraq's largest purchasers of dates, the value of Chinese imports from Iraq was always one-quarter to one-half of China's exports. There are no indications that China was interested in Iraq's oil, except in the context of the struggle against imperialism. In early 1962 the Chinese fully supported the Iraqi Government's measures concerning oil,[111] as 'just actions aimed at liquidating the vestiges of colonialism and upholding national sovereignty'.[112] The Chinese have probably been buying insignificant quantities of crude oil from Iraq since 1960.[113] In early July 1962 a Chinese delegation headed by Liu Fang, Vice Minister of the Petroleum Industry, left Peking to participate in Iraq's National Day celebrations. The delegation returned on 27 July but Liu Fang did not leave until 14 August, after having visited many oil installations and having allegedly conducted secret talks of which no details were revealed.[114]

On 8 February 1963, shortly after China and Iraq signed a new economic agreement, Kassem was overthrown in a bloody *coup d'état* along with his regime. Although the new Iraqi regime immediately started a systematic persecution of communists, it gained China's recognition within four days.[115] The Chinese, to be sure, duly protested: 'History has proved that the reactionary rulers of any country who suppress the people ruthlessly will only reap the whirlwind of their own sowing.'[116] But these protests were rather irresolute and did not come from the Government or the CCP: by that time, as Mao said later, the Iraqi Communist Party was opposing China, following the conductor's (Moscow's) baton and practising peaceful transition.[117] The persecution of the Iraqi communists became an issue in the 1964 Sino-Soviet polemics. Peking held the Soviets responsible for the misfortune of the Iraqi Communist Party:

The comrades of the Communist Party of Iraq were once full of revolutionary ardour. But acceptance of Khrushchev's revisionist line was forced on them by outside pressure, and they lost their vigilance against counter-revolution. In the armed counter-revolutionary *coup d'état*, leading comrades heroically sacrificed their lives, thousands of Iraqi Communists and revolutionaries were massacred in cold blood, the powerful Iraqi Communist Party was dispersed, and the revolutionary cause of Iraq suffered a grave setback. This is a tragic lesson in the annals of proletarian revolution, a lesson written in blood.[118]

On the other hand, the Soviets accused the Chinese of exploiting the difficulties of the Iraqi Communist Party:

How Peking understands proletarian solidarity can be judged by the CPC Central Committee's attitude towards the Baathist nationalists' repression of Salam Adil and other leaders of the Communist Party of Iraq. In conversations with foreign delegations, the Chinese leaders rejoiced openly and maliciously at the brutal murder of the Iraqi comrades. Immediately after the Baath take-over they began to seek contacts with the assassins. As has now become clear, the Chinese representatives in Iraq wanted to take advantage of the fact that the Iraqi Communist Party had become leaderless to create their own schismatic group there.[119]

China did not care much about the socio-political nature of Arab governments as long as they adhered to the struggle against imperialism or when the international scene was relatively calm. This was proved again shortly after the Iraqi *coup d'état* when on 15 March 1963 Peking recognised a new Syrian regime within a week after a *coup d'état* had taken place. Earlier, the Chinese adopted a similar procedure towards the Yemen. On 21 September 1962 they greeted Muḥammad al-Badr on his accession to the throne after the death of Imām Aḥmad.[120] A week later, on

28 September, the new Imām was overthrown and the Arab Republic of Yemen was proclaimed. On 6 October the PRC recognised the new Yemeni Republic, sending 'Abd-Allāh al-Sallāl, the new leader, a message of greetings almost identical to the one they had sent al-Badr only a fortnight earlier.[121]

Finally, a few words should be said about China's attitude towards Israel throughout this period. Following the Suez invasion, Peking seemed to have lost interest in relations with Israel. In 1957–9 Chinese attention was concentrated on the Arabs and their response to Western challenges. But after late 1959, when China's interest in the Arabs had declined, there were curious hints of renewed Chinese sympathy towards the Jewish people, including the people of Israel. Chinese expressions of hostility against Zionism became rare.[122] In December 1959 the Chinese commemorated one of the greatest Jewish writers.[123] The next month Peking condemned anti-Semitism[124] and in Tel Aviv an exhibition on modern China was opened. In May 1961 an Israeli woman writer visited Peking on the invitation of the Union of Chinese Writers,[125] and later that month the CCP Central Committee sent unprecedentedly warm greetings to the Israeli Communist Party, and through it to the people of Israel. It said:

The Central Committee of the Communist Party of China, on behalf of all the members of the Communist Party of China and all the people of China, extends its fraternal greetings to the Fourteenth Congress of the Communist Party of Israel, and through your Congress, wishes to convey its sincere respects to the Communist Party of Israel and to the people of Israel. . .

The Communist Party of China and the Chinese people are at all times in sympathy with and concerned about the struggles of your Party and your people and rejoice with you in every success which you have won. May your Party gain new successes in further uniting the labouring people of your country and all patriotic democratic forces in the struggle for world peace, democracy and socialism. May your people win new victories in defending democratic rights, struggling for a better life and realising social progress.[126]

China's more flexible attitude towards Israel should be understood not only against the background of the cool Sino-Arab relations and China's modified world outlook, but probably also as an early Chinese attempt to explore the position and win the support of communist parties in the approaching split with the Soviet Union.

4 : THE STRUGGLE AGAINST
IMPERIALISM AND REVISIONISM

In late 1963, after several years of limited interest, the Chinese increased their activity in the Middle East to an unprecedented level. The fact that at that time there was no particular development in the Middle East to have justified such an offensive reinforces the view that China's Middle East policy reflected primarily its perception of the global situation, rather than the local one.

In the summer of 1963 there were indications of a serious deterioration in China's relations with the Soviet Union. Disagreements with Moscow were as old as the Chinese communist movement. Yet, despite their growing misgivings, the Chinese had always tried to uphold the concept of unity and to follow Moscow's twists and turns, as far as was publicly possible. Even after 1960, when the controversy intensified, Mao still emphasised unity: 'We must unite with the Soviet Union, with fraternal parties . . . no matter what charges they make against us. . . . No matter what their attitude, we should adopt a policy of unity.'[1]

However, in the summer of 1963, after the Soviets together with the United States had signed the Nuclear Test Ban Treaty, the Chinese began to perceive Moscow as their enemy, though not yet as a short-term threat to China's security. The immediate threat came from the growing US involvement in Southeast Asia, particularly in Vietnam and Laos. This involvement, and what the Chinese believed to be the Soviets' tacit approval, made the world situation explosive. Consequently, the United States and the Soviet Union were seen as the chief enemies of China as well as of the rest of the world and were, therefore, to be firmly resisted: 'We are now principally in a struggle against imperialism and revisionism.'[2]

To accomplish this end the Chinese tried to mobilise the governments of Western Europe (primarily against the United States) and the communist parties all over the world (against the Soviet Union). But China's main field of activity remained in Asia and Africa. Even before the failure of their campaign in Europe and within the communist movement, the Chinese channelled most of their energies and efforts into Asia and Africa in an attempt to persuade their governments to hold a second 'Bandung' Conference and unite in the struggle against both the US and the USSR.

As early as 1961 the Chinese revealed their interest in holding a second Afro-Asian conference, though it was from late 1963 that most of China's foreign policy endeavours were devoted to enlisting the support of Asian and African governments for such a conference. Peking's main demands were that the second 'Bandung' Conference would exclude the Soviet Union and would adopt a militant and uncompromising attitude towards the United States. China's Middle East policy in the mid-1960s should be interpreted against this background.

In their Asian–African offensive the Chinese paid special attention to the Arab countries, and particularly to Egypt, for three main reasons: firstly, having detected the beginning of a new American onslaught, particularly in Southeast Asia, the Chinese once again became aware of the crucial position of the Middle East in a possible American encirclement of China: 'U.S. aggression against the Arab world occupies an important position in its "global strategy". The Arab world is rich in oil resources. It lies astride the three continents of Europe, Asia and Africa. And what is more important is the fact that this area forms a vital link in the chain of the U.S.-controlled NATO, CENTO and SEATO.'[3]

Secondly, the Chinese could not fail to observe that the Middle East had become one of the principal targets of Soviet foreign policy. They realised that despite the ups and downs in Soviet–Arab relations the Arabs had become increasingly dependent on Soviet support, in political, economic and military terms. It was, therefore, particularly important for Peking to gain Arab approval for the exclusion of the Soviet Union from the forthcoming Afro-Asian conference.

Finally, the Arabs, and particularly Egypt, provided the bridge between Asia and Africa, not merely in geographical terms, but in political terms as well. They represented, or so the Chinese believed, one of the most coherent and homogeneous groups within the Afro-Asian world. Furthermore, despite Nasser's hardly concealed pro-Indian outlook, the Chinese had apparently been quite impressed by his role as mediator in the Sino-Indian border conflict and by his considerable influence in Afro-Asian circles.

In other words, the Arabs and Egypt held the trump card to the success or failure of China's foreign policy in the mid-1960s. Under these circumstances, Peking needed their support vitally: 'The Chinese government and people are ready to make joint efforts with the governments and people of the United Arab Republic and other Asian–African countries to carry through the spirit of the 1st Asian–African Conference ... and prepare for the successful holding of the 2nd Asian–African Conference.'[4]

The Chinese offensive

Diplomatic and economic endeavours

In late 1963 China launched its most energetic campaign ever in the Middle East. This campaign, which gathered momentum as the Afro-Asian conference approached, consisted of diplomatic and political efforts, as well as of various economic appeals.

During two years, from the summer of 1963 to the summer of 1965, intensive Sino-Arab activity took place. China did almost everything it could to please the Arab governments. Arab National Days were celebrated profusely in China; Chinese messages of support and greetings were sent frequently to Arab leaders, organisations and conferences; China's communication media praised the Arabs lavishly and backed them on almost every issue, such as independence for South Yemen, opposition to West Germany and changing the course of the Jordan River. Inevitably, Peking also became more hostile to Israel: 'We Chinese people resolutely oppose U.S. imperialist efforts to make Israel a tool of aggression against the Arab countries. Therefore, whe have had nothing to do with Israel, neither will we have anything to do with it in the future.'[5]

Scores of Arab visitors, leaders and delegations, were invited to China. Most prominent among them were the Egyptian premier 'Alī Ṣabrī, who came in April 1963, 'the first UAR leader to have paid a visit to China',[6] and 'Abd-Allāh al-Sallāl, the Yemeni president, who came in June 1964. During Sallāl's visit a new Sino-Yemeni Friendship Treaty was signed to replace the one signed with the royalist regime in 1958.[7] It is still China's only Friendship Treaty with a Middle Eastern government. Altogether,

China signed more agreements with the Arab countries in 1964 than in any other year.[8]

In mid-August 1964 an Egyptian scientific delegation arrived in China to take part in a scientific symposium held in Peking. Many delegations participated but the Egyptians were accorded special treatment. They met Nieh Jung-chen, Vice Premier and Chairman of China's Scientific and Technological Commission, and at the end of the visit a joint communiqué on scientific and technical co-operation was signed between China's Scientific and Technological Commission and Egypt's Ministry of Scientific Research.[9]

This visit triggered widespread speculation regarding a possible Sino-Egyptian nuclear deal. Indeed, in November 1964, following China's first nuclear test, Nasser sent to Chou En-lai a private message, wherein he expressed his enthusiasm and congratulations about China's success in building its own atomic weapons. Allegedly, Chou En-lai replied that China would not try, like others, to maintain a monopoly on its scientific accomplishments but would 'share' its knowledge with 'everyone'.[10]

On the basis of the August joint communiqué and, perhaps, in view of Chou En-lai's November message, an agreement on scientific co-operation between China and Egypt was signed in Cairo in early 1965.[11] After Chou En-lai's visit to Egypt in April, on the eve of the forthcoming second 'Bandung' Conference, it was reported that Egyptian atomic scientists would visit China 'to become acquainted with the various aspects of progress achieved by the Chinese scientists in the field of atomic research' and to visit Chinese research centres which had been inaccessible to other scientific delegations.[12]

Apparently the Chinese exploited Egypt's nuclear hunger for political purposes. The prospect of China eventually sharing its nuclear knowledge with Egypt seems to have been very poor considering not only the circumstances in the Middle East (political instability, Soviet presence, distance from China, etc.), but also China's stand on nuclear proliferation. True, the Chinese doctrine held that, as long as the superpowers refused to destroy their nuclear weapons, the more other governments acquired such weapons, the better. In practice, however, Peking showed no sign of willingness to offer nuclear aid.[13] In September 1965 Vice Premier Ch'en Yi admitted that

As for the peaceful use of atomic energy and the building of atomic reactors, China has already been approached by several countries, and China is ready to render them assistance; as for the request for China's help in the manufacture of atom bombs, this question is not realistic... Any country with a fair basis in industry and agriculture and in science and technology will be able to manufacture atom bombs, with or without China's assistance.¹⁴

This vague statement reflected China's reluctance to share its nuclear technology. It is, of course, possible that the Chinese could have offered nuclear sharing in order to win Egypt's support for their policy, or even to get an opportunity to inspect Egypt's Soviet-built atomic reactor.¹⁵ But, as soon as the Chinese became convinced that Egypt had rejected their demands regarding the Afro-Asian conference, they declined to co-operate with the Egyptian scientists and refused to reveal China's nuclear secrets.¹⁶ This was demonstrated after the June 1967 war when Nasser wrote to Chou En-lai reminding him of his November 1964 promise to share China's nuclear knowledge and asked for Chinese help in developing Egypt's nuclear technology. The Chinese replied that the Egyptians would have to do it by themselves in the same way the Chinese had done.¹⁷

From late 1964 more Arab delegations visited China. A visit by an Egyptian economic and industrial delegation, headed by Vice Premier 'Azīz Ṣidqī, produced the first agreement for economic and technical co-operation between China and Egypt (more details below). In March 1965 a PLO delegation led by Aḥmad Shuqayrī arrived in China, as well as a Syrian delegation led by Foreign Minister Ḥasan Muraywid. In early April, Nasser's adviser on foreign affairs, Ḥusayn Dhū'l-Fiqār Ṣabrī, arrived in China. Numerous other Arab delegations and visitors came to China in those years, many of whom, quite contrary to China's practice in the past, were received by Mao Tse-tung.

Compared with the flow of Arab delegations to China, the number of Chinese delegations to the Middle East was rather small. The main burden of China's political offensive in the Middle East fell on Premier Chou En-lai and Foreign Minister Ch'en Yi.

In December 1963 Chou En-lai started his grand tour of Africa, undoubtedly one of China's greatest diplomatic initiatives up to that point, in Egypt. This was meant as a tribute to the first country in Africa and the Middle East to have established diplomatic relations with the PRC, and as an acknowledgement of Egypt's prominence in Africa, the Middle East and the Afro-Asian movement. In his first official visit to Egypt, Chou En-lai did his best to please his hosts by expressing China's support for

Arab unity, neutralism and non-alignment and by trying to belittle, or even ignore, previous Sino-Egyptian differences.

As the date of the Afro-Asian conference drew near, Chou En-lai's visits to the Middle East and meetings with Arab leaders became more frequent and intensive. In November 1964, when in Moscow, he had an opportunity to meet Marshal 'Abd al-Ḥakīm 'Āmir, Egypt's Vice President, who also happened to be there.[18] On 1 April 1965, Chou En-lai again arrived in Cairo. During his two-day visit he managed to meet Premier 'Alī Ṣabrī, President Nasser and PLO chairman Shuqayrī, and also to be interviewed by the Middle East News Agency.[19]

In June 1965, when the Afro-Asian conference was due to take place but had to be postponed because of the *coup d'état* in Algeria, China's leaders were rushing around in Asia, Africa and the Middle East. On 3 June, on his way to Tanzania, Chou En-lai made a stop-over in Iraq for talks with 'Abd al-Salām 'Ārif; the next day the Chinese premier landed in Cairo for two hours, and met 'Alī Ṣabrī; on his way back from Tanzania, on the night of 8 June, he again passed through Cairo and met the Egyptian Vice Premier as well as Nasser's adviser on foreign affairs; before dawn on 9 June his plane made a stop-over in Damascus, where, within three hours, he met President Amīn al-Ḥāfiẓ, Vice Premier Dr Ḥasan Muraywid and Secretary General of the ruling Ba'th Party, Munīf al-Razzāz. In this visit Chou En-lai was particularly responsive to Syria's anti-Israel and anti-Zionist stand, and reiterated that China was against any compromise over Palestine.[20]

Ten days later, on 19 June, Chou En-lai and Ch'en Yi, who were on their way to the conference in Algeria, paid another twelve-day friendship visit to Egypt. On the day of their arrival Ben Bella was overthrown by Boumedienne and the convocation of the conference as planned became questionable. There is little doubt that the Chinese urged the Egyptians and other participants to hold the conference without delay. This was Chou En-lai's fifth visit to Egypt since January 1964. After June 1965, it was Ch'en Yi who travelled to the Middle East (as well as to Asia and Africa) trying to persuade the governments to hold the conference on China's conditions.

China's intensive diplomatic activity in the Middle East in 1963–5 required some reorganisation and reinforcement of its Foreign Ministry and diplomatic network in the Middle East. These changes reflected not only the growing importance of the Middle

East in China's foreign policy, but also its anti-Soviet stimuli. One change concerned the areas of responsibility of the two Vice Foreign Ministers, Chi P'eng-fei and Tseng Yung-ch'üan. Both had been responsible for Soviet and East European affairs, with vast experience in these fields. From 1964, in addition to their previous responsibilities, Chi P'eng-fei was assigned African affairs and Tseng Yung-ch'üan Middle Eastern and North African affairs. This was probably the first time that the Arab world came under the specific responsibility of a Vice Foreign Minister.

Another important change occurred when the Department of African and West Asian Affairs, established in 1956, was divided into a Department of African Affairs and a Department of North African and West Asian Affairs. Although the new departments were created only in September 1964, the decision had probably been reached as early as February when Wang Yü-t'ien, Director of the former Department of African and West Asian Affairs, was appointed ambassador to Kenya.[21] As a result of this reorganisation China's Foreign Ministry had, for the first time, a department dealing exclusively with the Arabs. Ch'en Ch'u, who was appointed Director of the new department, also had rich experience in Soviet affairs. He had been attaché in Moscow from early 1959 to 1963 and previously Director of the Soviet and East European Department in China's Foreign Ministry.

To reinforce the Foreign Ministry, as well as China's representation in the Middle East, exchanges of personnel were undertaken. For example, Ho Kung-k'ai, who had been the senior Deputy Director of the Department of Africa and West Asia since September 1956, was sent to Egypt in June 1963 as counsellor and chargé d'affaires. And, in early 1964 Peking found it expedient to appoint Wang Jo-chieh, as first ambassador to the Yemen, where the PRC had been represented since 1957 only by a non-resident diplomat (Ch'en Chia-k'ang, concurrently ambassador to Egypt).

The Foreign Ministry was also reinforced. Lin Chao-nan, who had been counsellor and chargé d'affaires in Egypt since 1956, took up his new appointment as Deputy Director of the Department of Africa and West Asia in April 1964. He retained the same post when the new Department of North Africa and West Asia was formed in September of that year. Earlier, Kung Ta-fei, who had been Deputy Director of the Department of Africa and West Asia from July 1959 to August 1960, and was most familiar with Iraqi affairs, was recalled in September 1963 from his post of counsellor in Morocco to reassume his previous post as Deputy Director. (For more details and sources see Appendix i.)

In addition to diplomacy and politics, economics also played a role in China's mid-1960s offensive in the Middle East. Usually, the Chinese established economic relations with the Arab world mainly in order to realise their political aspirations. When in need of Arab support the Chinese were prepared to increase their Middle Eastern trade, particularly their imports, disregarding pure economic considerations. On the other hand, when Peking's interest in the Middle East declined, so did trade and aid.

In 1963 the Chinese began to employ economic means to secure Arab support for their political aims. For example, although trade with Egypt constituted only 1.2 per cent of their total foreign trade that year, the Chinese sent their Vice Minister of Foreign Trade especially to sign the 1963 protocol.[22] Previously, the annual Sino-Egyptian trade protocol had been concluded and signed at embassy level.

Furthermore, in 1965 Sino-Egyptian trade more than doubled compared with 1964 (from £15 million to £31 million) with a massive increase in Chinese imports from Egypt (from £7.2 million to £19.6 million). After four years of balanced trade with the Arabs, China again had a negative trade balance, most probably in a deliberate attempt to win the goodwill of the Arab governments. To this end Peking also used aid.

In 1964, China's aid offers to Third World countries reached an unprecedented peak. This was also a record year for Soviet foreign aid.[23] Thus both countries were competing to gain the support of the Asian and African governments. Until the end of 1964 China had offered non-communist countries aid of $786.5 million. Of this sum, $337.8 million, about 43 per cent, was offered in 1964 alone. Much of this aid offensive was directed towards the Middle East. Of the $143.1 million offered by the Chinese to the Arabs since 1956, almost 76 per cent, or $108.5 million, was offered in 1964. And if we regard 1963 as the beginning of this offensive and take into account the aid offered by the Chinese in that year,[24] then in 1963–4 the Arab countries were offered 85 per cent of China's entire aid to the Middle East over the period from 1956 to 1964.

Another indication of China's special interest in the Middle East was the latter's growing share in China's aid offers compared with Asia and Africa. Until the end of 1963 the Middle East was allocated 8 per cent of China's aid offers (with 61 per cent going to Asia and 31 per cent to Africa). In 1964, however, the Middle East share reached 32 per cent (compared with 34 per cent for Asia and Africa equally).[25]

China's aid was offered to Syria, the Yemen, and Egypt. Syria had already been offered 70 million Swiss francs (about $16.3 million) in 1963. The Yemen, in which the Chinese had been engaged in extensive aid operations since 1958, was offered $200,000 in 1963 and another £10 million (about $28.5 million) in 1964.[26] But particular attention was paid to Egypt.

In December 1964 the Egyptian Vice Premier visited China. At the end of his visit the parties signed an agreement for economic and technical co-operation according to which the Chinese undertook to supply Egypt with industrial equipment, valued at 345 million Swiss francs ($80 million), in support of its Second Five Year Plan.[27] This sum was offered as a loan without interest to be repaid in ten annual instalments starting in 1972.[28] It was immediately announced that a first group of Chinese experts would arrive in Egypt before the end of February 1965.[29] In 1964, this was the highest Chinese aid offer to any country and its terms were much easier than Soviet foreign aid terms.

Relations with the Palestinians

Until the mid-1960s, while maintaining a hostile attitude towards Israel, the Chinese never tried to exploit the Arab–Israeli conflict and the Palestine problem in order to improve their own position in the Arab world. Since 1964, however, Peking has not only adopted the Arab stand against Israel almost without reservation, but has also established relations with the PLO, newly created by the Arab governments at that time. Although China's interest in the Palestinians, particularly later, derived from long-term strategic and revolutionary considerations, it had originally been motivated by short-term tactical expediency: this was one of the important means employed by Peking to secure Arab goodwill.

In their initial exchanges with Arab leaders in 1963, the Chinese apparently remained unaware of the political value of the Palestine issue. Their few remarks on this issue were rather brief and vague, and neither implicated nor even mentioned Israel; e.g., 'The Chinese side reiterated its support. . .for the rights of the Arab people in Palestine.'[30] While visiting Egypt in late 1963, Chou En-lai sounded somewhat apologetic as he made the one brief remark on the Palestine issue in his long press conference: 'The Chinese people have always stood firmly behind the Arabs in Palestine in their just struggle for their legitimate rights. Our diplomatic actions [*sic*] have testified to this.'[31] The joint communiqué that concluded his visit stated that 'The Chinese side declared its full support to the people of Palestine in restoring their legitimate rights and in returning to their homeland.'[32]

Gradually, however, China's stand underwent considerable change. The Palestine problem came to be regarded no longer as merely an international dispute over refugees, but as a manifestation of the national liberation struggle of a distinct Palestinian people. The significance of this struggle extended far beyond the Middle East, having become part of the front against US imperialism. Typically, the Chinese analysed the Palestinian struggle from the standpoint of their own peculiar interests 'as a great assistance to themselves in their opposition to U.S. imperialist aggression'.[33] And when a PLO delegation visited China in March 1965, Mao allegedly told its members: 'Imperialism is afraid of China and the Arabs. Israel and Formosa are bases of imperialism in Asia. You are the front gate of the great continent, and we are the rear. They created Israel for you, and Formosa for us.'[34]

China's attitude towards Israel also changed. Whereas until the late 1950s the Chinese left a slightly open door for possible relations with Israel, in the mid-1960s they were no longer interested. The last known official Chinese communication with Israel came in August 1963 when Premier Chou-En-lai sent all Heads of Government a letter concerning the Nuclear Test Ban Treaty and other nuclear matters. In his reply, submitted to the Chinese ambassador in Stockholm, the Israeli premier not only upheld the Chinese proposals but also conveyed Israel's interest in establishing normal relations with the PRC.[35] As there was no Chinese response he sent Chou En-lai another letter, on 16 July 1965. In it he reviewed briefly Sino-Israeli exchanges in the past and invited Peking to send a delegation to visit Israel and provide a basis for normalised relations: 'such normalisation,' he wrote, 'might not only be of direct advantage to both countries but would also contribute to better conditions in the Middle East as a whole'. Peking, however, did not bother to reply.

By that time, China's concept of the Arab–Israeli conflict had been reformulated. In the 1950s the Chinese believed that the ultimate instigators of the conflict had been the Western powers;

therefore, the principal contradiction existed between them, on the one hand, and Israel *and* the Arabs, on the other; indeed, both Israel and the Arabs shared some of the blame for not complying with the 1947 United Nations Partition Plan but the contradictions between them were perceived as secondary and non-antagonistic. Consequently, Peking held in the 1950s that the Palestine problem could and should have been settled politically and peacefully through direct negotiation between the parties concerned without foreign interference and according to UN resolutions, primarily the 1947 Partition Plan.

In the mid-1960s, however, Israel was no longer considered a part of the Afro-Asian community but rather as an extension of US imperialism. Hence the principal and antagonistic contradictions existed now between the Arabs on the one hand, and Israel together with the United States on the other. Since antagonistic contradictions were in their view irreconcilable, the Chinese now rejected any suggestion that the Palestine question should be settled peacefully,[36] and advocated instead a people's armed struggle as the only way to settle the Arab–Israeli conflict.

Obviously, under these circumstances, China no longer approved of the United Nations as suitable for, and capable of, contributing to the settlement of the Palestine question. In China's retrospective view, the United Nations had been manipulated by Western imperialism not only to create the Palestine problem but also to prevent its settlement.[37]

These new concepts provided the basis for a significant change in China's relations with the Palestinians. In the past Peking confined itself to rare and casual verbal support of the Palestinians' right to return to their homeland. Any Chinese gesture towards the Palestinians was made indirectly through the Arab governments. However, beginning in the mid-1960s, China dealt directly with the Palestine liberation movement, to which it extended regular verbal as well as material support.

China's interest in the Palestinian liberation movement emerged after the First Arab Summit Conference of January 1964 had recommended the formation of a distinct Palestinian entity. Chou En-lai, then in Somalia, acclaimed the decision: 'We are glad to see the growing spirit of solidarity and co-operation among the Arab countries. China has always supported the Palestine people's just struggle for the restoration of their proper rights and for return to their homeland.'[38] Aḥmad Shuqayrī, who had been entrusted by the Arab leaders with organising the Palestinians, immediately called on the Chinese ambassador in Cairo to convey the Palestine people's gratitude for China's support of the Palestine cause.[39]

In March 1964 China's press began to express extensive support of the Palestinians, and huge demonstrations were held in Peking. Among those present were two Palestinian guests who later became well known: they were Khalīl al-Wazīr and Yasser Arafat, leaders of Fataḥ in its early organisational stages in Algeria.[40] In May 1964 the PLO was established; and in March 1965 its first delegation, headed by Shuqayrī, arrived in China. Throughout the visit the Chinese communication media discussed Middle Eastern, and particularly Palestinian, affairs in numerous articles and commentaries. China's top leaders, including Mao Tse-tung, met the delegation for talks. Judging from the wording of the joint statement published during the visit, China's commitment was quite considerable: 'The two parties agreed that the PLO shall set up a mission in Peking to strengthen mutual co-operation. *The Chinese people will make every effort to support the Arab people of Palestine in their struggle to return to their homeland by all means, political and otherwise.*'[41] [Italics added.] This was probably the strongest public commitment ever made by Peking towards the Palestinians. In addition to their approval of the opening of a PLO office with quasi-diplomatic status in Peking, the Chinese privately agreed to provide the PLO with arms and training. On 15 May 1965, Palestine Day was celebrated in China for the first time; the celebrations took place thereafter annually until 1971.

China's demonstration of friendship and support for the new-born PLO seemed somewhat exaggerated. In 1965 the PLO was not yet a 'national movement' and, more important, it was not yet engaged in a genuine liberation war. Moreover, the PLO deliberately eschewed any socialist pretensions and the image of its leader, Aḥmad Shuqayrī, was far from that of a revolutionary or a socialist leader. The Chinese were fully aware of the PLO's shortcomings. In 1965 they classified the peripheral Oman and Aden as centres of people's armed struggle, but not Palestine.[42] Mao also indirectly criticised Shuqayrī and the PLO leadership for giving priority to revolutionary training and indoctrination, instead of immediately launching an armed struggle and people's war. Although he regarded the Chinese revolution as a model to be followed in Asia, Africa and Latin America, Mao rejected the blind imitation of China's revolutionary experience by other national liberation movements. Speaking to the PLO delegation, he also dismissed the need to come from abroad for a long training in China:

All things can be divided. Imperialism is also a thing, it also can be divided, it also can be extinguished bit by bit. . . This principle is very simple, there is nothing deep and mysterious about it. There is no need to read boring books. Those who fight must do away with reading books. All the time we fought we did not read books. Read only a little, much reading is no good.

The battlefield is a school. I am not opposed to military schools. They can be conducted. However, they should not last too long. If they go for two or three years, that is too long. Several months is enough. . . The important thing is battlefield training. . .

There are some foreign people studying military matter in China. We advise them to go back, there is no need to study too long. Several months is quite enough, all classroom lectures are of no use. To go back and take part in fighting is more useful.[43]

According to another account he said:

Do not tell me that you have read this or that opinion in my books. You have your war and we have ours. You must make the principles and ideology on which your war stands. Books obstruct the view if piled up before the eye. What is important is to begin action with faith. Faith in victory is the first element of victory – in fact, it may mean victory itself.[44]

Yet, despite the fact that the Chinese were aware of the PLO's shortcomings, they responded positively to the emergence of the Palestine liberation movement and to its specific requests. This enthusiastic response reflected the perceived international situation, developments in the Afro-Asian community, the Middle East and China itself, and was based on short- as well as long-term considerations.

In a long-term view the Chinese, who had already concluded that the Palestine problem was the crux of the Middle East question and the key to the settlement of the Arab–Israeli conflict, recognised the PLO as the true representative of the Palestinian people. Furthermore, although in 1965 the PLO had not yet become a full-fledged liberation movement, the Chinese were convinced that it had strong national and revolutionary potential, particularly with regard to China's two main enemies, the United States and the Soviet Union.

In the first place, the Palestinians were firmly opposed to the United States at a time when Peking was deeply worried about the escalation of American involvement in Southeast Asia and elsewhere. The PLO, committed to armed struggle against Israel, the United States' 'tool of aggression', could not only cause concern but could even harm and undermine American interests in an extremely important and sensitive area and thus help to alleviate the pressure on China. Not less important was the fact that the PLO repeatedly tried to obtain the approval and support of the Soviet Union, but was consistently rejected or ignored.[45] Furthermore, the Soviets not only disapproved of the PLO and its methods but still maintained full diplomatic relations with Israel. Thus, willingly or not, the PLO was relatively independent of direct influence and pressure from both Moscow and Washington. The Chinese, whose fundamental interest in the Middle East was to diminish foreign-power intervention, considered this independence a revolutionary achievement and intended to sustain it, in order particularly to undermine Moscow's predominant position in the Middle East.

In addition to these long-term considerations, China's sudden interest in the Palestinians can be better explained and understood as a short-term expediency. Peking knew, of course, that the PLO had not emerged spontaneously but had been sponsored and created by the Arab governments and apparently enjoyed their unanimous approval. As the only non-Arab country to have so acted, China's alignment with the Arab governments on the Palestinian issue was clearly intended to please them and gain their support for one of China's most urgent objectives – the convening of the second 'Bandung' Conference which, without Soviet participation, would have urged armed struggle against 'US imperialism' throughout the Third World.

The failure

China's mid-1960s' policy in the Middle East, as well as in Asia and Africa, ended in total collapse and bitter disappointment. Despite China's extreme efforts, the Arab governments implicitly rejected its demands for the exclusion of the Soviet Union from the proposed Afro-Asian conference. Under these circumstances the Chinese declared that they would not participate and the conference was finally postponed indefinitely.

Much of the Arabs' rejection of China's Middle East policy in 1964–5 derived from a misunderstanding or simplified interpretation of China's foreign policy and the Sino-Soviet conflict. The Arabs, who identified with China's anti-imperialist impulses, could not understand China's anti-Soviet policy, at least not in the Middle East context. China's campaign against both the United States and the Soviet Union was a completely new

phenomenon in international politics. The Arabs tended to interpret it in the traditional terms to which they had been accus-
tomed under Western colonial rule, as well as under Soviet
patronage, namely, that China wanted to *replace* both the Soviets
and the Americans in the Middle East. Some of this misinterpretation is reflected in one of Haykal's important articles, where he
wrote:

> I am one of the people who watch the existing conflict between the Soviet
> Union and China in the heart of the Marxist–Leninist world, and follow its
> causes. Among other things the conflict results from the fact that China
> opposes the Soviet policy of co-operation with the national–revolutionary
> states which pursue a policy of non-alignment in the cold war between the
> communist East and the capitalist West.
>
> China's point of view, which is in my opinion wrong, is that the Soviet
> Union should restrict its support only within the limits of the Eastern camp,
> and refuse to help any country which does not hoist the flags of Marxism–
> Leninism.
>
> The leaders of the Soviet Union firmly resisted this narrow-mindedness
> and their view – which is in my opinion right – is that national revolutions
> are part of the world revolution against colonialism.[46]

Thus, much of the Arab attitude towards China was based on a
misconception, undoubtedly encouraged by the Soviets.

The Chinese apparently underestimated the Arabs' pre-
disposition towards the Soviet Union and the grudge they bore
China. As Sino-Soviet differences grew deeper, the Arabs moved
closer to the Soviet stand. They had many reasons for resisting
China's anti-Soviet attitudes. Apart from the massive political,
economic and military support they were obtaining from the
Soviets, and which the Chinese could never match, the Arabs on
balance preferred Moscow's Middle East policy to Peking's.

Arab reservations about China's mid-1960s' policy could be
detected at a very early stage. Chou En-lai's visit to Egypt in
December 1963, which the Chinese described as a great success,[47]
failed in fact to fulfil China's expectations.[48] Nasser's absence
from Egypt when the Chinese premier arrived was regarded as
an indication of Cairo's coolness towards Peking if not an insult.[49]
The message Nasser left Chou En-lai, in which he explained his
urgent visit to Tunisia, could not have changed this impression,
although the Chinese premier was said to have understood perfectly.[50]

Indeed, after his return Nasser made little effort to compensate
his guest. His speech at the reception for Chou En-lai contained
some barely concealed hints of criticism of China's Middle East
policy in the past. Nasser condemned, for example, the outside

forces which had tried to destroy the 1958–61 Egyptian–Syrian
union (of which the Chinese disapproved) and also pointed out
that dictatorial regimes would ultimately collapse, as had been
the fate of that of Kassem (whom the Chinese had allegedly
supported against Nasser). On the other hand, Nasser did not
forget to mention Moscow's valuable contributions to Egypt:
'The high dam is being built. . .with generous assistance from the
Soviet Union, for which we are grateful.'[51]

There is little doubt that Nasser was unwilling to approve of
the exclusion of the Soviet Union from the Afro-Asian conference.
'The Chinese party were told in Cairo they had no chance whatever of getting their way.'[52] Egypt's stand was reaffirmed in May
1964, some four months after Chou En-lai's visit, when Khrushchev arrived in Cairo. He was welcomed more warmly and
cordially than the Chinese premier. In the joint communiqué the
Egyptians praised the Soviet role in Africa,[53] thus persisting in
their opposition to the exclusion of Moscow from the conference.
In a memorandum written a few weeks before his death, Palmiro
Togliatti, the Italian communist leader, described Khrushchev's
visit to Egypt in May 1964 as one of the most important victories
obtained by the Russians over the Chinese.[54]

The Egyptians had already undergone the unpleasant experience of Sino-Soviet controversies within the AAPSO. Cairo was,
therefore, far from enthusiastic about the possibility of the second
'Bandung' Conference becoming an arena for Sino-Soviet propaganda and clashes. In April 1964, at the preparatory meeting for
the conference, Egypt (as well as Iraq and India) argued that the
time was not yet ripe for such a conference and proposed to postpone or even cancel it. Peking, on the other hand, wanted to
convene the conference, and as soon as possible.[55] In the end, the
conference was scheduled to begin on 18 April 1965, ten years
after the Bandung Conference (China insisted on September
1964), and was later postponed to 29 June. More important, a
sub-committee in charge of invitations decided not to invite the
Soviet Union, but the joint communiqué of the meeting stated
that no agreement had been reached on this question.[56]

As for the Chinese, while trying to win the Egyptians' goodwill,
they continued to offend them. China, provoked by Soviet–
Egyptian co-operation in the Afro-Asian movement, began to
form rival organisations which excluded both the Soviets and
the Egyptians. In June 1964, for example, the Asian–African

Economic Seminar met in North Korea, under Peking's auspices. Delegates from thirty-four countries were present but neither Egypt nor the Soviet Union had even been informed of the event.[57] In October 1964, at the second conference of the non-aligned countries in Cairo, Nasser was reportedly strongly hostile to the Chinese.[58] He continued to reject China's demands when Chou En-lai visited Egypt in April 1965. Summing up Chou En-lai's 'successful' journey in Rumania, Albania, Algeria, the UAR, Pakistan and Burma, the *People's Daily* mentioned the leaders of all these countries by name, except for Nasser.[59]

Despite the Egyptian stand, or perhaps because of it, the Chinese were very anxious to convene the conference at all costs and as soon as possible, as long as the issue of inviting Moscow remained unsettled. This is why the Chinese were so quick to recognise the new Boumedienne regime in Algeria, after a *coup d'état* had ousted Ben Bella on 19 June, just a few days before the conference was due to open.

China's haste to endorse the regime which had just deposed a leader who was said to have been one of China's best friends in the Afro-Asian world was regarded by many Asian and African leaders as unscrupulous and opportunistic. Yet there was nothing extraordinary in China's prompt recognition of Boumedienne. Ben Bella, who had undoubtedly respected and admired the Chinese, could by no means be regarded as China's *protégé*. Moreover, as we have seen, it was always Peking's practice in the past to accord recognition to new regimes shortly after they had seized power. In this case, the Chinese probably decided that the recognition of the new regime in Algeria was particularly justified in order to ensure that the change of government would not prevent or delay the holding of the conference: 'Some people hesitate to go to Algiers for the conference because they have reservations about the new Algerian Government. We hold that the change of leadership in Algeria is her internal affair in which no foreign state should interfere.'[60]

However, most of the countries that were to take part in the conference, and particularly Egypt, regarded the *coup d'état* as a pretext for postponing the conference.[61] Chou En-lai was already in Egypt when the Algerian *coup d'état* occurred. To his dismay, the conference was postponed to late October 1965.

In the meantime, Egypt moved even closer to the Soviet Union. In August 1965 Nasser arrived in Moscow. This was another blow to the Chinese. Nasser had been invited to visit China several times since 1956. In the past it had been announced that he would be coming to China 'soon'.[62] During his visit to Egypt in December 1963, Premier Chou En-lai renewed the invitation: 'We eagerly look forward to your visit to our country, Mr. President, in your capacity as a great Arab and African leader and for the sake of the welfare of the UAR people, the development of friendship between the UAR and CPR peoples, and world solidarity.'[63] In early August 1964 NCNA reported from Peking that Nasser would visit China at a suitable time on the invitation of Liu Shao-ch'i and Chou En-lai.[64] Yet, despite these repeated invitations, Nasser never came to China.

In early September 1965 Nasser completed his visit to the Soviet Union. In the joint communiqué Cairo and Moscow stressed their identity of opinion on many international questions. Furthermore, 'the UAR Government declared that the U.S.S.R.'s participation at the [Afro-Asian] Conference would enable the Conference to achieve its objectives successfully'.[65] In addition to this outspoken statement Nasser also wrote to Chou En-lai, reiterating that the Soviet Union was an Asian and not only a European country,[66] and that the Asian and African nations would only benefit from the Russians' presence at the conference. Allegedly, Chou En-lai's reply left no doubt about China's position: 'If the conference should be forcibly convened as scheduled in violation of the principle of consensus through consultation in spite of the opposition of China, the Kingdom of Cambodia and other countries, the Chinese Government will be compelled to absent itself from such a conference which will lead to a split.'[67]

Following these developments, the Chinese made a last-minute attempt to turn the wheels back. Disillusioned with the Egyptians, they concentrated their efforts on trying to enlist Syria's support. In early September 1965 Foreign Minister Ch'en Yi cut short his visit to Mali and hurried to Damascus. Although he was expected in Algeria on 5 September he did not leave Syria until the 7th. On his way back from Africa, skipping Egypt, he again made a 24-hour stop-over in Damascus between 18 and 19 September. If these visits had indeed anything to do with the forthcoming conference, they were too late. The Syrians had clarified several times that they regarded the Soviet Union as 'a reliable and trusty friend of the Arab peoples and that they would not let anyone destroy their friendship'.[68]

On 12 September the Chinese publicly confirmed they would

not take part in a conference convened in disregard of China's views.[69] A few days before the conference was due to open, Peking called for another postponement.[70] But, as the Arab and some Asian and African countries insisted on opening the conference as planned, the Chinese officially announced their withdrawal.[71] Without China it seemed impractical to hold the conference and it was finally postponed indefinitely.[72]

In fact, all the means employed by the Chinese to persuade the Arabs to support Peking's views had failed. China's diplomatic endeavours were rebuffed. The intensity and scope of the diplomatic effort invested by the Chinese in the Middle East in the mid-1960s have never been matched. In the decade since September 1965, not even *one* high-ranking Chinese official has visited the Arab countries. The economic offensive also failed. Cairo, for example, declined to use China's 1964 aid offer of $80 million, which by the end of 1973 was still unused. By late 1965 China was still unable, or unwilling, to implement its $16.3 million loan offered to Syria in February 1963.

Finally, China's anti-Israel attitude and its support for the Palestinians also failed to secure the Arabs' goodwill, at least as far as the Afro-Asian conference was concerned. Basically, Peking misinterpreted the Arab governments' stand on the Palestine issue. The Arab governments, which had monopolised, and in fact neglected, the management of Palestinian affairs since 1947, had no intention in the mid-1960s of providing their new creation, the PLO, with unlimited freedom of action and exclusive responsibility to liberate Palestine. There was no unanimous agreement among the Arab leaders on the PLO's future course of action and they, particularly Nasser, preferred to keep it under close control.

The Arab leaders still remembered China's intrigues and slanderous interference in Arab internal affairs in the late 1950s which had led to a serious deterioration in Sino-Arab relations. They could not but suspect Chinese motives in supporting the PLO. The generous offer of political indoctrination and of military aid made by China to the PLO in order to gain the goodwill of the Arab governments was, therefore, counter-productive. It not only threatened to reduce the PLO's dependence on the Arab governments, but had also been made in an unforgivable way, without consulting senior Arab leaders, primarily Nasser. For example, when Shuqayrī was in Peking, he instructed the Chinese to deliver arms shipments for the PLO directly to Alexandria,

without first obtaining Nasser's approval. The Egyptian ambassador in China warned Shuqayrī of the seriousness of his action.
Nasser was indeed furious, and refused to receive Shuqayrī after
the latter's return from China.[73]

In December 1965, following the collapse of their Middle
Eastern policy, the Chinese recalled their ambassadors from the
three main Arab capitals – Cairo, Damascus and Baghdad. This
step reflected China's displeasure and indignation with the Arab
governments rather than with the ambassadors; Ch'en Chia-k'ang
and Hsü Yi-hsin, China's ambassadors to Egypt and Syria respectively, were promoted Vice Foreign Ministers immediately on
their return to China.

The consequences

In late 1965 the Chinese revised yet again their analysis of the
world situation to reflect the changes in international affairs,
China's international experience in the preceding years, as well as
the growing radicalism at home. As a result of the events of the
mid-1960s – the failure to convene the Afro-Asian conference;
the setbacks in Africa; the Indo-Pakistan war; the abortive *coup*
in Indonesia; and primarily the increased US involvement in
Vietnam – the Chinese believed not only that the world's contradictions had become sharper but that their focus had moved to
Asia, very near to China.

China maintained that the Soviet Union, by refusing to take
firm measures against US aggression and even more by continuing to pursue the policy of *détente* with the United States at
that critical juncture, was in fact collaborating with the Americans and encouraging their intervention, particularly against
China. The Chinese maintained further that the governments of
Asia and Africa, let alone Europe, which were the target of Soviet–
American plots, did not realise this situation and were not prepared to form a united front to resist both.

Consequently, from 1966 on China's foreign policy became
more oriented towards national liberation movements and revolutionary organisations which were still committed to the struggle
against imperialism and, by implication, against Soviet revisionism as well. These assumptions were expounded in great detail in
Lin Piao's famous 1965 article 'Long Live the Victory of People's
War'.[74] This radical world outlook was influenced by the Cultural
Revolution (1966–8). The domestic onslaught against revisionism

and bourgeois thinking in the CCP, in the society and the political system in general, not only disrupted the daily operation of China's external relations, but also affected the concepts and perceptions underlying its foreign policy. There is little doubt that the Cultural Revolution reaffirmed and reinforced China's reliance on world revolution and its urge to armed struggle. It also increased Chinese hostility, particularly towards the Soviet Union but also towards orthodox communist parties and Third World governments.

Concentrating their attention on Southeast Asia, the Chinese no longer regarded the Middle East as a 'storm centre'. In 1966 this area remained beyond the perimeter of China's immediate interests; it was not even mentioned in Lin's article. Only from mid-1967, following the Arab–Israeli war, did the Chinese revive their interest in the Middle East.

China's Middle East policy reflected its basic analysis of the world situation and the lessons of China's setbacks in 1963–5. The first lesson was that Soviet influence was entrenched in the Arab countries to a much greater extent than Peking had realised. China's offensive in the Middle East was repulsed not so much because of American resistance but primarily because of Soviet opposition. Thus, although the United States still remained, particularly with its increased involvement in Vietnam, the main direct threat to China's security, it was the Soviet Union which had gradually become the major obstacle to China's policies in Asia and Africa. This realisation brought about a change in China's tactics. Whereas in the past Peking generally refrained from direct and public attacks on Soviet policy in the Middle East, from 1966 onwards such attacks became frequent and intensive.

The second lesson was that the Arab governments could not be expected to take an active part in the struggle against imperialism as long as they were under Soviet influence. For the Chinese, this was but another confirmation of their long-held belief that national–bourgeois regimes could not be trusted at times of crisis and, therefore, while being respected, should also be suspected. A very similar view was adopted by the Arabs towards China. Consequently, China lost much interest in cultivating relations with the Arabs; its relations with the Arab governments deteriorated, though formal exchanges did continue.

The third lesson was that, under these circumstances, national liberation movements and revolutionary organisations remained the only force which could persist in the struggle against American imperialism and Soviet revisionism. Thus from 1966 onwards the Chinese increased their support, rhetorical and material, to the national liberation movements in the Middle East, particularly to the Palestinians.

As the Cultural Revolution intensified, these policies became more radical, leading to deeper hostility towards the Soviet Union's role in the Middle East; to conflicts and incidents with the Arab authorities; and, finally, to greater expectations of revolutionary activity from the Palestine liberation movement.

Deterioration in governmental relations

Arab, and more particularly Egyptian, reservations about China grew in autumn 1965 following the abortive communist *coup d'état* in Indonesia. China's alleged encouragement of the attempted *coup* was said to have damaged the remnants of its prestige in the Afro-Asian world.[75] As a result of the events in Indonesia, Nasser decided to tighten his grip on those dissident communists who, unlike the orthodox communists, had refused to join the Arab Socialist Union (the only party permitted in Egypt) and continued to oppose the Government.[76]

In November 1965, several such groups were arrested, including members of the so-called 'Arab Communist Party' led by a certain Muṣṭafā Aghā. Allegedly, they had 'pro-Chinese' sympathies, and they were said to have plotted to overthrow Nasser and his regime and to have associated with Chinese officials in Cairo from whom they received financial help. Rumour held that an NCNA representative in Cairo was asked to leave the country following these arrests. It was also hinted that, because of his alleged connections with the Aghā group, Ch'en Chia-k'ang, China's ambassador in Egypt for almost ten years, left on 26 December 1965, earlier than planned.[77]

Moscow called the Aghā group 'political adventurers' and denied having any connection with them.[78] At that time the Soviets only alluded to China's relations with Aghā, but later they were explicit.[79] The allegation that Peking was involved in subversive communist activities in Egypt seems, in fact, doubtful and requires consideration.

In the late 1950s China's Middle East policy suffered irreparable damage as a result of similar accusations, whether justified or not. To ensure that this would not happen again, the Chinese did their utmost at the beginning of their political offensive in the Middle East and throughout it in the mid-1960s to placate the Arabs and assure them that 'China respects the sovereignty of the Arab countries' and that it 'never interferes in the internal affairs of any country'.[80] Peking had to adopt this policy not only to assure the Arabs of China's good intentions but also to warn them of other outside interference, presumably by the United States and, notably, the Soviet Union: 'The Chinese government and people...hold that the sovereignty of the Arab countries should be respected by all other countries and that encroachment and interference from any quarters should be opposed.'[81]

Adopting this policy to improve their prospects with the Arab governments, the Chinese, in the mid-1960s, ignored completely not only the persecution of communists in the Arab countries but also the existence of so-called 'radical' and 'extreme left' factions which had split from the orthodox communist parties. Such factions as the Socialist Revolution Party (Ḥizb al-Thawra al-Ishtirākiyya) in the Lebanon, or the Iraqi Communist Party Central Command (al-Qiyāda al-Markaziyya), were said to have opposed the Soviet Union as well as the Arab national–bourgeois regimes and very often were labelled by both as pro-Chinese.[82] There is, however, no evidence that China maintained any relationship or even identified publicly with these factions. Moreover, although these groups were basically opposed to Moscow and more radical on questions of Arab internal and external policy, they did not consider themselves pro-Chinese.[83]

It seems, therefore, odd that the Chinese should suddenly decide to support a small group of communist dissidents in a country like Egypt, where communism had been least developed and most strictly controlled, and had virtually no chance of success. True, such behaviour could have been a manifestation of China's fury over Egypt's role in rejecting its demands and thereby cancelling the Afro-Asian conference. Yet this was hardly China's style.

If the Chinese were indeed involved in Aghā's subversive attempt, this would have been a far more serious offence to Egypt than the Bakdāsh affair in 1959. Certainly, Cairo would have reacted firmly and mercilessly. In fact, Egypt has never officially implicated China in the Aghā affair and apparently did not consider China's links with the group, if there were any, as subversion. On the contrary, in his speech at the opening of Egypt's National Assembly in late November 1965, Nasser made some

favourable comments on China and on Egypt's relations with it.
He said:

We believe in the importance of the great role played by the Chinese
People's Republic, and the potentialities of that role... We work continuously to strengthen friendly relations between the UAR and this great
Asian country... We believe that the continued exclusion of this people...
from their lawful seat in the United Nations is a flagrant wrong to them, to
the United Nations and to world peace.[84]

This does not mean, however, that Sino-Egyptian relations became friendly again. Even if China had not been involved, or
had not been seriously involved, in the Aghā affair, and despite
Nasser's comments,[85] Peking still had many reasons to mistrust
and suspect the Egyptian regime, and *vice versa*.

While China's relations with Egypt remained lukewarm, there
was an impression in late 1965 of renewed friendship between
China and Syria. As we have seen, China's last-minute attempt
to secure Syria's support for the Afro-Asian conference failed,
but it gained Syria's sympathy in the context of the Arab–Israeli
conflict. Of all the Arab countries the Syrians were the most
impressed by China's firm stand in favour of the Palestinians and
against Israel:

We like the Chinese because they are revolutionaries and because they have
never stabbed us in the back, nor plotted against us and did not attempt to
hinder the construction of the Euphrates Dam. They did not lend us a
friendly hand, while hiding a dagger in the other...
    The Chinese openly said they were supporting us against Israel and,
indeed, they are standing by our side on the Palestine problem. They said,
moreover, that they regarded our frontier with the enemy as China's first
line of defence against Zionism and world imperialism.
    Why should we, therefore, hate the Chinese? Why shouldn't we co-operate
and maintain cultural and technical relations with them for mutual benefit –
aren't they revolutionaries like us?[86]

Subsequently, a Syrian Army mission visited China and it was
reported that 'hundreds' of Chinese experts had arrived in
Damascus. This allegedly aggravated the disagreements between
'pro-Soviet' and 'pro-Chinese' elements within the ruling Ba'th
Party.[87] When the February 1966 *coup d'état* took place in Syria,
it was said to have been engineered by so-called 'pro-Chinese'
elements.[88]

There is no evidence to substantiate any of these reports.
Indeed, a few among the officers who seized power in February
had been known as Marxist, and even as sympathisers of the
Viet Cong and China.[89] Basically, however, Syria's 'pro-Chinese'

inclination was largely rhetorical: 'Public opinion knows well that the Ba'th Party is a national–socialist party which does not identify with Peking in its struggle with Moscow. It is also known that the talk of Chinese influence in Syria is no more than a dream.'[90] Indeed, Syria could not afford to give up Soviet economic and military support. Very soon after the February *coup d'état* it became obvious that the new regime, although intending to seek a balanced position between Moscow and Peking, was in fact leaning towards the Soviets.[91] Syria's 'radicalism' had nothing to do with China: 'The ruling officers did not concern themselves much with ideology; their understanding of it is limited... To proclaim extreme revolutionary slogans came to be a ritual, behind which were hidden personal ambitions and rivalries.'[92] Maḥmūd Riyāḍ, Egypt's Foreign Minister, later expressed the opinion that 'the Chinese would never secure any permanent influence in Syria, because all the politicians and officers there were totally opportunistic, latching onto any issue of ephemeral interest or drawing in any outside power to overthrow their rivals'.[93]

The Chinese were not led astray by Syria's revolutionary uproar and treated the Syrian internal, as well as external, policy with some reservation. As far as Syria's internal politics were concerned, the Chinese avoided any public hint of criticism, although they apparently disliked, among other things, the predominance of the military in the Syrian political and social system. A 'pro-Chinese' faction in the Lebanon described the Syrian regime as

a petty-bourgeois regime consisting of two strata, a progressive one and a reactionary–opportunistic one... The Syrian regime is indeed opposing imperialist policy in the area but its seizure by the military prevents the revolutionary public from taking an active part in the success of the revolution. [This is] because the military mentality fears the masses' activity and consciousness which contradict the interests of this military class and its sheer existence as a representative of the petty-bourgeois class.[94]

Although there is no evidence of any Chinese association with this faction, the above description could very well reflect China's concealed attitudes towards Syria.

As far as Syria's foreign policy was concerned, the Chinese were not absolutely convinced about Syria's determination to fight imperialism in the Middle East. There were also some Chinese hints of dissatisfaction with Syria's fragile stand against Israel: 'According to the experience of the Chinese revolution, one must give imperialism and all reactionaries tit for tat and fight for every inch of land. Since the aggressors have taken up swords, the oppressed have to follow their example. Before wild beasts, one must not in the least show one's cowardice.'[95] In addition, Peking undoubtedly disapproved of Syria's close relationship with the Soviet Union. China most probably considered Soviet influence an important factor responsible for Syria's weak reaction to Western imperialism.

Sino-Arab relations had already gone from bad to worse when the Cultural Revolution erupted – and the worst was still to come. From late 1966 to mid-1967 Peking recalled all its ambassadors from the Arab capitals except for Huang Hua, China's ambassador to Egypt. He had been appointed in January 1966[96] and was the only Chinese ambassador to remain at his post during the Cultural Revolution.[97] This, however, did not shield the Arabs from the effects of the Cultural Revolution. During these years, particularly in early 1967, several incidents occurred which further damaged Sino-Arab relations. On the one hand, these incidents were the outcome of Chinese 'radicalism'. Yet some of the blame for provoking these incidents should be put on the Arab governments, whose somewhat irrational fear of the Chinese had no doubt been exacerbated by Red Guard extremism. Even more important, in order to protect their relations with the Soviet Union, and probably under Soviet pressure, they prevented the Chinese from demonstrating their grievances against Moscow. This led to several incidents. In Iraq, Chinese students tried to deliver a message of protest to the Soviet embassy in Baghdad in reaction to an incident in which Chinese students had been beaten in Moscow. This was prevented by Iraqi officials, and a week later the Chinese students were ordered to leave Iraq.[98] At the same time, seventeen Chinese students were told to leave Syria. Subsequently, the car of the Syrian ambassador in Budapest was attacked by several Chinese, and Damascus retaliated in February 1967 by imposing a ban on NCNA reports from Syria.[99] In Egypt, the authorities had been informed in advance of Chinese plans to demonstrate in front of the embassies of the Soviet Union and other East European countries. Measures were taken to prevent these demonstrations.[100] When two Chinese officials defected, one in Damascus in July 1966, and the other in Cairo in February 1968, both governments refused to extradite them. These refusals, particularly the Egyptian one, infuriated the Chinese and added more fuel to the already inflamed Sino-Arab relations.[101] It should be stressed however, that normal cultural and economic exchanges and mutual visits between China and the Arabs continued, though on a small scale, throughout the Cultural Revolution. Although the Cultural Revolution undoubtedly had some negative effects on Sino-Arab relations, the deterioration of these relations, as we have seen, had very little to do with the Cultural Revolution itself. Despite the disturbances of the Cultural Revolution, the daily management of China's relations with the Arabs was not much interrupted. In any case, the Chinese remained well informed of the situation in the Middle East and the world as a whole.

China's alertness to the situation in the Middle East became evident in May–June 1967. From the very beginning the Chinese interpreted the growing tension in the region not so much in terms of Arab–Israeli relations but primarily as a reflection of global power politics. China's firm and unreserved (though mostly rhetorical) support of the Arabs during the 1967 crisis should, therefore, be understood not merely as an attempt to regain the friendship of the Arabs and improve China's position in the Middle East, but mainly within the larger context of Peking's fundamental foreign policy concerns: the struggle to prevent the powers hostile to China, the United States and even more notably the Soviet Union, from seizing control over this strategic crossroads of the intermediate zone. In accordance with their fundamental analysis of Middle Eastern affairs, the Chinese regarded the June 1967 war as part of an American imperialist scheme to reassert its predominance in the Middle East and subvert national liberation and anti-imperialist movements. In this task the Americans had been assisted, in Peking's view, by the Soviets, whose aims were perceived as very similar. China had accused the Soviet Union of having betrayed the Arabs well before the fighting even started.[102] As tension mounted, culminating in war and eventually in an Arab defeat, Peking's attacks on the Soviet Union became more vituperative and fierce, to the point of accusing Moscow of collaboration with Washington in engineering the assault on the Arabs.

The Chinese interpreted the outcome of the war in the very same context as its origins had been analysed, that is, from the fundamental, strategic and long-term point of view. Referring to the Arab defeat as no more than a temporary setback, they said:

The Arab people's struggle against imperialist aggression will be a protracted one. Looked at in essence and from a long-term point of view, the

Arab people are really powerful. U.S. imperialism, British imperialism, Soviet revisionism, Israel – all are paper tigers. It is only a temporary phenomenon that Israel, by relying on the assistance of U.S. and British imperialism and Soviet revisionism, has been able to occupy some Arab territory by force of arms. The Arab people will sooner or later liberate all their territory now under forcible occupation by imperialism and its lackey. Without fail, the debt owed by imperialism to the Arab people will be repaid. No force on earth can stop the Arab people from exercising their sacred right... The reverses and setbacks which the Arab people will encounter in the course of their anti-imperialist struggle can under no circumstances halt their continuous advance.[103]

By this, however, the Chinese did not mean that final victory would be automatically guaranteed. Rather, it would depend on the drawing of correct lessons from the 1967 war, as well as from all previous 'acts of aggression' in the Middle East. The Chinese summed up these lessons in an important article published in the CCP organ *Red Flag*.[104] Analysing the war in the larger perspective of imperialism's world-wide attacks on 'the surging national liberation movement', the Chinese set forth four fundamental lessons. In the same manner as China had always perceived the Middle East, these lessons proceeded from the general, global and external, to the particular, local and internal, context.

The first lesson was that 'U.S. imperialism' had remained and would always remain the Arabs' 'sworn, number-one enemy'. Indicating again the crucial importance of the Middle East in world affairs and the history of American 'aggression' in the Middle East, the Chinese concluded that 'no illusions should be entertained about this ferocious enemy, U.S. imperialism, nor should any idea of winning easy victories through good luck be entertained; the only correct policy is to cast away illusions, prepare for struggle, give tit-for-tat and carry out a protracted and repeated trial of strength with the enemy'.

The second lesson was that Soviet revisionism had become 'the number-one accomplice of U.S. imperialism in every sense of the term'. Referring to the Soviets as traitors whose aid had only served their own 'neo-colonialist policies' and the 'counter-revolutionary line' of 'collaboration with the U.S. for world domination', the Chinese urged the Arabs not to be deceived and to carry through to the end the anti-imperialist and anti-revisionist struggle.

The third lesson was that 'to defeat the armed attacks of imperialism and its lackeys, the oppressed nations and people can only rely on the theory, strategy and tactics of people's war; any other strategy and tactics will not work'. Once again the

Chinese reiterated that people, and not modern weapons, were the decisive factor in war. They urged the Arabs to abandon conventional warfare, to unite their forces and employ the strategic principles of protracted war so as to carry on the struggle for a long period of time.

China's fourth lesson, which concerned the internal situation in the Arab world, was probably the most important since it summed up the Chinese rationale of the Arab defeat. 'Why did the Arab countries with 100 million people over more than 10,000 sq. km. of land suffer a setback in the war?' Peking's answer was that all the mistakes made by the Arab governments in the June war, as well as in previous crises (illusions about the principal enemy, dependence on the Soviets and the adoption of wrong strategy) had ultimately emanated from socio-political backwardness. In short, the Chinese believed that the Arab countries had not yet reached the stage of national–democracy and were still engaged in the national–democratic revolution:

The bourgeoisie in the Arab countries has a dual character. On the one hand, it suffers from imperialist oppression and has contradictions with the imperialists. In a given stage and to a certain extent it can take part in the anti-imperialist struggle. But on the other hand, being weak economically and politically, it vacillates and is prone to conciliation with the enemy.

Discrediting the leadership of the Arab bourgeoisie, the Chinese paid high tribute to 'the popular masses, first and foremost the workers and peasants, [who] are the *basic motive force* of the national–democratic revolution of the Arab countries' [italics added]. China's fourth lesson, which undoubtedly reflected the extremes of the Cultural Revolution, was far-reaching and inconsistent with previous Chinese conceptions of Arab politics and society. It indirectly urged Arab workers and peasants to seize control, unite all the revolutionary forces in their societies, and lead the revolution – otherwise the Arab countries would never reach the stage of national–democracy, let alone of socialism, and would suffer more defeats:

Now the revolutionary situation is excellent throughout the world. Likewise, the revolutionary situation in the Arab region is also excellent. So long as they adopt the correct policy, unite all the forces that can be united and, together with the people of the world, concentrate their attacks on neo-colonialism headed by the United States and on its running dogs, *the Arab proletariat and other revolutionary people* will surely be able *to lead* their revolutionary cause against imperialism from victory to victory. [Italics added.]

To sum up, the Chinese expected that the events of May and June 1967 in the Middle East would produce a thorough transformation in the Arab world, both externally and internally. They predicted that 'new-born forces will come to the fore from the masses. These new-born forces will grow, and become the mainstay of the Arab nations.'[105]

It was not long before the Chinese realised that their lessons of the June war fell on deaf ears. The Arabs continued to regard Israel as their principal enemy, rather than the United States (let alone the Soviet Union). This view was spelled out clearly, for example, by Yūsuf al-Sibāʿī, Secretary General of the AAPSO and chief editor of the Egyptian weekly *Ākhir Sāʿa*. In his view, Arab hostility towards the United States had little to do with the American involvement in Vietnam, Asia, Africa or Latin America. Rather, its chief cause was America's support for Israel, ultimately the Arabs' arch-enemy.[106] This stand was shared by many Arabs despite their anti-American rhetoric, as later events were to prove.

Similarly, although there were bitter expressions of disappointment at the Soviet attitude during the June 1967 crisis, the Arab governments refused to relinquish their dependence on the Soviet Union. As soon as the war was over, attempts began to exonerate the Soviets and to justify their 'responsible' reaction to 'America's war provocations'. Praising Soviet support of the Arabs, an editorial in *al-Ahrām* condemned the campaign to alienate the Arabs from the Soviet Union and thereby distract their attention from the real enemy.[107] Haykal, the editor of *al-Ahrām* and Nasser's close associate, continued to defend the Soviet Union, arguing that Moscow could not afford to abandon the Arabs because this would give the United States 'overwhelming strategic supremacy' and China a great 'revolutionary advantage'.[108] He firmly denied China's accusations that the Soviet Union had betrayed the Arabs: 'The UAR has a viewpoint which differs from that which China has on the U.S.S.R. and Yugoslavia. The Soviet Union stood on our side during the crisis and her aid to us has been inestimable. Yugoslavia, too, tries sincerely to do her utmost.'[109]

The Arab governments also rejected, in practice if not in theory, China's advice to adopt the strategy of a people's war as the only way to victory. In their view, 'the confrontation between the regular armies on the front line will continue to be the primary and decisive factor in the war'[110] whereas a people's war continued

to be regarded as a supplementary strategy, at best. After the
1967 war Nasser allegedly tried to explain to the Chinese that a
people's war could not be applied in the Arab–Israeli conflict.
When talking to Palestinian guerrillas who had been trained in
China, Nasser was said to have criticised Chinese methods as
unsuitable for the Arabs and for the conditions of the Middle
East.[111] In numerous articles, undoubtedly reflecting Nasser's
views, Haykal repeated this argument:

Those in the Arab world who consider that the main burden of the
[Palestine] problem could be solved by *fidā'iyīn* activity, only make it easy
for themselves and prepare the ground for escaping responsibility. *Fidā'iyīn*
activity would not be able to get Israel out of the West Bank [of the Jordan
River], the Syrian Heights or the Sinai Desert.[112]

The Arab leaders not only rejected China's call for people's war
but also disagreed, implicitly or explicitly, with China's presump-
tion that war was the only way of settling the Arab–Israeli conflict.
This was another indication that the Soviet Union still exerted
much influence on the Arab governments. When Nasser was in
Moscow in 1968, he allegedly said:

We gave and shall still continue to give any chance for a political solution
because we are convinced that war is not needed for its own sake but only
when there is no other alternative to guard the peace and freedom of states.
Although I know that a military solution has many advantages, particularly
for the morale of the Arab nation, I still give the priority to the fundamental
objective itself, namely – the liquidation of the consequences of aggression.
If I will manage to accomplish it in a political way – the better, but if the
accomplishment of this objective would call for war, this would be a sacrifice
my homeland would not hesitate to offer.[113]

Finally, China's hopes for a socio-political transformation in
the Arab countries were also frustrated. In no way could the
Arab 'proletariat' and 'revolutionary people' seize control over
the state apparatus: the Arab governments, particularly those
which were pro-Soviet, showed no sign of willingness to permit
greater political participation and suppressed groups and individuals who dared to criticise the Soviet role in the June 1967 war.
Indeed, there were indications of disillusionment and disappointment with Moscow within the Arab communist movement. In the
Lebanon, the 'pro-Chinese' Socialist Revolution Party published
a manifesto condemning the Soviet stand on the Palestine problem 'which is not different from the stand of any imperialist state
in the world'.[114] The statement also strongly attacked the Soviet
Union as well as the orthodox communist parties for having
represented 'the distorted capitulationist line' (*al-khaṭ al-taḥrīfī*

al-istislāmī) and turned into 'obedient puppets and followers of the Soviet deviationists'.[115]

The defeat also revived anti-Soviet feelings among the Syrian communists. It was reported in late June 1967 that the Syrian authorities had arrested the leaders of a 'pro-Chinese' communist faction, the Socialist Workers' Party (Ḥizb al-'Ummāl al-Ishtirākī), following its public statement accusing the Soviet Union of 'co-ordinating its actions with the United States against Arab interests' during and after the war.[116] In early 1968, a new 'pro-Chinese' communist party, the Arab Marxist–Leninist Party, was said to have been formed in Syria.[117] Later that year, members of the new party were arrested by the Syrian authorities.[118] There were also indications of a 'leftward turn' in the Iraqi Communist Party.[119]

Again, there was no evidence of any connection between China and these factions, most of which, in fact, refused to be called 'Chinese' communists and claimed that their relations with China were limited to adopting Mao Tse-tung's doctrines.[120] It seems highly unlikely that the Chinese had pinned their hopes on the emergence of these offspring as the 'new-born forces' which were to become 'the mainstay of the Arab nation'.

On the other hand, the orthodox communist parties in the Middle East firmly aligned themselves with the Soviet Union and, in fact, intensified their attacks on the Chinese:

> The propaganda of Mao Tse-tung's bloc against the cease-fire actually amounted only to one thing, i.e.: to let Israel take full advantage of her aggression to occupy more Arab lands and even invade the Suez Canal – and that is precisely what American imperialism wants.
>
> [The Chinese] would like the Arabs to embark upon adventures without any preparation and without taking into consideration the possible conse-quences of their action – and that is exactly what is wanted and hoped by the American imperialists and the rulers of Israel.[121]

Much of this anti-Chinese campaign was undoubtedly inspired and encouraged by Moscow to counter the Chinese anti-Soviet offensive. This offensive, though largely unsuccessful in the Middle East, managed to upset the Soviets' confidence in their position in the Arab countries.[122] It seems less likely that the Soviets really believed that the Chinese would be able to replace them physically in the Middle East. More probably they feared that Chinese ideas would replace Soviet ones and lead to what they considered disastrous consequences. To avert such a pos-sibility Moscow intensified its efforts in the Middle East in the following years. Thus, China's anti-Soviet offensive was, to a great extent, counter-productive as it motivated the Soviets to increase their presence and influence in the region.

The Chinese had failed yet again. They did not have the power, the influence or, indeed, the means to impose their 'lessons' on the Arabs or to retaliate when these 'lessons' were rejected. For example, in August 1967 the Chinese cancelled their participation in the Damascus International Fair after thirteen years of uninterrupted presence. Allegedly, this was done in protest at Syria's continued leaning towards the Soviet Union after the war.[123] It was also reported that the Chinese withdrew their $10 million 'gift' in hard currency offered to Egypt immediately after the war,[124] allegedly because the resolutions of the Khartoum summit conference (convened by the Arab leaders after the June 1967 war) 'had not been revolutionary enough'.[125] Both allegations should, however, be treated with much reserve since there is no substantial evidence to confirm either. There was also a marked drop in Sino-Arab trade. China's trade with the Middle East reached a record in 1966 – some $140 million. In 1967 and 1968, however, the annual average was only $80–90 million. This trend was particularly evident in China's trade with Egypt. In 1965 and 1966 the average annual trade stood at $72 million, whereas from 1967 to 1970 it was less than half – around $35 million each year.

Thus Sino-Arab relations, damaged in the mid-1960s, further deteriorated during the Cultural Revolution. But at the same time there was a growing Chinese interest in local national liberation movements, particularly the Palestinians.

Orientation towards the Palestinians

In 1964–5 the Chinese failed in their attempt to secure Arab support for the Afro-Asian conference by embracing the Palestinian cause. This failure, however, did not discourage Peking from preserving its relations with the Palestinians.

Although Arab leaders did not consider Chinese support for the Palestinians a sufficient incentive for submitting to China's conditions regarding the conference, they nevertheless appreciated China's hostility towards Israel. During the Cultural Revolution there was not much else China could have done to maintain a good image in the Arab world. The Chinese, therefore, continued to remind the Arabs of their attitude: 'The Chinese people are the most loyal and most dependable friend of the Arab people. We have consistently supported the Palestinian and Arab peoples in their struggles against imperialism and old and new colonialism, and for winning and safeguarding national independence.'[126] But, as we have seen, China's sudden interest in the Palestinians in 1964–5 was not based on short-term expediency alone; at a very early stage the Chinese had also realised the long-term revolutionary potential implicit in the Palestinian problem and, therefore, in the Palestine liberation movement.

Peking regarded the Palestinians, rather than the Arab governments, as the only force in the Middle East whose aims and methods contradicted the increased American involvement in Asia and the growing Soviet influence in the Third World:

The policy of U.S. imperialism and its collaborators, the Soviet modern revisionists, to preserve the status quo [in the Middle East meant] forbidding the Arab people to create 'disturbance' in the Middle East so as to make it possible for the U.S. to concentrate its forces to go on with the war of aggression in Vietnam in line with the eastward shift of the centre of gravity of U.S. strategy and with its needs of 'containing' China... Therefore, the struggle of the Palestinian people and the Arab people is linked up with the anti-U.S. struggle of the Vietnamese people and other revolutionary people of the world.[127]

China was fully aware of the 'disturbances' that Palestinian activities could cause: 'Just because the U.S. has a big stake in its oil, and because it has "strategic interests" in the Middle East, any single spark of revolution or any anti-imperialist outcry in this region will send cold shivers down the backs of the Americans in the White House.'[128]

In addition to contributing to the struggle against American imperialism, China's support of the Palestinians and uncompromising stand against Israel were one of its very few advantages over the Soviet Union in the Middle East, and Peking certainly had no intentions of giving it up. Throughout their offensive in the Arab world in 1964–5 the Chinese muted their grievances against Soviet policy towards Israel and the Palestine problem. This was probably done to avoid unnecessarily offending the Arabs. However, from 1966, after their offensive had failed anyway, the Chinese felt completely free to condemn publicly what they regarded as the subversive role played by the Soviets with regard to the Palestine problem. The Chinese accused the Soviet 'revisionist leading group' of having pretended to be the 'friends' of the Arab people and having hypocritically professed support for the Palestinian and Arab peoples while, in fact, acting in collusion with US imperialism and Zionism, playing the despicable game of selling out the national interests of the Arab people. In China's view, therefore, the Soviets had become accomplices of US imperialism in its aggression against, and oppression of, the Arab people.[129]

Peking no longer regarded Anglo-American machinations as the sole obstacle to the settlement of the Palestinian question. From mid-1966 the Chinese began to stress Soviet–American collusion as the primary reason for the persistence of the Arab–Israeli conflict:

> U.S. imperialism ... uses its softening tactics, trying by every means to bring the Arab people to a 'reconciliation' with the Zionists and an acceptance of the status quo of Israel, in other words, an acceptance of the humiliating position of the victimised Palestinian Arabs.
> It must be pointed out that the revisionist leading group of the Soviet Union is a partner of the U.S. in the latter's criminal plan against the Arabs. It is a well-known fact that the Soviet revisionists are linked with the Israeli Zionists. . . Obviously, a conspiracy is afoot in which the Soviet revisionists leading group works hand in glove with the U.S. imperialists in betraying the Palestinian and Arab peoples' interests and their anti-imperialist struggle.[130]

As early as February 1966 it was reported that Peking's Foreign Languages Press had published and distributed in the Middle East a booklet in Arabic entitled *Dawr al-Ittiḥād al-Sūfiyātī fī Khalq Isrā'īl* (*The Role of the Soviet Union in the Creation of Israel*). Allegedly, this booklet contained strong accusations against the Soviet Union as the principal state which had contributed to the establishment of Israel. It also contained quotations in favour of Israel from speeches of Gromyko, Malik, Zarapkin and other Soviet statesmen.[131] More than a month later, NCNA denied any connection between China or the PLO and this booklet.[132] Indeed, it seems unlikely that the Chinese would have gone as far as publishing such blatantly anti-Soviet accusations for distribution in the Arab countries. Nonetheless, the contents of this booklet faithfully reflected China's line of argument. Peking tried to belittle or deny any Soviet contribution towards the settlement of the Arab–Israeli conflict. The 1947 United Nations Partition Plan, which in the mid-1950s had been accepted by Peking as a basis for settlement, was no longer attributed to the Soviet Union. From 1964 it was completely rejected as an Anglo-American fabrication. Accordingly, the Chinese firmly persisted in their outright rejection of a peaceful settlement to the Arab–Israeli conflict. Although they had never denied in public Israel's right to exist, some of their own comments[133] and certainly their quoting of Palestinian statements[134] suggests that at that stage Peking would have welcomed a total Palestinian victory.

In sum, the Chinese believed that their relations with the Palestinians were of considerable international value. In 1966, they began to implement their March 1965 commitments to the PLO. Despite the upheavals of the Cultural Revolution, the Chinese carefully watched developments in the Middle East and continuously encouraged the Palestinians. Initial shipments of Chinese arms (mainly rifles, mines, explosives, grenades and machine-guns) reached Palestinian hands, and the first groups of Palestinian guerrillas (probably no more than a few dozen) returned to the Middle East after training on Chinese soil.[135]

Despite Chinese assistance, the PLO cautiously avoided too great an identification with Peking. Usually, it was the Chinese who quoted anti-Soviet remarks allegedly made by rank-and-file Palestinians: 'The Chinese people are the true friends of the Palestinian people. The Soviet revisionist group also professed support for Palestine, but in words only. It is colluding with Israel politically, economically and diplomatically.'[136] PLO leaders, however, were more careful. Aḥmad Shuqayrī often praised Soviet support for the Palestinian cause,[137] and Shafīq al-Ḥūt, chairman of the PLO Beirut Office, argued in early 1967: 'If Peking unrestrictedly supports the Arab right to restore Palestine *in theory* there is, however, no doubt that *in practice* it is Moscow that can translate this support into a language of international value.'[138] [Italics added.]

The Chinese expected that such comments would disappear after the June 1967 war which, in their view, had disgraced the Soviets and changed the situation in the Middle East in many respects. As we have seen, the Chinese regarded the war as an indisputable confirmation of their repeatedly stated analysis of the Arab–Israeli conflict and the Palestine problem: the war proved that Soviet–American interference in the region had been undermining the Arab position against Israel and had prevented a settlement of the Palestine problem; it also proved that the conventional strategy employed by the Arab governments in compliance with Moscow's dictates had failed completely. Thus, a self-reliant people's war led by the Palestinians, enjoying the co-operation of the Arab governments, was the only way to settle 'successfully' the Arab–Israeli conflict and defeat Soviet American schemes.[139]

Thus far, although the PLO had been created in 1964–5, its military activity against Israel remained sporadic and inefficient. Paradoxically, the Arab defeat in June 1967 provided the Palestinians with an essential asset for a people's war – a potential base inside enemy-occupied territory. As early as 1965, the Chinese Chief of Staff, with remarkable insight, had advised a visiting PLO delegation that it should have a base inside Israel because operations from outside would only enrage Israel and lead to retaliation campaigns against the Arab countries.[140] Israel's occupation of large Palestinian-inhabited areas was thus of immense revolutionary significance from Peking's point of view. Therefore, it was only in June 1967 that the Chinese, for the first time, endorsed the PLO as a national liberation movement and regarded Israel as a 'target of revolution':[141]

> The Arab people of Palestine and the Palestine Liberation Army have taken up their fighting posts and, together with the entire Arab armed forces and people, they are giving play to the spirit of courage in battle and fearing no sacrifice, and are dealing head-on blows at the aggressors. . .
>
> I believe that, having taken up arms, the revolutionary Arab people of Palestine and the entire Arab people will not lay down their arms and, like the heroic Vietnamese people, will fight on unflinchingly, resolutely and stubbornly until final victory. . .
>
> Today, the just war of the Arab States and peoples against aggression by U.S. imperialism, British imperialism and Israel is a fine *beginning* of the struggle to liberate Palestine.[142] [Italics added.]

This opportunity to launch a genuine armed struggle based on, and assisted by, the local population coincided with the revolutionary outbursts in China as the Cultural Revolution was reaching its climax. All these developments raised China's ideological and revolutionary expectations from the Palestine liberation movement.

Yet very soon it became evident that the Palestine liberation movement had neglected some of Mao's most fundamental stipulations for a people's war – unity, independence and perseverance. One result of the 1967 war was the gradual disintegration of the Palestine liberation movement into smaller factional organisations. Some of these factions, particularly the People's Front for the Liberation of Palestine (PFLP) and the People's Democratic Front for the Liberation of Palestine (PDFLP), claimed to be Marxist–Leninist. For many reasons, however, China always preferred to deal with the principal organisations, the PLO and, after the 1967 war, also Fataḥ. The radical and leftist groups were somewhat ignored because they never regarded

Mao Tse-tung's thoughts as the only or exclusive guide to revolution. Moreover, instead of concentrating on the liberation of
Palestine and the struggle against imperialism, they gave first
priority to the overthrow of the existing Arab regimes and the
launching of a social and political revolution. Drawing the
lessons of previous experience, the Chinese believed that such a
revolution was not only premature at that stage, but would also
divert the movement's efforts from the main target – the struggle
against imperialism. In addition to these shortcomings, the radical
organisations were small, detached from the masses, often perse-
cuted and outlawed, and had the effect of deepening the splits in
the Palestine liberation movement.

Fataḥ, on the other hand, never pretended to bear the standard
of Marxism–Leninism. It was ready to learn from the Chinese
revolutionary experience,[143] but also from the Vietnamese, the
Cuban and other models, and even claimed to have an 'original'
revolutionary experience which had preceded the Chinese.[144]
Moreover, the Chinese were well aware that Fataḥ provided a
major source of friction within the Palestine liberation movement
by criticising and challenging Shuqayrī's PLO,[145] an organisation
with which they had maintained close relations since 1965.

The Chinese, who harboured no illusions as to the shortcomings
of the PLO and its leader, realised that, despite having been
'imposed from above', Shuqayrī's PLO demonstrated a certain
degree of independence from the Arab leaders, particularly
Nasser. Contrary to Arab views and those of the Soviet Union,
Shuqayrī instructed PLO delegates at various Afro-Asian and
other conferences to support the Chinese stand or at least to avoid
offending China.[146] For these reasons the Chinese were apparently
disturbed by Shuqayrī's forced resignation in December 1967.
Nonetheless, it was Fataḥ that later, particularly since 1969,
received much of China's attention, support and encouragement,
because of its large popular base and its primary concern with
the national (i.e., anti-imperialist), rather than the socio-political,
task.

However, within a few months after June 1967, Israel's reprisals
and counter-measures brought guerrilla activities inside the
Israeli-administered territories to a virtual standstill. Palestinian
raids from outside Israel's borders, followed by Israeli retaliations,
were thereafter curbed and in some cases stopped altogether by
the Arab governments themselves.

Fundamentally, the Arab governments could not be reconciled

with either a people's war strategy or with the Palestinians playing the central role in the struggle against Israel. These views
were repeated again and again after June 1967. Haykal, undoubtedly reflecting Nasser's views, continued to underplay the
significance of the Palestinian organisations, stressing their
marginal and secondary role in the Arab–Israeli conflict.[147] The
Arab governments were also unwilling to take the risk and pay
the price of uncontrolled Palestinian operations against Israel.
And due to internal political considerations, Arab leaders could
not permit the stationing of independent Palestinian troops in
their countries. The result was that, while the Palestinians had
been unable to establish permanent guerrilla bases inside the
territories occupied by Israel, they became even more dependent
on the Arab regimes. Some organisations were no more than
agents or extensions of certain Arab governments, while practically all of them operated under their auspices, and often at their
mercy. Disillusioned, Nā'if Ḥawatma, leader of the PDFLP,
admitted that 'in its present conditions, the resistance movement
is more like a bargaining card in the hands of the Arab regimes
rather than a revolutionary vanguard capable of liberating Palestine, let alone the Arab homeland'.[148]

By late 1968, therefore, the Chinese had many reasons to be
disappointed with Palestinian revolutionary accomplishments and
politico-ideological inclinations. Apparently, China's military
assistance to the Palestinians had scarcely increased since June
1967 and, according to some reports, had even ceased altogether.[149]
Nevertheless, Peking continued to recognise the PLO as the true
representative of the Palestinian people. In the following years
China maintained its moral and material support to the Palestinians within the limits of its revolutionary strategy and military
potential and according to the existing circumstances in the
Middle East and, more important, in the world as a whole.

5 : THE STRUGGLE AGAINST
SOCIAL-IMPERIALISM

The end of the Cultural Revolution is usually regarded as the beginning of the pragmatic phase in China's foreign policy and its 'return' to the family of nations. This process allegedly started in the summer of 1968 when the Chinese began to view the Soviet Union as their principal enemy, and culminated in Peking's admission to the United Nations, and the Sino-American thaw. Yet, if we examine these developments in light of China's Middle Eastern policy, two different processes are revealed. In the first, which started in late 1968 and early 1969, the foundation was laid for a more pragmatic foreign policy, but its implementation was frustrated, apparently by Lin Piao and the radicals. Therefore, although diplomatic relations were restored, preference was still given to revolutionary organisations rather than governments and the Sino-American *rapprochement* was delayed until the summer of 1971, when Lin Piao disappeared. It was only from that time and early 1972 that China's foreign policy indeed became pragmatic, under the influence of Mao, Chou En-lai, Teng Hsiao-p'ing and Hua Kuo-feng.

In both periods the struggle against the Soviets was central but, whereas in the first they were depicted mainly as an immediate threat to China itself, in the second they were attacked as the main threat to the world, primarily to Europe and the Middle East and more recently to Africa. Accordingly, the role of the Middle East in China's foreign policy has changed: between 1969 and 1971 it played a marginal role, relations with governments remained tense and support to national liberation movements increased; from 1972 on, however, the role of the Middle East became much more important, preference was given to relations with established governments, while interest in revolution declined considerably.

The marginal role of the Middle East

In late 1968, when the Cultural Revolution was subsiding, a new phase in China's foreign policy began to emerge. Whether it was the end of the Cultural Revolution that relieved China's leaders of domestic pressures so as to enable them to watch and analyse the international situation more carefully; or whether it was their perception of changes in the world situation which, among other things, led to the termination of the Cultural Revolution – in either case it seems that China's modified world outlook reflected primarily perceived global developments, particularly the orientation of the two superpowers.

Around the November 1968 elections in the United States, initial signs came from Washington of American willingness to improve relations with the PRC and, what was more significant, to reduce its military involvement in Southeast Asia. Consequently, the Chinese were gradually relieved of the fear of American 'aggression', so deeply rooted in China's foreign policy since 1949. However, as the American threat was reduced, a new one emerged. Following the Soviet invasion of Czechoslovakia in August 1968, the Brezhnev Doctrine and the Soviet military build-up along China's northern borders, the Chinese began to regard the Soviet Union as their principal enemy and as the most imminent threat to China's security.

Basically, China interpreted these developments in a local Asian perspective. Although the Chinese continued to criticise Soviet policy vigorously all over the world, they concentrated most of their efforts on preparing against possible Soviet attack on China. Similarly, the United States' new Asia policy was still suspected by Peking. Therefore, China was very slow in responding positively to the American initiative and continued to encourage anti-imperialist struggles all over the world: while restoring normal governmental relations which had been suspended during the Cultural Revolution, the Chinese continued and in some cases even increased, their support of national liberation movements and people's wars, particularly in Asia.

Though it is difficult to substantiate, it seems that these perceptions were influenced or even articulated by Lin Piao, who emerged as the most powerful political figure in China after the Cultural Revolution. The Political Report he delivered at the Ninth CCP Congress in April 1969, which provided the basis for China's foreign policy until 1971, hardly mentioned Afro-Asian national–bourgeois governments and regarded China and the world's proletariat and 'revolutionary people' as the only force capable of resisting the United States and the Soviet Union. He laid particular emphasis on the Soviet threat to China.[1]

China's Middle Eastern policy in the first three years after the Cultural Revolution resembled, in these respects, pre-Cultural Revolution patterns. Distracted by the situation along their northern frontier and in Southeast Asia, the Chinese considered the role of the Middle East as rather marginal in their analysis of the international situation. Still, as in the past, Peking continued to interpret the situation there in terms of superpower involvement; although the Soviet Union had become China's principal enemy, the Chinese still laid the blame for the tension in the Middle East equally on the United States and the Soviet Union. *Any* Soviet–American plan or proposal to settle the Middle East problem was uncompromisingly rejected by Peking.

China's relations with the Arab governments, although formally restored, nevertheless remained lukewarm. On the other hand, the Chinese renewed their support, both verbal and material, to the local national liberation movements: the Palestinian organisations and the People's Front for the Liberation of the Occupied Arabian Gulf.

The restoration of suspended relations

In 1969 the Chinese began to restore their relations with the Arab countries, where all China's embassies, except for that of Egypt, had been operated by chargés d'affaires since 1966–7. Ambassadors were dispatched first to Syria (in June 1969), then to the Yemen (July 1969), Egypt (June 1970), the post having been vacant from July 1969) and Iraq (December 1970). In July 1969 a chargé d'affaires was sent to China's newly established embassy in South Yemen; he became ambassador in December 1970. Thus, by the end of 1970 all China's main diplomatic posts in the Middle East were filled.

The renewal of Chinese activity in the Middle East, and even more so the new analysis of the world situation, required a reorganisation of Middle Eastern affairs in China's Foreign Ministry. From September 1964 China's Middle East policy was supervised and executed by the Department of West Asia and North Africa. This department, which had been created to cope with China's intensive diplomacy in the Arab countries in the mid-1960s, became superfluous following the Chinese debacle, and apparently fell into oblivion during the Cultural Revolution.

From 1966 to 1969 there is almost no information on its staff or activities.

In September 1969, or probably earlier, the Department of West Asia and North Africa was recombined with that of Africa to form the Department of West Asia and Africa. This indicated a decline in importance of the Middle East in China's foreign policy. Still, after the upheavals of the Cultural Revolution, China's relations with the Middle East and Africa had to be restored and consolidated. To succeed in this, the best qualified diplomats in these fields were mobilised: Ho Ying, who became Director of the new department, and Ho Kung-k'ai and Kung Ta-fei, who became his deputies, had already held these positions in the past in addition to several diplomatic posts in both the Middle East and Africa.[2] Their assignment was not easy. China's relations with the Arab governments after the Cultural Revolution were governed by mutual suspicion inherited from the past, by their reserved attitude towards the Palestinians, whom the Chinese favoured, and particularly by the degree of their association with, and submission to, the Soviet Union.

When the Cultural Revolution ended and the Chinese were re-appraising the international situation, their relations with Egypt were at a low ebb. In mid-July 1969 Peking recalled Huang Hua, its ambassador to Cairo, precisely when new ambassadors were being dispatched to other capitals. He left his office some three and a half years after his appointment (compared with almost ten years of his predecessor), allegedly for his encouragement and support of the student riots in Alexandria in November 1968 and also as a result of pressure by the Soviets, who did not like his influence and connections with African liberation movements.[3] Whether these reports were true or, as is more probable, exaggerated, Huang Hua was recalled only to be promoted to a higher post. His office in Cairo stood vacant for almost a year until, in late June 1970, Peking appointed a new ambassador to Egypt. This delay could be regarded as a diplomatic retaliation: in July 1968 Cairo had recalled its ambassador from Peking; he was not replaced until fourteen months later, in September 1969.

One of the main reasons for the cool Sino-Egyptian relations was the Soviet–Egyptian alliance, which time and again Peking sought to undermine. In early 1970 the Chinese tried to exploit what seemed to be growing strains in Soviet–Egyptian relations. In a letter to Nasser, Chou En-lai briefly reviewed the latest

US-backed Israeli attacks on Egypt and other Arab countries. He implied that similar support for the Arabs had not, and would not, come from the Soviet Union and urged Nasser to launch an armed struggle: 'In the common struggle against imperialism, the Chinese people will forever remain *the most* reliable friend of the people of the UAR, Palestine and other countries.'[4] [Italics added.]

Nasser's reply came more than a fortnight later. In polite and diplomatic style, he told Chou En-lai to mind his own business: 'The people of our country believe that the forces of the UAR and the Arab nation will triumph eventually. *They have faith in their own principles as well as in their friends.*'[5] [Italics added.] Speaking shortly afterwards, Nasser again implicitly denied Chinese arguments by firmly defending and justifying Egypt's friendship and co-operation with Moscow and by insisting on the need to find a *political* settlement to the Arab–Israeli conflict. He expressed deep appreciation and gratitude for Soviet support, particularly military aid: 'The truth is that the Soviet Union is the only power that can help us to realise our aims. It is the only power that wanted to help us therein, otherwise the enemy and his associates could have imposed their conditions upon us.'[6]

Nasser was also furious about China's anti-Soviet propaganda among the Palestinians and particularly about China's allegations that Egypt was selling-out the guerrillas to Moscow. In March, following his exchange of letters with Chou En-lai, Nasser told Arafat, who was about to leave for China, to inform the Chinese premier that he (Nasser) was not selling-out anyone to the Soviet Union.[7] But he continued to irritate Peking. In June 1970 he accepted the Rogers Plan which the Chinese had rejected as a 'superpowers' plot to impose a Middle East Munich'; they also rejected the cease-fire agreement along the Suez Canal which came into force, following Nasser's approval, on 8 August 1970.

These Sino-Egyptian disagreements, as well as the controversies of the past, were probably responsible for what appeared as China's restrained reaction to the death of Nasser in late September 1970.[8] China's message of condolence was nothing more than mere formality and Kuo Mo-jo, China's special envoy to the funeral, was a secondary figure compared with other countries' envoys. Consequently, Egypt's interim president, Anwar Sadat, did not meet with him although he managed to meet other leaders. Several months later Chou En-lai reportedly blamed the Soviets for Nasser's death: 'They deceived him. They pushed him into a situation and they left him. They allowed his heart to be broken.'[9] He was speaking to an Egyptian goodwill delegation led by the Speaker of the National Assembly that visited China from 26 to 29 January 1971. Although this delegation, the first after several years, was regarded as an Egyptian gesture to improve relations with Peking, the Chinese did not seem very enthusiastic. Apparently, the main disagreement during the visit concerned the Palestinians, whom the Chinese mentioned repeatedly and who were completely ignored by the Egyptian delegation. Chou En-lai made no speech in honour of the delegation.[10]

China's relations with Syria also reflected the degree of the latter's dependence on the Soviet Union. Although Syria has always been regarded as more radical and militant than the other Arab countries, the Chinese did not seem impressed. In practice, Syria was not less, but probably more, dependent on Moscow than the other countries. Similarly, despite Syria's unreserved rhetorical support of the Palestinians, Peking was undoubtedly aware that their activities in and from Syria were kept under strict control.

However, by the spring of 1969 there were indications of a serious deterioration in Syria's relations with Moscow, involving not only Syria's external posture (such as the refusal to abide by the United Nations Security Council Resolution 242 and the resultant Soviet retaliation of suspending arms supplies), but also internal struggle between rival factions.[11] As a result of this deterioration President Nūr al-Dīn al-Atāsī cancelled his visit to Moscow at the last minute. Instead, a Syrian military delegation led by Major General Muṣṭafā Ṭallās, then Chief of Staff of the Syrian Army and First Deputy Minister of Defence, rushed to Peking. Press reports during the visit (13 to 21 May 1969), and for some time afterwards, suggested that China had agreed to supply Syria with a variety of arms including light weapons, tanks, aircraft and even missiles. The visit and the alleged 'arms deal' were described not only as the culmination of the Sino-Soviet conflict in the Middle East but also as the beginning of large-scale Chinese penetration into the region and intervention in the Arab–Israeli conflict.[12]

These reports were grossly inaccurate. It is inconceivable that the Syrians believed they would get weapons, particularly of sophisticated types, from China. In fact, Syria's President Atāsī admitted that news reports of Ṭallās' visit had been exaggerated and stressed that, aware of China's limited capabilities, Ṭallās had

had no intention of seeking military aid in Peking.[13] Moreover, during the visit the Chinese themselves urged the Syrians and the Arabs not to depend on outside sources of support: 'We are deeply convinced that so long as the Arab countries *firmly rely on their own people*, carry out the policy of *maintaining independence* and *keeping the initiative in their own hands and relying on their own efforts* and steadfastly take the road of armed struggle, they will assuredly win final victory.'[14] [Italics added.]

Rather than intending, or having the capacity, to replace the Soviets in Syria, the Chinese used the visit to demonstrate their sympathy with Syria's rejection of a superpower-engineered political settlement of the Arab–Israeli conflict and to encourage the Syrians to continue resisting Soviet pressure. In June, immediately after the visit, the Chinese dispatched an ambassador to Syria, their first to the Middle East since the Cultural Revolution.

Damascus, however, did not conceive of the visit to China as a point of departure from Soviet patronage but, on the contrary, as an attempt to force the Soviets to increase their commitments. This was proved during the visit as well as by later events. Ṭallās carefully avoided criticising the Soviets, and the Syrians omitted Chinese attacks on the Soviets from the NCNA dispatches published in Damascus.[15] By July the Soviet–Syrian crisis was over and a Syrian delegation, which included President Atāsī and Defence Minister Ḥāfiẓ Asad, was cordially welcomed in Moscow. Following this visit came a further improvement in Soviet–Syrian relations and in late September Atāsī paid another visit to Moscow on his way to North Korea. He did not visit China.

South Yemen (the People's Democratic Republic of Yemen (PDRY) since November 1970) provided another example of China's attempts to outmanoeuvre the Soviet Union in the Middle East. The new South Yemeni regime tried from the beginning to maintain a balance between Moscow and Peking, accepting military aid mainly from the Russians and economic aid mainly from the Chinese. However, until July 1969, when a new leadership seized power, the Soviets had much more influence than the Chinese and China's relations with South Yemen made rather slow progress. The situation changed later. In July 1969 a Chinese embassy was established in Aden (an agreement on diplomatic relations had already been reached in January 1968). Li Ch'iang-fen, the Chinese chargé d'affaires, who in December 1970 became

China's first ambassador to South Yemen, had been counsellor and chargé d'affaires in the Yemen since May 1961 and was thus very familiar with the situation in the Arabian Peninsula.

The establishment of a Chinese embassy in Aden also improved China's relations with the People's Front for the Liberation of the Occupied Arabian Gulf (PFLOAG). This immediately triggered Soviet criticism,[16] and enabled the Chinese to increase their economic activities. A previous loan of $12 million (offered in September 1968) began to be implemented and another loan of $43 million was offered in August 1970, following the visit to China by the South Yemeni president. China's aid to South Yemen consisted of the construction of various textile enterprises, salt works and medical aid, but primarily the building of a strategically important road to connect the third district with the fifth (about 500 km), including wells and bridges along it. Several hundred Chinese worked on these projects. Consequently, South Yemen became the only country in the Middle East to receive more economic aid from China than from the Soviet Union and Eastern Europe together.

Increased interest in liberation movements

Following the Cultural Revolution Peking maintained a rather radical policy in the Middle East. Despite the restored relations with the Arab governments it was the national liberation movements which attracted Chinese attention: 'The Arab people's mass movement against imperialism and aggression, the Palestinian people's armed struggle and the armed struggle of the people of the Dhufar area have now converged into a raging storm of revolution striking at imperialism, revisionism and reaction. It is the main current that decides the situation in the Middle East.'[17] The fact that this ideological–revolutionary outlook was endorsed by the Ninth CCP Congress reflected the internal political struggle in China. Apparently, Mao did not share these views. He made no statement in support of the Middle Eastern liberation movements and received none of their numerous delegations and representatives who came to China after the Cultural Revolution.

Notwithstanding Mao's presumed reservations, the Chinese resumed their support of, and relations with, the two main liberation movements in the Middle East, the Dhufār Liberation Front and the PLO. Dhufār is the Southwestern district of the Sultanate of Oman, which had been under British colonial rule by treaty since the end of the eighteenth century and still maintains special ties with Britain. The Dhufār Liberation Front started its military operations in June 1965 and from the beginning established close relations with the National Liberation Front of South Yemen. Soon after South Yemen gained independence, its sixth district, adjacent to the Omani border and to Dhufār, became the main base of the Dhufār liberation movement. In September 1968, at the movement's second congress, the old leadership was overthrown and the organisation changed its name and objectives to 'The People's Front for the Liberation of the Occupied Arabian Gulf' (PFLOAG). The doctrines of the new Marxist–Leninist leadership were very similar to those of the PFLP and particularly the PDFLP – all of them offspring of the same movement: 'al-Qawmiyūn al-'Arab' (The Arab Nationalists). The PFLOAG, whose aim by then was not merely to 'liberate' Dhufār or Oman but to establish an Arab People's Republic in the entire Gulf, officially remained uncommitted in the Sino-Soviet conflict and apparently adopted the revolutionary principles of Cuba and Che Guevara.[18]

In June 1970 it was reported that a new organisation had been founded, 'The National Democratic Front for the Liberation of Oman and the Arabian Gulf' (NDFLOAG).[19] It was particularly active in Northern Oman and in December 1971 merged with the PFLOAG to form the 'People's Front for the Liberation of Oman and the Arabian Gulf' (still PFLOAG).[20]

China's interest in South Arabia dates back to the 1950s, but was irregular and superficial. It was during the Cultural Revoluction, and especially afterwards, that China began to encourage the Dhufār Liberation Front, and later the PFLOAG, more systematically. From early 1969, the NCNA office in Aden maintained extensive coverage of the military operations of the PFLOAG (previously, this coverage had been carried out from Cairo), and NCNA correspondents were sent from Aden to report directly from the battlefield.[21] China's press and radio often acclaimed the 'Dhufāri guerrillas'. Several PFLOAG delegations visited China, the most important staying for five weeks in March–April 1970. It was not received by Mao but held talks with Chou En-lai. At that time the Chinese apparently approved of the PFLOAG maximalist plans: 'The excellent situation of the victoriously developing armed struggle of the Dhufār people is bound to promote and inspire the development of the national liberation struggle of the people of the *entire Arabian Gulf region.*'²² [Italics added.]

Beyond the rhetoric, China's material support to the PFLOAG was rather small. In fact, only after July 1969, when a PRC embassy was first established in Aden, did China's relations with the PFLOAG improve. Although exact details of China's aid are unknown, it seems that the Chinese provided the Dhufāri revolutionaries with no more than a few hundred rifles and machineguns. These were delivered either directly or, more likely, through the South Yemeni authorities. According to some reports, there were also several Chinese instructors at a PFLOAG base in South Yemen near the Omani border. China's support to the PFLOAG was frequently acknowledged by its members and leaders: 'The PFLOAG expresses its heartfelt thanks to socialist countries, particularly the People's Republic of China, for their moral and material support and aid to our revolution.'²³

China's relations with the Palestinians were much more complicated. After the Cultural Revolution, and in fact since June 1967, the Palestinians were the only group in the Middle East which accepted China's interpretation that the Palestine problem, not merely the problem of the territories occupied during the war, was the root of the Arab–Israeli conflict and the key to its settlement. Not less important, they consistently opposed outside intervention and rejected any peace or settlement formula which emanated from the United States, the Soviet Union or the United Nations. In China's view, the Palestinians had become 'an important revolutionary force in the Middle East', being the main obstacle to the realisation of the superpowers' schemes in that region. There were many indications that after the Cultural Revolution the Chinese considered the Palestinian struggle as second in importance only to the liberation wars of Indochina.

China's Middle East policy in that period definitely preferred the Palestinians, notwithstanding its efforts to restore and rehabilitate relations with the Arab governments. The consistent Chinese support of the Palestinians between 1969 and 1971 provided a major source of friction in Sino-Arab relations. As we have seen, again and again Peking tried in vain to persuade the Arab governments to adopt the Palestinian strategy and to assist the Palestinian struggle.

This does not mean, however, that China's attitude towards the Palestinians was uncritical. From past experience the Chinese were well aware of the shortcomings of the Palestine liberation movement. Thus, although they repeatedly urged the Palestinians to adopt armed struggle and a people's war, they could not fail to observe that Palestinian military operations were at a standstill from the late 1960s onward. They also did not approve of, let alone inspire, terror and hijacking, which had been introduced by both the radical and the so-called moderate Palestinian organisations, as a substitute for military activity.[24] From the beginning Peking almost completely ignored Palestinian acts of terror, in itself an obvious sign of disapproval. Later, Chinese diplomats and officials privately condemned Palestinian terrorism,[25] although there was no public condemnation at that stage. It was also reported that the Chinese had reproached the Palestinians directly, stressing that terror and hijacking constituted a waste of energy and resources which diverted the people's attention from the main targets and created hostile public opinion. As such, terror contradicted Mao's revolutionary doctrines.[26]

Another development which damaged China's relations with the Palestinians was the latter's growing association with Moscow. As was the case with several other national liberation movements, China's connections with the Palestinians only stimulated further Soviet commitment.[27] Despite their reservations, the Palestinians welcomed the Soviet gestures. Indeed, they criticised Soviet pressure for a political settlement; in their view 'the Soviet Union was so far not convinced that the Palestinian people's struggle to restore their homeland and to drive out the gangster State of Israel was a legitimate one'.[28] In response to an article in *Pravda* which had praised Nasser for 'opposing extremist tendencies in the Arab world', *Fath*, the daily organ of the PLO Central Committee, said: 'The Palestinian cause is our cause. Nobody else has the right to interfere in it. If one wants to take an internationalist stand, one should side with us, or else keep silent – otherwise one should expect a reply if one knocks at the door.'[29] Nevertheless, to China's displeasure, the Palestinians realised that they would not be able to further their cause without seeking the friendship of Moscow. Even the so-called 'extreme-leftist' organisations, which the Soviets in any case continued to ignore, were careful not to alienate Moscow:

Imperialism and the reactionary forces are trying to find a loophole in the relations between the progressive Palestinian and Arab nationalist movements and the Soviet Union and the countries of the socialist camp. Our duty it to prevent imperialism from succeeding in fulfilling this aim. The

Soviet Union has been a main supporter of the Arab people in their war against imperialism and its plans in our homeland.[30]

Although there is no evidence of overt Chinese criticism of the Palestinians' overtures towards Moscow, Peking undoubtedly considered it an example of failure to distinguish between enemies and friends or between true and false friends:

Social-imperialism has always been colluding with U.S. imperialism and hostile to the Palestinian people. It has wildly slandered and abused the Palestinian people's armed struggle and greatly discrediting itself. Recently, it has changed its tactics and hypocritically pretended to 'support' the Palestinian people's armed struggle. It is clear to everyone that its aim is merely to place the Palestinian armed forces under its control, using them as capital in making dirty deals with U.S. imperialism in the Middle East, so as to realise its criminal plot of stamping out the Palestinian armed struggle and divide up the Middle East with U.S. imperialism.[31]

Finally, the Chinese were undoubtedly disappointed by the slow progress towards unity within the Palestine liberation movement. In the late 1960s and early 1970s the Palestine liberation movement further disintegrated. Although the various organisations formally co-operated under PLO auspices, each still retained its independence and relied not only on different tactics but even on a different strategy.

All these considerations underlay China's relations with the Palestinians in the three years following the Cultural Revolution. Adhering to their consistently reiterated call for unity among the Palestinians, the Chinese continued to regard the PLO as the only organisation truly representative of the Palestinian people. Most of China's relations with the Palestinians were carried out through the PLO, which still maintained a permanent office in Peking, or through Fataḥ, which, despite some reservations, was acknowledged by Peking as the backbone of the PLO.

As we have seen, China's interest in Fataḥ was based not only on its being the largest, most united and most powerful of all Palestinian organisations. Paradoxically, China was also attracted to it by its lack of socialist or Marxist inclinations. Contrary to the commonly-held view, China never insisted that national liberation movements should adopt Mao's revolutionary doctrines or copy China's revolutionary experience *verbatim et litteratim.* Rather, China insisted on adoption of only the fundamental principles, primarily that of combining theory and practice and adapting the revolutionary strategy to local circumstances. This is exactly what Fataḥ claimed to be doing: 'We acquaint our cadres, without complications, with world experience in national liberation. We believe that we should benefit from such experiences, but at the same time we believe that attaining victory necessitates that we produce from our actual circumstances a national experience which will also enrich world experience.'[32] Fārūq al-Qaddūmī (alias Abū Luṭf), one of Fataḥ's important leaders, enlarged on the topic:

There is an infantile leftism among those who propagate socialist thought by applying the experiences of others. On this basis such movements can be described as idealistic and infantile, because any movement must study the given reality. These movements have not studied the given reality but described it according to descriptions of other societies. As a result, their understanding and description is abstract. Our description is nearer to reality. Thus Al-Fateh is the only actual revolutionary movement in the Palestinian field.[33]

Rejecting the leftist organisations' calls for class struggle to precede the liberation of Palestine, Fataḥ insisted that national tasks should take precedence over all other considerations and should be implemented under a national (i.e., Fataḥ) leadership. Apparently, China fully endorsed and approved of this view and conducted its relations with Fataḥ and the PLO on this basis. Consequently, there is little evidence of any Chinese preference given to the Marxist organisations, or of relations with them. In fact, the Chinese very rarely mentioned or praised military operations by the radical groups. Although representatives of these groups occasionally visited China, they came not independently but rather as members of the PLO delegations.

Still, in the latter half of 1970 there were reports that the Chinese had become more interested in the leftist organisations and even offered them considerable military aid. These reports, however, could not be verified. Most likely, the PFLP and the PDFLP only received their share of one of the Chinese arms shipments that reached the Palestinians via Damascus and Latakia. Other reports said that the PFLP leader, George Ḥabash, had visited China in mid-October 1970 after visiting North Korea (2–14 September);[34] but there was not even a hint from China that such a visit did actually take place. Moreover, the Chinese completely ignored Ḥabash's visit to North Korea, which was highly publicised and extensively treated there. Some Beirut newspapers reported that Ḥabash had not been invited by the Chinese.[35] Even if there was a secret visit, during which the Chinese allegedly criticised Ḥabash for his 'wrong tactics' (this was immediately after the PFLP's spectacular hijackings and the fighting in Jordan), it seems that they continued to maintain their reservations about the radical Palestinian groups. There is no indication that China considered any group other than Fataḥ and the PLO as capable of leading the Palestine liberation war.

Notwithstanding China's preference for the Palestinians over the Arab governments, there was evidence that the content, intensity and scope of China's rhetorical support as well as material assistance to the PLO and Fataḥ had also declined after the Cultural Revolution.[36] The most obvious indication was China's reduced coverage of Palestinian operations. To some extent, this merely reflected the reduction in Palestinian activities. Yet this selective coverage was probably another way of implying Chinese disapproval of certain Palestinian actions and policies. Similarly, quite often Peking referred cynically to 'twists and turns', 'difficulties', 'temporary difficulties', 'difficult circumstances', or even 'the most difficult circumstances' that the Palestinians were encountering in their struggle. Palestinian delegations continued to visit China but none received the same treatment or the firm commitment accorded to Shuqayrī's PLO delegation in 1965. Arafat's visit to China in March 1970 provided a good example.

As we have seen, the Chinese were not particularly enthusiastic about Shuqayrī's dismissal in late 1967, if only because Moscow was obviously pleased about it. Apparently, China also had some reservations about Arafat, who became PLO chairman in February 1969, mainly because of his association with Nasser (whose relations with Peking were very cool at that time), whom he had accompanied on his visit to Moscow in August 1968.

Arafat, who had unofficially visited the PRC as early as March 1964, paid his first official visit to China, leading a Fataḥ (not a PLO) delegation in March 1970, precisely five years after Shuqayrī's visit. There were many differences between the two visits. Arafat came to China after spending twelve days in Moscow a month earlier – apparently with trifling results but, nevertheless, sufficient to make the Chinese suspicious. In China Arafat was generally received by 'deputies' rather than by leaders of high rank. Unlike Shuqayrī he was not received by Mao, who shortly afterwards met the presidents of the Sudan and South Yemen. Chou En-lai met Arafat on 27 March but made no speech in honour of the delegation. In his speech, Vice Premier Li Hsien-nien completely ignored Arafat's position as PLO chairman: 'The

Palestine National Liberation Movement [Fataḥ] led by Chairman Arafat has persevered in armed struggle, united with other anti-imperialist armed organisations of Palestine and dealt repeated blows at the enemy, thereby playing an active role in promoting the liberation cause of Palestine.'[37] In addition, the *People's Daily* did not publish the customary editorial on such occasions and no joint communiqué was issued.

It is difficult to determine what aid the Chinese offered Arafat during his visit, if any. However, in August and September 1970 there were reports, mentioned above, on the arrival and distribution of Chinese arms shipments to the Palestinian guerrillas.[38] As some of these reports had come from sources hostile to the PRC, their accuracy should be suspect. Other reports suggested that Chinese arms supplies 'have accounted for only a small percentage of the armoury of the Palestinian guerrillas', and questioned claims of Chinese participation in the fighting in Jordan or in the training of Palestinian guerrillas in the Middle East.[39] Still, in October 1970 Arafat cabled the Chinese: 'The Central Committee of the Palestine Revolution [*sic*] expresses acknowledgement of China's great assistance which has the biggest influence in supporting our revolution and strengthening its perseverance.'[40]

The next year, however, brought about a decisive change in China's attitude towards the Palestinians. As a result, China's interest in and support of, the Palestinians was drastically reduced and they were no longer regarded as the core of the resistance to the superpowers in the Middle East.

The central role of the Middle East

By late 1971 and early 1972 China's stand on international affairs had undergone a significant change. The previous analysis of the world situation, apparently formulated by Lin Piao, had reflected mainly regional developments – the Soviet threat to China's security; suspicions of American intentions in Southeast Asia; continuing reservations about Third World governments, despite normalising relations with them; the belief in the dominant role of national liberation movements in the fight against imperialism.

It seems that the settlement of the first phase in the post-Cultural Revolution political struggle, following the fall of Lin Piao, enabled Mao and Chou En-lai to regain control and revise China's world outlook. In a typical Maoist manner the new analysis of the world situation reflected the situation in the world as a whole with a clearer distinction between principal and secondary enemies. Western Europe, rather than China, was now regarded as the immediate target of Soviet military expansion. Peking maintained that the Soviets, planning to dominate Europe, channelled most of their efforts towards the countries of the intermediate zone, in an attempt to seize control particularly in key areas such as the Middle East and more recently Africa. American signals to China were now no longer rejected. Washington's determination to end its involvement in Vietnam and to improve relations with Peking convinced the Chinese that the United States finally was on the decline.

These changes were linked to a general historical trend and were spelled out most clearly in a confidential document circulated in the Chinese army:

Both Soviet revisionism and U.S. imperialism are our arch enemies. At present Soviet revisionism is our most important enemy. After World War II, at first it was U.S. imperialism which lorded it over the world; so we said that U.S. imperialism was the No. 1 enemy. Later, Soviet revisionist, social-imperialism emerged. A situation presented itself in which the United States and the Soviet Union contended for hegemony in the world and demarcated spheres of influence. These two big villains carried out aggression, subversion, control and intervention everywhere and bullied the people of all countries, turning the world into a very unpeaceful place. Since then, U.S. imperialism and Soviet imperialism, the two superpowers, have been the common enemies of the people of the world. The present situation is: U.S. imperialism's counterrevolutionary global strategy has met with repeated setbacks; its aggressive power has been weakened; and hence, it has had to make some retraction and adjustment of its strategy. Soviet revisionism, on the other hand, is stretching its arms in all directions and is expanding desperately. It is more crazy, adventurist and deceptive. That is why Soviet revisionism has become our country's most dangerous and most important enemy.[41]

According to Peking, the fact that the United States was on the decline created vacuum areas, particularly in Asia, and thus only aggravated the contradictions between it and the expansionist policies of the Soviet Union. A similar situation had existed in the 1950s, when the decline of Britain and France had, in China's view, aggravated the contradictions between them and the expansionist policies of the United States. Then as now, Peking believed that the ever-intensifying contest between the superpowers offered new and better opportunities to the peoples and countries lying between them to oppose superpower hegemony and to achieve genuine revolution, liberation, and independence.

Indeed, since 1971–2 the Chinese perceived signs of increased resistance to the superpowers, particularly the Soviet Union. Furthermore, since Peking considers that the Soviet–American competition is bound to lead eventually to collision and to another world war, the resistance of the Second World (the developed countries other than the United States and the Soviet Union) and the Third World (the developing countries of Asia, Africa and Latin America) has become, in China's view, the main defence against such an eventuality.[42]

This new analysis of the world situation led to far-reaching changes in China's foreign policy. Its relations with the United States began to improve gradually, culminating dramatically in President Nixon's visit to China in February 1972 and the opening of semi-diplomatic missions. Not only have bilateral Sino-American relations been normalised but China implicitly, and sometimes even explicitly, also began to approve of US policy on certain issues and in some areas, with a view to restraining and blocking the Soviet advance.

Improved Sino-American relations, particularly after Henry Kissinger's first visit to China in July 1971, as well as China's belief in the crucial importance of Second and Third World countries in resisting superpower hegemony, brought about a decisive change in China's position in the world. In October 1971 the PRC was admitted to the United Nations and seated as a permanent member of the Security Council. In addition to the governments which had already recognised the PRC, more than thirty other governments did so within a short period after late 1970. Peking established full diplomatic relations with all of them and ceased its support of revolutionary groups which opposed them.

Thus China's new foreign policy was designed not merely to improve bilateral relations, and certainly not to increase the 'Chinese presence' or 'Chinese control' in other countries; primarily, the Chinese intended to use their extensive foreign relations network and their new status in the world to convince Second and Third World governments to unite in jointly opposing the superpowers' (particularly Moscow's) attempts to gain control over Europe, the Middle East, Asia and the rest of the world. Accordingly, the Chinese supported and encouraged any sign of independence and unity among these countries. On the assumption that the United Nations was controlled by the superpowers, they acted to limit its involvement in local affairs and disputes as far as possible. They used the organisation to attack the United

States and more particularly the Soviet Union, and to rally support against both.

The Middle East, which had played a rather marginal role in China's world outlook after the Cultural Revolution, became extremely important to it after late 1971. China's renewed interest in the Middle East stemmed from its revised analysis of the global situation, regional developments and also the stabilised domestic political scene.

As in the past, the Chinese continued to regard the Middle East as a major bone of contention among the superpowers because of its extremely important strategic location and rich oil resources: 'In the Middle East the main interest of Soviet revisionism is to contend with U.S. imperialism for oil and strategic positions... The Middle East is situated at the junction between Europe, Asia and Africa, and the Suez Canal connects the Mediterranean, the Red Sea and the Indian Ocean. The Middle East is thus a pivotal area.'[43] While having maintained this view for many years, following the Paris peace agreements and the settlement of the Indochinese problems, the Chinese anticipated an intensification of the Soviet–American struggle in the Middle East: 'From Asia and Vietnam, U.S. imperialism has moved its forces over to Europe and the Middle East. This has greatly aggravated the contradictions between the United States and the Soviet Union, putting the two dogs at loggerheads. This struggle of theirs is advantageous to the revolution of ours and the world's people.'[44]

Although after 1971–2 the Chinese came to believe that the Middle East and Europe had become the immediate targets of Soviet expansionism, they were undoubtedly aware that the success of this policy would ultimately be to China's detriment. Thus, as in the past, the developments in the Middle East were linked by the Chinese with the impaired American position in Asia and with the parallel increase in the Soviet potential threat to China's security: 'We can see very clearly that all actions of Soviet revisionism in Asia are intended to encircle China. Its spearhead is pointed at us in an attempt to achieve a great strategic encirclement of us.'[45]

Elaborating on this issue, the Chinese underlined the central position of the Middle East, particularly the Suez Canal, in this Soviet attempt, which not only threatened China but made the Middle East a key to the control of the world. The way the

Chinese described the Soviet scheme to encircle China was very reminiscent of the way they had treated the German attempt to join forces with Japan in the early 1940s, as well as the Anglo-American attempt to organise a crescent of military pacts in Asia, the Middle East and Europe in the 1950s:

At present, a noteworthy move of the Soviet revisionist Navy is its desperate expansion in the Indian Ocean. Its intention is to use the Indian Ocean as the 'connecting point', and to have two prongs of a naval pincer form an arc-shaped sea lane connecting the three continents of Europe, Africa and Asia. In the half arc in the Eastern Hemisphere, the Pacific Fleet based in Vladivostok will be despatched to the Indian Ocean via the Sea of Japan, the West Pacific Ocean and the Malacca Strait. In the half arc in the Western Hemisphere, the Black Sea Fleet will be despatched to enter the Indian Ocean via the Mediterranean Sea. (Because the Suez Canal is not open at present, this fleet will have to sail around the Cape of Good Hope.) In this way, Soviet revisionism will be able not only to have supremacy in the ocean but also to effect complete strategic naval encirclement of our country.[46]

China's perception of the crucial position of the Middle East in Soviet expansionist schemes is also confirmed by the length at which the Chinese analysed Soviet Middle East involvement in this confidential document. The space devoted to Soviet intentions and activity in the Middle East equalled that which dealt with Soviet intentions and activity in Asia and Europe together. There is little doubt that in China's mind Europe and the Middle East are the most immediate targets of the Soviets prior to their turning on China:

One of the two superpowers (the United States) is desperately trying to hold to the many places it has occupied; the other (the Soviet Union) is reaching out in every direction and worming its way into every crevice. Strategically, Europe is the focus of their contention. At the same time their fierce contention extends also to the Middle East, the Arab world, the Mediterranean as well as the Indian Ocean.[47]

An unnamed Chinese official, said to be 'close to the latest thinking on the problem', was quoted as saying that China would not be attacked before the Soviet rear had been secured through the control of Europe and the Middle East.[48]

It should be stressed, however, that, despite their *rapprochement* with the United States, which they perceive as being on the defensive, the Chinese have never ceased – even though they have greatly muted – their support and encouragement for the struggle against 'US imperialism'. The Middle East is regarded as one of those areas which the Americans would be the least prepared to leave. Although in the short range the Chinese implicitly prefer American supremacy in the Middle East rather than Soviet, fundamentally they await the expulsion of both. This is why Peking still insists on continuing the struggle against the United States as well: 'The Middle East has become an important battlefield where the Arab people and the people of the world strike at U.S. imperialism.'[49]

Finally, China's renewed interest in the Middle East corresponded to the growing resistance among Middle Eastern countries to superpower hegemony, and particularly to Soviet expansion and patronage. These signs of independence were evident in several fields: in the co-ordinated activity of the Organisation of the Oil Producing and Exporting Countries (OPEC), which included such governments as Iran, Kuwait and Saudi Arabia; in the Persian Gulf where the local governments headed by Iran rejected a Soviet-proposed Asian Collective Security Pact and resisted Soviet intervention in the area; in the success of the Afro-Arab conference; in the Arab Middle East where governments, particularly Egypt and the Sudan, had become disillusioned with the Soviets and took independent measures in both the military fields (i.e., the October 1973 war) and the political (i.e., the acceptance of the United States' diplomatic initiative); and, no less significantly, in the recognition of the PRC by seven more Middle Eastern governments. Under these circumstances, local national liberation movements, particularly those in South Arabia, but also the Palestinian organisations, were no longer regarded by China as playing the central role in the struggle against the superpowers. Instead, it is the Middle Eastern governments which have become the main force capable, together with other Third and Second World countries, of blocking the United States and more particularly, the Soviet Union.

These considerations, and China's foreign policy in general, remained unchanged after the death in January 1976 of Chou En-lai and in September of Mao:

The Soviet Union and the United States are the source of a new world war, and Soviet social-imperialism in particular presents the greater danger. The current strategic situation in their contention is that Soviet social-imperialism is on the offensive and U.S. imperialism on the defensive... Soviet–U.S. contention extends to every corner of the world, but its focus is still Europe.

The Soviet Union has massed its troops in Eastern Europe and at the same time accelerated its plunder of strategic resources and its scramble for strategic bases in Africa and the Middle East in an attempt to encircle Europe from the flanks by seizing the Persian Gulf in the east, thrusting round the Cape of Good Hope in the south and blocking the main navigation routes of the Atlantic Ocean in the west.[50]

Although paying lip service to the Palestinians, the Chinese continue to cultivate relations with Middle Eastern governments, primarily Egypt, the Sudan and Iran, praising their resistance to superpower hegemony, in particular that of the Soviets.[51] China's Middle Eastern policy has been conducted on the basis of these principles since 1971–2.

Orientation towards governments

From 1971 on China's position in the Middle East changed decisively. In addition to the five Arab governments which already maintained diplomatic relations with China (Egypt, Syria, the Yemen, Iraq and South Yemen), another five Middle East governments recognised the PRC in 1971. These were Kuwait (29 March), Turkey (4 August), Iran (16 August), the Lebanon (9 November) and Cyprus (14 December). On 14 April 1977 Jordan recognised the PRC and on 25 May 1978 Oman followed suit. Full diplomatic relations were established with all these countries.

These diplomatic successes were part of the general expansion of China's foreign relations which included the admission of the PRC to the United Nations in October 1971. For the first time, Peking had the opportunity of taking an active part in the attempts to settle the Middle East's problems. The Chinese seemed very much interested in Middle Eastern issues in the United Nations and their delegations included several well known experts on Middle Eastern affairs. Huang Hua, China's first permanent representative to the United Nations, was ambassador to Egypt from early 1966 to July 1969, the only one to remain in his post during the Cultural Revolution. Ch'en Ch'u, permanent representative to the United Nations since May 1977, who was also Huang's deputy there until February 1973, had been Director of the Department of West Asia and North Africa in the Foreign Ministry from 1964 to 1966. Chou Chüeh, who took part in the debates on the Middle East in the 29th session of the General Assembly in November 1974, has since 1970 been Deputy Director and is now Acting Director of the Department of West Asia and

North Africa. Lin Chao-nan, who participated in the October–November 1977 debates, had been counsellor and chargé d'affaires in Egypt from 1956 to 1964 and then Deputy Director of the Department of West Asia and North Africa from 1964 to 1967, an office he reassumed in October 1975. And Chang Shu, who in April 1973 took office as Deputy Director of the Department of Political and Security Council Affairs of China's permanent mission to the UN, had been First Secretary and chargé d'affaires in Iraq (April 1965–December 1971) and then Deputy Director of the Department of West Asia and Africa (1972).

The sudden increase in China's relations with the Middle East; its access to Middle Eastern affairs in the United Nations; and its perception of Soviet attempts to penetrate the Middle East, the Persian Gulf and the Indian Ocean, called for another re-organisation of China's diplomatic apparatus. In April 1972 Ho Ying, Director of the Department of West Asia and Africa, was appointed Vice Foreign Minister. There is no doubt that his sector of responsibility still covered the Middle East and Africa,[52] two fields in which he is probably China's most experienced and competent diplomat. In August 1972 his former Department of West Asia and Africa was again divided into a Department of African Affairs and a Department of West Asian and North African Affairs. The change was not merely an administrative one but also reflected China's renewed interest in the Middle East, as well as a revised concept of its relative world position.

In the past the Middle East was very much associated in China's world outlook with Africa, both in terms of the anti-imperialist struggle and even more so in the actual operation of China's foreign relations. Since 1972 the Middle East has again been perceived as a link between Europe and Asia. This is evident in both China's strategic considerations and its diplomatic performance. Thus, Ts'ao K'o-ch'iang, who was appointed Director of the new West Asia and North Africa Department in August 1972, had acquired rich experience and familiarity with Asian affairs. Similarly, whereas in the past China's diplomats in the Middle East usually had an 'African' background, many of the second generation of its ambassadors to the Middle East since the Cultural Revolution, appointed in 1973–4, had particularly rich experience in Asia and Europe. (See Appendix I.)

China's orientation towards the Arab governments is best exemplified in Sino-Egyptian relations. After several years of friction,

Egypt became again the centre of China's interest in the Arab World. Following the death of President Nasser, whose close association with the Soviet Union had been a thorn in China's flesh, the Chinese welcomed the remarkable flexibility of his successor. In February 1971 President Sadat, without consulting the Soviets and definitely without their approval, initiated negotiations with the United States concerning an 'interim settlement' with Israel. In early May, when American Secretary of State William Rogers was in Cairo, Sadat dismissed Vice President 'Alī Sabrī along with other top officials, including the Ministers of War and the Interior and the Chief of Intelligence. All had been associated in one way or another with Moscow and resented Sadat's orientation towards Washington.[53]

Both developments were a slap in the face for the Soviets. Although the Chinese avoided public comment, it could be easily understood from their extremely restrained reaction to Rogers' visit and his 'interim settlement' proposals, compared with their uncompromising opposition to previous American plans, that they welcomed Sadat's independent initiative.[54]

Shortly afterwards, compensating Moscow for the events of May, Sadat signed a Treaty of Friendship with the Soviet Union. Again, China's reaction was extremely cautious. Peking, whose 1950 Treaty of Friendship with the Soviet Union was still in force, did not take the Soviet–Egyptian treaty too seriously, as might have been expected. China was always more concerned with the actual, not the formal, aspects of foreign relations. The Soviet–Egyptian treaty, as its abrogation in 1976 proved, was more symbolic than real; indeed, in July 1971, less than two months after Sadat had signed the treaty, he supported President Numayrī of the Sudan in quelling, with China's reticent agreement, a communist, probably Soviet-inspired, *coup d'état*.[55]

In March 1972 Maḥmūd Riyāḍ, Sadat's special adviser on foreign affairs and former Foreign Minister, visited China after several delays. Although no joint communiqué was issued and disagreements remained – apparently concerning the Palestinians – Riyāḍ had a series of talks with Chinese officials, including two meetings with Chou En-lai. The Chinese advised him that Egypt should not rely on superpower-sponsored negotiations, which would only reflect the existing frontlines, but should rather change the situation by force.

In view of the deadlock reached with the United States over the 'interim settlement' issue, it seems – and the October 1973 war later proved – that Sadat fundamentally concurred with the Chinese advice. The Soviets, however, were reluctant or unwilling to supply Egypt with offensive weapons needed for a military operation. Gradually many people in Egypt, among them Haykal as well as Sadat himself, reached the conclusion, which the Chinese had reiterated since 1967 and even earlier, that the Soviets indeed had no intention of changing the situation of 'no war, no peace' in the Middle East.[56] This conviction, among other things, led Sadat to expel the Soviet military advisers from Egypt in July 1972.

China completely approved of Sadat's action, which Chou En-lai, speaking at a reception in honour of the Yemeni premier in Peking, described as the beginning of a new Arab policy 'fully independent from the superpowers who seek to serve only their own interests'.[57] Sadat's *tour de force* further improved Sino-Egyptian relations. Chinese leaders granted Egyptian journalists interviews which were later published extensively in the Middle Eastern press. In one of these important interviews Ho Ying, Vice Foreign Minister in charge of Middle Eastern affairs, elaborated on China's stand on the Middle East:

We do not seek to replace others, nor do we want to change our relations with other parties. What we are keen to do is to put our better experience before your eyes so that you will be on your guard when dealing with outside forces.

In circumstances such as yours, foreign aid, especially the military aspect of that aid, is a question of vital importance to you. You must get your needs from any source you can, however great the difficulties.[58]

Ho Ying also stressed the need for unity among the Arab countries, as well as among the people within each country. In China, he said, this unity had been accomplished by the Communist Party. 'You in Egypt have the [Arab] Socialist Union which can play a similar role so as to achieve national unity among the people.'

Muḥammad Ḥasanayn Haykal, who also visited China early in 1973, published a series of articles in February, including a long interview with Chou En-lai. These articles infuriated the Soviets, who accused Haykal of having written lies and fabrications about Moscow's Middle Eastern and Afro-Asian policy, and particularly its military aid to the Arabs.[59] On 12 March 1973, shortly after the Soviet accusations were published, Egypt's Foreign Minister, Muḥammad Ḥasan al-Zayyāt, arrived in China for a four-day visit. This was the first visit ever by an Egyptian Foreign Minister to China. Chou En-lai was reportedly absent from the capital so that Zayyāt only met Foreign Minister Chi P'eng-fei.

A completely different welcome was accorded by the Chinese to Ḥusayn al-Shāfiʿī, Egypt's Vice President, who visited China from 21 to 24 September 1973. Shāfiʿī, whose veiled criticism of the Soviet Union the NCNA had already quoted earlier in 1973, not only met with Chou En-lai but was also honoured by an audience with Mao. He was the first Egyptian leader to see Mao since the mid-1960s. During his visit Shāfiʿī again criticised the superpowers' role in the Middle East,[60] but his pilgrimage to Peking probably had more to do with the planned Egyptian–Syrian attack on Israel, which began just ten days after he had left. It is unlikely that Shāfiʿī disclosed the secret of the attack to the Chinese but it is possible that he tried to explore what China's reaction would be.

When the war broke out, the Arabs received China's full blessings.[61] In China's view, the most important aspect of the war, disregarding territorial gains or losses, was that it had been planned and executed by the Arabs independently and thus terminated the long stalemate of 'no war, no peace' in the Middle East. For precisely this reason the Chinese believed that the Arabs had spoiled their initial advantage by accepting the ceasefire agreement, which Peking regarded as the very first step undertaken by the superpowers to reimpose a deadlock.

Following the war, it seems that China welcomed the Egyptian–American *rapprochement* and the American initiative in the Middle East which resulted in the disengagement agreements between Israel and Egypt and Syria and caused the Soviets a considerable setback. Yet, in China's view, progress towards a settlement in the Middle East has been too slow. Some two years after the October 1973 war, the Chinese again argued that the Arabs had lost their initiative. As a result there has been a return to the superpower-controlled situation of 'no war, no peace'.[62]

But then, in March 1976, the Egyptians abrogated their Friendship Treaty with the Soviet Union and denied naval facilities to Soviet warships. The Chinese could not hide their satisfaction.[63] Later that month it was reported that China had supplied Egypt, free of charge, with thirty engines and thousands of spare parts for its Soviet-built MiG jet fighters, as well as with other military equipment.[64] Subsequently, Vice President Ḥusnī Mubarak visited China from 18 to 26 April, heading a delegation which included the Minister of State for War Production. He met with China's political and military leaders and was also received by Mao. On 21 April, a protocol of military co-operation was signed. Although no details were released, it appears that China was to supply Egypt with spare parts and strategic raw materials to the value of $10 million, under a reactivated 1964 loan of 345 million Swiss francs.[65] Although offered in 1964, it had remained untouched until 1973. Only 28 per cent (97.4 million) was used between 1973 and early 1976.[66] In May, another military delegation, headed by War Minister and Deputy Premier General Jamasī, visited China.

These visits and agreements were often described as *the* major Chinese breakthrough and first foothold in the Middle East.[67] Yet the Sino-Egyptian *rapprochement* is of little more than symbolic value. The Egyptians, and even more so the Chinese, are well aware of the fact that China's military–economic capabilities are extremely limited, compared with Egypt's needs. Still, for the first time the Chinese have been able to offer Egypt at least some political support. This was exemplified by China's sympathetic though restrained reaction to the beginning of the Israeli–Egyptian dialogue following Sadat's visit to Jerusalem in November 1977. The Chinese reaction was sympathetic not only because Sadat's move had inflicted another blow to the Soviets, but also because it conformed to China's fundamental stand that the Arab–Israeli conflict should be settled through direct negotiations without outside interference. The reaction was restrained mainly because public and straightforward approval of Sadat's initiative would have added more strain to the already lukewarm relations between China and the so-called radical Arab governments, that categorically rejected the initiative.

China's relations with the other Arab governments were governed mainly by its perception of their attitude towards the Soviet Union and the degree of their independence. Generally, the Chinese have been disappointed by the Arab regimes, with the exception of Egypt and the Sudan. In December 1971, when China's recent foreign policy took shape, Chou En-lai said: 'In the Middle East the Soviet revisionists have enlarged their military bases in Iraq, Syria, Yemen and South Yemen.' And in March 1973 he added: 'Since the worsening of the relations between the U.S.S.R. and Egypt, the Middle East policy of the Soviet revisionists has shifted from the management of key points to diversified management. Lately, they have vigorously aided Syria and Iraq.'[68]

Under these circumstances, there has been little improvement in Sino-Syrian relations since 1971. In May 1972 a Syrian delegation headed by Foreign Minister ʿAbd al-Ḥalīm Khaddām arrived in China. The visit apparently had more economic than political significance (Khaddām had previously been Foreign Trade Minister) and China offered Syria an interest-free loan of $45 million, the first since 1963.

Unlike Egypt, which had adopted a more flexible foreign policy, Syria remained rigidly oriented towards the Soviets. This orientation changed slightly only after the October 1973 war when Syria very reluctantly accepted Kissinger's step-by-step diplomacy. China undoubtedly approved of this change and welcomed the US-sponsored disengagement agreement between Israel and Syria in May 1974 as a further setback to the Soviets.[69] More recently, however, the Chinese have obviously been annoyed by the Syrian contribution to the deterioration in the Lebanon.

China's relations with the Yemen remained limited mainly to the economic field. In July 1969 Wang Jo-chieh, China's ambassador to the Yemen, returned to the same post which he had left two years earlier. Subsequently, the Chinese resumed their work on the Ṣanʿāʾ-Ṣaʿda Road disrupted not so much because of the Cultural Revolution in China as because of the civil war in the Yemen. In July 1972, during the visit to China of the Yemeni Prime Minister, Peking offered the Yemen another interest-free loan of $21 million. The Yemen received relatively little Chinese attention in the early 1970s not only because of its relations with Moscow but also because its role is marginal in the two poles of attraction of China's Middle East policy – the Arab–Israeli conflict and the Persian Gulf.

As a result of its growing interest in the Persian Gulf China's relations with Iraq assumed new significance. Whereas in the past the Chinese perceived Iraq more within the context of the Arab–Israeli conflict, from 1971–2 onwards Iraq was linked much more to the situation in Asia, the Indian Ocean and particularly the Persian Gulf. Within this context, China has become more concerned about Iraq's close association with Moscow, not so much about its formal aspects (such as the Soviet–Iraqi Friendship Treaty of April 1972) as about its concrete manifestations (such as providing naval facilities to Soviet ships). Apparently, one of the main reasons for China's eagerness to consolidate its relations with the Gulf states, particularly Kuwait and even more so Iran, was to create and support a balance against Iraq. Both Kuwait and Iran have always been at odds with Iraq and their stand was implicitly endorsed by Peking. When a high-ranking Iraqi delegation visited China from 25 December 1971 to 3 January 1972, no joint communiqué was issued. It was assumed that the Chinese disapproved of some of the extremist Iraqi expressions against Israel and also refused to support Iraq's claims to several Persian Gulf islands which had been occupied by Iran shortly before the Iraqi visit.

On the other hand, China tried to improve relations with Iraq so as to loosen its dependence on the Soviet Union. In June 1971 China offered Iraq, for the first time ever, an interest-free loan of about $40 million, to be repaid in Iraqi products over a ten-year period beginning in 1984. Only in November 1973 did the Chinese begin to implement the offer by signing a protocol for building a bridge over the Tigris River. This gesture, however, did not improve Sino-Iraqi relations, particularly since Iraq became the main supporter of the People's Front for the Liberation of Oman, contrary to China's policy. However, since 1975 there has been a significant change in Iraq's policy: as the Kurdish revolt ended in March 1975, Iraq normalised relations with Iran and loosened its ties with Moscow in favour of Western aid and investment. In March 1976 it established diplomatic relations with Oman.[70]

Peking's quest for stability in the Persian Gulf with a view to disrupting the Soviet advance into the Indian Ocean also affected China's relations with South Yemen. Whereas since 1969 the Chinese had used South Yemen as a base for providing the PFLOAG with material support, training and encouragement, they ceased doing so in 1971. Furthermore, there were indications that the South Yemeni authorities had become less militant and had reduced their support to the PFLOAG, as well as to the Eritrean Liberation Front, preferring greater stability in the area. This was confirmed in March 1976 when South Yemen and Saudi Arabia established diplomatic relations. These changes, which apparently did not receive Moscow's blessing, were probably linked to the South Yemeni complaints about Soviet subversion and the quantity and quality of recent Soviet aid.[71] The Chinese undoubtedly welcomed both developments as signs of independence. Yet in July 1978 China suffered a setback in South Yemen when a Soviet-engineered *coup d'état* overthrew the pro-Chinese leadership.

By that time, however, the Chinese more than doubled their diplomatic representation in the Middle East, following the decision of seven Middle Eastern governments to recognise Peking. In 1971, almost thirteen years after a Middle East government had last recognised the PRC (South Yemen, as a new state, was an exception), several other governments finally did the same. Kuwait was the first, in March. As early as 1961 Peking had implicitly supported Kuwait's independence against Iraq's claim to the territory, but Kuwait preferred to establish diplomatic relations with Taiwan. Nonetheless, Kuwait also developed trade relations with Peking at the same time and the two countries occasionally exchanged economic delegations. The NCNA had set up an office in Kuwait as early as 1966.

The main obstacle to diplomatic relations with Peking had been Kuwait's refusal to give up its recognition of Taiwan as the only legal government of China. In an interview, the Kuwaiti foreign minister was asked about diplomatic relations with the PRC. He replied that in the past Peking had sought diplomatic relations with Kuwait on the condition that the latter severed relations with Taiwan. This demand was rejected.[72] In March 1971, however, Kuwait gave in and a Chinese embassy was immediately established. From the strategic point of view, China's relations with Kuwait were intended to contribute to further stability in the Persian Gulf against intervention from the outside, by the Soviet Union, or by local regimes (Iraq) or movements (the PFLOAG). From the economic point of view, although Kuwait had very little to offer China, it proved to be an enormous market, relative to its size, for Chinese exports. In 1975, the value of China's exports to Kuwait was around $55 million, similar to the figure for Iraq or Iran and more than any other country in the Middle East. (Kuwait, Bahrain and Qatar in 1975 absorbed 28 per cent of China's exports to the region.)

In August 1971 Turkey and Iran extended diplomatic recognition to the PRC. Probably because of the importance of the Persian Gulf in their strategic outlook, the Chinese concentrated their attention on Iran. Basically, China's relations with Iran were motivated by common fears of Soviet expansion. In recent years Iran has become the most powerful state in the Middle East with an unmistakable determination to play *the* dominant role in the Persian Gulf and to deny such a role to any other state or power. Although the Shah maintained close relations, particularly economic, with the Soviet Union, the fear of Soviet invasion or subversion has always been a fundamental consideration in Iran's foreign policy. Soviet attempts to penetrate the Middle East, the Indian Ocean and the Persian Gulf, and particularly Moscow's association with Iraq, caused Iran to adopt a firmer stand towards the Soviets. These were probably the basic motivations behind Iran's recognition of the PRC. China's attitude towards Iran had never been entirely hostile. In the 1950s the Chinese approved of the nationalisation of Iran's oil industry, and regarded the country as a target of exploitation, first by Anglo-American capitalism, and later by Soviet–American competition. China itself imported Iranian oil from 1960 to 1966, about 200,000 tons a year, or 1.4 million tons altogether.[73] Apparently the Chinese had never interfered or become directly involved in Iran's internal affairs, although occasionally they quoted 'articles' of 'Iranian revolutionaries' (probobly an offshoot of the communist People's Party, or Tudeh, which the Chinese considered reformist and revisionist). Most of these 'articles', which were still quoted in 1969 and 1970, dealt mainly with the international situation rather than with domestic developments.[74] Yet sometimes the Chinese alluded, very briefly and cunningly, to the internal struggle in Iran: 'We hope that in this New Year [1345 according to the Irani tradition] the heroic Iranian people may become victorious against Zahak the Tyrant by keeping their traditional standard and Kaveh's flag flying.'[75] In pre-Sassanian mythology Kāveh was a blacksmith who overthrew the tyrant Zahāk. The allusion to the Shah was unmistakable.

However, in 1971 Sino-Iranian relations began to improve, leading to recognition and the establishment of diplomatic relations. There is little doubt that China considers Iran to be one of the most serious obstacles to the expansion of Soviet influence and presence in the Persian Gulf, as well as a major contributor to organising and uniting the members of OPEC and other Third World countries against 'superpower hegemony'.

Suspecting Iraq as a possible outlet and outpost for Soviet penetration into the Persian Gulf and Asia, the Chinese implicitly endorsed Iran's occupation of several Gulf islands, also claimed by Iraq. China also ceased its support of the PFLOAG, established normal relations with Kuwait, and later with Oman, and improved relations with other Gulf states. Incidentally, unlike the Arab countries which refer to the Gulf as 'Arabian', the Chinese usually refer to it as 'Persian'.[76] Trade between China and Iran has developed steadily. Chinese exports, for example, rose from $3.2 million in 1971 to more than $100 million in 1974. From 1974, the Chinese also imported 200,000 to 300,000 tons of oil every year, paying hard cash at OPEC prices (in those years China itself became an oil exporter). But probably the best indication of the importance of Iran in China's foreign policy was the visits to Iran of Foreign Minister Chi P'eng-fei (in June 1973), of Vice Premier Li Hsien-nien (in April 1975) and of Chairman Hua Kuo-feng (in August 1978). No Chinese leader of such high rank had visited the Middle East or the Arab countries since 1965.

On 9 November 1971 the PRC was recognised by the Lebanon. For many years the issue of recognising China was subject to parliamentary and governmental debates in the Lebanon, under the pressure of the opposition. However, diplomatic relations with Taiwan did not prevent the Lebanon from exchanging delegations and developing trade with the PRC. Indeed, in the late 1960s Beirut's trade with Peking surpassed that with Taiwan and the Lebanese authorities even became worried about Chinese goods flooding the local markets. They were also concerned about possible clandestine relations between China and radical groups and the 'spreading' of Maoist doctrines. In fact, as we have seen, there is no evidence that such relations or even intentions existed although Chinese diplomats from Damascus often travelled to Beirut to meet Palestinian, as well as Lebanese, personalities.

Usually, Chinese hostility towards the Lebanon was demonstrated only when measures had been taken against the Palestinians. In October 1969, for example, the Chinese blamed the 'Lebanese reactionary authorities' for making 'pincer attacks in co-ordination with the Israeli aggressor forces against the Palestinian guerrilla fighters on the southern borders of Lebanon'.[77] Still, most of the blame fell on US imperialism and Zionism.

China's diplomatic relations with the Lebanon had an unfortunate start. When the question of China's admission to the United Nations was put to the vote in October 1971, negotiations between China and the Lebanon were already taking place in Paris. Yet, in the United Nations the Lebanon first supported the American resolution to regard the expulsion of Taiwan as an 'important question' which required a two-thirds majority; and then, after this resolution had been defeated and when China's admission seemed inevitable, the Lebanon still abstained on the Albanian resolution.[78]

Beirut's speedy recognition of Peking on 9 November was

probably designed to offset the mistake in the United Nations, even though it seems that for some time after the recognition the Chinese continued to maintain a cool attitude towards Beirut. Soon, however, relations did develop, particularly in the economic field. China regarded the Lebanon not simply as a market for its exports (which reached about $18 million in 1974), but mainly as the financial and economic centre of the Middle East. Already in early 1972 the Iraqi News Agency reported that Peking decided to open a branch of the National Bank of China in Beirut and to make full use of the city's banking and free-zone facilities.[79] Hsü Ming, China's first ambassador to Beirut, who arrived in March 1972, was particularly well qualified for the job. He had rich diplomatic, as well as economic, experience as China's commercial representative in Italy (1965–6) and as China's representative to the PRC–Japan Memorandum Trade Office since the early 1970s.

Later in 1972 Khalīl Abū Ḥamad, the Lebanese Foreign Minister, made his first visit to China (24 November–5 December). The main visible results were again in the economic field. A new trade agreement provided for mutual most-favoured-nation treatment and mutual transit facilities, as well as the promotion and expansion of mutual trade. If Peking indeed meant to use Beirut as a centre for financial, economic and even political activity in the Middle East, its plans were disrupted by the civil war which erupted in 1976. True to form, the Chinese blamed the superpowers, especially the Soviet Union, and indirectly criticised Syria for inciting, complicating and sustaining the conflict, which it felt should be settled by the peoples concerned without outside intervention.

Jordan recognised the PRC only on 14 April 1977. As in the case of the Lebanon, there has always been a group in Jordan sympathetic to the PRC. Once, in 1957, Jordan came very near to recognising Peking. With this attempt thwarted, there was very little development in Sino-Jordanian relations thereafter. China's attitude towards the Jordanian Government became particularly hostile during its clashes with the Palestinians in November 1968, September 1970 and early 1971. While branding the Jordanian Government as 'reactionary', the Chinese nevertheless laid most of the blame for these incidents on the United States.[80]

Later in 1971 a visit to China by a Jordanian economic delegation triggered reports that Jordan would establish diplomatic relations in early 1972. These reports were immediately denied,[81] but in the field of trade, despite the fact that Jordan maintained diplomatic relations with Taiwan, imports from the PRC by far exceeded those from the island (Chinese exports in 1976 reached almost $14 million).

On 25 May 1978 the PRC was recognised by Oman. This is probably the most striking example of the transformation in China's position in the Middle East. It was only in 1971 that Peking ceased supporting the PFLOAG, determined to subvert Oman and seize power there. Since then China has changed course and became an eager champion of stability in the Persian Gulf, so much so that even the Sultan of Oman considered it in his interest to establish normal relations with Peking.

There are still five Middle Eastern states which do not maintain diplomatic relations with the PRC. Four are in Arabia – Bahrain, Qatar, the United Arab Emirates and Saudi Arabia. China's interest in the stability of the Gulf area, based on firm anti-Soviet motivations, has already paved the way for recognition. This is particularly true in the case of Saudi Arabia, whose independent stance in international affairs the Chinese have approved in the past (against American imperialism) as well as more recently (against Soviet social-imperialism). After years of hostility to pro-Soviet regimes in the Middle East in general, and in the Arabian Peninsula in particular, Riyad now aims at containing Soviet influence in the area by establishing diplomatic relations (e.g., with South Yemen in March 1976), and by providing funds and arms to substitute for Moscow. There is little doubt that Peking is pinning its faith on Saudi Arabia and is willing to establish full diplomatic relations with it as soon as it agrees. This much, however, cannot be said about Israel, the fifth Middle Eastern country which still does not maintain diplomatic relations with Peking.

In 1950 Israel was the first country in the Middle East to recognise the PRC; it had never recognised Taiwan and, moreover, it expressed its readiness, particularly in recent years, to establish normal relations with Peking; Israel's role in containing Soviet penetration in the Middle East is beyond doubt. Nevertheless, the Chinese have consistently refused to have any form of relations with Israel. For example, it was reported from Jerusalem in June 1971 that direct telephone communications between Israel and the PRC were about to be established. This report was firmly refuted by the Chinese: 'The question of China instituting telephone communications with Israel simply does not exist... The

Chinese Government and people have no contact whatsoever with the Israeli Zionists. This has been the case in the past and will remain so in future. This stand of the People's Republic of China is firm and unshakable.'[82] This refusal derives not only from the decision not to antagonise the Arabs and thereby lose their support (on which the Chinese in any case no longer rely), but mainly from the realisation that such a step is unnecessary so long as the Chinese cannot influence the situation in the Middle East.

Yet China's new analysis of the world situation, primarily from the standpoint of the perceived Soviet expansion, did bring about a change, though as yet a very subtle one, in Peking's attitude towards Israel. Hints of such a change were spelled out not only in private talks but even in public pronouncements. Despite their continuing support of the Palestinians, the Chinese have always been very careful not to identify themselves with the latter's maximalist aims or, in fact, with any specific 'plan', Palestinian or otherwise. There is little doubt that fundamentally the Chinese regard Israel as a *fait accompli*. While they reiterate, particularly in the United Nations, and contrary to the facts, that 'ever since the founding of the People's Republic of China we have refused to have any contact with the Israeli Zionists who persist in aggression',[83] they immediately made it clear that they were not opposed to the Jewish people or the people of Israel but only to 'Israeli Zionist policies of aggression and expansion'.[84] Such a distinction between the Government and the people of Israel, very rarely expressed in the 1960s, was also made by Chou En-lai immediately after China's admission to the United Nations. He was quoted as saying: 'Among the 76 countries which voted for the Albanian resolution there are, of course, some countries which cannot have official governmental relations with China although their peoples are friendly with the Chinese people. One example is Israel. This does not mean that we cannot become friendly with the Jewish people.'[85]

From the early 1970s the NCNA began to report quite frequently and with unprecedented familiarity on the situation in Israel, trying to underline the so-called 'widening gap' between the Government and 'the broad masses of the Israeli people and particularly the labouring people [who] are bitterly disappointed at the existing state of affairs'.[86] Such an attitude could be regarded as preparing the ground for Chinese 'people's diplomacy' towards Israel.

Indeed, there were some intentional or unintentional exchanges between Israeli and Chinese officials. In July 1971 it was reported that an Israeli member of the leftist United Workers Party (which participated in the coalition government) had met privately with Chinese officials in Paris during the preceding three years.[87] Since 1972, Israel's representatives in the United Nations have met several times with Chinese officials in the organisation. And in May 1973 came the incredible story of China's ambassador in Greece who had attended a Twenty-fifth Anniversary reception in the Israeli embassy in Athens, thus triggering widespread speculation. He later said he had thought he was visiting the Kuwaiti embassy (though no such embassy existed in Athens).[88] These 'meetings' were followed by a wave of 'reports' about an alleged *rapprochement* between China and Israel. Most of these rumours apparently came from Soviet sources in an unmistakable attempt to drive a wedge between China and the Arabs:

Despite loud anti-Israel propaganda from Peking and protestations of friendship towards the Arabs, the Chinese leaders are playing a dishonest double game; their only contribution to the Palestinian struggle has been a supply of books of quotations and Mao badges. Israel started a series of broadcasts of sketches from the History of Jews in China, in a tone friendly to Peking and the latter reciprocated by pronouncements in the United Nations which were welcome to Israel.[89]

However, all these reports and allegations were firmly denied by the Chinese and so far nothing has come of these 'contacts'.

Similarly, nothing as yet has come out of the Israeli Government's marked willingness and repeated attempts to initiate a dialogue with Peking with a view to normalising relations. Shortly after Israel voted for the admission of the PRC to the United Nations, an Israeli consulate was established in Hong Kong. As there was no progress in relations with China, the consulate closed down three years later. After the October 1971 vote, Israel also asked a number of personalities who were invited to China to raise the issue of Sino-Israeli relations during their visits. These visitors included, among others, Anthony Wedgwood Benn, Pierre Mendès-France, Pietro Nenni, Giuseppe Medici, Georgio Macovescu, James Schlesinger and even the late Emperor Haile Selassie of Ethiopia. China's response was not as negative as might have been expected. All these visitors shared the impression that the Chinese admitted, sometimes in marked embarrassment, that, although the establishment of the State of Israel had been a grave mistake from the very beginning, Israel's right to exist must now be reckoned with and recognised *post-factum*.[90] As far as relations with Israel were concerned, the Chinese implied that their current negative attitude might be modified in the future once a solution to the Middle Eastern crisis could be reached in a way satisfactory also to the Arabs.[91] A similar message was brought back by Maḥmūd Riyāḍ, President Sadat's adviser on foreign affairs and formerly Foreign Minister, after his visit to China in March 1972. He was also under the impression that the Chinese disapproved of the annihilation of Israel but would not recognise Israel before the Arab–Israeli conflict had been settled.[92]

Public opinion in Israel today generally tends to sympathise with the Chinese, despite their support of the Arabs and the Palestinians, even as far as regarding China as Israel's tacit ally against the Soviet Union. While these views reflect more wishful thinking than objective realities, it is nonetheless true that the changing international situation has affected China's attitude towards Israel, and for the better.

Dissociation from liberation movements

China's appreciation of the Middle East governments' resistance to superpower hegemony, and particularly to Soviet intervention, led to a significant change in its attitude towards the local national liberation movements. Continued Chinese support for some revolutionary struggles became incompatible with Peking's new orientation.

The Chinese had come to realise that some governments which were threatened by national liberation movements made a valuable contribution to uniting Third and Second World countries against the superpowers, and provided a more reliable and effective barrier against their expansion than the revolutionaries who fought against them. In the Middle East, for example, this was notably true of Oman and also of Iran, Kuwait, the Lebanon and Turkey, where the Chinese had previously supported, to a greater or a lesser degree, opposition and insurgent elements. This was also the case of Israel, the continued existence of which is now implicitly regarded by the Chinese as conforming with their short-term interests.[93]

The Chinese had additional reasons to suspect national liberation movements. Very often, China's relations with them, far from excluding the Soviets, only motivated them to increase their commitment to these movements, which they had otherwise been reluctant and unwilling to support. Furthermore, after gaining independence, some liberation movements, which had been supported by Peking, made way for Soviet expansion and permitted a Soviet presence in their countries. In South Yemen, whose struggle for independence the Chinese had encouraged for many years, the authorities not only began to rely heavily on the Soviets but also granted them naval facilities. The Chinese are very sensitive to the issue of the Soviet naval build-up in the Indian Ocean which, in their view, is directed ultimately against China. For this reason, perhaps, the Chinese do not seem very enthusiastic about a possible 'Palestinian State' and apparently prefer a different settlement of the Palestinian problem.[94]

Under these circumstances the Chinese became more careful and selective and less committed in their support of national liberation movements, and in some cases withdrew such support entirely.[95] Accordingly, the Chinese adopted a more flexible stand on armed struggle. Implicitly, they began to advise liberation movements to hold negotiations while persisting in armed struggle. There was nothing extraordinary in this approach which conformed with China's revolutionary doctrines, based on the CCP experience. 'Political bargaining was an intrinsic part of the military and political struggle.'[96] The above-mentioned considerations and assumptions are evident in China's relations with the two main liberation movements in the Middle East – the PFLOAG and the Palestinian organisations.

China's attitude towards the PFLOAG changed dramatically not only because of the revised Chinese world outlook but also because the local situation had changed. After suffering several defeats by the Sultan of Oman and his supporters, the PFLOAG began to decline.[97] In addition, the Arab governments, including South Yemen and, since 1975, also Iraq, probably became disillusioned by the possible disruptive consequences of PFLOAG activities against the independent states of the Gulf.[98] As a result of these attitudes and its own failures, the PFLOAG in August 1974 shortened its name as well as its aim to 'The People's Front for the Liberation of Oman' (PFLO), and adopted the new strategy of political, along with armed, struggle.[99] By late 1975 it was virtually defeated.

These developments apparently received Peking's blessing. From 1971 on the Chinese began to regard the Persian Gulf governments, particularly Iran and Kuwait, as a potential and effective obstacle to Soviet expansion and as a balance against Iraq. By establishing full diplomatic relations with both Kuwait and Iran, and eventually with Oman itself, and by endorsing the independence of the Persian Gulf states, Peking in fact rejected the PFLOAG maximalist plans to dominate the entire Gulf area.

China's relations with the Gulf states, particularly with Iran, which in late 1973 sent several hundred troops to help the Sultan of Oman against the insurgents, became incompatible with continued relations with the PFLOAG. Consequently, China ceased entirely its encouragement and coverage of the PFLOAG operations; Chinese instructors with the Dhufāri guerrillas were withdrawn; and the Chinese discontinued their supplies. 'Chinese support is now insignificant.'[100] When he was in Iran in June 1973, Foreign Minister Chi P'eng-fei declared that China had not been involved in the operation of leftist rebels in the Gulf and said that 'China believes that Iran is correct in strengthening its forces to combat subversive activity in the Persian Gulf' and that it was 'Iran's duty to do everything possible to combat this serious threat'.[101]

Certainly, China's Foreign Minister did not regard the PFLOAG as a 'serious threat'. Rather, he probably had in mind the Soviets, who had become the main supporters of the insurgents. Remote as this possibility was, the last thing the Chinese wanted to witness in the Persian Gulf was a repetition of their experience in South Yemen; they probably preferred a British-backed Sultanate of Oman to a Soviet-controlled People's Democratic Republic of Oman.

The change in China's attitude towards the Palestinians was not as acute as that towards the PFLOAG. Basically, unlike its experience with the Persian Gulf states, China's new orientation towards the Arab governments has so far not been jeopardised by its simultaneous cultivation of relations with the Palestinians. This is because the Arabs and the Palestinians have a firm common interest in fighting Israel, with which Peking has no intention of normalising relations.

However, despite their common interest, Arab and Palestinian views on both the ends and means of the struggle against Israel have never been identical. Whereas in the past the Chinese had approved of the Palestinian strategy and rejected that of the Arab governments, since late 1971 the opposite seems to have been true. Encouraging independent Arab policies, such as Sadat's, the Chinese no longer press the Arab governments to adopt the Palestinian strategy. In fact, there are indications that the Chinese believe that it is no longer possible to achieve a *complete* restoration of the Palestinians' 'rights'. From 1971 the Chinese became more outspoken in their criticism of the Palestine liberation movement. Already in May 1971, at a meeting with Arab journalists, Chou En-lai expressed his disappointment at the lack of unity among the guerrillas and the prolonged stagnation in their activities. He was quoted as saying that he did not understand the meaning of 'the temporary retreat in the Palestinian struggle, which could imply that there was no conflict with the enemy'.[102] Later he repeated: 'The struggle of the Palestinian guerrillas is beset by pressure and difficulty. This is induced by the disunity of the Arabian countries.'[103] The Chinese undoubtedly regard the fragmentation of the Palestine liberation movement as its main disadvantage: 'The protracted struggle of the Palestinian people proves another truth: the Palestinian revolution will advance when the unity within the Palestinian revolutionary ranks and their unity with other parties are reinforced; otherwise, *it will suffer setbacks*.'[104] [Italics added.]

The Chinese also no longer concealed their disapproval of Palestinian terror. Ho Ying, China's Vice Foreign Minister in charge of Middle Eastern and African affairs, told a visiting Turkish journalist that, although China supported the Palestinians, it did not approve of hijacking and terrorism.[105] These views were also expressed publicly. Ch'iao Kuan-hua, then China's senior Vice Foreign Minister, who in October 1972 headed China's delegation to the United Nations, declared there: 'The Chinese Government has always opposed assassination and hijacking of individuals as a means for waging political struggles and is also opposed to terrorist acts by individuals or a handful of people divorced from the masses, because they are harmful to the cause of national liberation and people's revolution.'[106]

Under these circumstances, China's material support to the Palestinians was further reduced. Some Palestinians admitted that the Chinese had not fulfilled their pledges, even the minor ones, and sources in Beirut said that actual Chinese aid was less than a quarter of what had been promised.[107] In May 1971 a Palestinian delegation visited China to participate in the 'Palestine International Week' which had been organised by the Chinese; neither Palestine Day, celebrated in China every year since 1965, nor Palestine Week, were held after 1971. That the Palestinians were in difficulties and that China's support was not forthcoming, at least not as they had expected, was confirmed in the visit of yet another Fatah delegation to China in September 1971. Its leader, Khalīl al-Wazīr (alias Abū Jihād), Arafat's closest friend and second-in-command, said among other things:

It is our ardent wish that the militant friendship between the Palestinian Revolution and the Arab people and the Chinese people will be deepened and that their revolutionary unity will be strengthened so that the struggle in our region will be pushed forward more resolutely and with greater confidence. . .

In the past the great Chinese Revolution stood on our side with the ardour of a revolutionary, with the sincerity of a close friend. Today, at a most difficult time, we have come to you again.[108]

This was shortly before the PRC was admitted to the United Nations. On the eve of China's admission, the Palestinians expressed their belief that China's membership of that body would promote the Palestinian cause. Indeed, in all the debates on Middle Eastern issues the Chinese remained very consistent in their views that the full restoration of Palestinian 'rights' was the first step towards the settlement of the Middle East conflict. A Palestinian leader described as being 'in close touch with the Chinese Government' admitted that China's attitude towards the Palestinians 'has changed for the better since China took its natural place on the United Nations rostrum, because its unswerving attitude became stronger, more influential and more efficacious in favour of the Palestinian revolution'.[109]

Sino-Palestinian bilateral relations, however, did not improve much. China's attitude towards the Palestinians in the context of the October 1973 war was remarkably different from its attitude in the previous war. In June 1967 Chou En-lai had met the PLO representative in Peking along with the other Arab ambassadors, and sent messages of support to the heads of the Arab states, as well as to PLO Chairman Shuqayrī. In 1973, on the other hand, the PLO representative was not present at Chou's meeting with the Arab ambassadors and no message of support was sent to Arafat (messages were sent to Presidents Sadat and Asad). The Chinese, to be sure, did not ignore, and even praised, the role played by the Palestinians in the war. Yet, whereas the 1967 war had confirmed China's disappointment with the Arab governments and consolidated its orientation towards the Palestinians, the 1973 war only confirmed China's disappointment with the Palestinians and consolidated its orientation towards the Arab governments.

Modified stand on the Arab–Israeli conflict

China's new orientation, motivated by the drive against the Soviets and the thaw with the Americans, led to a modified stand on the Arab–Israeli conflict. This conflict has consistently been linked by the Chinese to the global situation: in the 1950s and 1960s more in Marxist–Leninist terms, as a struggle of oppressed people against Western colonialism and neo-colonialism which had created the conflict and sustained it; in the 1970s more in terms of power-politics, as a struggle of oppressed people against two great powers which are preventing a settlement in order to perpetuate and increase their control.

Contending and at the same time colluding in the Middle East, the two superpowers, taking advantage of the temporary difficulties of the Palestinian and other Arab people on their road of struggle, have tried to make political deals by sacrificing their national rights and territorial sovereignty so as to grab strategic areas and oil resources in the Middle East. Here lies the root cause of the fact that there has been no reasonable settlement of the Middle East issue for the past five years.[110]

While the Chinese have condemned *both* superpowers for complicating the Arab–Israeli conflict, there is little doubt that in recent years they have concentrated their attacks on the Soviet Union. This reflects China's conviction that the Soviets, by professing to be the Arabs' friends, have been able to gain considerable influence and were therefore in a position to undermine any Arab intentions to change the status quo. This is why the Chinese were so satisfied with the Arab attempts to free themselves from Soviet patronage.

Consequent to the growing Arab disillusion with Moscow since 1971, Peking has greatly reduced its opposition to American initiatives in the Middle East. In late October 1973 the Chinese tacitly justified the alert of American forces: 'The Soviet Revisionists were forced under U.S. pressure to give up their attempt to send troops to the Middle East unilaterally.' Peking also did not oppose, and in fact privately approved of, Kissinger's step-by-step diplomacy, not only because of the progress it had made towards a settlement, but primarily because of the setbacks it inflicted on the Soviet position in the Middle East:

[Soviet] relations with Egypt have rapidly deteriorated and some of its vested positions in the Middle East are in danger of being replaced by the United States.

Both superpowers have had a number of big trials of strength there since the last October's Middle East war, with the United States taking the lead again and again.[111]

Because of the superpowers' involvement, Peking consistently and systematically opposed any 'plan', 'proposal' or 'resolution' for a political settlement of the Arab–Israeli conflict and urged the Arabs instead to rely on themselves, to unite and persist in armed struggle. This Chinese stand was very often misunderstood. It was alleged that Peking considered the status-quo situation of 'no war, no peace' in the Middle East as advantageous to China's interests since it engaged the United States and particularly the Soviet Union in an area far away from China's borders, kept the Suez Canal closed and thus reduced the threats to China's security. It was also alleged that Peking was opposed in principle to a political and peaceful settlement, including even a cease-fire agreement, and instead glorified armed struggle as the one and only way to settle the Middle East problem. Finally, it was alleged that on the basis of both convictions Peking had attempted to stir up the Middle East situation, hoping to embroil the two superpowers in a confrontation (preferably nuclear) which would lead to their destruction and eventually to China's supremacy.

These allegations deserve detailed consideration. There is little reason to believe that Peking considered continued stagnation in the Middle East, which could stabilise and consolidate definite spheres of superpower influence, as conforming to its long-term interests. In fact, this is exactly what the Chinese had always tried to prevent by urging the local people to persist in struggle so as to achieve eventually a complete withdrawal of the superpowers.

True, since the June 1967 war the Chinese consistently rejected, and refused to take part in, any attempt to reach a political settlement of the Arab–Israeli conflict: they opposed Security Council Resolution 242 of November 1967; the Rogers Plan of December 1969; the cease-fire agreements between Israel and Egypt in August 1970, as well as that of October 1973; and also most United Nations and Security Council resolutions on the Middle East, even those commonly regarded as pro-Arab. For all these motions without exception failed to stipulate what China regarded as basic preconditions for a settlement: an immediate Israeli withdrawal from *all* the occupied territories and a *full* restoration of Palestinian 'rights'. They also failed to condemn Israel firmly and to distinguish between aggression and resistance. Fundamentally, China believed that all these 'resolutions' and 'plans' were defective because they had been designed and manufactured by the superpowers, not in order to settle the Middle East conflict but rather to sustain it and thereby prolong the stalemate and maintain their presence and influence.

Therefore, the Chinese in principle rejected peaceful settlement or political negotiations whenever the superpowers were directly or indirectly involved. Thus, when they opposed the cease-fire resolution in October 1973, it was not, as some people believed, because they wanted the war to continue for its own sake; it was because China regarded the resolution as a deal between the two superpowers, which not only ignored and offended the other Security Council members (i.e., the PRC) but also aimed to re-impose on the Middle East the situation of 'no war, no peace', temporarily terminated by the war.[112] China also opposed the dispatch, and later the extension of the mandate, of the United Nations Emergency Force. Such a force, in China's view, would be under superpower manipulation and, therefore, subservient to their schemes.[113]

China's opposition to these resolutions did not necessarily entail the use of its veto power. As a rule the Chinese preferred not to participate in the votes rather than veto them or abstain, thereby antagonising the Arabs who had believed they needed and, there-fore, accepted these resolutions.[114] The Chinese explained their refusal to vote as a response to Arab appeals: 'Out of respect for the countries concerned, we would give consideration to that draft resolution [of 23 October 1973, on supervising the cease-fire]... If the countries concerned – I repeat, the countries concerned – want such a thing, we have no alternative, but the maximum we can do is to refrain from opposing it.'[115] And with regard to the resolution to dispatch a United Nations Emergency Force, the Chinese said: 'It is only out of consideration for the requests repeatedly made by the victims of aggression that China feels not in a position to veto it.'[116]

China's opposition to any superpower-controlled settlement in the Middle East was also manifested and reinforced by its con-sistent encouragement of armed struggle. Again, this is not regarded as an end in itself but rather as a symbol of indepen-dence and a reaction to outside intervention. So long as the United States and the Soviet Union remained involved, any *political* settlement would, in China's view, reflect the existing inferior Arab positions. Under these circumstances the only way the Arabs could change the situation in their favour was by *military* means. This message was delivered very clearly to Maḥmūd Riyāḍ, then Sadat's adviser on foreign affairs, who visited China in March 1972. Foreign Minister Chi P'eng-fei told him that 'the Chinese Government believes that it is impossible to gain at the conference table what one cannot win on the battle-field'.[117]

Consciously or unconsciously, it was exactly on the basis of this assumption that Egypt and Syria attacked Israel in October 1973. As the Chinese had predicted, the Arabs' military gains were not only confirmed but also extended when the political agreements were concluded. The Chinese were very pleased with the results of the war, with the degree of unity achieved not only among the Arab countries but among Afro-Asian countries in general, and with the variety of weapons employed, particularly the oil embargo: 'The war of resistance of the Arab people, including the Palestinian people, against the Israeli aggressors upset the prolonged state of "no war, no peace" created by the superpowers in the Middle East, and exerted a positive influence on the struggle of the Asian and African peoples against imperialism and hege-monism.'[118]

In China's view, war was necessary because the superpowers had continuously prevented a just settlement. The only alter-native to war was to reject and drive out any outside intervention and to settle all conflicts locally. This, and not armed struggle, has in fact been the essence of China's Middle East policy.

CONCLUSION

China's Middle East policy has been analysed in this study as an interaction between continuity and change. Apparently, the considerable changes in this policy, particularly the transformation of the Cultural Revolution's radicalism, which won China almost universal hostility, into the moderation of recent years, which won China almost universal respect, could very easily be misinterpreted as opportunism. Yet to understand China's Middle East policy only in terms of these changes would be totally misleading.

One of the main conclusions of this study is the rather remarkable continuity and consistency of China's fundamental attitudes towards the Middle East. From a very early stage, even before they seized power, let alone established relations with Middle Eastern countries, the Chinese had revealed a considerable interest in the Middle East situation. This interest stemmed from the belief that the Chinese revolution was not an isolated phenomenon but a part of a world-wide historical trend. Therefore, China's enemies were also the enemies of the rest of the world, particularly the colonial and semi-colonial countries, and they all shared the same common interest: the struggle against imperialism and outside intervention, and for independence.

Thus, despite the changes in China's Middle East policy, at any given time China's primary, continuous and long-term interest in the Middle East has been to encourage and support opposition to hostile global powers. To some extent, this interest has been even more important than gaining formal diplomatic recognition although, in China's view, recognition of the PRC certainly implied opposition to imperialism and increased independence.

The continuous interest in the Middle East by the Government of the PRC – a government which did not exist before 1949, had had no previous relations with this area, and which has been facing enormous problems both at home and abroad since then –

should be regarded as an outstanding phenomenon in international politics. Furthermore, the nature of China's interest in the Middle East was also outstanding. Unlike the other powers, whose interest was to acquire territories, bases, spheres of influence and economic benefits, China's interest was to urge the local governments and peoples to resist these powers without itself becoming involved or intending to replace others.

China's attitudes were different not only from those of the Western powers but also, at a very early stage, from those of the Soviet Union. Unlike the Soviets, the Chinese regarded the intermediate zone, in which the Middle East occupied an extremely important strategic position, as the main battlefield against the West. Whereas the Soviets were reluctant to use or advocate the use of force in the Middle East, fearing a deterioration to a world war and damage to their already consolidated interests, the Chinese urged them and the Arabs firmly to resist the West precisely to avoid another world war. Earlier than the Soviets and to a greater extent, the Chinese believed in the potential, long-term force of Arab nationalism as partner in the anti-imperialist front. Unlike the Soviets, they revealed little interest in the socio-political nature of the Middle Eastern regimes. This approach was based on a principle Mao had articulated as early as 1940:

No matter what classes, parties, or individuals in the oppressed nations join the revolution [i.e., the proletarian–socialist world revolution], and no matter whether they are conscious of the point mentioned above [that such revolution has the proletariat of the capitalist countries as its main force and the oppressed peoples of the colonies and semi-colonies as its allies], or whether they understand it subjectively, so long as they oppose imperialism, their revolution becomes part of the proletarian–socialist world revolution, and they themselves become its allies.[1]

Accordingly, the Chinese tended to judge the Middle East governments in view of their attitude towards 'imperialism' or any outside intervention. Unlike Moscow, Peking did not bother itself with ideological definitions and classification of the Arab regimes.[2] However, from the very few remarks Peking did make on this issue, it seems that the Chinese were not misled by the slogans of Arab socialism and, in fact, believed that the Arabs have not yet reached the stage of national democracy, let alone socialism.[3]

This Chinese attitude towards the Middle East, which until recently was largely misunderstood, was far from a mere rationalisation of the distance between China and the Middle

East or China's limited economic and military capabilities. Rather, it was deeply rooted in China's fundamental world outlook. It is only within this framework that the changes in China's Middle East policy, far from being regarded as opportunistic, become meaningful and systematic. This is also evident in the way decisions on the Middle East were formulated.

Very little is known of the foreign policy-making process in China. Yet, if we take the Middle East as an example, China's policy, within the framework mentioned above, was the result of the interaction of three major 'inputs': the basic analysis of the world situation; the interpretation of the situation in the Middle East in light of the basic analysis; and the domestic situation in China.

Despite the isolation imposed on them by the international community until the early 1970s, the Chinese always watched carefully and soberly what was going on in other parts of the world. As we have seen, the general analysis of the world situation has always provided the basis for China's Middle East policy. Very often it was made, in a brief but exhaustive manner, by Mao Tse-tung himself. Typically, he looked at the situation as a whole and perceived the fundamental trends in the world in a long-term and optimistic perspective.[4]

The analysis of the situation in the Middle East, although sometimes incorporated in Mao's general analysis, was usually made by other Chinese statesmen, notably Liu Shao-ch'i and Ch'en Yi, but particularly Chou En-lai. His regular 'reports' on the international situation and the work of the Government provided the link between theory and practice by applying Mao's general remarks about the international situation to the concrete circumstances in the Middle East (as well as other parts of the world) and by taking into account China's domestic needs.

The relationship between China's domestic situation, on the one hand, and its world outlook and foreign policy, on the other, is much more problematic. The Chinese themselves regarded this relationship as a two-way process:

Foreign policy is an extension or expansion of domestic policy, and it is impossible to have a foreign policy that is completely isolated from the domestic policy. It is closely co-ordinated with the economic, cultural and military policies. On the other hand, though the formulation of a foreign policy is based on the [domestic] character of the country concerned, it is also necessary to analyse the immediate international situation, i.e., to decide from this objective matter its diplomatic action and steps. Consequently, the foreign policy also affects in turn the domestic policy.[5]

The influence of each of the 'inputs' on the final product of China's Middle East policy varied. Usually, the analysis of the world situation was the predominant 'input' but sometimes the Middle East situation or China's domestic situation provided the major contribution to the decision-making process. For example, the events in the Middle East from early 1957 and throughout 1958 offered Peking the rationale for a re-evaluation of the world situation, which in turn affected China's foreign, as well as domestic, policy. In the mid-1950s, on the other hand, all three 'inputs' contributed to a tolerant and moderate policy of peaceful co-existence: the perceived relaxation in international tension caused by Western setbacks; the emergence of anti-imperialist tendencies in the Middle East; and China's Five Year Plan, which required a period of peaceful transition.

Finally, if we try to evaluate Chinese achievements in the Middle East in traditional terms of power politics, then China's Middle East policy must be admitted a complete failure. Yet, if we bear in mind that Peking has never sought direct involvement and presence in the Middle East, nor economic or other gains, the conclusion would be somewhat different.

As far as China's long-term ends are concerned, the Chinese had never anticipated easy and swift victories in the struggle against foreign intervention in the Middle East. For many years the Arab governments did not accept China's point of view and, when they had taken measures against imperialism or social-imperialism, this derived from local circumstances and pressures, and probably had nothing, or very little, to do with Chinese encouragement and support.

However, in recent years there have been indications that some Middle East governments have begun to grasp the nature of China's Middle East policy and the peculiarities of its attitudes as corresponding to their own interests. Considering the fact that, ever since relations with the Middle East were established, the Chinese have been unable to apply any kind of pressure on the local governments, this change should be regarded as an initial success.

THE MIDDLE EAST IN CHINA'S FOREIGN MINISTRY: STRUCTURE AND PERSONNEL

China's foreign policy has been implemented in the Middle East, as elsewhere, by many organisations and agencies. These include Friendship Associations; the Chinese People's Institute of Foreign Affairs; the Chinese People's Association for Friendship with Foreign Countries; the CCP International Liaison Department; the Foreign Affairs Bureau of the Ministry of National Defence; the New China News Agency; and so on. As implied by their names, each of these organisations has a separate and specific function in China's foreign relations system. However, the main burden falls naturally on China's Ministry of Foreign Affairs.

The purpose of this Appendix is to supplement background information on the departments and officials connected with China's Middle East policy, some of whom have already been discussed in this study. The additional information reaffirms the remarkable degree of flexibility of the Foreign Ministry and its adaptability, in terms of both structure and personal qualifications, to the changes in China's world outlook and Middle Eastern policy.

The data were assembled from scattered references in China's press and NCNA reports, as well as from biographical compilations which complemented one another.

Note. In this Appendix PE refers to previous experience and LE to later experience.

DEPARTMENTS

First period: Department of West Asia and Africa
(September 1956–September 1964)

DIRECTORS

K'o Hua (September 1956–January 1960)
  PE: Director, Department of Protocol (March 1955–September 1956)
  LE: Ambassador, Guinea (March 1960–May 1964)
         Director, Department of Africa (September 1964–July 1967)
         Ambassador, Ghana (September 1972–August 1974)
         Director, Department of Asia (April 1975–December 1975)
         Ambassador, the Philippines (December 1975–April 1978)
         Ambassador, Britain (September 1978–   )

Ho Ying (January 1960–February 1962)
- PE: Counsellor, Indonesia (January 1952–October 1952).
  Deputy Director, Department of Asia (October 1952–September 1954)
  Ambassador, Mongolia (September 1954–September 1958)
  Deputy Director, Department of Asia I (March 1959–January 1960)
- LE: Ambassador, Tanganyika (February 1962–July 1964)
  Ambassador, Uganda (April 1963–April 1964)
  Ambassador, Tanzania (July 1964–1967)
  Director, Department of West Asia and Africa (September 1970–April 1972)
  Vice Foreign Minister (April 1972–   )

Wang Yü-t'ien (June 1962–January 1964)
- PE: Attaché and chargé d'affaires, East Germany (1953–1956)
  Deputy Director, Department of Protocol (August 1956–January 1958)
  Director, Department of Protocol (February 1958–January 1959)
  Director, Department of the Soviet Union and Eastern Europe (January 1959–June 1959)
  Ambassador, the Sudan (June 1959–March 1962)
- LE: Ambassador, Kenya (February 1964–1967)
  Ambassador, Congo-Brazzaville (June 1969–December 1972)
  Ambassador, West Germany (February 1973–September 1974)

DEPUTY DIRECTORS

Ho Kung-k'ai (September 1956–June 1963)
- PE: Deputy Director, Department of West Europe and Africa (?–August 1956)
- LE: Counsellor and chargé d'affaires, Egypt (August 1963–1967)
  Deputy Director, Department of West Asia and Africa (July 1970–August 1972)
  Director, Department of Africa (August 1972–   )

Kung Ta-fei (July 1959–August 1960)
- PE: First Secretary, Burma (August 1953–1957)
- LE: Counsellor, Morocco (August 1960–1963)
  Deputy Director, Department of West Asia Africa (September 1963–September 1964)
  Deputy Director, Department of Africa (September 1964–1969)
  Deputy Director, Department of West Asia and Africa (October 1969–December 1970)
  Ambassador, Iraq (December 1970–December 1972)
  Ambassador, Zaïre (January 1973–July 1978)

Meng Ying (March 1961–March 1964)
- PE: Counsellor, Mongolia (1956–1961)
- LE: Ambassador, Zanzibar (March 1964–July 1964)
  Deputy Director, Department of Africa (September–December 1964)
  Ambassador, Central African Republic (December 1964–1966)

Li Chün (August 1961–January 1962)
- PE: Unknown
- LE: Counsellor, Tanganyika and Uganda (1962–?)

Hsieh Feng (October 1962–September 1964)

PE: Deputy Director, General Office of the Foreign Ministry (1956)
        Counsellor, Hungary (1956–1962)
LE: Deputy Director, Department of Africa (September 1964–?April
        1967)
Kung Ta-fei (September 1963–September 1964)
    See above
Lin Chao-nan (April 1964–September 1964)
PE: Counsellor and chargé d'affaires, Egypt (1956–1964)
LE: Deputy Director, Department of West Asia and North Africa
        (September 1964–December 1967, October 1975–)
        Alternate Representative, UN (September–November 1977)

ASSISTANT DIRECTORS

Shih Ku (January 1961–June 1963)
PE: Deputy Chief, China's Trade Agency in Syria (August 1956–
        December 1958)
        Consul General, Damascus (December 1958–April 1960)
LE: Counsellor, Tanganyika (June 1963–?February 1965)

Second period: Department of West Asia and North Africa
      (September 1964–October 1969)

DIRECTORS

Ch'en Ch'u (September 1964–January 1966)
PE: Director, Department of the Soviet Union and Eastern Europe
        (1955)
        Counsellor and attaché, Soviet Union (January 1956–1963)
LE: Ambassador, Ghana (January 1966–November 1966).
        Director, Department of Information (August 1970–October
        1971)
        Deputy Permanent Representative, UN (November 1971–
        December 1972)
        Ambassador, Japan (February 1973–April 1977)
        Permanent Representative, UN (May 1977–)

DEPUTY DIRECTORS

Lin Chao-nan (September 1964–December 1967)
    See above
Ch'en T'an (April 1965–January 1966)
PE: ?Director, General Office, Ministry of Railways (1959)
LE: Ambassador, Syria (January 1966–April 1967)
        Ambassador, Guinea (March 1971–August 1974)
Wang Jen-san (September 1964–?April 1966)
PE: Deputy Director, Propaganda Department, Kiangsu CP
        Committee (1958–1961)
        First Secretary, Suchow CP Committee (1961–?1964)
LE: Ambassador, Chad (April 1973–May 1977)
        Ambassador, Liberia (July 1977–)
Chao Yüan (May 1967–September 1969)
PE: Counsellor and chargé d'affaires, Guinea (December 1959–1963)
LE: Deputy Director, ?Department of West Asia and Africa (October
        1969–?)
        Deputy Director, Department of Africa (April 1973–1975)

Chargé d'affaires, Mozambique (June 1975–1977)
Ambassador, Mauritania (May 1978–   )

Third period: Department of West Asia and Africa
(October 1969–August 1972)

DIRECTORS
Ho Ying (September 1970–April 1972)
    See above

DEPUTY DIRECTORS
Ho Kung-k'ai (July 1970–August 1972)
    See above
Kung Ta-fei (October 1969–December 1970)
    See above
Chao Yuän (October 1969–?)
    See above.
Chou Chüeh (November 1970–August 1972)
    PE: Unknown
    LE: Deputy Director, Department of West Asia and North Africa
            (August 1972–August 1974)
            Acting Director, Department of West Asia and North Africa
            (August 1974–   )
Ts'ui Chien (May 1972–July 1972)
    PE: Unknown
    LE: Ambassador, South Yemen (August 1972–May 1977)
            Ambassador, Tunisia (August 1977–   )
Chang Shu (January 1972–May 1972)
    PE: First Secretary and chargé d'affaires, Iraq (April 1965–December
            1971)
    LE: Deputy Director, Department of Political and Security Council
            Affairs, Permanent Mission, UN (April 1973–   )

OTHER OFFICIALS
Chu Ch'i-chen (October 1971–August 1972)
    PE: First Secretary, Egypt (January 1965–?)
    LE: Deputy Director, Department of West Asia and North Africa
            (August 1972–?January 1973)
            Minister and chargé d'affaires, Australia (1973–1977)
            Deputy Director, Department of America and Oceania (June
            1977–   )
Chao Wei (October 1970–October 1971)
    PE: Consul, Calcutta (August 1956–January 1960)
            Attaché, Tanganyika and Tanzania (October 1962–?)
    LE: Secretary, PRC delegation to UN (November 1971–   )
Chu Hsien-sung (November 1971–?August 1972)
    No details available
Lin Ai-li (October 1970–August 1972)
    PE: Unknown
    LE: Deputy Director, Department of West Asia and North Africa
            (August 1972–?July 1974)
            Chargé d'affaires, Iran (February 1976–   )

*Fourth period: Department of West Asia and North Africa
(August 1972–   )*

DIRECTORS

Ts'ao K'o-ch'iang (August 1972–August 1974)
PE: Counsellor, North Korea (January 1956–May 1960)
        Deputy Director, Department of Asia II (February 1961–January
        1970)
        Deputy Director, Department of Asia (April 1970–March 1971)
LE: Ambassador, Syria (August 1974–   )

ACTING DIRECTOR

Chou Chüeh (August 1974–   )
        See above

DEPUTY DIRECTORS

Chou Chüeh (August 1972–August 1974)
        See above
Ch'eng Yuan-hsing (September 1974–   )
        No details available
Wang P'u-ch'ing (October 1973–November 1974)
PE: First Secretary, Finland (July 1958–November 1959)
        Cultural Counsellor, Cuba (June 1964–1965)
        Deputy Director, China–Latin America Friendship Association
        (1966–?)
LE: Counsellor and chargé d'affaires, Syria (January 1975–   )
Lin Ai-li (August 1972–?July 1974)
        See above
Lin Chao-nan (October 1975–   )
        See above
Chu Ch'i-chen (August 1972–?January 1973)
        See above
Wen Yeh-chan (June 1976–   )
PE: Attaché, the Sudan (July 1959–?)
        Deputy Director, Department of Africa (December 1972–
        November 1973)

AMBASSADORS

EGYPT

Ch'en Chia-k'ang (June 1956–December 1965)
PE: Deputy Director, Department of Asia (May 1950–August 1952)
        Director, Department of Asia (August 1952–1954)
        Assistant Foreign Minister (?November 1954–June 1956)
LE: Vice Foreign Minister (January 1966–?)
        Disappeared during the Cultural Revolution
Huang Hua (January 1966–June 1969)
PE: Director, Department of West Europe and Africa (October 1954–
        September 1956)
        Director, Department of West Europe (September 1956–January
        1959)
        Ambassador, Ghana (August 1960–December 1965)

LE: Ambassador, Canada (July 1971–November 1971)
          Permanent Representative, UN (November 1971–November 1976)
          Foreign Minister (December 1976–   )

Ch'ai Tse-min (June 1970–September 1974)

PE: Director, Communications Department, Peking Municipal CP
          Committee (1959–1960)
          Ambassador, Hungary (May 1961–July 1964)
          Ambassador, Guinea (August 1964–1967)

LE: President, Chinese People's Association for Friendship with
          Foreign Countries (September 1974–August 1975)
          Ambassador, Thailand (January 1976–May 1978)
          Chief Liaison Officer, USA (May 1978–   )

Chang T'ung (September 1974–May 1977)

PE: Colonel, Military Attaché, India (August 1956–1960)
          Chargé d'affaires, Congo-Stanleyville (July 1961–September 1961)
          Deputy Director, Department of Asia I (May 1962–September 1964)
          Director, Department of Asia I (September 1964–1967)
          Ambassador, Pakistan (June 1969–August 1974)

LE: Ambassador, West Germany (August 1977–   )

Yao Kuang (July 1977–   )

PE: Counsellor, Poland (November 1957–October 1963)
          Deputy Director, Department of Asia II (April 1964–August 1964)
          Director, Department of Asia II (August 1964–?1969)
          Ambassador, Poland (August 1970–December 1971)
          Ambassador, Canada (February 1972–September 1973)
          Ambassador, Mexico (September 1973–May 1977)

SYRIA

Ch'en Chih-fang (October 1956–February 1958)

PE: Deputy Mayor, Canton (January 1955–April 1956)

LE: Ambassador, Iraq (August 1958–September 1960)
          Director, College of Diplomacy (June 1962–February 1964)
          ?Vice President, Chinese People's Institute of Foreign Affairs
          (June 1962–?1964)
          Ambassador, Uganda (April 1964–1967)
          Ambassador, Switzerland (December 1970–August 1975)
          Ambassador, Vietnam (September 1977–   )

Hsü Yi-hsin (March 1962–December 1965)

PE: Deputy Director, Department of the Soviet Union and Eastern
          Europe (June 1950–August 1952)
          Director, Department of the Soviet Union and Eastern Europe
          (August 1952–June 1954)
          Ambassador, Albania (June 1954–May 1957)
          Ambassador, Norway (April 1958–March 1962)

LE: Vice Foreign Minister (January 1966–November 1970)

Ch'en T'an (January 1966–April 1967)

PE: ?Director, General Office, Ministry of Railways (1959)
          Deputy Director, Department of West Asia and North Africa
          (April 1965–January 1966)

LE: Ambassador, Guinea (March 1971–August 1974)

Ch'in Chia-lin (June 1969–May 1974)

PE: Chargé d'affaires and Counsellor, London (June 1957–October
          1962)

Deputy Director, Information Department (October 1962–1964)
Director, Information Department (March 1965–1969)
LE: Director, Department of Information (1974–?1976)
Ambassador, Denmark (August 1977–   )

Ts'ao K'o-ch'iang (August 1974–   )
PE: Counsellor, North Korea (January 1956–May 1960)
Deputy Director, Department of Asia II (February 1961–January 1970)
Deputy Director, Department of Asia (April 1970–March 1971)
Director, Department of West Asia and North Africa (August 1972–August 1974)

YEMEN

Wang Jo-chieh (February 1964–January 1967, July 1969–December 1972)
PE: Director, Political Department, Chekiang Military District (November 1955–January 1960)
Major General (January 1960–   )
LE: Ambassador, South Vietnam Provisional Revolutionary Government (June 1973–?1976)
Ambassador, Mauritius (September 1977–)

Chang Ts'an-ming (February 1973–July 1975)
PE: Deputy Director, East China Office of Trade Unions (February 1952–October 1955)
Director, Consular Department (October 1955–May 1957)
Ambassador, Ceylon (May 1957–August 1962)
Ambassador, Mongolia (September 1963–1966)
LE: Ambassador, Finland (September 1975–   )

Chao Chin (September 1975–   )
PE: Counsellor, Mongolia (1960–1964)
Ambassador, Bulgaria (March 1971–July 1975)

IRAQ

Ch'en Chih-fang (August 1958–September 1960)
See *Syria*.

Chang Wei-lieh (September 1960–December 1965)
PE: Second Secretary, CP Committee Hainan (1955–1956)
Counsellor, Soviet Union (October 1956–1959)
LE: Vice Chairman, PRC–Cuba Friendship Association (July 1970–?)
Ambassador, Morocco (February 1971–May 1974)
Ambassador, Mongolia (October 1974–April 1978)
Ambassador, Thailand (July 1978–   )

Ts'ao Ch'ih (January 1966–May 1967)
PE: Mayor and CP Secretary, Ch'angsha (1949–1964)
Director, United Front Work Department, Hunan CP Committee (1960–?)
LE: Ambassador, Nepal (September 1972–November 1977)
Ambassador, Cyprus (December 1977–   )

Kung Ta-fei (December 1970–December 1972)
PE: First Secretary, Burma (August 1953–?1957)
Deputy Director, Department of West Asia and Africa (July 1959–August 1960)
Counsellor, Morocco (August 1960–1963)
Deputy Director, Department of West Asia and Africa (September 1963–September 1964)

Deputy Director, Department of Africa (September 1964–1969)
Deputy Director, Department of West Asia and Africa (October 1969–December 1970)
LE: Ambassador, Zaïre (January 1973–July 1978)
Hu Ch'eng-fang (February 1973–May 1974)
PE: Deputy Director, Department of Asia I (September 1960–November 1962)
Counsellor, Czechoslovakia (December 1962–1966)
LE: Ambassador, Chile (March 1978–   )
Chao Hsing-chih (August 1974–November 1976)
PE: Consul General, Geneva (April 1963–January 1971)
? in the Department of West Asia and Africa (February 1971–May 1971)
Ambassador, Cameroon (August 1971–May 1974)
LE: Vice Chairman, Shanghai Municipal Revolutionary Committee (February 1977–   )
Hou Yeh-feng (September 1977–   )
PE: Member, Council of the China-Japan Friendship Association (October 1963–?1965)
Deputy Director, Department of Africa (November 1965–?)
Ambassador, Tunisia (February 1972–May 1977)

SOUTH YEMEN

Li Ch'iang-fen (December 1970–June 1972)
PE: Director, Liaoning Provincial Office of Foreign Affairs (June 1955–?1959)
Deputy Director, Department of Asia II (April 1959–1960)
Chargé d'affaires and Counsellor, Yemen (May 1961–?1967)
Chargé d'affaires, South Yemen (July 1969–December 1970)
LE: Ambassador, Zambia 1972–September 1977)
Ts'ui Chien (August 1972–May 1977)
PE: Deputy Director, Department of West Asia and Africa (May 1972–July 1972)
LE: Ambassador, Tunisia (August 1977–   )
Huang Shih-hsieh (November 1977–   )
PE: Counsellor, Ghana (1965–1966)
Ambassador, Rwanda (June 1972–August 1977)

KUWAIT

Sun Sheng-wei (August 1971–May 1977)
PE: Counsellor, Burma (April 1960–October 1970)
LE: Ambassador, Sri Lanka (June 1977–   ) and the Maldives (October 1977–   )
Ting Hao (September 1977–   )
PE: Member, 3rd CC, Chinese Communist Youth League (1957)
Counsellor and chargé d'affaires, Denmark (September 1964–1968)
?Deputy Director, Department of West Europe (?)
Counsellor and chargé d'affaires, Chile (January 1971–March 1973)

TURKEY

Liu Ch'un (May 1972–May 1976)

PE: Chargé d'affaires, Laos (July 1962–September 1962)
Ambassador, Laos (September 1962–January 1967)
Director, Department of Asia (October 1969–March 1972)
LE: Ambassador, Tanzania (May 1976–) and the Seychelles (April 1978–)
Wei Yung-ch'ing (May 1976–September 1978)
PE: Assistant Director, Department of Protocol (June 1962–March 1965)
Chargé d'affaires, Mauritania (September 1965–February 1969)
Member, Council of the Chinese People's Institute of Foreign Affairs (September 1971–)
Chargé d'affaires, Ghana (June 1972–1976)

IRAN

Ch'en Hsin-jen (March 1972–November 1974)
PE: Ambassador, Finland (1954–1958)
President, Chinese People's Institute of Foreign Affairs (December 1958–November 1961)
Deputy Director, College of Diplomacy (November 1961–?)
Member, Chinese People's Institute of Foreign Affairs (September 1971)
LE: Ambassador, The Netherlands (January 1975–July 1978)
Ambassador, Philippines (September 1978–)
Hao Te-ch'ing (December 1974–January 1977)
PE: Secretary, CP Committee, Ch'engtu (1954)
Ambassador, Hungary (September 1954–April 1961)
Ambassador, North Korea (July 1961–November 1965)
Deputy Director, General Office of Foreign Affairs (November 1965–?)
Vice Chairman, Commission for Cultural Relations with Foreign Countries (April 1966–?)
Ambassador, Norway (February 1971–September 1972)
Ambassador, The Netherlands (October 1972–October 1974)
LE: President, Chinese People's Institute of Foreign Affairs (March 1977–)
Chiao Jo-yü (February 1977–)
PE: Deputy Mayor, Shenyang (November 1948–August 1954)
Secretary, Shenyang Municipal CP Committee (August 1954–1965)
Political Commissar, Shenyang Military District (June 1960–1965)
Ambassador, North Korea (November 1965–1967)
Ambassador, Peru (December 1971–January 1977)

LEBANON

Hsü Ming (March 1972–September 1978)
PE: Counsellor, East Germany (January 1955–August 1960)
Deputy Director, Department of the Soviet Union and Eastern Europe (May 1960–1964)
Commercial Representative, Italy (February 1965–1966)
Council Member, PRC–Japan Friendship Association (July 1970–February 1972)
Member, Council for Promotion of International Trade (1971)
Representative, PRC–Japan Memorandum Trade Office (February 1971–December 1971)

CYPRUS

Tai Lu (August 1972–October 1977)
    PE: First Secretary, North Vietnam (June 1959–July 1960)
           ? in the Department of Asia II (September 1961–1962)
           First Secretary, Economic and Cultural Mission, Laos (January
               1962–February 1963)
           Chargé d'affaires, Laos (March 1963–1965)
           Counsellor, North Korea (September 1971–March 1972)
    LE: Ambassador, Uganda (March 1978–)
Ts'ao Ch'ih (December 1977–)
           See *Iraq*

JORDAN

Ku Hsiao-po (December 1977–)
    PE: Member, Presidium, 8th Executive Committee, All-China
           Federation of Trade Unions (December 1957)
           Deputy, 2nd NPC (April 1959)
           Ambassador, the Sudan (April 1962–November 1965)
           Ambassador, Benin (June 1973–October 1977)

SOURCES

Wolfgang Bartke, 'The Diplomatic Service of the People's Republic of China', *Mitteilungen des Instituts für Asienkunde* (Hamburg), nos. 20 (1967) 46 (1972), 53 (1973), 64 (1975).
    'Die Strukturellen und Personellen Komponenten der Chinesischen Aussenpolitik', in Erik von Groeling and Marie-Luise Näth (eds.), *Die Aussenpolitik Chinas* (München: R. Oldenbourg Verlag, 1975), pp. 189–220.
Chinese Communist Who's Who (Taipei: Institute of International Relations, 1970–1).
Directory of Chinese Communist Officials, no. A 66–B, March 1966 (US Government publication).
Gendai chūgoku jinmei jiten (*A Biographical Dictionary of Contemporary Chinese*) (Tokyo: Kazan Kai, 1966).
Institute of Asian Affairs, Hamburg, *China Aktuell* (monthly).
Donald W. Klein, 'Sources for Elite Studies and Biographical Material on China', in Robert A. Scalapino (ed.), *Elites in the People's Republic of China* (Seattle: University of Washington Press, 1972), pp. 609–56.
    'The Men and Institutions Behind China's Foreign Policy', in Roderick MacFarquhar (ed.), *Sino-American Relations 1949–1971* (Newton Abbot: David and Charles, 1972), pp. 43–56.
    and Anne B. Clark, *Biographic Dictionary of Chinese Communism, 1921–1965* (Cambridge, Mass.: Harvard University Press, 1971).
Malcolm Lamb, *Directory of Central Officials in the People's Republic of China, 1968–1975* (Australian National University, Contemporary China Papers no. 10, 1976).
Union Research Institute, Hong Kong, *Biographical Service*.
United States Department of State, Bureau of Intelligence and Research, *Directory of Party and Government Officials of Communist China*, Biographical Directory no. 271, 2 vols. (Washington D.C., 20 July 1960).
Who's Who in Communist China, revised edn, 2 vols. (Hong Kong: Union Research Institute, 1969 and 1970).

THE MIDDLE EAST IN CHINA'S ECONOMIC RELATIONS

China's relations with the Middle East provide one of the best examples of the use of economic policies for political ends. The primary motive for China's continued interest in the Middle East was to mobilise and encourage the local peoples and governments to resist imperialism, social-imperialism, or both. Economic considerations probably played an extremely marginal role in this interest, if any. Although China has maintained economic relations with the Middle East since the early 1950s, these relations have been uneven and correlated not so much with the fluctuations of the Chinese economy as with those of China's Middle East policy.

China's economic relations in the Middle East have been treated in this study along with, and as part of, the political changes. The purpose of this appendix is to provide a more general picture of these relations with the Middle East and a comparison between these relations and China's economic relations with other groups of developing countries.

Trade

China's trade with the Middle East, apart from its (limited) economic value, had an important dual political function. Trade relations with countries which had not yet recognised the PRC were exploited as sub-diplomatic ties to bypass the question of recognition and at the same time create a favourable atmosphere for it. 'Under international custom, trade treaties and agreements can be conducted between two states which have not yet established diplomatic relations. Therefore, concluding trade treaties and agreements can lay the groundwork for the establishment of diplomatic relations. China's [diplomatic] relations with Ceylon and Egypt were developed in this way.'[1] More recent examples of this practice are Kuwait, the Lebanon and Jordan which had maintained extensive trade relations with Peking, which exceeded those with Taiwan, long before they decided to recognise the PRC.

The other function of China's Middle East trade, particularly imports, was to enlist Arab goodwill and support. Egypt, which the Chinese have usually regarded as a key government, not only in the Middle East but in Africa and the Afro-Asian context as well, provides the best example of China's political manipulation of economic relations.

In 1957–60, China's trade with Egypt reached an annual average of more than $61 million, approximately one-third in exports and two-thirds in imports. In other words, in order to consolidate their political position the Chinese were ready to sell less and buy more, not necessarily according to their economic needs. The negative trade balance they accumulated in these years reflected the relatively friendly relations between the two countries.

However, as soon as Sino-Egyptian relations deteriorated, trade patterns changed. In 1961–4 China's trade with Egypt fell to an annual average of $37 million, of which more than half was exports and less than half imports. In other words, when the Arab governments rejected China's Middle East policies the Chinese reacted, among other things, by cutting their trade, particularly imports. Again, the case of Egypt is outstanding: China's imports decreased drastically from $44.5 million in 1960 to $14.6 million in 1961.

This trend was reversed in the mid-1960s. Whereas in 1964 Chinese imports from Egypt were still as low as $16.7 million, they jumped to $45.1 million in 1965, reflecting China's efforts to win the support of the Arab governments for the convention of the second Afro-Asian conference. In 1965–6, Sino-Egyptian trade reached an annual average of more than $72 million, twice the annual average of the previous four years.

During the Cultural Revolution trade dropped yet again. It was resumed as a part of China's attempts since 1969 to restore relations with the Middle East governments. However, it was only in 1972, when China's interest in these governments became explicit, that its trade with Egypt approached the volume of the 1965–6 period. In March 1972, a Chinese trade delegation headed by Pai Hsiang-kuo, Minister of Foreign Trade, came to Cairo to sign the annual trade agreements. Considering the fact that a year earlier Sino-Egyptian trade had constituted less than one per cent of China's total foreign trade, the visit should be interpreted in the political rather than the economic context.

China's economic policy in the Middle East after the Cultural Revolution became more rational and 'economic'. The establishment of diplomatic ties boosted already existing economic relations, particularly China's exports: these increased steadily from about $80 million in 1970–1, to $125 million in 1972 (50 per cent increase), $175 million in 1973 (40 per cent), and about $300 million in 1974–5 (70 per cent). On the basis of this policy, China gradually succeeded in eliminating the $150 million deficit accumulated in its Middle East trade before 1965–6. In fact, in 1972–5, China's exports to the Middle East surpassed imports by more than $400 million.

Still, despite the improvement in absolute terms in China's Middle East trade, its volume relative to the growth of China's total trade has constantly declined. In 1957 China's trade with non-communist countries reached $1,090 million, about 30 per cent of China's total trade. The share of the Middle East was 7 per cent. In 1965, when China's trade with non-communist countries was 2.5 times larger than in 1957 ($2,570 million), the share of the Middle East dropped to 5 per cent. In the mid-1970s, China's trade with non-communist countries constituted more than 80 per cent of its total trade, yet the Middle East share fell to 3–4 per cent. However, its share in China's trade with developing countries, which declined from 17 per cent in 1968 to 12 per cent in 1970 and to 8 per cent in 1971, reached 14 per cent in 1974.

Aid

If China's trade with the Middle East has greater political than economic significance then even more so has its aid policy. Until 1963, Chinese aid offers to the Arab countries amounted to the very modest sum of $18 million, extended to Egypt (in 1956), and the Yemen (in 1958–9). Then in 1963–4 China agreed to give Arab countries $125 million in loans, an unprecedented offer which was undoubtedly meant to win Arab goodwill for the Afro-Asian conference. As we have seen, this gesture did not persuade the Arabs to support China's demands, and Sino-Arab relations deteriorated further.

In fact the Arabs, and particularly Egypt, which had been offered the largest loan of 345 million Swiss francs ($80 million), were very reluctant to use Chinese aid. Moreover, it seems that the Chinese themselves, disappointed by the Arabs and preoccupied with the Cultural Revolution, were in no hurry to fulfil their promises. In January 1969, the four-year period within which the $80 million aid offer to Egypt had to be used expired, and the loan remained unused. China then agreed to change the conditions and extended the offer for another three years, to the end of 1971.[2] However, in March 1971 the Egyptians revealed that only 45 million out of the 1964 offer (about 13 per cent) had, in fact, been used.[3] There was no further progress until 26 June 1973 when a Sino-Egyptian protocol for building a sand brick factory was signed. In 1976, following the Sino-Egyptian *rapprochement*, the 1964 loan began to be extensively exploited.[4] Still, by early 1977, only 162.3 million Swiss francs had been used, with 182.7 million left. Other Arab countries were also slow in using China's aid offers.

Whereas in terms of offers Egypt is still the largest recipient of Chinese aid, in terms of consumption the Yemen and the PDRY have been the primary beneficiaries of Chinese aid in the Middle East. In both countries China has been engaged in extensive road-building in addition to textile enterprises and medical, educational and agricultural aid. Chinese aid was particularly successful in these countries not only because of the generous terms (loans are usually free of interest with a long grace period and could be repaid in local currency or even goods), but also because the Chinese, unlike the Soviets, adapted themselves to the local way of life, maintained a low living standard and never refused hard work.

These principles of foreign aid, which had been first formulated in 1964,[5] were reiterated by Vice Premier Teng Hsiao-p'ing in his speech at the Special Session of the United Nations General Assembly in April 1974:

We hold that economic aid to the developing countries must strictly respect the sovereignty of the recipient countries and must not be accompanied by any political or military conditions and the extortion of any special privileges or excessive profits. Loans to the developing countries should be interest-free or low-interest and allow for delayed repayment of capital and interest, or even reduction and cancellation of debts in case of necessity. We are opposed to the exploitation of developing countries by usury or blackmail in the name of aid.

We hold that technology transferred to the developing countries must be practical, efficient, economical and convenient for use. The experts and other personnel dispatched to the recipient countries have the obligation to pass on conscientiously technical know-how to the people there and to respect the laws and national customs of the countries concerned. They must not make special demands or ask for special amenities, let alone engage in illegal activities.[6]

Altogether the Middle East's share in China's aid offers was rather small, except for 1964 and 1976 when about one-third of China's total aid was offered to Arab countries. In 1970, still a record year for China's aid offers ($709 million, some 20 per cent of China's total aid offers to 1976), the share of the Middle East was merely 6 per cent, compared with Africa's 64 per cent and Asia's 30 per cent. Since then, China's aid offers have declined steadily, to a level of $88 million in 1976. The Middle East share was 31 per cent ($27 million offered to the Yemen). In the previous two years it had not been offered any Chinese aid. Apparently, the reduction in China's aid offers is also related to a more rational approach to economics in general and economic relations in particular. In the words of Vice Premier Li Hsien-nien: 'It is our bounden internationalist duty to provide such aid as we can to Third World countries. However, since China is also a developing country with limited capabilities, our aid is but modest. With the further development of our socialist revolution and construction, we hope we shall make a greater contribution.'[7]

Finally, although China's aid to the Arab countries as a whole is very small, 8 per cent compared with 52 per cent by the Soviet Union and 40 per cent by Eastern Europe, it is considerable in the case of the Yemen and particularly of South Yemen, where China's aid offers almost equal those of the Soviet Union and Eastern Europe together.

Table 3. *China's trade with developing countries, 1968–75: the share of the Middle East (in million US dollars and per cent)*

	1968		1969		1970		1971		1972		1973		1974		1975	
	$	%	$	%	$	%	$	%	$	%	$	%	$	%	$	%
Middle East	120	17	125	9	121	10	125	9	181	10	274	10	518	14	418	11
Asia	403	58	952	70	886	70	906	62	1,054	59	1,816	64	2,147	56	2,320	61
Africa	162	23	278	20	235	19	370	25	373	21	530	19	698	18	721	19
Latin America	11	2	11	1	10	1	50	4	175	10	202	7	449	12	317	9
Total	696	100	1,366	100	1,252	100	1,451	100	1,783	100	2,822	100	3,812	100	3,776	100

Table 4. *China's aid offers to the Middle East, 1956–76 (in million US dollars)*

	1956	1958	1959	1963	1964	1967	1968	1970	1971	1972	1973	1976	Total	%
Egypt	4.7				80.0	21.0					28.0		133.7	35
Syria				16.3						45.0			61.3	16
Yemen		12.7	0.7	0.2	28.5					21.0	1.0	27.0	91.1	24
South Yemen							12.0	43.0					55.0	14
Iraq									40.0				40.0	11
Total	4.7	12.7	0.7	16.5	108.5	21.0	12.0	43.0	40.0	66.0	29.0	27.0	381.1	100

Table 5. *China's aid offers to developing countries, 1956–76: the share of the Middle East (in million US dollars and per cent)*

	1956–65		1956–76		1964		1970		1971		1972		1973		1974		1975		1976	
	$	%	$	%	$	%	$	%	$	%	$	%	$	%	$	%	$	%	$	%
Middle East	143	17	381	10	109	32	43	6	40	8.5	66	13	29	7	–	–	–	–	27	31
Asia	483	51	1,027	28	114	34	212	30	89	19	89	18	64	15	25	13	81	30	3	3
Africa	269	32	2,068	57	115	34	454	64	295	63	210	42	335	78	172	87	182	67	57	65
Latin America	–	–	144	4	–	–	–	–	44	9.5	89	18	–	–	–	–	10	3	1	1
Europe	–	–	45	1	–	–	–	–	–	–	45	9	–	–	–	–	–	–	–	–
Total	845	100	3,665	100	338	100	709	100	468	100	499	100	428	100	197	100	273	100	88	100

Table 6. *Aid offers by communist countries to the Middle East,
1954–76: the Chinese share (in million US dollars and
per cent)*

	China	%	Eastern Europe	%	USSR	%	Total	%
Egypt	134	6	796	36	1,300	58	2,230	100
Syria	61	5	778	59	467	36	1,306	100
Iraq	40	4	419	36	699	60	1,158	100
Yemen	91	44	17	8	98	48	206	100
South Yemen	55	48	21	18	39	34	115	100
Total	381	8	2,031	40	2,603	52	5,015	100

SOURCES TO TABLES

Robert Loring Allen, *Middle Eastern Economic Relations with the Soviet Union, Eastern Europe, and Mainland China* (Charlottesville, Virginia: Woodrow Wilson Department of Foreign Affairs, University of Virginia, 1958).

Wolfgang Bartke, *China's Economic Aid* (London: C. Hurst and Co., 1975).

Nai-Ruenn Chen, 'China's Foreign Trade, 1950–74', in Joint Economic Committee, Congress of the United States, *China: A Reassessment of the Economy* (Washington: US Government Printing Office, 1975), pp. 617–52.

Chiang Tao, 'Chung-kung tui Ya-Fei kuo-chia ti ching-chi yüan-chu' ('Communist China's Economic Aid to Asian–African Countries'), *Fei-ch'ing yen-chiu (Studies on Chinese Communism)* (Taipei), vol. I, no. 2 (February 1967), pp. 65–75.

'China's Foreign Aid', *China News Summary*, no. 338 (24 September 1970).

China Trade Report, Hong Kong (monthly).

John F. Copper, *China's Foreign Aid* (Lexington, Mass.: Lexington Books, 1976).

Alexander Eckstein, *Communist China's Economic Growth and Foreign Trade* (New York: McGraw-Hill, 1966).

Far Eastern Economic Review, Hong Kong (weekly).

Carol H. Fogarty, 'China's Economic Relations With the Third World', in Joint Economic Committee, Congress of the United States, *China: A Reassessment of the Economy* (Washington: US Government Printing Office, 1975), pp. 730–7.

Sydney Klein, 'China's Trade and Aid Relations with Africa and the Middle East, 1951–1966', *China Mainland Review*, vol. II, supplement (June 1967), pp. 357–68.

Politics versus Economics – the Foreign Trade and Aid Policies of China (Hong Kong: International Study Group, 1968).

Milton Kovner, 'Communist China's Foreign Aid to Less-Developed Countries', in Joint Economic Committee, Congress of the United States, *An Economic Profile of Mainland China*, vol. II (Washington: US Government Printing Office, 1967), pp. 609–20.

Robert L. Price, 'International Trade of Communist China, 1950–1965', in Joint Economic Committee, Congress of the United States, *An Economic*

Profile of Mainland China, vol. II (Washington: US Government Printing Office, 1967), pp. 579–608.

Special Focus, 'Focal Points in China's Foreign Aid', *Asia Research Bulletin*, 1–31 July 1972.

Leo Tansky, 'Chinese Foreign Aid', in Joint Economic Committee, Congress of the United States, *People's Republic of China: An Economic Assessment* (Washington: US Government Printing Office, 1972), pp. 371–82.

United Nations, *Yearbook of International Trade Statistics* (annual).

United States Government, Department of State, Bureau of Intelligence and Research, *Communist States and Developing Countries: Aid and Trade* (annual).

A. H. Usack and R. E. Batsavage, 'The International Trade of the People's Republic of China', in Joint Economic Committee, Congress of the United States, *People's Republic of China: An Economic Assessment* (Washington: US Government Printing Office, 1972), pp. 335–70.

NOTES

PREFACE

1 ' "Chung-tung" ho "Chin-tung" ' (' "Middle East" and "Near East" '), *Shih-chieh chih-shih* (*World Knowledge*) (hereafter *SCCS*), no. 23 (December 1951), p. 9.
2 *Ibid.*
3 *Chung-chin-tung lieh-kuo chih* (*Records of the Middle and Near Eastern Countries*) (Peking: Shih-chieh chih-shih she, 1956), p. 1.

CHAPTER 1

1 See for example: [Chang] Han-fu, 'Ying-Yi chan-cheng yü chin-tung' ('The Anglo-Iraqi War and the Near East'), *Hsin-hua jih-pao* (*New China Daily*), 7 May 1941; Ju Shui, 'Yi-la-k'o tsai Ying-kuo ching-chi shang ti chung-yao hsing' ('The Importance of Iraq in Britain's Economy'), *ibid.*, 13 May 1941; and the following editorials in *Chieh-fang jih-pao* (*Liberation Daily*): 'Ti-chung-hai ti hsing-shih' ('The Situation in the Mediterranean'), 19 May 1941; 'Chin-tung chan-cheng k'uo-ta' ('The Near East War Spreads'), 22 May 1941; 'Ti-chung-hai feng-huo yü T'ai-p'ing-yang an-yun' ('The Mediterranean's Warning Fire and the Dark Clouds of the Pacific'), 11 June 1941.
2 Ch'iao Mu (Ch'iao Kuan-hua), 'Kuo-chi hsin hsing-shih' ('A New International Situation'), *Ta-chung sheng-huo* (*Public Life*) (Hong Kong), no. 1 (17 May 1941), pp. 7–8.
3 Editorial, 'Ch'ing k'an chin-jih chih yü-chung, ching-shih shui-chia chih t'ien-hsia' ('Please Look at the World Today and to Whom it Really Belongs'), *Chieh-fang jih-pao*, 18 May 1941.
4 See for example the following editorials in *Chieh-fang jih-pao*: 'Hsu-li-ya chan-cheng chieh-shu' ('The Syrian War Ended'), 12 July 1941 and 'Yi-lang shih-chien chih chiao-hsün' ('The Lesson of the Iranian Affair'), 4 September 1941. See also Tseng Yung-ch'üan, 'Tsai pei-Fei ti la-chu chan' ('The Push-and-Pull War in North Africa'), *ibid.*, 14 and 15 September 1941.
5 'A Turning Point in World War II' (12 October 1942), *Selected Works of Mao Tse-tung*, vol. III (Peking: Foreign Languages Press, 1965), p. 105.
6 'Mao chu-hsi ch'ang-t'an kuo-nei-wai chü-shih' ('Chairman Mao Talks on Internal and External Situation'), *Chieh-fang jih-pao*, 13 June 1944.
7 Anna Louis Strong, 'A World's Eye View from a Yenan Cave – an Interview with Mao Tze-tung', *Amerasia*, vol. XI, no. 4 (April 1947), pp. 124–5; official version in *Selected Works of Mao Tse-tung*, vol. IV (Peking: Foreign Languages Press, 1961), pp. 97–100.
8 Lu Ting-yi, 'Explanation of Several Basic Questions Concerning the

Postwar International Situation', *Chieh-fang jih-pao*, 4 and 5 January 1947, English translation in United States Department of State, *United States Relations with China, with Special Reference to the Period 1944–1949* (Washington: US Government Printing Office, 1950), pp. 713–14.

9 Editorial in *JMJP*, 9 December 1953, in *SWB/FE*, no. 311 (15 December 1953), pp. 5–7. See also Chou En-lai, 'Political Report to the First National Committee of the CPPCC' (4 February 1953), in *CB*, no. 228 (8 February 1953), p. 7.

10 NCNA, 25 March 1954, in *SWB/FE*, no. 341 (1 April 1954), p. 3, and NCNA, 17 June 1954, in *SWB/FE*, no. 373 (22 July 1954), p. 8. See also Chou En-lai, 'Political Report' (delivered on the opening day of the 2nd Session of the National Committee of the CPPCC on 21 December 1954), NCNA, *Daily Bulletin*, no. 1207 (29 December 1954), p. 2.

11 See for example: Chang Pi, 'Suo-wei "Chung-tung ssu-ling pu"' ('The So-Called "Middle East Command"'), *SCCS*, no. 10 (15 March 1952), pp. 16–17; Yuan Fang, 'Ya-chou jen-min fan-tui Mei-kuo p'in-ts'ou Chung-tung ch'in-lüeh chi-t'uan' ('Peoples of Asia Oppose the Rigging-Up of an Aggressive Bloc in the Middle East by the United States'), *SCCS*, no. 4 (20 February 1954), pp. 12–14.

12 Li Ping, *Jen-shih wo-men ti shih-chieh* (*Recognise our World*) (Peking: Kung-jen ch'u-pan she, 1952), pp. 22–3.

13 I Hsin, *Hsin Chung-kuo ti wai-chiao* (*New China's Foreign Affairs*) (Hong Kong: Nan-fang shu-tien yin, 1950), pp. 26–7.

14 Mao Tse-tung, 'On New Democracy', *Chieh-fang* (*Liberation*), nos. 98–9 (20 February 1950). English translations in *Selected Works of Mao Tse-tung*, vol. II (Peking: Foreign Languages Press, 1965), p. 356; Stuart R. Schram and Hélène Carrère d'Encausse, *Marxism and Asia* (London: Allen Lane, The Penguin Press, 1969), p. 255, and Stuart R. Schram, *The Political Thought of Mao Tse-tung*, revised and enlarged edn (New York: Praeger, 1970), p. 377. See also Mao Tse-tung, *On People's Democratic Dictatorship* (Peking: New China News Agency, 1949), p. 7, and Liu Shao-ch'i. *Internationalism and Nationalism* (Peking: Foreign Languages Press, 1949), p. 32.

15 Liu Ssu-mu, *Tzen-yang hsüeh-hsi kuo-chi shih-shih* (*How to Study Current International Affairs*) (Peking: Shih-chieh chih-shih ch'u-pan she, 1951), pp. 102–3.

16 Lu Ting-yi, 'Explanation Concerning the International Situation', p. 715.

17 *JMJP*, 22 October 1951, in *SWB/FE*, no. 132 (30 October 1951), p. 25. On the 'contradictions' between the United States and Great Britain see also: 'A Realistic Picture', *Chan-wang* (*Outlook*), 20 October 1951, in American Consulate General, Hong Kong, *Chinese Communist Propaganda Review*, no. 42 (15 June 1953), pp. 2–3; Kuang Tao, 'American Imperialism Meets with Frustration Everywhere', *Shih-shih shou-ts'e* (*Current Affairs Handbook*), no. 3 (10 February 1952) in *Chinese Communist Propaganda Review*, no. 13 (1 March 1952), pp. 15–17.

18 'Chung-tung, pei-Fei ho La-ting Mei-chou jen-min wei ho-p'ing erh tou-cheng' ('The Peoples of the Middle East, North Africa and Latin America Fight for Peace'), *SCCS*, no. 8 (1 March 1952), p. 3.

19 Liu Ssu-mu, *Tzen-yang hsüeh-hsi kuo-chi shih-shih*, pp. 92, 96.

20 Which sent troops to fight in Korea. See, for example, Wang Ch'ing, 'Mei-ti nu-i hsia ti T'u-erh-ch'i' ('Turkey Under American Imperialist Enslavement'), *SCCS*. no. 17 (3 November 1951), pp. 19–20.

21 'Chung-tung, pei-Fei ho La-ting Mei-chou j'en-min wei ho-p'ing erh tou-cheng', p. 3.
22 Liu Ssu-mu, *Tzen-yang hsüeh-hsi kuo-chi shih-shih*, p. 79.
23 *JMJP*, 23 October 1951, in *SWB/FE*, no. 132 (30 October 1951), p. 26.
24 See also Peter Van Ness, *Revolution and Chinese Foreign Policy* (Berkeley, Los Angeles: University of California Press, 1971), ch. 3.
25 *Khrushchev Remembers*, with an introduction, commentary and notes by Edward Crankshaw (London: Sphere Books, 1971), pp. 394–6.
26 Schram and d'Encausse, *Marxism and Asia*, pp. 64–7.
27 Commentary in *JMJP*, 22 October 1951, in *SWB/FE*, no. 132 (30 October 1951), pp. 25–6.
28 *JMJP*, 8 December 1951, in *SWB/FE*, no. 139 (18 December 1951), p. 19.
29 Chang Pi, 'Lun Chung-tung, Chin-tung ti min-tsu tu-li chieh-fang yun-tung' ('Discussing the Middle East and Near East National Independence and Liberation Movement'), *SCCS*, no. 9 (8 March 1952), p. 9. See also NCNA, 13 March 1952, in *SWB/FE*, no. 152 (18 March 1952), p. 26.
30 NCNA, 5 April 1950, in *SWB/FE*, no. 51 (11 April 1950), p. 24; NCNA, 28 May 1952, in *Hsin-hua yüeh-pao* (*New China Monthly*), no. 6 (1952), p. 218, and *People's China*, vol. v, no. 12 (16 June 1952), p. 37.
31 See, for example, Shih Chih, 'Double Crossing Diplomacy, Britain and Iran Oil', *JMJP*, 29 March 1953, in NCNA, *Daily Bulletin*, no. 760 (31 March 1953), p. 5.
32 Walter Z. Laqueur, *The Soviet Union and the Middle East* (London: Routledge and Kegan Paul, 1959), pp. 139–43.
33 For further details see 'Communiqué of the Results of the Census and Registration of China's Population', NCNA, 1 November 1954, in *CB*, no. 301 (1 November 1954). See also 'Figures and Tables of Non-Chinese Races', *China News Analysis*, no. 569 (18 June 1956), pp. 1–3; Amrit Lal, 'Sinification of Ethnic Minorities in China', *Current Scene*, vol. viii, no. 4 (15 February 1970), pp. 1–24, and the tables in Henry G. Schwartz, *Chinese Policies towards Minorities* (Western Washington State College, Occasional Paper no. 2, 1971), pp. 29–45.
34 See 'Communism and Islam, the Chinese Aspects', in *CB*, no. 195 (25 June 1952); Yang I-fan, *Islam in China* (Hong Kong: Union Research Institute, 1957), pp. 69–81, and *Moslem Unrest in China* (Hong Kong: Union Research Institute, 1958).
35 Arab News Agency, 4 May 1950, in *SWB/FE*, no. 56 (16 May 1950), p. 27.
36 Cairo radio, 31 March 1951, and Arab News Agency, 2 April 1951, in *SWB/FE*, no. 103 (10 April 1951), pp. 3–4.
37 For example: United Press, Taipeh, 30 January 1951, in *SWB/FE*, no. 94 (6 February 1951), p. 36, and Pusan radio, 2 and 3 April 1951, in *SWB/FE*, no. 103 (10 April 1951), p. 4. On 14 July 1954 Taipeh radio reported that a Chinese Muslim pilgrim mission was to leave shortly to visit the Arab countries: *SWB/FE*, no. 372 (20 July 1954), p. 24.
38 Mohamed Heikal (Muḥammad Haykal), *Nasser: the Cairo Documents* (London: New English Library, 1972), pp. 46–7.
39 'Canton Moslems Voice Support for People of Iran, Morocco', *Nan-fang jih-pao*, 10 April 1951, in *SCMP*, no. 93 (10–12 April 1951), pp. 7–8.
40 Wuhan radio, 30 April 1951, in *SWB/FE*, no. 107 (8 May 1951), p. 4.

41 For example: article by Ma Chien (Muslim Professor in Peking University) in support of the Iranian people's fight for nationalisation of the oil industry, *JMJP*, 29 July 1951, in *SCMP*, no. 146 (31 July 1951), pp. 5–6; Saifudin, 'The Just Struggle of the Iranian People', *People's China*, vol. IV, no. 3 (1 August 1951), p. 11; letters to the Egyptian people sent by two imams of the mosque in Peking, four Professors of Arabic and students of the Arabic section of the Department of Oriental Languages in Peking University. NCNA, 1 November 1951, in *SWB/FE*, no. 133 (6 November 1951), p. 31; rally held by the Muslim community of the Hankow area in support of Egypt, Wuhan radio, 12 November 1951, in *SWB/FE*, no. 135 (20 November 1951), pp. 16–17. See also Han Tao-jen, 'The Emancipation of Islamic Nationals of China', *JMJP*, 6 June 1952, in *CB*, no. 195 (25 June 1952), pp. 6–11.

42 Address by Ma Chien at a meeting on 31 October 1951 of the Third Session of the First National Committee of the CPPCC, *JMJP*, 2 November 1951, in *CB*, no. 139 (22 November 1951), p. 6.

43 China's Islamic Association, *Moslems in China* (Peking, 1953). See also Banquet for Moslem Delegates (to the Asia and the Pacific Peace Conference), NCNA, 20 October 1952, in *SWB/FE*, no. 194 (28 October 1952), p. 11.

44 J. D. Simmonds, *China's World* (New York: Columbia University Press, 1970), pp. 36–7.

45 Chinese text in *Chung-hua jen-min kung-ho-kuo tui-wai kuan-hsi wen-chien chi* (*Collected Documents on the Foreign Relations of the People's Republic of China*), vol. I (Peking: Shih-chieh chih-shih ch'u-pan she, 1957), p. 23

46 The cable said: 'Sir, on behalf of the Central People's Government of the People's Republic of China, I hereby acknowledge the receipt of Your Excellency's telegram of the 9th instant with regard to the decision made by the Government of Israel concerning the Central People's Government of the People's Republic of China and Your Excellency's hopes for the Chinese people and greetings to myself. I extend to Your Excellency on behalf of the Central People's Government of the People's Republic of China our welcome and thanks.' *Chung-hua jen-min kung-ho-kuo tui-wai kuan-hsi wen-chien chi*, pp. 22–3.

47 For example: NCNA, *Daily News Release*, no. 259 (17 January 1950), p. 68; *People's China*, vol. I, no. 3 (1 February 1950), p. 19; *Hsin-hua yüeh-pao*, vol. I, no. 4 (February 1950), p. 1080; 'Ta-shih jih-chih' ('Diary of Major Events'), p. 3, in *Jen-min shou-ts'e 1951* (*People's Handbook*) (Peking: Ta-kung pao she, 1951).

48 For example: Chou En-lai, 'Fight for the Consolidation and Development of the Chinese People's Victory', report rendered at a meeting of cadres called by the National Committee of the CPPCC to commemorate the first anniversary of the founding of the People's Republic of China, 30 September 1950. Chinese text in *K'ang-Mei yüan-Ch'ao; pao-chia wei-kuo* (*Resist America Aid Korea; Protect the Nation Defend the Country*) (Shanghai: Wen-hui pao fa-hsing, 1950), p. 5. English translation: NCNA, 30 September 1950, in *SWB/FE*, no. 77 (10 October 1950), p. 41, and *CB*, no. 12 (5 October 1950), p. 4. See also *Shih-chieh chih-shih shou-ts'e 1955* (*World Knowledge Handbook*) (Peking: Shih-chieh chih-shih she, 1955), p. 120.

49 Article 56 of the Common Program of the CPPCC, *China Digest*, 5 October 1949, supplement.

50 Liao Kai-lung and Wang Tsung-i, 'Great Achievements of the People's

Republic of China during the Past Two Years', *Shih-shih shou-ts'e*, no. 22 (5 September 1951). NCNA, 24 September 1951, in *CB*, no. 120 (3 October 1951), p. 7.

51 Chu Jung-fu, 'Hsin Chung-kuo wu nien lai ti wai-chiao' ('Foreign Relations of New China during the Past Five Years'), *SCCS*, no. 19 (5 October 1954), p. 8. English translation in *CB*, no. 307 (6 December 1954), p. 6.

52 Mordecai Namir, *Shliḥut be-Mosqva, Yeraḥ Dvash ve-Shnot Za'am (Israeli Mission in Moscow)* (Tel Aviv: 'Am 'Oved, 1971), pp. 147–9. See also *Jerusalem Post*, 18 February 1972.

53 *Shih-chieh chih-shih shou-ts'e 1955*, p. 448.

54 Israel radio, 12 June 1950, and Denmark radio, 14 June 1950, in *SWB/FE*, no. 61 (20 June 1950), p. 31.

55 Namir, *Shliḥut be-Mosqva*, pp. 147, 149. For an extensive analysis of Israel's attitudes towards China see Michael Brecher, *Israel, the Korean War and China: Images, Decisions and Consequences* (Jerusalem: The Jerusalem Academic Press, 1974).

56 Chinese text in *Ts'ung sheng-li tao sheng-li (From Victory to Victory)* (Shanghai: Wen-hui pao fa-hsing, 1951), p. 83. English translation: NCNA, 30 November 1950, in *CB*, no. 36 (5 December 1950), p. 3, and United Nations, *Security Council Official Records*, 5th year, 527th meeting, no. 69 (28 November 1950), pp. 2–3.

57 Wang Yün-sheng, 'Ts'ung shih-san kuo ti t'i-an t'an-ch'i' ('Start Discussions from the 13 Countries' Proposal'), in *Ch'ao-hsien chan-chu yü shih-chieh hsing-shih (The Korean War and the World Situation)* (Shanghai: Ta-kung pao ch'u-pan, 1951), p. 80.

58 Editorial in *Kuang-ming jih-pao*, 2 February 1951, in *SWB/FE*, no. 95 (13 February 1951), pp. 9–10.

59 NCNA, *Daily News Release*, no. 818 (4 October 1951), p. 13.

60 'The anti-state conspiratorial centre headed by Slansky was a typical U.S. espionage agency. It was no accident that U.S. imperialism chose these people as its henchmen; members of the centre were all Trotskyites, Zionists, Titoites and bourgeois nationalists. They were all traitors to the revolution.' Editorial, 'Tremendous Victory of Czechoslovak People', *JMJP*, 30 November 1952, in NCNA, *Daily Bulletin*, no. 679 (4 December 1952), pp. 7–8.

61 'This group of assassins donned the garb of physicians, scientists and professors and appeared to be intellectuals of high calibre. Yet because of their reactionary, bourgeois and Jewish Zionist ideology and their hostile feeling towards the working people, they degenerated into murderers.' Editorial, 'Arrests in the Soviet Union an Important Achievement of State Security Work', *JMJP*, 16 January 1953, in NCNA, *Daily Bulletin*, no. 709 (19 January 1953), pp. 3–4.

62 See, for example, article on Judaism and Zionism in *Kuo-chi wen-t'i i-ts'ung (Translations on International Questions)*, no. 2 (February 1953), pp. 92–9, translated from *L'Humanité* (Paris), 20 and 22 December 1952.

63 'Kuan-yü Yu-t'ai-fu-kuo-chu-i' ('About Zionism'), *SCCS*, no. 1 (1 January 1953), p. 30.

64 Yang Hsüeh ch'un, 'Hsia-ai min-tsu-chu-i t'ung-chih hsia ti I-ssu-lieh' ('Israel Under the Rule of Narrow-Minded Nationalism'), *SCCS*, no. 9 (25 February 1953), pp. 19–20.

65 Brecher, *Israel, the Korean War and China*, p. 56. See also Meron Medzini, 'Israel and China: a Missed Opportunity?' *Wiener Library*

218   *Notes to pages 25–7*

Bulletin, vol. xxv, nos. 1–2 (1971), p. 35, and *Ha'aretz Weekly Magazine* (Tel Aviv), 9 August 1974, p. 8.

66 David Hacohen, *Yoman Burma* (*Burmese Diary*) (Tel Aviv: 'Am 'Oved, 1963), pp. 61–2, and the author's additional notes in *Ma'ariv* (Tel Aviv), 6 May 1973. See also David Hacohen, 'Behind the Scenes of Negotiation between Israel and China', *New Outlook* (Tel Aviv), vol. vi, no. 9 (November–December 1963), pp. 29–44.

67 Chou En-lai, *Cheng-fu kung-tso pao-kao* (*Report on the Work of the Government*) (Peking: Jen-min ch'u-pan she, 1954), p. 34. English translation: Chou En-lai, *Report on the Work of the Government* (Peking: Foreign Languages Press, 1954), p. 44.

68 Hacohen, *Yoman Burma*, p. 158.

69 *Ibid.*, p. 234.

70 *Ibid.*, pp. 244–5. It was also in June that relations between Israel and the Soviet Union greatly improved following the upgrading of their missions to the status of embassies.

71 Hacohen, *Yoman Burma*, p. 304.

72 *Ibid.*, pp. 62, 180.

73 Chou En-lai, *Cheng-fu kung-tso pao-kao*, p. 33.

74 Hacohen, *Yoman Burma*, pp. 318–19. See also Louis Shub, 'China–Israel', *Jewish Affairs Background Reports* (The University of Judaism, Center for the Study of Contemporary Jewish Life), vol. i, no. 3 (October 1972), p. 5. However, on the eve of the Bandung Conference and after negotiations with Israel had already failed, the Chinese commented on Israel's performance in the United Nations, including the 1954 vote: 'In the United Nations it, as usual, took measures to follow U.S. imperialist policy, agreeing to the U.S. calumniating our country as "aggressors" and to the proposal of "blockade and embargo" against our country. Then, at the 9th General Assembly it also agreed to the proposal raised by the U.S. in 1954 not to discuss our place in the United Nations. However, afterwards the Government of Israel also published a communiqué explaining this act.' *Shih-chieh chih-shih shou-ts'e 1955*, p. 452.

75 NCNA, 1 October 1954, in *SWB/FE*, no. 395 (7 October 1954), p. 21.

76 *Ha'aretz Weekly Magazine*, 9 August 1974, pp. 8–9. Israel radio (12 January 1955) said, however, that 'although trade talks would be the primary objective of this visit, the prospects of establishing diplomatic relations would also be discussed'. *SWB/FE*, no. 423 (18 January 1955), p. 14.

77 Michael Brecher, *The Foreign Policy System of Israel* (London: Oxford University Press, 1972), p. 241. See also Hacohen, *Yoman Burma*, p. 393, and *Ha'aretz Weekly Magazine*, 9 August 1974, p. 9.

78 Hacohen, *Yoman Burma*, p. 405.

79 NCNA, for example, reported on the arrival of the delegation only on 31 January, and even then very briefly. *SWB/FE*, no. 429 (8 February 1955), p. 16.

80 Whereas in September Chou En-lai had mentioned the likelihood of establishing normal relations with Israel and Afghanistan, in December he said that progress had been made in the talks on diplomatic relations with Afghanistan and Nepal, completely ignoring Israel. Chou En-lai, 'Political Report' (delivered on the opening day of the 2nd Session of the National Committee of the CPPCC, on 21 December 1954), NCNA, *Daily Bulletin*, no. 1207 (29 December 1954), p. 3.

81 Menahem Mansoor, *Arab World Political and Diplomatic History*

1900–1967: A Chronological Study (Washington: NCR Microcard Editions, 1972), vol. II, 20 August 1950. The Chinese regarded the Arab League as a creation of imperialism divided into pro-American and pro-British factions and therefore incapable of ensuring unanimous action on important issues. See 'Kuan-yü A-la-po lien-mang' ('About the Arab League'), *SCCS*, no. 17 (5 September 1951), p. 17, and *Shih-chieh chih-shih shou-ts'e 1955*, p. 860.

82 See the editorial by Wang Yün-sheng, 'The Shameless Cadaver at the UN Security Council', *Ta-kung pao*, 18 January 1950, in American Consulate General Shanghai, *Chinese Press Review*, no. 1069, p. 1.

83 *New York Times*, 1 and 2 July 1950.

84 See 'U.S. Chides Egypt on Korean Policy', *New York Times*, 4 July 1950.

85 Mansoor, *Arab World*, vol. II, 5 December 1950.

86 On 3 August 1950 the Security Council rejected a Soviet proposal to discuss the question of recognition of the PRC as representative of China; on 19 September the General Assembly rejected a similar Indian resolution. The Lebanon, Saudi Arabia, Syria and the Yemen abstained as well; Iran, Iraq and Turkey voted against, and Israel for the Indian resolution. Again on 29 September and 27 November Egypt abstained when the Security Council voted to invite a representative of the PRC to participate in the discussion of Peking's complaint of US armed aggression against Korea and Taiwan.

87 For example, Damascus radio, 11 May 1950, in *SWB/FE*, no. 56 (16 May 1950), p. 27; *New York Times*, 28 June 1950.

88 *New York Times*, 13 December 1950. Egypt decided not to recognise China under the pressure not only of the West but also of religious circles, particularly Muslim refugees from China. See *Christian Science Monitor*, 25 January 1951.

89 'Chou En-lai Proposes 7-Nation Conference', NCNA, 17 January 1951, in *SWB/FE*, no. 92 (23 January 1951), p. 9.

90 I An, 'Ai-chi kai-k'uang' ('General Situation in Egypt'), *SCCS*, no. 5 (5 March 1951), p. 14.

91 Wang Yün-sheng, 'Ts'ung shih-san kuo t'i-an t'an-ch'i', p. 83.

92 *New York Times*, 20 January 1951, and *La Bourse Egyptienne*, 18 January 1951.

93 See *La Bourse Egyptienne*, 10, 23, 25 and 26 January 1951, quoting from *al-Muqaṭṭam*, *Rūz al-Yūsuf*, *al-Miṣrī* and *al-Muṣawwar*.

94 Editorial, 'The Chinese People Cannot Tolerate American Aggressors' Resolution of Slander', *Kuang-ming jih-pao*, 2 February 1951, in *SWB/FE*, no. 95 (13 February 1951), pp. 9–10. See also Chou En-lai's statement on the resolution, 'U.S. Has Blocked Path to Peaceful Settlement', NCNA, 2 February 1951, in *SWB/FE*, no. 94 (6 February 1951), pp. 5–7.

95 Editorial, 'The U.S. Government Again Proves Itself the Deadly Enemy of Peace', *JMJP*, 3 February 1951, in *SWB/FE*, no. 94 (6 February 1951), p. 7.

96 Saifudin, 'The Just Struggle of the Iranian People', p. 11, and NCNA, 8 July 1951, in *SWB/FE*, no. 117 (17 July 1951), pp. 13–14.

97 Peking broadcast in Tonkinese, 10 December 1951, in *SWB/FE*, no. 139 (18 December 1951), p. 19.

98 *JMJP*, 12 January 1952, in *SWB/FE*, no. 144 (22 January 1952), p. 17.

99 *JMJP*, 15 October 1951, in *SWB/FE*, no. 131 (23 October 1951), pp. 16–17. Also in *SCMP*, no. 196 (17 October 1951), pp. 4–5.

100 *JMJP*, 26 November 1951, in *SWB/FE*, no. 137 (4 December 1951), pp. 12–13.
101 'Ai-chi ti "cheng-pien"' ('Egypt's *"Coup d'Etat"*'), *SCCS*, no. 31 (9 August 1952), p. 10; 'Na-chi-pu ti hou-t'ai lao-pan' ('Naguib's Back-Stage Manager'), *SCCS*, no. 45 (5 November 1952), p. 13.
102 I An, 'Na-chi-pu fan-tung t'ung-chih hsia ti Ai-chi' ('Egypt Under Naguib's Reactionary Rule'), *SCCS*, no. 4 (20 February 1953), pp. 18–19.
103 See *Daily Telegraph* and *Le Monde*, 1 January 1953.
104 Chu li-ju, 'Mei-kuo p'in-ts'ou Chung-tung ch'in-lüeh chi-t'uan ti hsin i-mou' ('U.S. New Conspiracy to Rig-Up a Middle East Aggressive Bloc'), *SCCS*, no. 22 (20 November 1954), p. 13.
105 *Shih-chieh chih-shih shou-ts'e 1955*, p. 763, and 'Ya-Fei hui-i kuo-chia chieh-shao' ('Introducing the Countries of the Asian–African Conference'), *SCCS*, no. 4 (20 February 1955), p. 24.
106 *Shih-chieh chih-shih shou-ts'e 1955*, p. 765.
107 For example: 'President of Egypt Opposes U.S.–Pakistan Agreement', *JMJP*, 7 February 1954, and 'Deputy Premier of Egypt Nasser Opposes Middle East Aggression Bloc', *JMJP*, 9 February 1954, both in *SCMP*, no. 748 (16 February 1954), p. 35. See also 'U.S.–Pakistani and Turko–Pakistani Pacts Rousing Protests in Asia and Middle East', *JMJP*, 23 March 1954, in *SCMP*, no. 773 (24 March 1954), p. 17.
108 For example: *New York Times*, 7 January 1954; NCNA, 22 February 1954, in *SCMP*, no. 757 (28 February 1954), p. 19; *al-Jumhūriyya* (Cairo), 22 May 1954; and Peking radio, 24 May 1954 (quoting TASS), in *SWB/FE*, no. 358 (1 June 1954), p. 4.
109 NCNA, 25 June 1954, in *SWB/FE*, no. 367 (1 July 1954), p. 3.
110 Al-*Ahrām* (Cairo), 25 June 1954, and NCNA, 27 June 1954, in *SWB/FE*, no. 368 (6 July 1954), p. 10.
111 NCNA, 1 July 1954, in *SWB/FE*, no. 369 (8 July 1954), p. 6. See also *The Hindu* (Delhi), 1 July 1954.
112 'Interview with Egypt's Prime Minister Lieut. Col. Gamal Abdel Nasser', *U.S. News and World Report* (3 September 1954), p. 31. Arabic text in *Majmū'āt Khuṭab al-Ra'īs Jamāl 'Abd al-Nāṣir (Collection of Speeches of President Jamāl 'Abd al-Nāṣir)*, part i. 30 August 1954 (Cairo: UAR Information Department, n.d.), pp. 209–11. See also *Khuṭab wa Taṣrīhāt al-Ra'īs Jamāl 'Abd al-Nāṣir 1952–1959 (Speeches and Declarations of President Jamāl 'Abd al-Nāṣir)*, vol. iii (Cairo: Maṭābi' Sharkat al-A'lānāt al-Sharqiyya, n.d.), p. 499.
113 *The Hindu*, 5 September 1954.
114 Kao Ping-shu, 'Hsin Chung-kuo ti tui-wai ching-chi kuan-hsi' ('New China's Economic Relations with Foreign Countries'), *SCCS*, no. 19 (5 October 1954), p. 11. Translated in *CB*, no. 307 (6 December 1954), pp. 10–17.
115 *La Bourse Egyptienne* and *The Times*, 5 January 1953; *Financial Times*, 6 January 1953. See also *JMJP*, 3 January 1953, in *SCMP*, no. 485 (1–5 January 1953), p. 4; Arab News Agency, 4 January 1953, in *SWB/FE*, no. 215 (13 January 1953), p. 4.
116 Report by Tso Chung-shu, acting manager of the China National Import and Export Corporation. NCNA, 22 April 1955, in *SWB/FE*, no. 452 (28 April 1955), p. 16.
117 *Shih-chieh chih-shih shou-ts'e 1955*, p. 469.
118 NCNA, 5 October 1954, in *SWB/FE*, no. 396 (12 October 1954), p. 16. See also Chi Yin, 'Hsu-li-ya jen-min je-ai hsin Chung-kuo' ('The

Syrian People Ardently Love New China'), *SCCS*, no. 21 (5 November 1954), p. 32.

119 This argument was put forward as early as 1941. See, for example, Hsiao Yu (Li Wei-han), 'Chin-tung ti ch'i-chü' ('The Near East Chessboard'), *Chieh-fang jih-pao*, 23 May 1941.

120 *Shih-chieh chih-shih shou-ts'e 1955*, p. 448, and p. 23 above.

121 Yang Hsüeh-ch'un, 'Hsia-ai min-tsu-chu-i t'ung-chih hsia ti I-ssu-lieh', p. 20.

122 *Shih-chieh chih-shih shou-ts'e 1955*, p. 451.

123 Chung Lin, 'Chung-chin-tung kuo-chia ti min-tsu chieh-fang yun-tung' ('The National Liberation Movement of the Middle and Near Eastern Countries'), *SCCS*, no. 3 (5 February 1955), p. 14.

124 *Shih-chieh chih-shih shou-ts'e 1955*, p. 451.

125 *Ibid*. These places – which were to form the Palestine Arab state according to the Partition Plan – were regularly marked on Chinese maps as the 'Arab Zone' (*A-la-po ch'ü*); as a rule the Chinese have shown the Partition borders along with the actual armistice borders agreed upon by Israel and the Arab states. Peking also fairly consistently used in its maps the term 'Palestine' together with the name 'Israel', probably accepting the Soviet definition of Palestine as those areas which are outside Israel (*Pa-li-ssu-tan ch'u I-ssu-lieh ti ti-ch'ü*). ' "Chung-tung" ho "Chin-tung" ', p. 9. Quite often when the Chinese were naming the countries of the Middle East they mentioned Israel as well as Palestine, as two different countries. See, for example, Li Ping, *Jen-shih wo-men ti shih-chieh*, p. 34.

126 Chung Lin, 'Chung-chin-tung kuo-chia ti min-tsu chieh-fang yun-tung', p. 14.

127 *Shih-chieh chih-shih shou-ts'e 1955*, p. 860.

128 *Ibid*., pp. 451–2.

CHAPTER 2

1 'Statement by the Government of the PRC on the Question of the Suez Canal', 15 August 1956, *Shih-chieh chih-shih shou-ts'e 1957*, pp. 1171–2. English translation in *SWB/FE*, no. 588 (21 August 1956), pp. 4–5.

2 Saudi Arabia, for example, was praised because it 'has pursued a policy of independence and peace. It is defending its sovereignty and national interests and is opposing participation in military blocs established by the Western countries in the Asian and African area.' 'Observer' in *JMJP*, 14 December 1955, in *SWB/FE*, no. 519 (20 December 1955), p. 7. See also *SCCS*, no. 24 (20 December 1955), p. 3.

3 Chou En-lai's political report at the 2nd Plenary Session of the 2nd National Committee of the CPPCC, 30 January 1956. NCNA, *Daily Bulletin*, supplement no. 237 (1 February 1956), p. 5. See also Vice Premier Ho Lung's speech at a meeting celebrating the Bandung Conference in Peking, 18 April 1956. *SWB/FE*, no. 554 (24 April 1956), p. 12.

4 Speech by Comrade Ch'en Yi, 'The Present International Situation and Our Foreign Policy, 25.9.56', *Eighth National Congress of the Communist Party of China*, vol. II (Peking: Foreign Languages Press, 1956), pp. 329, 330–1.

5 'Summing-Up at the 6th Enlarged Plenum of the 7th Central Committee', September 1955, *Mao Tse-tung ssu-hsiang wan-sui (Long Live*

Mao Tse-tung's Thought) (n.p., August 1969), pp. 14–15. English translation in *Miscellany of Mao tse-tung Thought*, JPRS, no. 61269–1 (20 February 1974), p. 16. Official version, dated 11 October 1955, in *Selected Works of Mao Tse-tung*, vol. v (Peking: Foreign Languages Press, 1977), pp. 214–15. See also Mao's opening speech at the National Conference of the CCP, 21 March 1955, *ibid.*, p. 156.

6 *Eighth National Congress*, vol. ii, p. 329.

7 P'eng Chen's speech, representing the CCP Central Committee in a rally in Peking. Peking radio, 3 November 1956, in *SWB/FE*, no. 611 (8 November 1956), pp. 5–6. Throughout his speech he did not mention the Soviet Union at all.

8 Pai Shou-yi, 'Historical Ties Between China and the Arab World', *People's China*, no. 7 (1 April 1955), p. 27. See also Feng Chia-sheng, 'China and the Arab World', *China Reconstructs*, vol. iv, no. 4 (April 1955), pp. 24–6. A more documented work was prepared at that time and published after the Bandung Conference: Chou I-liang, *Chung-kuo yü Ya-chou ko-kuo ho-p'ing yu-hao ti li-shih* (*History of the Peaceful and Friendly Relations Between China and the Asian Countries*) (Shanghai: Jen-min ch'u-pan she, 1955), pp. 64–71.

9 NCNA, 8 April 1955, in *SWB/FE*, no. 448 (14 April 1955), p. 10.

10 *New York Times*, 18 and 26 April 1955.

11 *Ibid.*, and see also Muḥammad Ḥasanayn Haykal in *Akhbār al-Yawm* (Cairo), 23 April 1955.

12 Heikal, *Nasser: the Cairo Documents*, pp. 54–5, 226–7; also in *al-Ahrām*, 22 January 1958.

13 Uri Ra'anan, *The U.S.S.R. Arms the Third World* (Cambridge, Mass.: MIT Press, 1969), pp. 57–60, 138–44.

14 'Egypt and Syria's cotton and other products can be exchanged for our tobacco, silk, paper, tea, wool, wooden goods and some manufactured goods that they need. There are good prospects for the development of trade between China and Egypt, Syria and other Arab states.' Talk by Li Che-jen, Vice Minister of Foreign Trade, on trade with Asia and Africa, on Peking radio, 16 April 1955, in *SWB/FE*, no. 450 (21 April 1955), p. 16.

15 *New York Times*, 26 April 1955; NCNA, 9 August 1955, in *SWB/FE*, no. 483 (16 August 1955), p. 9.

16 For more details see: NCNA, 14 October 1955, in *SWB/FE*, no. 503 (25 October 1955), p. 2, and *Economic Supplement*, no. 187 (27 October 1955); NCNA, 1 December 1955, in *SWB/FE*, no. 516 (8 December 1955), p 13; and NCNA, 3 January 1956, in *SWB/FE*, no. 524 (10 January 1956), p. 15.

17 Text in *SCMP*, no. 1151 (15–18 October 1955), pp. 64–8.

18 NCNA, 3 September 1955, in *SWB/FE*, no. 490 (8 September 1955), p. 8.

19 Allen, *Middle Eastern Economic Relations*, p. 21.

20 Article by Chen Szu in *Ta-kung pao*, 24 November 1955, in *SWB/FE*, no. 514 (1 December 1955), p. 7.

21 11 August 1955, in *SWB/FE*, no. 484 (18 August 1955), p. 9.

22 'Trade May Bring Cairo–Peiping Tie', *New York Times*, 22 April 1955; 'Red China Talks Cotton to Draw Egypt Closer', *Christian Science Monitor*, 7 June 1955.

23 'The Story of Cotton', *China News Analysis*, no. 188 (12 July 1957), pp. 1–7; Alexander Eckstein, *Communist China's Economic Growth and Foreign Trade* (New York: McGraw-Hill, 1966), pp. 111–12.

24 Yeh chi-chuang, 'China's Economic Relations with Asian and African

Countries: Progress and Prospects', *People's China*, no. 6 (16 March 1956), p. 14.

25 Cairo radio, 16 May 1956 and 'Peking and Cairo', *China News Analysis*, no. 158 (22 November 1956), p. 6. Li Fu-ch'un, Chairman of the State Planning Commission, told the 8th CCP Congress that excessive exports of steel products in 1955 had done harm to China's economy. See *CB*, no. 416 (9 October 1956), p. 3.

26 The Chinese tended to exaggerate the volume of their trade with the Arabs. For example, on 11 November 1956, *JMJP* said that China's trade with Egypt in 1955 was three times higher than in 1954 (*SWB/FE*, no. 604 (14 October 1956), p. 13). Yet in reality it was only twice as much. See also *Shih-chieh chih-shih shou-ts'e 1957*, p. 1358.

27 NCNA, 4 September 1956, in *SWB/FE*, no. 594 (11 September 1956), p. 4. See also NCNA, 23 May 1956, in *SWB/FE*, no. 564 (29 May 1956), p. 2.

28 National Bank of Egypt, *Economic Bulletin*, vol. xvii, no. 3 (1964), p. 357. See also Allen, *Middle Eastern Economic Relations*, p. 77.

29 Chang Yüeh, the deputy chief representative in Egypt, had been Deputy Director of the Department of West Europe and Africa in China's Foreign Ministry since 1951. When diplomatic relations were established with Egypt in 1956, he became counsellor in China's embassy ranking second only to the ambassador. He was later appointed chargé d'affaires in the Yemen, ambassador to Somalia and, in September 1974, ambassador to the Sudan. Shih Ku, the deputy chief representative in Syria, became consul-general in Damascus in December 1958, thus being China's senior diplomat in Syria after China's embassy had been closed down following the union between Syria and Egypt. In mid-1960 he was appointed assistant director in the Department of West Asia and Africa in China's Ministry of Foreign Affairs, and from June 1963 served in Dar-es-Salaam, Tanganyika (later Tanzania), first as attaché and then as counsellor.

30 Prior to the Bandung Conference, as well as during its meetings, there were pleas by Muslim refugees from Turkestan to present their case at the conference. See *Dawn* (Pakistan), 17 April and 27 May 1955.

31 More details in Donald W. Klein and Anne B. Clark, *Biographic Dictionary of Chinese Communism, 1921–1965* (Cambridge, Mass.: Harvard University Press, 1971), pp. 5–9. See also François Joyaux, 'Les Musulmans de Chine et la Diplomatie de Pekin', *L'Afrique et l'Asie*, no. 77 (1er trimestre, 1967), pp. 17–24.

32 NCNA, 31 May 1956, in *SWB/FE*, no. 567 (7 June 1956), p. 11.

33 NCNA (Cairo), 19 August 1956, in *SWB/FE*, no. 589 (23 August 1956), p. 14.

34 *JMJP*, 21 October 1955, in *SWB/FE*, no. 504 (27 October 1955), p. 5; *Ta-kung pao*, 8 January 1956, in *SWB/FE*, no. 525 (12 January 1956), p. 7.

35 On 20 September 1955 Egypt, Saudi Arabia, Syria and the Yemen still abstained in the vote to postpone the China issue.

36 Simmonds, *China's World*, p. 40.

37 See, for example, *Washington Post*, 17 May 1956.

38 *New York Times*, 22 April 1956. See also *al-Jumhūriyya*, 22 May 1956.

39 Heikal, *Nasser: the Cairo Documents*, p. 62.

40 Humphrey Trevelyan, *The Middle East in Revolution* (London: Macmillan, 1970), p. 34. See also Robert St John, *The Boss* (London: Arthur Barker, 1960), p. 187.

41 Ra'anan, *The U.S.S.R. Arms the Third World*, p. 69, and *Who's Who in the Arab World 1974–1975* (Beirut: Publitec Publications, n.d.), pp. 1607–8.

42 NCNA, 24 and 25 May 1956, in *SWB/FE*, no. 565 (31 May 1956), p. 5. See also *New York Times* and *La Bourse Egyptienne*, 25 May 1956. Neither Nasser nor 'Āmir ever visited China. An Egyptian military delegation headed by the Chief of Staff did come to China, but not before April 1958.

43 A similar manoeuvre occurred in May 1969 when, following a Soviet refusal to supply them with arms, the Syrians immediately sent a military delegation to China. The result was a renewal of Soviet military shipments to Syria.

44 Chou En-lai, 'The Present International Situation, China's Foreign Policy, and the Question of the Liberation of Taiwan', report to the 3rd Session of the 1st NPC, 28 June 1956. NCNA, *Daily Bulletin*, supplement no. 245 (29 June 1956), p. 6.

45 Editorial in *JMJP*, 19 May 1956, in *SWB/FE*, no. 563 (24 May 1956), p. 3.

46 'At the same time when Egypt recognised People's China, it attempted to keep its relations with the Western bloc countries friendly.' *Al-Akhbār* (Cairo), 30 May 1956.

47 'The Egyptian People Are Not Easily Scared', *JMJP*, 22 July 1956, in *SWB/FE*, no. 581 (26 July 1956), p. 5.

48 'Observer' in *JMJP*, 1 July 1956, in *SWB/FE*, no. 575 (5 July 1956), p. 4.

49 The problem of the Suez Canal, particularly from the aspect of international law, attracted much Chinese attention. See for example: Fang Te-chao, *Su-i-she yun-ho ho Su-i-she yun-ho wen-t'i* (*The Suez Canal and the Suez Canal Problem*) (Peking: Shih-chieh chih-shih she, 1957); Mi Hsien-pi, *Ti-kuo-chu-i yü Su-i-she yun-ho* (*Imperialism and the Suez Canal*) (Shanghai: Jen-min ch'u-pan she, 1957); Chao Li-hai, 'Su-i-she yun-ho wen-t'i yü kuo-chi fa' ('The Problem of the Suez Canal and International Law'), *Cheng-fa yen-chiu* (*Studies in Government and Law*), no. 1 (2 February 1957), pp. 12–19.

50 *The Hindu*, 5 August 1956.

51 NCNA, 5 August 1956, in *SWB/FE*, no. 585 (9 August 1956), p. 2.

52 *Ta-kung pao* of 28 July 1956 described Egypt as 'a giant of the Middle East who has recently risen to its feet and whose steps have awakened those in sleep and inspired those striving for freedom and independence'. *SWB/FE*, no. 583 (2 August 1956), p. 5. It seems that Peking considered the nationalisation not only a major blow to the West but also an example for other governments, particularly in the oil producing states. This was the barely concealed message of *JMJP* on 8 October 1956. It said that the oil of the Middle East did not form part of the wealth of that area because it was siphoned off through pipelines by the Western powers. The oil companies reaped enormous profits, only a small fraction of which found their way back as royalties to the oil producing countries. The nationalisation of the Suez Canal Company, the paper concluded, had greatly encouraged the Arab countries in their struggle for independence. *JMJP*, 8 October 1956, in *SWB/FE*, no. 604 (16 October 1956), p. 4.

53 Mao Tse-tung, 'Opening Address', *Eighth National Congress*, vol. I, Documents, p. 9.

54 NCNA, 17 September 1956, in *SWB/FE*, no. 598 (25 September 1956), pp. 3–4.

55 For example, Article (5) of the Chinese Government Note of 17 Septem-
    ber 1956 to Egypt: 'Egypt will never be alone. China will, together
    with all peace-loving countries and peoples in the world, firmly stand
    by the side of Egypt and give full support to the righteous struggle of
    the Egyptian people...' Defence Minister P'eng Teh-huai said in his
    Order of the Day on 1 October 1956 that 'the schemes of the colonial-
    ists who attempt to intimidate and carry out armed intervention against
    Egypt are doomed to failure. The Chinese people should lend support
    to Egypt in her just struggle.' Peking radio, 1 October 1956, in *SWB/
    FE*, no. 602 (9 October 1956), p. 6; and press editorials of that day.
56 *JMJP*, 25 October 1956, in *SWB/FE*, no. 609 (1 November 1956), p. 7.
57 It was mentioned for the first time when the Egyptian ambassador
    presented his credentials to Mao on 17 September 1956.
58 For more details see Appendix I.
59 *SWB/FE*, no. 598 (25 September 1956), p. 10, and no. 606 (23 October
    1956), p. 4.
60 Text of the Chinese Government Statement in *Shih-chieh chih-shih
    shou-ts'e 1957*, pp. 1185–6. English translation in *SWB/FE*, no. 610
    (6 November 1956), p. 5.
61 Editorial in *JMJP*, 3 November 1956, in *SWB/FE*, no. 611 (8 Novem-
    ber 1956), p. 7.
62 Chinese text of the official protest in *Shih-chieh chih-shih shou-ts'e
    1957*, p. 1186. English translation in *SWB/FE*, no. 611 (8 November
    1956), p. 2.
63 Chinese text in *Jen-min shou-ts'e 1957*, p. 405. English translation in
    SWB/FE, no. 612 (13 November 1956), p. 3.
64 Cf. Allen S. Whiting, 'Foreign Policy of Communist China', in Roy C.
    Macridis (ed.), *Foreign Policy in World Politics*, 4th edn (Englewood
    Cliffs, New Jersey: Prentice-Hall, 1972), pp. 314–15.
65 China's limited capabilities were particularly manifested over the issue
    of possible transportation for volunteers. Illustrating the impractic-
    ability of such a plan were remarks made by Chiang Ming, Deputy
    Minister of Foreign Trade, on the question of carrying out the trade
    protocol which he had just signed in Cairo. He said there were trans-
    port difficulties, but that China was doing its best to continue the
    shipment of goods to Egypt. NCNA, 24 November 1956, in *SWB/FE*,
    no. 617 (29 November 1956), p. 3.
66 Mohamed Abdel Khalek Hassouna (Muḥammad 'Abd al-Khāliq
    Ḥassūna), *The First Asian–African Conference Held at Bandung,
    Indonesia (April 18–24, 1955)*, report submitted to the League of the
    Arab States' Council (Cairo: Imprimerie Misr, 1955), p. 22.
67 David Kimche, *The Afro-Asian Movement, Ideology and Foreign Policy
    of the Third World* (Jerusalem: Israel Universities Press, 1973), p. 52.
68 *JMJP*, 5 January 1955, in *SWB/FE*, no. 421 (11 January 1955), p. 7.
69 The Delhi resolution stated: 'We also condemn pressure of all types
    that is being exerted by certain powers, especially through Israel and
    Turkey, to coerce the Arab countries to join military blocs... This
    conference expresses its sympathies for the plight of the Arab refugees
    and upholds their right to return to Palestine. This conference con-
    demns the aggressive policy of the ruling circles of Israel.' NCNA,
    10 April 1955, in *SWB/FE*, no. 448 (14 April 1955), p. 21.
70 NCNA, 8 April 1955, *ibid.*, p. 10.
71 Aḥmad al-Shuqayrī, *Min al-Qimma ilā 'l-Hazīma (From Zenith to
    Defeat)* (Beirut: Dār al-'Awda, 1971), p. 218, and Munaẓẓamat al-Taḥrīr

al-Filasṭīniyya, *Munaẓẓamat al-Taḥrīr al-Filasṭīniyya wa-Jumhūriyyat al-Ṣīn al-Sha'abiyya* (*The Palestine Liberation Organisation and the People's Republic of China*) (n.p., n.d. ?Cairo, ?1966), pp. 23–4. See also *New York Times*, 21 April 1955.

72 NCNA, 19 April 1955, in *SWB/FE*, no. 451 (26 April 1955), p. 13.
73 Indian Information Service, 21 April 1955, *ibid.*, p. 18; Hassouna, *The First Asian–African Conference*, p. 94; 'Chou Backs Arabs on Israel Dispute', *New York Times*, 21 April 1955.
74 Hassouna, *The First Asian-African Conference*, p. 119; George McTurnan Kahin, *The Asian-African Conference, Bandung, Indonesia, April 1955* (Ithaca, New York: Cornell University Press, 1956), p. 16; G. H. Jansen, *Zionism, Israel and Asian Nationalism* (Beirut: The Institute for Palestine Studies, 1971), p. 258.
75 For example: Kimche, *The Afro-Asian Movement*, p. 67.
76 Kahin, *The Asian–African Conference*, p. 16.
77 According to *Dawn* (Pakistan), 25 April 1955.
78 Compare, for example, the Indian Information Service report of the speech of the Lebanon's premier, 20 April 1955, with that of NCNA, in *SWB/FE*, no. 451 (26 April 1955), p. 10.
79 *JMJP*, 25 April 1955, in *SWB/FE*, no. 453 (3 May 1955), p. 19.
80 P'ei Min, 'Pa-le-ssu-tan wen-t'i' ('The Palestine Problem'), *SCCS*, no. 10 (20 May 1955), pp. 32–3.
81 *Ibid.*
82 'Premier Chou En-lai's Report on the Asian–African Conference' (delivered at the meeting of the Standing Committee of the National People's Congress on 13 May 1955), NCNA, *Daily Bulletin*, supplement no. 226 (19 May 1955), p. 4.
83 Brecher, *Israel, the Korean War and China*, pp. 78–9.
84 Hacohen, *Yoman Burma*, pp. 479–80.
85 *Ha'aretz Weekly Magazine*, 9 August 1974, p. 9, and Brecher, *Israel, the Korean War and China*, p. 102.
86 *Ibid.*, pp. 102–3.
87 For example: 'What Kind of a Country is Israel?', *Ta-kung pao*, 7 December 1955, as summarised in *China News Analysis*, no. 116 (20 January 1956), p. 6.
88 Chou En-lai, 'The Present International Situation, China's Foreign Policy and the Question of the Liberation of Taiwan', 28 June 1956, NCNA, *Daily Bulletin*, supplement no. 245 (29 June 1956), pp. 6, 8.
89 Liu Shao-ch'i, 'The Political Report of the Central Committee of the Communist Party of China to the 8th National Congress of the Party, 15.9.56', *Eighth National Congress*, vol. I, Documents, p. 93.
90 Speech by Comrade Ch'en Yi, 'The Present International Situation and Our Foreign Policy, 25.9.56', *ibid.*, vol. II, p. 345.
91 'Wei-le Chin-tung ti ho-p'ing ho an-ch'üan' ('For Peace and Security in the Near East'), *Kuang-ming jih-pao*, 21 April 1956, p. 4.
92 'Mei-kuo pu-ying kan-she Pa-le-ssu-tan chü-shih' ('The U.S. Should Not Interfere in the Situation in Palestine'), *JMJP*, 1 October 1955; 'Observer' in *JMJP*, 20 April 1956, and *Ta-kung pao*, 21 April 1956, in *SWB/FE*, no. 555 (26 April 1956), p. 3; *Kung-jen jih-pao*, 13 November 1955, in *SWB/FE*, no. 510 (17 November 1955), p. 6; *Ta-kung pao*, 15 November 1955, in *SWB/FE*, no. 511 (22 November 1955), p. 6.
93 P'ei Min, 'I-ssu-lieh' ('Israel'), in *Chung-chin-tung lieh-kuo chih*, pp. 169–85.

94 *Ibid.*, p. 171.
95 *Ibid.*, p. 169.
96 *Ibid.*, pp. 183–4.
97 *Ibid.*, pp. 175–6.
98 'Observer' on 'British-Instigated Attack on Jordan', *JMJP*, 17 October 1956, in *SWB/FE*, no. 606 (23 October 1956), p. 5.
99 For example, whereas up to the war China said that, in May 1948, under the instigation of colonialism, the Arabs had attacked Israel, or that a war had 'broken out', it now said that 'Israel, immediately after its proclamation, started a war against its neighbouring Arab countries'. See 'Pa-le-ssu-tan wen-t'i' ('The Palestine Problem'), *Shih-chieh chih-shih shou-ts'e 1957*, pp. 910–11.
100 In Chou En-lai's message to Nasser dated 10 November 1956. Chinese text in *Jen-min shou-ts'e 1957*, p. 406. English translation in *SWB/FE*, no. 613 (15 November 1956), p. 2.
101 *Ta-kung pao*, 17 February 1957, in *SWB/FE*, no. 640 (21 February 1957), p. 4.
102 Peking home service, 3 April 1957, in *SWB/FE*, no. 653 (9 April 1957), p. 4.
103 NCNA (Cairo), 16 April 1957, in *SCMP*, no. 1515 (24 April 1957), p. 35.
104 NCNA (Cairo), 18 April 1957, in *SCMP*, no. 1516 (25 April 1957), p. 54. See also *JMJP*, 14 November 1957, in *SWB/FE*, no. 717 (19 November 1957), p. 5.
105 NCNA, 16 June 1957, in *SWB/FE*, no. 674 (20 June 1957), p. 2.
106 Yang Chen-ch'ien, *Hsi-nan Ya-chou (South-West Asia)* (Shanghai: Hsin chih-shih ch'u-pan she, 1957), p. 111.
107 *Jen-min shou-ts'e 1958*, p. 388, still referred to Israel as a country which had already recognised the PRC but with which it had not yet exchanged representatives.
108 NCNA, 29 May 1957, in *SCMP*, no. 1543 (4 June 1957), p. 52.
109 *Yedi'ot Aharonot* (Tel Aviv), 6 May 1973. Generally, Mao had no interest in the Jewish people, and only rarely, when discussing nationalities problems in China, mentioned that 'Marx was a Jew'.
110 *Khrushchev Remembers, the Last Testament* (London: André Deutsch, 1974), p. 246.
111 Ra'anan, *The U.S.S.R. Arms the Third World*, pp. 109–22, 138–44.
112 Peking did not seem unduly to regret the fact that the Soviet Union had not been invited. However, the usual tribute was paid: 'It should be pointed out in particular that the Soviet Union is a country situated both in Europe and Asia ... the position maintained by the Soviet Union in international relations is consistent with the aims of the Asian–African conference.' *JMJP*, 5 January 1955, in *SWB/FE*, no. 421 (11 January 1955), p. 7. This view was completely reversed ten years later.
113 *Khrushchev Remembers*, p. 367. See also 'Soviet Foreign Ministry Statement on the Situation in the Middle East', 17 April 1956, *Soviet News*, 18 April 1956.
114 *Ta-kung pao*, 5 February 1956, in *SWB/FE*, no. 533 (9 February 1956), p. 5.
115 This was China's comment on the announcement of the arms deal between Egypt and Czechoslovakia in September 1955. See, for example, *JMJP*, 3 October 1955, and *Kuang-ming jih-pao*, 6 October 1955, in *SWB/FE*, no. 499 (11 October 1955), p. 6, and Peking's

service to Taiwan, 8 October 1955, in *SWB/FE*, no. 500 (13 October 1955), p. 3.

116 *JMJP*, 1 November 1955, in *SWB/FE*, no. 507 (7 November 1955), p. 6. See also *JMJP*, 3 October, and *Kuang-ming jih-pao*, 6 October 1955, in *SWB/FE*, no. 499 (11 October 1955), p. 6.

117 Statement issued on 5 August by the spokesman of the Information Department of the Ministry of Foreign Affairs. NCNA, 5 August 1956, in *SWB/FE*, no. 585 (9 August 1956), p. 2.

118 Editorial in *JMJP*, 14 August 1956, in *SWB/FE*, no. 588 (21 August 1956), p. 6.

119 *Shih-chieh chih-shih shou-ts'e 1957*, pp. 1171–2. English translation in *SWB/FE*, no. 588 (21 August 1956), pp. 4–5.

120 NCNA, 17 August 1956, in *SWB/FE*, no. 589 (23 August 1956), p. 6. See also article (2) of 'Reply Note of the Government of the People's Republic of China to the Note of the Republic of Egypt of 10.9.1956 on the Question of the Suez Canal', *Shih-chieh chih-shih shou-ts'e 1957*, pp. 1181–2. English translation in *SWB/FE*, no. 598 (25 September 1956), pp. 1–2.

121 Based on data in United Arab Republic, *Suez Canal Report 1958* (? Ismāʿīliya: Suez Canal Authority, 1958), pp. 85–117.

122 Editorial in *JMJP*, 21 September 1956, in *SWB/FE*, no. 599 (27 September 1956), p. 2.

123 Ch'en Yi, 'The Present International Situation and Our Foreign Policy', *Eighth National Congress*, vol, II, p. 342.

124 *Ibid.*, p. 12. See also Ch'en Yi's speech, *ibid.*, p. 333; the Chinese Statement of 15 August, *op. cit.*; *JMJP*, 17 August 1956, in *SWB/FE*, no. 589 (23 August 1956), p. 5.

125 Mao's speech in State banquet in honour of Sukarno, NCNA, 2 October 1956, in *SWB/FE*, no. 602 (9 October 1956), p. 12.

126 *Ta-kung pao*, 25 August 1956, in *SWB/FE*, no. 591 (30 August 1956), p. 5.

127 Editorial, 'Long Live the Soviet Union, the Great Defender of Peace', *JMJP*, 7 November 1956, in *SWB/FE*, no. 612 (13 November 1956), pp. 11, 5. See also Chou En-lai's speech at the Anniversary of the October Revolution reception given by the Soviet ambassador, NCNA, 7 November 1956, *ibid.*, p. 9; *JMJP*, 15 January 1957, in *SWB/FE*, no. 631 (22 January 1957), p. 5.

128 *JMJP*, 8 November 1956, in *SWB/FE*, no. 612 (13 November 1956), p. 6.

129 Declaration issued by the Chinese People's Committee to Support Egypt's Resistance against Aggression, NCNA, 9 November 1956, in *SWB/FE*, no. 613 (15 November 1956), p. 3.

130 *Jen-min shou-ts'e 1957*, pp. 147–8. English translation in NCNA, *Daily Bulletin*, no. 1689 (16 November 1965), p. 3. Mao's speech in *Selected Works*, vol. v, pp. 332–49.

131 'On the Struggle of the CPSU for the Solidarity of the International Communist Movement: Report by M. A. Suslov on February 14, 1964, at the Plenum of the CPSU Central Committee', *Pravda*, 3 April 1964, in William E. Griffith (comp.), *Sino-Soviet Relations, 1964–1965* (Cambridge, Mass.: MIT Press, 1967), p. 232.

132 Soviet Government Statement, 21 August 1963, in William E. Griffith (comp.), *The Sino-Soviet Rift* (Cambridge, Mass.: MIT Press, 1964), p. 365.

133 *Khrushchev Remembers,* p. 399. See also Khrushchev's address to the

Rumanian Communist Party Congress, 21 June 1960, in David Floyd (comp.), *Mao Against Khrushchev* (New York: Praeger, 1963), p. 280; 'Statement' of the Moscow Conference, 6 December 1960, *ibid.*, p. 299; and editorial, 'Strengthen the Unity of the Communist Movement for the Triumph of Peace and Socialism', *Pravda*, 7 January 1963, *ibid.*, p. 348.

134 Editorial in *JMJP*, 13 November 1956, in *SWB/FE*, no. 614 (20 November 1956), p. 4.

135 'Statement by the Spokesman of the Chinese Government – A Comment on the Soviet Government's Statement of August 21, September 1, 1963', *PR*, no. 36 (6 September 1963), p. 13. On 22 March 1959, when Egypt's relations with the Soviet Union were strained, Nasser revealed in a speech that, up to 6 November 1956 when the fighting virtually ended, Egypt had been alone without even a hint of the slightest help from the Soviet Union. Heikal, *Nasser: the Cairo Documents*, pp. 134–8.

136 Chou T'ien-ch'ih, 'Lessons of the Arab War against Aggression', *Hung Ch'i (Red Flag)*, no. 13 (17 August 1967), p. 54, in *PR*, no. 37 (8 September 1967), p. 24.

137 Muḥammad Ḥasanayn Haykal, *Aḥādīth fī Āsiyā (Dialogues in Asia)* (Beirut: Dār al-Maʿārif, 1973), pp. 87–8. See also in *al-Anwār* (Beirut), 23 February 1973.

138 Editorial in *JMJP*, 5 November 1956, in *SWB/FE*, no. 612 (13 November 1956), p. 5.

139 *JMJP*, 11 November 1956, in *SWB/FE*, no. 613 (15 November 1956), p. 6.

140 Chou En-lai, 'Report on Visit to Eleven Countries in Asia and Europe', delivered to the 3rd session of the 2nd National Committee of the CPPCC, 5 March 1957, NCNA, *Daily Bulletin*, supplement no. 251 (6 March 1957), p. 17.

CHAPTER 3

1 'Summing Up of Provincial and Municipal Party Secretaries Conference' (January 1957), *Mao Tse-tung ssu-hsiang wan-sui*, pp. 82–3. English translation in *JPRS*, no. 61269-1, p. 55. Official version in *Selected Works of Mao Tse-tung*, vol. v, pp. 361–2.

2 For example, 'Talks with Directors of Various Co-Operative Areas' (speech of 12 December 1958), *Mao Tse-tung ssu-hsiang wan-sui*, p. 256. English translation in *JPRS*, no. 61269-1, p. 137. See also John Gittings, 'New Light on Mao – His View of the World', *China Quarterly*, no. 60 (December 1974), pp. 756–7.

3 'Address at the Supreme State Conference' (speech of 5 September 1958), *Mao Tse-tung ssu-hsiang wan-sui*, p. 232; see also speech of 8 September, p. 239. English translation in *Chinese Law and Government*, vol. ix, no. 3 (Fall 1976), pp. 82, 91.

4 Editorial on the current situation in the Middle East, *JMJP*, 10 September 1957, in *SWB/FE*, no. 699 (17 September 1957), pp. 2–3.

5 5 September 1958 address at the Supreme State Conference, p. 233. English translation in *Chinese Law and Government*, p. 83.

6 8 September 1958 address at the Supreme State Conference, pp. 237–240. English translation in *Chinese Law and Government*, p. 89. See also NCNA, 8 September 1958, in *SWB/FE*, no. 801 (11 September 1958), p. 43.

7 'Speech at the Sixteenth Supreme State Conference' (15 April 1959),

Mao Tse-tung ssu-hsiang wan-sui (n.p., 1967), p. 54. English translation in *Chinese Law and Government*, p. 100.

8 8 September 1958 address at the Supreme State Conference, p. 240. English translation in *Chinese Law and Government*, p. 93.

9 Shuqayrī, *Min al-Qimma ilā 'l-Hazīma*, p. 261.

10 Kuo Mo-jo's speech in the rally on Bandung Conference Anniversary, NCNA, 23 April 1959, in *SWB/FE/10/A3/2*.

11 'The strength of the world anti-imperialist camp has surpassed that of the imperialist camp. It is we, not the enemy, who are in the superior position.' 'The Present Situation and Our Tasks' (25 December 1947), *Selected Works of Mao Tse-tung*, vol. IV, p. 172.

12 Editorial in *JMJP*, 10 September 1957, in *SWB/FE*, no. 699 (17 September 1957), p. 2.

13 Burhān's message of greetings to Nasser, NCNA, 26 July 1957, in *SWB/FE*, no. 686 (1 August 1957), p. 16.

14 United Nations, *Yearbook of International Trade Statistics 1960* (New York: Statistical Office of the United Nations, Department of Economic and Social Affairs, 1961), p. 562. Most Chinese imports from Egypt consisted of raw cotton.

15 NCNA, 21 December 1957, in *SWB/FE*, no. 728 (30 December 1957), p. 8.

16 NCNA, 17 October 1957, in *SWB/FE*, no. 710 (24 October 1957), p. 2.

17 *Al-Difāʿ* (Jordan), 12 and 22 November 1956, and *The Times*, 21 November 1956.

18 NCNA (Cairo), 24 March 1957, in *SCMP*, no. 1498 (27 March 1957), p. 21. Jordan in fact recognised the PRC only in April 1977.

19 *Kuang-ming jih-pao*, 25 July 1957, in *SWB/FE*, no. 685 (30 July 1957), p. 4.

20 *SWB/FE*, no. 690 (15 August 1957), p. 4; no. 694 (29 August 1957), p. 1; no. 702 (26 September 1957), p. 7.

21 Yu Chao-li (pseud.), 'A New Upsurge of National Revolution', *Hung Ch'i*, no. 5 (1 August 1958), translated in *PR*, no. 26 (26 August 1958), p. 9.

22 See above, pp. 17–18.

23 On the Egyptian–Syrian union see: Malcolm Kerr, *The Arab Cold War 1958–1967, A Study of Ideology in Politics* (London: Oxford University Press, 1967), ch. 1.

24 Heikal, *Nasser: the Cairo Documents*, p. 119.

25 Chou En-lai, 'The Present International Situation and China's Foreign Policy', NCNA, 11 February 1958, in *CB*, no. 492 (14 February 1958), p. 3.

26 'Report on the Work of the Central Committee of the Communist Party of China to the Second Session of the Eighth National Congress', delivered by Liu Shao-ch'i on 5 May 1958, in *PR*, no. 14 (3 June 1958), p. 7.

27 *New York Times*, 2 January 1959; *The Times*, 2 and 5 January 1959.

28 For example, NCNA, 3 and 6 January 1959, in *SWB/FE*, no. 835 (13 January 1959), p. 10.

29 *JMJP*, 19 June 1957, in *SCMP*, no. 1556 (24 June 1957), p. 38.

30 Ch'en Yi's speech at the UAR ambassador's reception, NCNA, 22 February 1959, in *SWB/FE*, no. 848 (26 February 1959), p. 16.

31 Editorial, 'Victory Belongs to the Arab People', *JMJP*, 3 August 1958, in *SWB/FE*, no. 791 (7 August 1958), p. 11.

32 *JMJP*, 5 February 1957, in *SCMP*, no. 1466 (8 February 1957), pp. 35–6.

33 Charles Neuhauser, *Third World Politics, China and the Afro-Asian People's Solidarity Organization 1957–1967* (Cambridge, Mass.: Harvard East Asian Monographs, 1968), pp. 11–21.

34 For example, 'At the moment when the national countries in Asia and Africa, above all the Arab states, urgently need to strengthen unity among themselves and among all anti-imperialist forces in their respective countries, Tito acted as a provocateur to undermine this unity everywhere.' Editorial, 'Tito's Trip to Asia and Africa', *JMJP*, 18 March 1959. See also *PR*, no. 12 (24 March 1959), pp. 9–10.

35 Heikal, *Nasser: the Cairo Documents*, p. 232.

36 See Nasser's speeches on 13, 15 and 20 March 1959, UAR Information Department, *Press Release*, no. 46/59 and 50/59. Excerpts in Walter Laqueur, *The Struggle for the Middle East: The Soviet Union and the Middle East 1958–68* (London: Routledge and Kegan Paul, 1969), pp. 229–35.

37 Yu Chao-li (pseud.), 'Imperialism Is the Sworn Enemy of Arab National Liberation', *Hung Ch'i*, no. 7 (1 April 1959), pp. 1–8; in *PR*, no. 14 (7 April 1959), pp. 10–14. See also editorial, 'What Are the True National Interests of the Arab Peoples', *JMJP*, 20 March 1959, in *PR*, no. 12 (24 March 1959), pp. 6–9.

38 Chou En-lai, 'Report on the Work of the Government' (delivered at the 1st Session of the 2nd NPC, 18 April 1959), in *SWB/FE/5/c2/24*.

39 The UAR Information Department published a special 60-page pamphlet entitled *The Tibetan Revolution*. NCNA, 23 April 1959, in *SCMP*, no. 2002 (29 April 1959), p. 42.

40 Editorial in *Akhbār al-Yawm*, 2 May 1959.

41 For example, *Akhbār al-Yawm*, 18 July 1959, and NCNA, 22 July 1959, in *SWB/FE/86/A4/1*.

42 Texts in *SWB/FE*, no. 735 (23 January 1958), pp. 10–16.

43 *Ḥawl al-ʿĀlam* (Jordan), 24 September 1959; *Newsweek*, 24 November 1959, and *al-Ḥayāt* (Beirut), 25 November 1959.

44 *JMJP*, 30 September 1959, in *CB*, no. 594 (2 October 1959), pp. 72–3.

45 *Al-Ahrām*, 1 October 1959, p. 4.

46 *An Interview with President Nasser* (Washington: Press Department, Embassy of UAR, 1959), p. 7, quoted by Joseph E. Khalili, *Communist China's Interaction With the Arab Nationalists Since the Bandung Conference* (New York: Exposition Press, 1970), pp. 22–3.

47 For example, Ṣalāḥ Sālim, 'We – and China', *al-Jumhūriyya*, 1 October 1959; *al-Akhbār*, 2 and 9 October 1959, and Egypt's press, 1 to 25 October 1959.

48 *New York Times*, 26 October 1959, and *La Bourse Egyptienne*, 25 October 1959.

49 Heikal, *Nasser: the Cairo Documents*, p. 273.

50 Khālid Bakdāsh, 'A-la-po min-tsu yun-tung chung-ti liang t'iao tao-lu' ('Two Trends in the Arab National Movement'), *Ho-p'ing ho she-hui-chu-i wen-t'i* (*Problems of Peace and Socialism*), no. 11 (November 1959), pp. 32–9, published simultaneously in *World Marxist Review*, vol. II (November 1959), pp. 26–32.

51 'On the Anti-China Question' (22 March 1960), *Mao Tse-tung ssu-hsiang wan-sui*, pp. 316–18. English translation in *JPRS*, no. 61269–1, p. 227.

52 Chou En-lai, 'The Current International Situation and China's Foreign Relations' (speech at the 2nd Session of the 2nd NPC, 10 April 1960), NCNA, in *SWB/FE/308/c/3*.

53 See, for example, Nasser's view on the problem of Taiwan, *al-Ahrām*, 3 September 1958; also p. 98 above.

54 Editorial, 'Hail to the Iraqi People's Great Victory', *JMJP*, 16 July 1958, in *PR*, no. 21 (22 July 1958), p. 8.

55 *Japan Times*, 8 October 1959. See also Nasser-Eddine Mon'im (Naṣir al-Dīn Mun'im), *Arab-Chinese Relations 1950–1971* (Beirut: The Arab Institute for Research and Publishing, n.d.), pp. 211ff.

56 See for example, Maḥmūd al-Durra, *al-Tajriba al-Shuyu'iyya fī 'l-Ṣīn* (*The Communist Experience in China*) (Beirut: Dār al-Kātib al-'Arabī, 1964). The author visited China with the first Iraqi Friendship Delegation in 1958 and later became a political refugee in the UAR; Fu'ād al-Rikābī, *al-Ḥall al-Awḥad* (*The Only Solution*) (Cairo: al-Sharika al-'Arabiyya li 'l-Ṭibā'a wa 'l-Nashr, 1963). The author was a Ba'thist and Minister of Development in Kassem's first government, and later became a political refugee; Harry B. Ellis, *Challenge in the Middle East, Communist Influence and American Policy* (New York: Ronald Press, 1960). See also *al-Ahrām*, 3 October 1959, and *al-Ḥawādith* (Beirut), 6 November 1959, and other Egyptian and pro-Egyptian newspapers in the Arab world.

57 Uriel Dann, *Iraq Under Qassem, A Political History, 1958–1963* (London: Pall Mall, 1969), pp. 227, 233 and n. 16. See also Neuhauser, *Third World Politics*, pp. 84–5, n. 31.

58 Editorial, 'A New Stage of the International Communist Movement', *JMJP*, 19 November 1958, in *PR*, no. 39 (25 November 1958), p. 8.

59 'Speech at the Tenth Plenum of the Eighth Central Committee' (24 September 1962), *Mao Tse-tung ssu-hsiang wan-sui*, p. 433. English translation in Stuart Schram (ed.), *Mao Tse-tung Unrehearsed, Talks and Letters: 1956–71* (Harmondsworth: Penguin Books, 1974), p. 192.

60 *Al-Waqāi' al-'Irāqiyya* (*Iraqi Official Gazette*), 14 December 1959.

61 *New York Times*, 19 January 1957, and *Middle Eastern Affairs*, vol. VIII, no. 3 (March 1957), p. 124.

62 Text in Yaacov Ro'i, *From Encroachment to Involvement, A Documentary Study of Soviet Policy in the Middle East, 1945–1973* (Jerusalem: Israel Universities Press, 1974), pp. 210–15.

63 'Foreign Ministry Statement on the Soviet Union's Middle East Proposal' (17 February 1957), *Jen-min shou-ts'e 1958*, p. 432. English translation in *SCMP*, no. 1474 (20 February 1957), pp. 36–7.

64 Editorial in *JMJP*, 20 February 1957, in *SWB/FE*, no. 641 (26 February 1957), p. 2.

65 Chou En-lai, 'Report on Visit to Eleven Countries in Asia and Europe', 5 March 1957, NCNA, *Daily Bulletin*, supplement no. 251 (6 March 1957), pp. 19, 22.

66 *JMJP*, 7 September 1957, in *SWB/FE*, no. 698 (12 September 1957), p. 2.

67 Joint Statement by the China Peace Committee, the Chinese Islamic Association and the China–Syria and China–Egypt Friendship Association, 18 October 1957, *Jen-min shou-ts'e 1958*, p. 433. English translation, NCNA, 18 October 1957, in *SWB/FE*, no. 710 (24 October 1957), p. 3.

68 Commentary in *Ta-kung pao*, 19 October 1957, in *SWB/FE*, no. 710 (24 October 1957), p. 4.

69 Editorial, 'Hands off Syria!' *JMJP*, 18 October 1957, *ibid.*, p. 4.

70 Editorial in *JMJP*, 22 October 1957, in *SWB/FE*, no. 711 (29 October 1957), p. 4.

71 Mao Tse-tung, 'Speech at Moscow Celebration Meeting' (delivered on November 6, 1957, in celebration of the 40th Anniversary of the October Revolution), *JMJP*, 7 November 1957, in *CB*, no. 480 (13 November 1957), p. 3.

72 The suggestion was put forward by Khrushchev himself: *Khrushchev Remembers, the Last Testament,* p. 254.

73 Statement on the Lebanon by the Spokesman of the PRC's Foreign Ministry, 29 June 1958, in *SWB/FE*, no. 781 (3 July 1958), pp. 5–6.

74 *JMJP*, 19 June 1958, in *SWB/FE*, no. 778 (24 June 1958), p. 4.

75 According to Haykal who accompanied Nasser. Heikal, *Nasser: the Cairo Documents,* pp. 127–8. Khrushchev's account is somewhat different: 'We counteracted the U.S. landing in Lebanon, not by military means but by mobilising world public opinion... We also began demonstrative military preparations to show that we would be ready and willing to extend military aid in the Near East if it were needed.' *Khrushchev Remembers, the Last Testament,* p. 340.

76 Editorial, 'The World Cannot Look On with Folded Arms', *JMJP*, 20 July 1958. Abridged translation in *PR*, no. 22 (29 July 1958), pp. 5–6.

77 NCNA, 23 July 1958, in *SWB/FE*, no. 788 (29 July 1958), p. 2.

78 *Khrushchev Remembers,* p. 433; *Khrushchev Remembers, the Last Testament,* pp. 258–61; Mao Tse-tung, 'Talks with Directors of Various Co-Operative Areas' (speech of 30 November 1958), in *Mao Tse-tung ssu-hsiang wan-sui,* p. 254. English translation in *JPRS*, no. 61269–1, p. 135. See also 'Speech at the Tenth Plenum of the Eighth Central Committee' (24 September 1962), *Mao Tse-tung ssu-hsiang wan-sui,* p. 432, English translation in Schram, *Mao Unrehearsed,* p. 190; and the note by Allen S. Whiting in *China Quarterly,* no. 63 (September 1975), p. 611

79 *Khrushchev Remembers, the Last Testament,* pp. 258–61; *Mao Tse-tung ssu-hsiang wan-sui,* p. 255.

80 'Standing at the Forefront to Safeguard Peace', *JMJP*, 3 August 1958, in *SWB/FE*, no. 791 (7 August 1958), p. 5.

81 Editorial in *Ta-kung pao,* 5 August 1958, in *SWB/FE*, no. 792 (12 August 1958), p. 4.

82 NCNA, 8 August 1958, in *SWB/FE*, no. 793 (14 August 1958), pp. 3–4.

83 *JMJP*, 8 August 1958, *ibid.*, pp. 1–3.

84 Yu Chao-li (pseud.), 'An Excellent Situation for the Peace Struggle', *Hung Ch'i,* no. 1 (1 January 1960), pp. 33–9, in *SCMP*, no. 2171 (7 January 1960), pp. 3–10. See also Chou En-lai, 'The Current International Situation and China's Foreign Relations' (speech at the 2nd Session of the 2nd NPC, 10 April 1960), in *SWB/FE/308/c/1–5.*

85 People's Liberation Army, General Political Department, 'Source Material: Several Important Problems Concerning the Current International Situation', *Kung-tso t'ung-hsün (Bulletin of Activities),* no. 17 (25 April 1961), English translation in J. Chester Cheng (ed.), *The Politics of the Chinese Red Army* (Stanford, California: Hoover Institution of War, Revolution and Peace, 1966), p. 484.

86 Neuhauser, *Third World Politics,* pp. 24–7.

87 For example, *Akhbār al-Yawm,* 16 January 1960, and Muḥammad Ḥasanayn Haykal, 'Naḥnu wa 'l-Shuyū'iyya: 7 Fawāriq bayn al-Shuyū'iyya wa bayn al-Ishtirākiyya al-'Arabiyya' ('Communism and Ourselves: Seven Differences between Communism and Arab Socialism'), *al-Ahrām,* 4 August 1961.

88 *Egyptian Gazette,* 26 April 1960.

89 United Nations General Assembly, General Debate Proceedings, Provisional Edition, A/PV, 873, 27 September 1960.
90 There were a few indirect accusations. For example, in their condolences over the death of a Lebanese communist leader in a Syrian jail the Chinese blamed the reactionary, presumably UAR, authorities for his brazen murder. *PR*, no. 24 (16 June 1961), p. 26.
91 Cheng, *The Politics of the Chinese Red Army*, pp. 481, 487.
92 *Ibid.*, p. 484.
93 National Bank of Egypt, *Economic Bulletin*, vol. XXIV, no. 3 (Cairo, 1971), table 5/2b.
94 As early as 1954 Nasser said in an interview: 'India with a 2,000-mile common frontier with China has a delicate problem and must follow the policy it deems fit to ensure her own safety and to ensure peace in the areas surrounding and affecting her – that is, in South East Asia. Only time will tell how successful that policy will be.' *The Hindu*, 5 September 1954.
95 Heikal, *Nasser: the Cairo Documents*, p. 237.
96 *Ibid.*
97 NCNA, 26 October 1962, in *SCMP*, no. 2850 (31 October 1962), p. 39, and 'Alī Ḥamdī al-Jamāl, *al-Nizāʿ bayn al-Hind wa 'l-Ṣīn (The Conflict between India and China)* (Cairo: Dār al-Qalām, 1964), pp. 19–25.
98 G. H. Jansen, *Nonalignment and the Afro-Asian States* (New York: Praeger, 1966), pp. 331–2.
99 Al-Jamāl, *al-Nizāʿ bayn al-Hind wa 'l-Ṣīn*, p. 27.
100 Editorial in *al-Jumhūriyya*, 6 November 1962; see also Muḥammad Ḥasanayn Haykal in *al-Ahrām*, 9 November 1962.
101 Jansen, *Nonalignment and the Afro-Asian States*, p. 335.
102 See *Chairman Mao Tse-tung's Important Talks with Guests from Asia, Africa and Latin America* (Peking: Foreign Languages Press, 1960), pp. 2–8.
103 Quoted in *Middle East Record 1960*, p. 76.
104 For example, an editorial from Ṣawt al-Aḥrār of 3 March 1960 entitled 'Who Is Responsible for This Confusion in the Progress of Our Republic?' was published in *JMJP*, 31 March 1960 and later broadcast by Peking radio in Arabic. *SWB/FE/301/A4/1*.
105 NCNA, 4 March 1961, in *SCMP*, no. 2453 (10 March 1961), p. 25.
106 NCNA, 29 June 1961, in *SCMP*, no. 2531, p. 4, and *PR*, no. 26 (7 July 1961), p. 29.
107 See, for example, editorial, 'British Troops Must Withdraw Immediately from Kuwait', *JMJP*, 11 July 1961, in *SCMP*, no. 2539 (18 July 1961), pp. 30–2.
108 Editorial, 'Stop British Armed Intervention Against Kuwait', *JMJP*, 4 July 1961, in *SCMP*, no. 2534 (11 July 1961), pp. 30–2.
109 NCNA, 14 July 1961, in *SCMP*, no. 2541 (20 July 1961), p. 36.
110 *Ibid.*, p. 37.
111 In December 1961 the Iraqi Government announced that the combined concessions of foreign oil companies, which had previously covered almost the whole country, would be restricted to an area of less than 1920 sq. km.
112 'Iraq Fights Foreign Monopolies', *PR*, no. 8 (23 February 1962), p. 22. See also *SCCS*, no. 5 (1962), pp. 10–11, and *JMJP*, 16 February 1962, in *SCMP*, no. 2683 (21 February 1962), p. 27.
113 According to the Sino-Iraqi trade agreements of 1960 and 1961, Iraq was to sell China crude oil and oil products. In July 1960 the Iraqi

Minister of Oil Affairs said that Iraq had sold (unspecified) quantities of crude oil to China at 4 per cent above the 'world price'. Earlier, on 9 January, it was reported that China had intended to buy 50,000 tons of crude oil (*Middle East Record 1960*, p. 76). This amount, 0.125 per cent of Iraq's oil exports, constituted no more than 1.5 per cent of China's oil imports in 1960, or 0.6 per cent of China's total oil supply.

114 *Le Commerce du Levant* (Beirut), 6, 25, and 28 July and 1 August 1962.

115 *PR*, no. 7 (15 February 1963), p. 19.

116 NCNA, 15 March 1963, in *SCMP*, no. 2942 (20 March 1963), pp. 27–8. See also 'The Persecution of Patriots', *PR*, no. 9 (1 March 1963), pp. 25–6; NCNA, 22–7 February 1963, in *SCMP*, no. 2927 (27 February 1963), pp. 29–31 and no. 2928 (28 February 1963), pp. 24–6.

117 See 'Conversation with Zanzibar Expert M. M. Ali and his Wife' (18 June 1964), *Mao Tse-tung ssu-hsiang wan-sui*, p. 510. English translation in *JPRS*, no. 61269–2, pp. 367–8.

118 'The Proletarian Revolution and Khrushchev's Revisionism: Comment on the Open Letter of the Central Committee of the CPSU (8)', by the Editorial Departments of *Jen-min Jih-pao* and *Hung Ch'i* (31 March 1964), in Griffith, *Sino-Soviet Relations, 1964–1965*, p. 201.

119 'The Soviet–Chinese Polemic: Suslov Speech – II', *Current Digest of the Soviet Press*, vol. XVI, no. 14 (29 April 1964).

120 NCNA, 22 September 1962, in *SCMP*, no. 2827 (27 September 1962), p. 40.

121 NCNA, 6 October 1962, in *SCMP*, no. 2837 (11 October 1962), p. 30.

122 One example: 'Struggle of the Arab People Against CENTO and Israel, the Tool of Imperialism', *PR*, no. 51 (22 December 1961), pp. 12, 16.

123 'Schiller and Sholem Aleichem Commemorated', *PR*, no. 48 (1 December 1959), p. 20. See also Ch'en Chen-kuang. 'T'an Hsiao-lo-mu A-lai-han-mu ho t'a-ti tsuo-p'in' ('Discussing Sholem Aleichem and His Works'), *Chung-shan ta-hsüeh hsüeh-pao* (*Chung-shan University Magazine*), no. 1–2 (1959), pp. 91–7, and a collection of translated stories, *I-ch'ang huan-hsi, i-ch'ang k'ung* (Peking: Jen-min wen-hsüeh ch'u-pan she, 1959). Yiddish writers had been translated into Chinese also in 1957. I am grateful to Dr Irene Eber of the Hebrew University for bringing these translations to my attention.

124 'Anti-Semitism – An International Conspiracy', *JMJP*, 11 January 1960, in *PR*, no. 3 (19 January 1960), pp. 20–1.

125 NCNA, 5 May 1961, in *SCMP*, no. 2494 (11 May 1961), p. 36.

126 NCNA, 1 June 1961, in *Daily Bulletin*, no. 1237 (2 June 1961), p. 28.

CHAPTER 4

1 'Speech at the Ninth Plenum of the Eighth CCP Central Committee' (18 January 1961), *Mao Tse-tung ssu-hsiang wan-sui* (1967), p. 262. English translation in *JPRS*, no. 61269–2, p. 241.

2 'Remarks at a Briefing' (March 1964), *Mao Tse-tung ssu-hsiang wan-sui* (1967), *ibid.*, p. 339.

3 NCNA report of *JMJP* editorial, 16 March 1964, in *SWB/FE/1509/* A4/1.

4 Vice Premier Li Hsien-nien in Egypt's National Day reception, NCNA, 23 July 1964, in *SCMP*, no. 3267 (28 July 1964), p. 25.

5 Commentator, 'Support the Just Stand of the Arab People', *JMJP*, 14 March 1965, in *SCMP*, no. 3419 (18 March 1965), p. 28.
6 *Ta-kung pao*, 26 April 1963, in *SCMP*, no. 2969 (1 May 1963), p. 43.
7 'Text of the Sino-Yemeni Friendship Treaty', NCNA, 15 June 1964, in *SCMP*, no. 3241 (18 June 1964), p. 38.
8 See Donald W. Klein, 'The Management of Foreign Affairs in Communist China', in John M. H. Lindbeck (ed.), *China, the Management of a Revolutionary Society* (Seattle: Washington University Press, 1971), p. 324.
9 NCNA, 24 August 1964, in *SCMP*, no. 3288 (27 August 1964), p. 40.
10 Heikal, *Nasser: the Cairo Documents*, p. 268.
11 Cairo radio, 12 January 1964, in *Mizan*, vol. vii, no. 2 (1965), p. 30.
12 See, for example, *al-Ahrām*, 9 April 1965, and *Rūz al-Yūsuf*, 19 April 1965.
13 See Oran R. Young, 'Chinese Views on the Spread of Nuclear Weapons', in Morton H. Halperin (ed.), *Sino-Soviet Relations and Arms Control* (Cambridge, Mass.: MIT Press, 1967), pp. 13–71, and especially p. 63; George H. Quester, 'Paris, Pretoria, Peking... Proliferation?' *Bulletin of the Atomic Scientists* (October 1970), pp. 12–16.
14 Vice Premier Ch'en Yi's press conference on 29 September 1965, *PR*, no. 41 (8 October 1965), p. 8. For a slightly different version see Harold C. Hinton, *China's Turbulent Quest* (Bloomington and London: Indiana University Press, 1973), pp. 187–8.
15 Rumours that China had offered, or was going to offer, nuclear aid to the Arabs usually came from Soviet sources. See Walter C. Clemens, 'Chinese Nuclear Tests: Trends and Portents', *China Quarterly*, no. 32 (October–December 1967), p. 126.
16 *New York Times*, 31 January 1966.
17 Heikal, *Nasser: the Cairo Documents*, pp. 274–5.
18 NCNA (Moscow), 8 November 1964, in *SCMP*, no. 3336 (13 November 1964), p. 39.
19 NCNA (Cairo), 1–2 April 1965, in *SCMP*, no. 3432 (6 April 1965), pp. 33–4, and no. 3433 (7 April 1965), pp. 25–8, 41–3.
20 *New York Times, The Times, Daily Telegraph*, 10 June 1965.
21 Simmonds, *China's World*, pp. 100–1.
22 NCNA (Cairo), 7 July 1963, in *SCMP*, no. 3021 (18 July 1963), p. 38.
23 Charles B. McLane, 'Foreign Aid in Soviet Third World Politics', *Mizan*, vol. x, no. 6 (November–December 1968), p. 222.
24 In February 1963 China signed three economic agreements with Syria. *PR*, no. 9 (1 March 1963), p. 5.
25 Data adapted from Eckstein, *Communist China's Economic Growth and Foreign Trade*, p. 307; Milton Kovner, 'Communist China's Foreign Aid to Less-Developed Countries', in Joint Economic Committee, Congress of the United States, *An Economic Profile of Mainland China*, vol. ii (Washington: US Government Printing Office, 1967), pp. 609–20. See also Appendix ii.
26 Union Research Institute, *Communist China 1964* (Hong Kong, 1965), p. 111.
27 NCNA, 21 December 1964, in *SCMP*, no. 3364 (24 December 1964), p. 27.
28 *Communist China 1964*, p. 111.
29 Cairo radio, 28 December 1964, in *Mizan*, vol. vii, no. 2 (1965), p. 29; *al-Ahrām*, 29 December 1964; *al-Jumhūriyya*, 2 and 19 January 1965.

30 'Sino-UAR Joint Communiqué', NCNA, 25 April 1963, in *SCMP*, no. 2969 (1 May 1963), pp. 37–8.
31 'Premier Chou En-lai's Press Conference', *PR*, no. 52 (27 December 1963), p. 12.
32 *Ibid.*, p. 11.
33 Editorial in *JMJP*, 17 March 1964, in *SWB/FE/*1509/A4/1.
34 *Al-Anwār*, 6 April 1965 (from NCNA), quoted by John K. Cooley, *Green March, Black September, The Story of the Palestinian Arabs* (London: Frank Cass, 1973), p. 176. See also *Al-Ḥawādith*, 30 April 1965.
35 Government of Israel, Prime Minister's Office, *Government Year Book 5724 (1963/4)* (Jerusalem, 1964), p. 155, and Brecher, *Israel, the Korean War and China*, p. 104.
36 For example, *PR*, no. 19 (7 May 1965), p. 4, condemning Bourguiba's proposal for Arab–Israeli peaceful co-existence.
37 China's view was reinforced by Indonesia's withdrawal from the UN early in 1965. See, for example, 'The United Nations – Tool of U.S. Imperialist Aggression', *PR*, no. 3 (15 January 1965), p. 14; 'Justice Cannot Be Upheld in U.N.', *PR*, no. 4 (22 January 1965), p. 13; 'U.N. Must Be Thoroughly Reorganised', *PR*, no. 5 (29 January 1965), p. 6.
38 Press Conference in Mogadishu (Somalia), NCNA, 3 February 1964, in *SCMP*, no. 3157 (10 February 1964), p. 33.
39 NCNA, 5 February 1964, in *SWB/FE/*1486/A4/1.
40 Without mentioning these names *Dawn* (Pakistan) of 28 March 1964 reported that they had come from the Palestine Bureau in Algeria which, according to one of them, was the strongest private organisation after the Arab League struggling for the Palestine cause. The Chinese, who named the guests as Muḥammad Khalīl and Muḥammad Rifa'at, gave no clue to their real identities. Other sources confirmed that Khalīl al-Wazīr had visited China at that time. See Ehud Ya'ari, *Fataḥ* (Tel Aviv, 1970), pp. 27–8, 227; Cooley, *Green March, Black September*, p. 91. On 16 January 1973 the Egyptian daily *al-Jumhūriyya* said that both Abū-'Amār and Abū-Jihād had visited China in 1964. These are the pseudonyms of Yasser Arafat and Khalīl al-Wazīr. See also, 'Al-'Alāqāt al-Filasṭīniyya al-Ṣīniyya' ('Sino-Palestinian Relations'), *Filasṭīnunā (Our Palestine)*, no. 36 (March 1964), pp. 16–18. April–May 1963 as the date of the visit is given in Thomas Kiernan, *Arafat, the Man and the Myth* (New York: W. W. Norton, 1976), pp. 226–7).
41 'Joint Statement of the Chinese People's Institute of Foreign Affairs and the PLO', *JMJP*, 23 March 1965, in *SCMP*, no. 3425 (26 March 1965), p. 36.
42 Van Ness, *Revolution and Chinese Foreign Policy*, ch. 4, and especially pp. 85–6, 92–3.
43 'You Fight Your Way, We Fight Ours', A Talk with the Palestine Liberation Organisation Delegation (March 1965), *Mao Tse-tung ssu-hsiang wan-sui*, pp. 614–15, English translation in *JPRS*, no. 61269–2, pp. 447–8. Part of the talk is also in *Mao Tse-tung wen-hsüan (Selected Writings of Mao Tse-tung)* (n.p., n.d.), English translation in *Translations on Communist China*, no. 90, *JPRS*, no. 49826 (12 February 1970), p. 23.
44 Quoted in Cooley, *Green March, Black September*, p. 176. Cf. Shuqayrī, *Min al-Qimma ilā 'l-Hazīma*, p. 260.
45 Shuqayrī, *Min al-Qimma ilā 'l-Hazīma*, pp. 269–71. He and other

Palestinian leaders were very careful not to alienate the Soviets. They paid frequent tribute to the positive contribution of the USSR towards the Palestinians, especially in the United Nations and the Security Council (where China, of course, had no say). See, for example, Markaz al-Abḥāth, Munaẓẓamat al-Taḥrīr al-Filasṭīniyya (PLO Research Centre), *al-Yawmiyāt al-Filasṭīniyya* (*Palestinian Diary*), 1965, pp. 204, 252.

46 Muḥammad Ḥasanayn Haykal, 'Communists in Iraq', *al-Ahrām*, 29 March 1963.

47 For example, 'A Milestone in Sino-Arab Friendship and Unity', *JMJP*, 23 December 1963.

48 See also W. A. C. Adie, 'Chou En-lai On Safari', in Roderick Mac-Farquhar (ed.), *China Under Mao: Politics Takes Command* (Cambridge, Mass.: MIT Press, 1966), p. 471.

49 For example, 'The Mandarin Meets the Sphinx', *The Economist*, 21 December 1963, pp. 1257–8.

50 Heikal, *Nasser: the Cairo Documents*, p. 267.

51 NCNA (Cairo), 14 December 1963, in *SCMP*, no. 3132 (6 January 1964), p. 30.

52 A personal communication from Egypt's Foreign Minister Maḥmūd Riyāḍ, quoted by W. A. C. Adie, 'China, Israel and the Arabs', *Conflict Studies*, no. 12 (May 1971), p. 15.

53 Text of the joint statement in Ro'i, *From Encroachment to Involvement*, pp. 385–94. See also Malcolm H. Kerr, 'The Middle East and China, the Scope and Limits of Convergent Interests', in A. M. Halpern (ed.), *Policies Toward China – View from Six Continents* (New York: Mc-Graw-Hill, 1965), pp. 441–2.

54 *New York Times*, 5 September 1964, quoted in Walter Laqueur, *The Struggle for the Middle East* (New York: Macmillan, 1969), p. 71.

55 Franklin B. Weinstein, 'The Second Asian–African Conference: Preliminary Bouts', *Asian Survey*, vol. v, no. 7 (July 1965), pp. 361, 363.

56 Jakarta home service, 15 April 1964, in *SWB/FE*/1529/c1/1 and *SWB/FE*/1530/c/3.

57 Kimche, *The Afro-Asian Movement*, pp. 184–5.

58 Colin Legum, 'Africa and China', in Halpern, *Policies Toward China*, p. 419.

59 Editorial, 'For the Common Victory of a Common Cause', *JMJP*, 7 April 1965, in *SCMP*, no. 3436 (12 April 1965), pp. 27–8.

60 Vice Premier Ch'en Yi's press conference on 29 September 1965, *PR*, no. 41 (8 October 1965), p. 11. Later, however, Red Guard publications revealed Chou En-lai's admission that Chinese officials, both in the Middle East and in the International Liaison Department of the Party's Central Committee, had 'overestimated and miscalculated the bourgeois coup of Algeria'. *SCMM*, no. 636 (9 December 1968), p. 8.

61 Muḥammad Ḥasanayn Haykal, 'A Possibility of Postponing the Great Algerian Conference', *al-Ahrām*, 24 June 1965. See also Griffith, *Sino-Soviet Relations 1964–1965*, p. 126. It was argued that Egyptians had been connected to the explosion in the conference hall: Guy J. Pauker, 'The Rise and Fall of Afro-Asian Solidarity', *Asian Survey*, vol. v, no. 9 (September 1965), p. 430.

62 See above, p. 46.

63 Cairo radio, 20 December 1963.

64 NCNA, 2 August 1964, in *SCMP*, no. 3274 (7 August 1964), p. 29.
65 'U.S.S.R.–U.A.R. Communiqué', *Pravda*, 2 September 1965. English text in Ro'i, *From Encroachment to Involvement*, pp. 413–19. See also Laqueur, *The Struggle for the Middle East*, p. 72.
66 One of China's main arguments in calling for the exclusion of Moscow from the conference was that the Soviet Union was primarily a European country. For example, Observer, 'The Soviet Union Is Not Qualified to Participate in the Afro-Asian Conference', *JMJP*, 18 June 1965, in *SCMP*, no. 3482 (22 June 1965), pp. 18–23. Compare with China's stand in 1955, above, p. 227, n. 112.
67 Heikal, *Nasser: the Cairo Documents*, pp. 271–2.
68 *Krasnaya Zvezda (Red Star)*, 27 July 1965, in *Mizan*, vol. vii, no. 8 (1965), p. 12.
69 NCNA, 12 September 1965, in *PR*, no. 38 (17 September 1965), pp. 8–9.
70 Editorial, 'Second Asian–African Conference Should be Postponed', *JMJP*, 23 October 1965, in *SWB/FE/1994/A4/1–4*.
71 NCNA, 26 October 1965, in *SWB/FE/1997/A4/1–2*.
72 Alaba Ogunsanwo, *China's Policy in Africa 1958–71* (Cambridge University Press, 1974), p. 134. For more details on China's efforts concerning the conference, see pp. 122–34.
73 Shuqayrī, *Min al-Qimma ilā 'l-Hazīma*, pp. 233, 269–70.
74 *JMJP*, 3 September 1965, in *PR*, no. 36 (3 September 1965), pp. 9–30.
75 *Al-Ahrām*, 26 November 1965.
76 *New York Times*, 17 October 1965.
77 As we have seen, not only had his and the other ambassadors' recall been planned, but he was promoted to the post of Vice Foreign Minister.
78 Ye. Primakov in *Pravda*, 12 December 1965, in *Mizan*, vol. viii, no. 1 (January–February 1966), p. 3.
79 For example, S. G. Yurkov, *Pekin: Novaya Politika? (Peking: A New Policy?)* (Moscow: Izdatel'stvo Politicheskoi Literaturui, 1972), p. 138. For more details on the Aghā incident see 'The Chinese Penetration into the Arab World', *al-Ḥayāt*, 27 November 1965; *al-Jumhūriyya*, 10 January 1966; *New York Times*, 31 January and 16 February 1966; *Le Figaro*, 24 January 1966. The trial of Aghā's group started on 5 February 1966; in September he was sentenced to life imprisonment with hard labour. *Al-Ahrām*, 9 September 1966.
80 NCNA, 15 March 1965, in *SCMP*, no. 3419 (18 March 1965), p. 27. 'We must... resolutely, thoroughly, wholly and completely... in no circumstances interfere in the internal affairs of others or impose our own ideas upon others.' Editorial, 'Guarantee of New Victories for Socialism – New Year Message 1965', *JMJP*, 1 January 1965, in *SCMP*, no. 3371 (6 January 1965), pp. 3–6.
81 Ch'en Yi in Iraqi National Day reception, NCNA, 14 July 1964, in *SCMP*, no. 3260 (17 July 1964), p. 32.
82 For example, *Izvestiya*, 19 August 1964, in *Mizan*, vol. vii, no. 4 (1965), p. 8; Yurkov, *Pekin: Novaya Politika?*, p. 138; *al-Jarīda* (Beirut), 1 September 1965; *al-Ṣafā* (Beirut), 1 October 1965; *al-Ḥayāt*, 23 October 1965. See also *New York Times*, 24 October 1964, quoting Khālid Bakdāsh from *World Marxist Review*: 'In Syria, the Lebanon and in other Arab countries, the Chinese leaders are trying to build up splinter groups of shady elements.'
83 See, for example, Uriel Dann, 'The Communist Movement in Iraq since

1963', in Michael Confino and Shimon Shamir (eds.), *The U.S.S.R. and the Middle East* (Jerusalem: Israel Universities Press, 1973), pp. 381–2; Avigdor Levy, 'The Syrian Communists and the Ba'th Power Struggle, 1966–1970', *ibid.*, p. 402. See also Laqueur, *The Struggle for the Middle East*, p. 169.

84 Cairo radio, 25 November 1965, in *Mizan*, vol. vIII, no. 1 (January–February 1966), p. 17. See also *al-Jumhūriyya*, 28 November 1965.

85 In an interview in May 1966, Nasser again spoke about China with much restraint. He admitted that the Sino-Indian and Sino-Soviet conflicts had undermined the position of the national liberation movement in Asia and Africa and encouraged imperialist pressure everywhere, and that some aspects of China's Asian policy were arguable. He added, however, that with regard to Africa he did not perceive indications of Chinese radicalism either in words or in deeds. *Al-Ahrām*, 9 May 1966.

86 *Al-Ba'th* (Damascus), 15 November 1965.

87 *Al-Ḥayāt*, 14 December 1965. Some reports even traced these disagreements to the aftermath of Chou En-lai's June visit to Syria. *Al-Ḥurriyya* (Beirut), 28 June 1965. See also *al-Anwār*, 23 December 1965 and *al-Ḥayāt*, 24 December 1965.

88 *Al-Ḥayāt*, 26 February, 1 and 4 March 1966; *al-Jarīda*, 24 February 1966.

89 For example, Ạhmad Suwaydānī, formerly Chief of Army Intelligence who was appointed Chief of Staff following the *coup d'état*. He was said to have been fascinated by the writings of Giap and Mao, and visited Moscow as well as Peking. *Al-Ḥayāt*, 24 February 1966. See also Eliezer Be'eri, *Army Officers in Arab Politics and Society* (London: Praeger, 1970), p. 165.

90 *Al-Akhbār* (Beirut), 14 November 1965.

91 *Al-Ḥayāt*, 16 March 1966. See also M. S. Agwani, *Communism in the Arab East* (London: Asia Publishing House, 1969), p. 104.

92 Aryeh Yodfat, 'The U.S.S.R., Jordan and Syria', *Mizan*, vol. xi, no. 2 (March–April 1969), pp. 82, 83, 88, 91.

93 Adie, 'China, Israel and the Arabs', p. 6.

94 *Al-Jadīd* (Beirut), 21 October 1966.

95 Commentary in *JMJP*, 22 October 1966, on Syria's response to the 'plot' of Israeli aggression, in *SWB/FE/2298/A4/1*.

96 China's ambassador to Syria, Ch'en T'an, and to Iraq, Ts'ao Ch'ih, had also been appointed in January 1966.

97 There is still no sound explanation for this fact. Cairo had been for a long time a co-ordination centre for Chinese activities in Africa, the Middle East and the Afro-Asian movement, but other capitals were no less important. Allegedly, Chou En-lai told Nasser that Huang Hua had remained in Cairo as 'proof of respect' for Nasser. Heikal, *Nasser: the Cairo Documents*, p. 278.

98 *Al-Manār* (Baghdad), 3 February 1967.

99 *Al-Ḥayāt*, 28 January 1967.

100 *Rūz al-Yūsuf*, 13 February 1967.

101 See *Christian Science Monitor*, 5 June 1967, and Heikal, *Nasser: the Cairo Documents*, pp. 275–6.

102 For example, Commentator, 'The True Colours of False Friends', *JMJP*, 2 June 1967, in *SWB/FE/2481/A4/1*.

103 Editorial, 'Arab People, Unite, Make Sustained Efforts, and Fight Imperialism to the End', *JMJP*, 11 June 1967, in *SWB/FE/2489/A4/2*.

104 Chou T'ien-ch'ih, 'Lessons of the Arab War against Aggression', *Hung*

Ch'i, no. 13 (17 August 1967), pp. 51–7, English translation in *PR*, no. 37 (8 September 1967), pp. 22–6.
105 Editorial, 'Arab People's Anti-U.S. Storm is Irresistible', *JMJP*, 15 June 1967, in *SWB/FE/2492/A4/2*.
106 Editorials in *Ākhir Sā'a* (Cairo), 4 and 11 October 1967.
107 Quoted by Cairo radio, 13 June 1967, in *Mizan*, vol. IX, no. 4 (July–August 1967), p. 4. See also statement by Syrian trade union leader, Khālid al-Jundī, Damascus radio, 14 June 1967.
108 *Al-Ahrām*, 25 August 1967. See also Ro'i, *From Encroachment to Involvement*, p. 465.
109 Haykal in *al-Ahrām*, quoted by the *Egyptian Mail*, 23 September 1967. See also *al-Jumhūriyya*, 8 July 1967. The reference to Yugoslavia was a reaction to a Chinese attack on Tito. See, for example, Commentator, 'Renegade Tito's Dirty Mission to Middle East', *JMJP*, 28 August 1967, in *SWB/FE/2555/A4/1–2*.
110 Ṭāhir 'Abd al-Hakīm, 'The People's Army, Its Tasks and Composition', *al-Jumhūriyya*, 19 September 1968.
111 Heikal, *Nasser: the Cairo Documents*, pp. 274, 276–7.
112 *Al-Ahrām*, 26 and 18 January 1968, and 20 September 1968. See also Dr Ṣādiq Jalāl al-'Aẓm, 'al-Muqāwama al-Musallaḥa wa 'l-Mawāqif al-Haykaliyya' ('Armed Resistance and the Haykalian Position'), *Dirāsāt 'Arabiyya (Arab Studies)*, vol. V, no. 10 (August 1969), pp. 17–57.
113 Haykal, according to the Middle East News Agency, 11 July 1968. See also Muṣṭafā Ṭayba, 'The Political Struggle as a Means to Liquidate the Consequences of Israeli Aggression', *al-Akhbār* (Cairo), 16 August 1967.
114 *Al-Ḥayāt*, 30 May 1967.
115 *Al-Ḥayāt*, 6 August and 15 September 1967; *al-Ṣayyād* (Beirut), 10 August 1967; *al-Ṣafā*, 19 August 1967.
116 *Al-Jadīd*, 30 June 1967, and *Middle East Record 1967*, p. 497.
117 *L'Orient* (Beirut), 22 February 1968; *al-Jarīda*, 22 February and 3 March 1968; *al-Nahār* (Beirut), 22 February 1968.
118 *Al-Ḥawādith*, 1 November 1968.
119 See *al-Ṣayyād*, 2 November 1967, and 'The U.S.S.R. and the Persian Gulf', *Mizan*, vol. X, no. 2 (March–April 1968), p. 54.
120 *Al-Ḥawādith*, 18 October 1968.
121 Khālid Bakdāsh, 'Syrian Communists Call for Arab Unity', *al-Akhbār* (Beirut), 3 September 1967, in Laqueur, *The Struggle for the Middle East*, pp. 309–11. See also 'Resolution of the third conference of the Iraqi Communist Party', *Ṭarīq al-Sha'ab*, January 1968, in *SWB/ME/2702/4*; Fahmi Salfiti, 'The Situation in Jordan and Communist Tactics', *World Marxist Review* (October–November 1968), pp. 43–6.
122 'The Middle East: Soviet Anxieties', *Mizan*, vol. IX, no. 4 (July–August 1967). See also John K. Cooley, 'Moscow Wary of Peking Advances in Arab World', *Christian Science Monitor*, 5 June 1967; James Reston, 'China Is A Factor in Soviet Position', *New York Times*, 23 June 1967.
123 *Al-Ḥayāt*, 24 August 1967. The cancellation might in fact, merely have reflected the disturbances of the Cultural Revolution.
124 China offered this sum, as well as 150,000 tons of wheat, without conditions and without a date of repayment, as a token of admiration and appreciation of 'the Egyptian people's stand in face of the mighty imperialist conspiracy engineered and carried out with the actual and practical planning and participation of U.S. imperialism'. Cairo radio, 11 June 1967.

125 *China News Summary* (Hong Kong), no. 326 (2 July 1970), p. B1. The wheat shipments were already in Egypt by early July 1967. See *al-Ahrām*, 5 July 1967.
126 Editorial in *JMJP*, 15 May 1966, in *SWB/FE/2164/A4/3*.
127 NCNA, 15 May 1966, in *SWB/FE/2164/A4/4*.
128 NCNA, 4 May 1966, in *SWB/FE/2155/A4/1*.
129 Kuo Chien, vice-chairman of the Chinese Committee for Afro-Asian Solidarity, at a rally in Peking in support of Palestine. NCNA, 20 May 1966, in *SWB/FE/2167/A4/1*.
130 Editorial in *JMJP*, 15 May 1966, in *SWB/FE/2164/A4/3*.
131 *Al-Ḥayāt*, 12 February 1966.
132 *Al-Ḥayāt*, 24 March 1966.
133 For example, Commentator, 'Break this Aggressor Dagger Israel into Pieces', *JMJP*, 16 November 1966, in *SWB/FE/2319/A4/1*.
134 For example, 'The Palestinian people are more convinced than ever that people's liberation war is the only way to *eliminate* the colonialist base – Israel – and to liberate Palestine *completely*.' Statement from Peking Office of the PLO, NCNA, 10 November 1966, in *SWB/FE/2316/A4/2*. [Italics added.]
135 More details in Zeev Schiff and Raphael Rothstein, *Fedayeen – The Story of the Palestinian Guerrillas* (London: Valentine, Mitchell, 1972), pp. 71, 209–10. Chinese aid was generally given free.
136 NCNA, 26 October 1966, in *SWB/FE/2303/A4/2*. See also Samīr Ḥakīm (a Palestinian working in China), 'Mao Tse-tung's Thought Is Guide For Palestinian People', *JMJP*, 17 May 1967, in *SWB/FE/2470/A4/1–2*.
137 For example, in Ṣawt Filasṭīn (The Voice of Palestine), 24 June 1966, in *Mizan*, vol. VIII, no. 4 (1966), p. 8. Also interview in *al-Anwār*, 31 May 1967.
138 *Al-Ḥawādith* (Beirut), 3 February 1967, and other Arab newspapers of that day. See also *al-Yawmiyāt al-Filasṭīniyya*, 15 February 1967 and 15 July 1966.
139 Chou T'ien-ch'ih, 'Lessons of the Arab War against Aggression'.
140 He pointed out that the Galilee mountains were of great military advantage, being close to vital Israeli targets, as well as to Syria and Lebanon, where rear bases could be established. See Shuqayrī, *Min al-Qimma ilā 'l-Hazīma*, pp. 237–8.
141 Van Ness, *Revolution and Chinese Foreign Policy*, pp. 217–20.
142 Chou En-lai's message of support to Shuqayrī, NCNA, 6 June 1967, in *SWB/FE/2485/A4/3*.
143 For example, Fatḥ, Ḥarakat al-Taḥrīr al-Waṭanī al-Filasṭīnī (Fatah, the Palestinian National Liberation Movement), *Dirāsāt wa Tajārib Thawriyya (Revolutionary Trials and Lessons)*, no. 4, *al-Tajriba al-Ṣīniyya (The Chinese Experience)* (n.p., August 1967). p. 40.
144 Y. Harkabi, 'Fedayeen Action and Arab Strategy', *Adelphi Papers*, no. 53 (December 1968), pp. 13–14.
145 For example, 'It must be acknowledged that the PLO...headed by Ahmed Shukairy failed to liberate Palestine... Today the PLO, this pseudo-liberation organisation, is no longer playing any significant role in the liberation of Palestine. The reason being that it did not spring from the masses themselves, but was artificially imposed from above. Al-Fatah, the Palestine National Liberation Movement, *Press Release*, no. 1 (January 1968), p. 6.
146 For example, *al-Ḥawādith*, 21 February and 3 March 1967.

147 See *al-Ahrām*, 15 September 1967, 18 and 26 January, 15 August and 19 September 1968.
148 *Al-Ṣayyād*, 30 January 1969.
149 *Christian Science Monitor* (London edn), 11 July 1968, and Edgar O'Ballance, *Arab Guerrilla Power 1967–1972* (London: Faber and Faber, 1974), p. 124.

CHAPTER 5

1 *PR*, special issue (28 April 1969), pp. 25–9. 'Peking hint of aid for Asian armed revolts', *The Times*, 6 April 1969.
2 For more details see Appendix ɪ.
3 *Al-Ṣafā*, 17 May 1969; *Christian Science Monitor*, 14 August 1969; *Daily Telegraph*, 19 August 1969.
4 NCNA, 2 February 1970, in *SWB/FE/3296/ᴀ4/1*. See also Tillman Durdin, 'China's Note to Nasser Is Seen As Bid to Widen Mideast Role', *New York Times*, 8 February 1970; Stanley Karnow, 'China's Only a Paper Tiger Despite Middle East Bombast', *Washington Post*, 23 February 1970.
5 NCNA, 18 February 1970, in *SWB/FE/3309/ᴀ4/1*.
6 *Al-Ahrām* and the Middle East News Agency, 25 March 1970.
7 Heikal, *Nasser: the Cairo Documents*, p. 277.
8 For example, 'China and the Death of President Nasser', *China News Summary* (Hong Kong), no. 339 (1 October 1970), pp. ʙ4–ʙ5.
9 Heikal, *Nasser: the Cairo Documents*, pp. 23–4.
10 'Peking Seeks Better Ties with Egypt', *International Herald Tribune*, 8 February 1971; *Le Monde*, 31 January–1 February 1971.
11 Avigdor Levy, 'The Syrian Communists and the Baʿth Power Struggle, 1966–1970', in Shamir and Confino, *The U.S.S.R. and the Middle East*, pp. 407–11.
12 These views were put forward particularly by the Lebanese press and were quoted in the Western press. See for example, *al-Ḥayāt*, 16 and 22 May and 9 June 1969; *al-Jarīda*, 25 May 1969; *Egyptian Gazette*, 14 May 1969. See also Paul Martin, 'China Enters Scene in Middle East', *The Times*, 19 May 1969; *The Observer*, 18 May 1969, and *Le Monde*, 22 May 1969.
13 *Al-Ṣayyād*, 22 May 1969.
14 Huang Yung-sheng, China's Chief of Staff, at a banquet given in honour of the Syrian military delegation, NCNA, 14 May 1969, in *SWB/FE/3075/ᴀ4/1*.
15 *Al-Ḥayāt*, 9 June 1969.
16 See Radio Peace and Progress, 13 August 1969, and *Pravda*, 14 September 1969.
17 NCNA Correspondent, 'Destiny of Middle East determined by Arab revolutionary people', 10 April 1970, in *SWB/FE/3353/ᴀ4/2*.
18 *Al-Ḥawādith*, 20 February 1970.
19 See NCNA, 19 July 1970, in *SWB/FE/3436/ᴀ4/1*.
20 D. L. Price, 'Oman: Insurgency and Development', *Conflict Studies*, no. 53 (January 1975), p. 5.
21 For example, *PR*, no. 4 (24 January 1970), p. 25, and *SWB/FE/3487/ᴀ4/5*
22 NCNA, 21 March 1970, in *SWB/FE/3338/ᴀ4/1–3*.
23 Ḥasan Ghasānī (alias Ṭalāl Saʿad), Director of the PFLOAG office in Aden, NCNA, 10 June 1970, in *SWB/FE/3406/ᴀ4/1*.

24 There were allegations that the Chinese had stood behind the hijackings, if not in practice then in theory. See 'Guerrillas claim the "right"
of revolutionaries to disregard international law', *The Times*, 21 September 1970.
25 For example, *Christian Science Monitor*, 5 November 1970. See also
Ross Terrill, *800,000,000 The Real China* (Harmondsworth: Penguin
Books, 1975), p. 127.
26 *Christian Science Monitor*, 14 November 1970. See also Cooley, *Green
March, Black September*, p. 143.
27 For more details on the change in Soviet attitude in favour of the
Palestinians, see Moshe Ma'oz, 'Soviet and Chinese Influence on the
Palestinian Guerrilla Movement', in Alvin Z. Rubinstein (ed.), *Soviet
and Chinese Influence in the Third World* (New York: Praeger, 1975),
pp. 116–19. See also Galia Golan, 'The Soviet Union and the PLO',
Research Paper no. 19 (The Hebrew University of Jerusalem, The
Soviet and East European Research Centre, December 1976), p.
105.
28 Talāl Salmān, in *al-Ṣayyād*, 6 February 1969.
29 Commentary, 'A Word to Pravda', *Fatḥ*, 4 August 1970.
30 'The Political, Organizational and Military Report of the Popular Front
for the Liberation of Palestine' (February 1969), in Leila S. Kadi,
*Basic Political Documents of the Armed Palestinian Resistance Move-
ment* (Beirut: Palestine Liberation Organisation Research Centre,
December 1969), pp. 219–20.
31 Commentary, 'The Armed Struggle of the Palestinian People Is Forging
Ahead in Victory', *JMJP*, 7 January 1970, in *SWB/FE/3274/A4/1*.
32 'The Resistance, How Does It Think and Act? How Does It Face the
Present? How Does It See the Future?' a dialogue with Fatah, *al-
Ṭalī'a* (Cairo), June 1969, in Kadi, *Documents*, p. 70.
33 Quoted in Kadi, *Documents*, pp. 102–3.
34 *Al-Hadaf* (Beirut), 17 October 1970, and Cooley, *Green March, Black
September*, p. 143.
35 *Al-Ḥawādith*, 11 September 1970, and *Niḍā al-Waṭan*, 16 September
1970.
36 For example, Abdullah Schleifer, 'La Percée Chinoise au Proche-
Orient', *Jeune Afrique*, no. 537 (20 April 1971), p. 41.
37 NCNA, 22 March 1970, in *SWB/FE/3337/A4/2*.
38 'Chinese on Secret "Arms for Arabs" Mission', *Daily Telegraph*,
26 August 1970; 'Chinese train Arabs', *Sunday Times*, 30 August 1970;
'Maoists Train Arab Units', *Free China Weekly*, vol. XI, no. 37 (13
September 1970), p. 2; *Egyptian Gazette*, 26 August 1970.
39 Paul Martin, 'Arab guerrillas look to China', *The Times*, 19 August
1970; Alain Bouc, 'Le soutien matériel de Pekin à la guérilla reste
d'une ampleur limitée', *Le Monde*, 27–8 September 1970.
40 Arafat's National Day Message to Chou En-lai, NCNA, 3 October 1970,
in *SWB/FE/3502/A4/1*.
41 'Soviet Revisionism Is Our Country's Most Dangerous and Most
Important Enemy', Outline of Education on Situation for Companies
(Lesson Two), *Reference Materials Concerning Education on Situation*,
no. 42 (Propaganda Division, Political Department, Kunming Military
Region, 2 April 1973), in *Issues and Studies*, vol. X, no. 9 (June 1974),
p. 98.
42 See address on the international situation by Teng Hsiao-p'ing, Vice
Premier and Chairman of the delegation of the PRC to the Sixth

Special Session of the United Nations General Assembly, 10 April
1974, in *PR*, supplement to no. 15 (12 April 1974), p. I.
43 *Reference Materials*, no. 42, in *Issues and Studies*, vol. x, no. 9 (June
1974), p. 99.
44 'The Great Victory of Chairman Mao's Revolutionary Diplomatic Line',
Lesson Two, *Reference Materials Concerning Education on Situation*,
no. 43 (4 April 1973), in *Issues and Studies*, vol. x, no. 9 (June 1974),
p. 105.
45 *Reference Materials*, no. 42, in *Issues and Studies*, vol. x, no. 9 (June
1974), p. 99.
46 *Ibid.*, pp. 101–2.
47 Speech by Politburo member Wang Hung-wen, 3 April 1974, in *PR*,
no. 15 (12 April 1974), p. 11. See also 'Acute Struggle Between Social
Revisionism and U.S. Imperialism Viewed from the October Mideast
War', *JMJP*, 4 January 1974, and Teng Hsiao-p'ing's address to the
United Nations, p. II.
48 *New York Times* and *Toronto Globe and Mail*, 5 October 1974.
49 'The Historical Current of the People's Revolution in the World is
Irresistible', Lesson One, *Reference Materials Concerning Education
on Situation*, no. 41 (30 March 1973), in *Issues and Studies*, vol. x,
no. 9 (June 1974), p. 95.
50 Hua Kuo-feng, 'Political Report to the 11th National Congress of the
Communist Party of China' (Delivered on 12 August and adopted on
18 August 1977), *PR*, no. 35 (26 August 1977), p. 40. See also 'Speech
by Huang Hua, Chairman of Chinese Delegation', *PR*, no. 41 (7 October 1977), p. 33, and interview with Vice Premier Li Hsien-nien,
Sunday Times, 27 March 1977.
51 '1976 in Review, Soviet Union Runs Into Snags in Middle East', *PR*,
no. 6 (4 February 1977), pp. 23–5. See also 'Soviet Social-Imperialism –
Most Dangerous Source of World War', *Hung Ch'i*, no. 7 (1977), in *PR*,
no. 29 (15 July 1977), pp. 4–10.
52 See interview with Ho Ying in *al-Jumhūriyya*, 4 January 1973.
53 Malcolm H. Kerr, 'Soviet Influence in Egypt, 1967–73', in Rubinstein,
Soviet and Chinese Influence in the Third World, pp. 100–2.
54 In his December 1971 Report on the International Situation, Chou
En-lai allegedly said: 'The Soviet revisionists do not fare well in the
Middle East. Egypt toppled Ali Sabri and Sudan crushed the *coup
d'état* machinated by the Soviet revisionists.' *Issues and Studies*, vol.
XII, no. 7 (January 1977), p. 116.
55 Kerr, 'Soviet Influence in Egypt', p. 102. See also 'China and the Arab
World' (3), *An-Nahar Arab Report*, vol. II, no. 44 (1 November 1971).
56 Kerr, 'Soviet Influence in Egypt', pp. 102–3.
57 'China Is Jubilant over Sadat Move', *New York Times*, 6 August 1972.
See also 'People of Egypt Cannot Be Bullied', *PR*, no. 30 (28 July
1972), pp. 15–16.
58 *Al-Jumhūriyya*, 4 and 11 January 1973.
59 Haykal's interview with Chou En-lai appeared in *al-Anwār*, 23 February
1973; his article on China's foreign policy was summarised by the
Middle East News Agency, 25 February 1973. Both were also published
in his book *Aḥādīth fī Āsiyā (Dialogues in Asia)* (Beirut: Dār al-Ma'ārif,
1973), pp. 33–171. For the Soviet reaction see, for example, Moscow
radio, 5 March 1973 and *Izvestiya*, 9 March 1973. See also 'Arab States
– China: A Friendly Dialogue', *An-Nahar Arab Report Backgrounder*,
vol. IV, no. 13 (26 March 1973).

60 *PR*, no. 39 (28 September 1973), pp. 4–5.
61 For example, Commentator, 'Firmly Support Egyptian and Syrian Resistance to Israeli Military Aggression', *JMJP*, 8 October 1973.
62 Ch'iao Kuan-hua on 26 September 1975, in *PR*, no. 40 (3 October 1975), p. 12.
63 For example, 'Angry Roar of the Egyptian People', *PR*, no. 13 (26 March 1976), pp. 11–14; Jen Ku-ping, 'The Egyptian People Cannot Be Crushed by Pressure or Abuse', *PR*, no. 14 (2 April 1976), pp. 15–18.
64 Middle East News Agency, 25 March 1976.
65 *Al-Ahrām*, 27 April 1976; *International Herald Tribune*, 22 and 26 April 1976.
66 *Al-Akhbār*, 19 and 28 April 1976; *Washington Post*, 25 April 1976.
67 For example, 'Major Gain Seen in China–Arab Ties', *New York Times*, 23 April 1976.
68 Chou En-lai's 1971 Report on the International Situation, p. 118, and 1973 Report, p. 121.
69 *PR*, no. 23 (7 June 1974), pp. 26–7.
70 D. L. Price, 'Stability in the Gulf: The Oil Revolution', *Conflict Studies*, no. 71 (May 1976), pp. 7, 10.
71 *Financial Times*, 25 March 1976; Price, 'Stability in the Gulf', pp. 10–11.
72 *Al-Ra'y al-'Ām* (Kuwait), 17 February 1969.
73 Sevinc Carlson, 'China's Urgent Need for Stability in the Middle East', *New Middle East*, no. 36 (September 1971), pp. 27–8.
74 For example, National Day greetings from Iranian revolutionaries, NCNA, 4 October 1970, in *SWB/FE/3501/A4/1*. See also NCNA, 8 August 1969, in *SWB/FE/3160/A4/1*, and NCNA, 15 March 1970, in *SWB/FE/3332/A4/1*.
75 Peking radio in Persian, 21 March 1966, in *SWB/FE/2126/A4/2*.
76 Sometimes they used both terms together but with clear distinction: 'The Persian Gulf (the Arabian Gulf).' See, for example, *Kuo-chi chih-shih (International Knowledge)*, no. 3 (Peking: Jen-min ch'u-pan she, 1972), pp. 56–9.
77 'U.S. Imperialist Plot to Stamp Out Palestinian People's Armed Struggle Will Never Be Realised', NCNA, 26 October 1969, in *SCMP*, no. 4528 (31 October 1969), p. 23.
78 *An-Nahar Arab Report*, vol. III, no. 8 (21 February 1972), p. 2.
79 8 January 1972, quoted in *Arab Report and Record 1972*, p. 10.
80 For example, 'Chinese Government Statement on Jordan', NCNA, 21 September 1970, in *SWB/FE/3489/A4/1–2*.
81 *'Ammān al-Masā* (Amman), 25 October 1971, according to Middle East News Agency and United Press International of the same day. See also *al-Ḥayāt*, 17 November 1971.
82 Statement by the General Administration of Telecommunications, NCNA, 28 June 1971, in *SWB/FE/3722/A4/1*. See also *SWB/ME/w628/B1*.
83 There are also some subtle changes of style in China's reference to 'Israeli Zionism'. Terms like 'a dagger thrust into the Arab hearts', 'tool of aggression', or 'running dog of U.S. imperialism', are now used less frequently than in the 1960s. The Chinese have also been careful not to endorse extremist Arab vituperations of Israel. For example, on 17 July 1969 NCNA quoted the Iraqi chargé d'affaires referring in an Iraqi National Day reception in Peking to 'the new Nazi expansionist Zionism' (*SWB/FE/3129/A4/1*). *Peking Review*,

however, reported on the same occasion mentioning only 'Zionism'. *PR*, no. 30 (25 July 1969), p. 4.

84 For example: 'Ch'iao Kuan-hua's Speech on Middle East Question', *PR*, no. 51 (17 December 1971), p. 9; 'Huang Hua's Speech on Palestine Question', *PR*, no. 48 (29 November 1974), p. 13.

85 Interview on 28 October 1971, *Asahi Shimbun*, 6 November 1971.

86 'Israel Beset with Crises', *News from Hsinhua News Agency* (London), no. 5570 (4 July 1973), p. 11.

87 Brecher, *Israel, the Korean War and China*, p. 105.

88 *International Herald Tribune*, 12–13 May 1973.

89 Moscow radio, 22 February 1972, in *Arab Report and Record 1972*, p. 98. See also Novosti dispatches by Pavel Demchenko on 3 August 1971 and by V. Katin on 10 August 1971; David Bonavia, 'Chinese linked to "Zionist plot"', *The Times*, 25 June 1970; and D. Volsky, 'Middle East Schemes of Peking', *New Times* (Moscow), no. 3 (22 January 1969), p. 16.

90 For example: Pierre Mendès-France, *Dialogues avec l'Asie d'Aujourd'hui* (Paris: Editions Gallimard, 1972), pp. 147, 150–1. See also Francesco Gozzano (who accompanied Pietro Nenni on his tour in China and participated in Nenni's talks with Chou En-lai and other Chinese leaders), 'China's Stand on the Middle East', *New Outlook*, vol. xv, no. 1 (1972), p. 41. On Rumanian attempts to mediate between China and Israel see, for example, *Christian Science Monitor*, 28 July 1971.

91 Associated Press, quoting Medici's report on his talks in China from *Il Globo* and *Il Populo* (Italy), 9 January 1973.

92 See his remarks in a symposium on China, its international position and its stand on the Middle East crisis, *al-Ahrām*, 28 April 1972.

93 This view was expounded in a speech allegedly made by Foreign Minister Ch'iao Kuan-hua in Tientsin in May 1975 and 'reproduced' in *Issues and Studies*, vol. xi, no. 12 (December 1975), pp. 93–108. Although there are doubts about the authenticity of this document, which had apparently been composed of several original statements and supplemented with fabrications, the comments on Israel basically conform to Peking's stand.

94 Analysing the conditions of an Arab–Israeli settlement, the Chinese have always insisted on complete Israeli withdrawal and restoration of the Palestinians' legitimate rights, but never mentioned the establishment of a Palestinian state. One recent exception, expressed indirectly, is in *PR*, no. 13 (31 March 1978), p. 24. Another is in a confidential speech allegedly delivered on 30 July 1977 by Foreign Minister Huang Hua. See *Issues and Studies*, vol. xiv, no. 1 (January 1978), p. 101. Parts of the speech, reproduced in full by *Issues and Studies* starting November 1977, seem fabricated.

95 Cf. Deidre M. Ryan, 'The Decline of the "Armed Struggle" Tactic in Chinese Foreign Policy', *Current Scene*, vol. x, no. 12 (December 1972).

96 Tang Tsou and Morton H. Halperin, 'Mao Tse-tung's Revolutionary Strategy and Peking's International Behavior', *American Political Science Review* (March 1965), pp. 94–5.

97 Cf. Bettie M. Smolansky and Oles M. Smolansky, 'Soviet and Chinese Influence in the Persian Gulf', in Rubinstein, *Soviet and Chinese Influence in the Third World*, p. 140.

98 The Egyptian authorities, for example, ordered the PFLOAG office in Cairo to close down and end its activities in Egypt by the end of

May 1972. See *An-Nahar Arab Report*, vol. III, no. 23 (5 June 1972), p. 4.
99 Price, 'Oman: Insurgency and Development', p. 7.
100 *Ibid.*
101 *An-Nahar Arab Report*, vol. II, no. 26 (25 June 1973), p. 2.
102 *Al-Kifāḥ* (Beirut), quoted by the Middle East News Agency, 10 May 1971. See also Tsai Ching-lang, *Chinese Communists' Support to Palestinian Guerrilla Organizations* (Republic of China: World Anti-Communist League, February 1973), p. 17.
103 Chou En-lai's 1973 Report on the International Situation, p. 121; see also p. 116.
104 'Iron Will of Palestinian People', *PR*, no. 28 (8 July 1977), p. 21.
105 Ankara radio, 12 December 1973, quoted in *China Topics*, no. 592 (January 1974). See also John Gittings, 'Popular rights, yes – terrorism, no', *Guardian*, 21 December 1973.
106 *New York Times*, 4 October and 22 November 1972. See also 'China's Stand on International Convention Against Taking Hostages', *PR*, no. 50 (10 December 1976), p. 32.
107 *New York Times*, 10 February 1971. Tanyug reported on 29 March 1971 that there had been complaints by the Palestinians of the slowness of Chinese aid. *SWB/FE/3648/A4/1*.
108 NCNA, 21 September 1971, in *SWB/FE/3793/A4/2–3*.
109 Interview in Voice of Palestine (Cairo), 15 January 1973, quoted in *Arab Report and Record 1973*, p. 23.
110 Editorial, 'Arab People's Just Struggle Will Triumph', *JMJP*, 5 June 1972, in *PR*, no. 23 (9 June 1972), p 10.
111 *PR*, no. 23 (7 June 1974), pp. 26–7.
112 *PR*, no. 43 (26 October 1973), pp. 11–12. See also 'China Accuses Superpowers on Mideast', *New York Times*, 25 October 1973.
113 *PR*, no. 44 (2 November 1973), pp. 5–11. The Chinese also refused to pay for it. *PR*, no. 49 (3 December 1976).
114 Not only the Arabs but reportedly also the United States persuaded the Chinese not to cast their veto. See Mohamed Heikal, *The Road to Ramadan* (London: Collins, 1975), pp. 249–50.
115 Ch'iao Kuan-hua in the Security Council, 23 October 1973, *News from Hsinhua News Agency*, no. 5712 (25 October 1973), pp. 3–6.
116 *News from Hsinhua News Agency*, no. 5714 (27 October 1973), pp. 3–5.
117 *PR*, no. 13 (31 March 1972), p. 4.
118 *JMJP* New Year editorial, 1 January 1974, in *PR*, no 1 (4 January 1974), and Teng Hsiao-p'ing's speech, p. II. See also 'China, the Mideast and the Oil Crisis', *Current Scene*, vol. XII, no. 4 (April 1974), pp. 13–17.

CONCLUSION

1 'On the New Democracy' (20 February 1940), *Selected Works of Mao Tse-tung*, vol. II, pp. 346–7.
2 See Jaan Pennar, *The U.S.S.R. and the Arabs, the Ideological Dimension 1917–1972* (London: C. Hurst, 1973).
3 Khrushchev and his successors considered that Egypt was following a 'non-capitalist path of development', and was 'building socialism'. See Schram and d'Encausse, *Marxism and Asia*, p. 89.
4 See also Lin Wei, 'Chairman Mao's Method of Appraising Situations',

Chung-kuo ch'ing-nien pao (China Youth), 1 February 1962, in *SCMP*, no. 2717 (11 April 1962), pp. 6–8.
5 Yeh Mang, 'Foreign Policy of New China', *SCCS*, no. 3 (20 January 1951), in *CB*, no. 65 (15 March 1951), p. 5.

APPENDIX II

1 Wang Yao-t'ien, *Kuo-chi mao-yi t'iao-yüeh ho hsieh-ting (International Trade Treaties and Agreements)* (Peking: Finance and Economic Publications, 1958), p. 116, quoted in James Chieh Hsiung, *Law and Policy in China's Foreign Relations, A Study of Attitudes and Practice* (New York: Columbia University Press, 1972), p. 392, n. 49.
2 Maḥmūd al-Marāgh, 'What in the Talks between Egypt and People's China', *Rūz al-Yūsuf*, 23 February 1970.
3 *Rūz al-Yūsuf*, 30 March 1970.
4 *Al-Akhbār*, 19, 28 April 1976.
5 See eight principles of foreign aid, *PR*, no. 34 (21 August 1964), p. 16.
6 Supplement to *PR*, no. 15 (12 April 1974), p. v.
7 At a banquet for a Yemeni visitor, 23 December 1976, in *SWB/FE/5400/A4/1*.

BIBLIOGRAPHY

The bibliography is divided into three parts: Chinese sources, Arabic sources, and Western or other sources. Listed are those which deal exclusively or predominantly with China's relations with or policy towards the Middle East. More general works have not been included unless they contribute, in my view, to a better understanding of China's Middle East policy.

CHINESE SOURCES

One of the myths this study has tried to dismiss is the suggestion that the Chinese had very limited knowledge of the Middle East. However, the numerous articles, commentaries, NCNA dispatches and even books on the Middle East which were published in China, particularly in the 1950s, indicate that the Chinese were not only greatly interested in Middle Eastern affairs but were also very well informed. These sources were extensively used in this study. One example is the periodical *Shih-chieh chih-shih* (*World Knowledge*). This was not merely China's main mouthpiece on foreign affairs in the 1950s but was also said to have been closely connected to the Ministry of Foreign Affairs, whose officials were on its editorial board, often writing semi-officially on foreign policy. Also used were several handbooks, both general and dealing with foreign affairs, which provided a rare chance to compare Chinese attitudes on the same issue over a span of time.

After the early 1960s Chinese-language publications on the Middle East began to disappear, ceasing almost entirely during the Cultural Revolution. The main sources for that period were China's daily press, radio broadcasts, and the New China News Agency (NCNA) dispatches. In the early 1970s there were first signs of renewed Chinese interest in publishing on foreign affairs, including the Middle East. The volumes of *Kuo-chi chih-shih* (*International Knowledge*) published since 1971 provide an example.

It has been impossible and impractical to list here all, or even the important, articles and commentaries on the Middle East in Chinese periodicals, let alone the daily press. Additional sources on China's Middle East policy are quoted throughout the study.

Chairman Mao Tse-tung's Important Talks with Guests from Asia, Africa and Latin America. Peking: Foreign Language Press, 1960.

Chang Pi. 'Lun Chung-tung, Chin-tung ti min-tsu tu-li chieh-fang yun-tung' ('Discussing the Middle East and Near East National Independence and Liberation Movement'), SCCS, no. 9 (8 March 1952), p. 9.

'Suo-wei "Chung-tung ssu-ling pu"' ('The So-called "Middle East Command"'), SCCS, no. 10 (15 March 1952), pp. 16–17.

Chao Li-hai. 'Su-i-she yun-ho wen-t'i yü kuo-chi fa' ('The Question of the

Suez Canal and International Law'), *Cheng-fa yen-chiu (Studies in Government and Law)*, no. 1 (February 1957), pp. 12–19.

China Supports the Arab People's Struggle for National Independence. Peking: the Chinese People's Institute of Foreign Affairs, 1958.

The Chinese People Firmly Supports the Arab People's Struggle Against Aggression. Peking: Foreign Language Press, 1967.

Chou I-liang. *Chung-kuo yü Ya-chou ko-kuo ho-p'ing yu-hao ti li-shih (History of the Peaceful and Friendly Relations Between China and the Asian Countries).* Shanghai: Jen-min ch'u-pan she, 1955.

Chou Nan. 'I-la-k'o kung-ho-kuo ti nei-cheng wai-chiao cheng-ts'e' ('Domestic and Foreign Policy of the Republic of Iraq'), *Kuo-chi wen-t'i yen-chiu (Studies of International Problems)*, vol. 1 (May 1959), pp. 19–31.

Chou T'ien-ch'ih. 'Lessons of the Arab War Against Aggression', *Hung Ch'i*, no. 13 (17 August 1967), pp. 51–7, English translation in *PR*, no. 37, 8 September 1967, pp. 22–6.

Chung-chin-tung lieh-kuo chih (Record of the Various Countries of the Middle and Near East). Peking: Shih-chieh chih-shih she, 1956.

Chung-hua kung-ho-kuo tui-wai kuan-hsi wen-chien chi (Collected Documents on the Foreign Relations of the People's Republic of China). Peking: Shih-chieh chih-shih ch'u-pan she, 1957.

Chung Lin. 'Chung-chin-tung kuo-chia ti min-tsu chieh-fang yun-tung' ('The National Liberation Movement of the Middle and Near Eastern Countries'), *SCCS*, no. 3 (5 February 1955), p. 14.

'Chung-tung, pei-Fei ho La-ting Mei-chou jen-min wei ho-p'ing erh tou-cheng' ('The People of the Middle East, North Africa and Latin America Fight for Peace'). *SCCS*, no. 8 (1 March 1952), p. 3.

Chung-tung wen-t'i wen-chien hui-pien (Collection of Documents Concerning the Middle East Problems). Peking: Shih-chieh chih-shih she, 1958.

Editorial. 'What Are the True National Interests of the Arab Peoples', *PR*, no. 12 (24 March 1959), pp. 6–9.

Fang Te-chao. *Su-i-she yun-ho ho Su-i-she yun-ho wen-t'i (The Suez Canal and the Suez Canal Problem).* Peking: Shih-chieh chih-shih she, 1957.

I An. 'Ai-chi kai-k'uang' ('General Situation in Egypt'), *SCCS*, no. 5 (5 March 1951), p. 14.

'Na-chi-pu fan-tung t'ung-chih hsia ti Ai-chi' ('Egypt Under Naguib's Reactionary Rule'), *SCCS*, no. 4 (20 February 1953), pp. 18–19.

I Hsin. *Hsin Chung-kuo ti wai-chiao (New China's Foreign Affairs).* Hong Kong: Nan-fang shu-tien yin, 1950.

'Kuan-yü Yu-t'ai-fu-kuo-chu-i' ('About Zionism'). *SCCS*, no. 1 (1 January 1953), p. 30.

Li En-ch'iu. 'Tzen-yang jen-shih tang-mu ti Chung-tung ching-shih' ('How to Understand the Current Situation in the Middle East'), *Chung-kuo ch'ing nien (China Youth)*, no. 15 (1 August 1958), pp. 2–4.

Li Ping. *Jen-shih wo-men ti shih-chieh (Recognise Our World).* Peking: Kung-jen ch'u-pan she, 1952.

Liu Ssu-mu. *Tzen-yang hsüeh-hsi kuo-chi shih-shih (How to Study Current International Affairs).* Peking: Shih-chieh chih-shih ch'u-pan she, 1951.

Mao Tse-tung ssu-hsiang wan-sui (Long Live Mao Tse-tung's Thought). n.p.: 1969.

Mei-Ying ch'in-lüeh chün-tui pi-hsü ch'e-ch'u Li-pan-nung ho Yüeh-tan (Anglo-American Aggressive Troops Must Withdraw from the Lebanon and Jordan). Peking: Shih-chieh chih-shih ch'u-pan she, 1958.

Mi Hsien-pi. *Ti-kuo-chu-i yü Su-i-she yun-ho (Imperialism and the Suez Canal).* Shanghai: Jen-min ch'u-pan she, 1957.

Min-tsu wen-t'i yen-chiu hui (Institute for the Study of Nationalities Problems). *Hui-hui min-tsu wen-t'i (Problems of the Chinese Muslims)*. Peking: Min-tsu ch'u-pan she, 1958.

Nan-k'ai ta-hsüeh li-shih hsi (Nankai University, History Department). 'Chung-tung jen-min ti min-tsu chieh-fang tou-cheng' ('The National Liberation Struggle of Middle East Peoples'). *Li-shih chiao-hsüeh (Historical Education)*, no. 8 (1 August 1958), pp. 2–19.

P'ei Min. 'Pa-le-ssu-tan wen-t'i' ('The Palestine Problem'), *SCCS*, no. 10 (20 May 1955), pp. 32–3.

Shao Tsung-han. 'Ch'in-lüeh che pei-p'o ch'e-ping i-hou ti Chung-tung hsing-shih' ('The Situation in the Middle East after the Forced Withdrawal of the Aggressors'), *SCCS*, no. 24 (20 December 1956), pp. 4–7.

Teng T'o. 'Mu-ch'ien Chung-tung hsing-shih' ('Current Situation in the Middle East'), *Hsüeh-hsi (Study)*, no. 15 (3 August 1958), pp. 2–8.

Tso-t'an (Symposium). 'Fan-tui Mei-Ying ch'in-lüeh che p'o-huai kuo-chi fa ho lien-ho-kuo hsien-chang ti tsui-hsing, Mei-Ying ch'iang-tao pi-hsü li-chi tsung Chung-tung kun-ch'u ch'ü' ('Resist the Criminal Act of Subverting International Law and the United Nations Charter by the Anglo-American Aggressors, Anglo-American Gangsters Must Withdraw Immediately from the Middle East'), *Cheng-fa yen-chiu (Studies in Government and Law)*, no. 4 (5 August 1958).

Wang Ch'ing. 'Mei-ti nu-i ti T'u-erh-ch'i' ('Turkey Under American Imperialist Enslavement'), *SCCS*, no. 17 (3 November 1951), pp. 19–20.

Wei Shen-san. 'Ying-Mei cheng-tuo Chung-tung shih-yu ti li-shih fa-chen' ('The Historical Development of Anglo-American Plunder of Middle Eastern Oil'), *SCCS*, no. 9 (5 May 1957), pp. 5–7.

Wei Tao-hsü. 'Chung-tung shih-yu tui hsi-Ou ching-chi ti ying-hsiang' ('The Effects of Middle Eastern Oil on the Economy of Western Europe'), *SCCS*, no. 24 (20 December 1956), pp. 9–10.

Yang Chen-ch'ien. *Hsi-nan Ya-chou (South-West Asia)*. Shanghai: Hsin chih-shih ch'u-pan she, 1957.

Yang Hsüeh-ch'un. 'Hsia-ai min-tsu-chu-i t'ung-chih hsia ti I-ssu-lieh' ('Israel Under the Rule of Narrow-Minded Nationalism'), *SCCS*, no. 9 (25 February 1953), pp. 19–20.

Yu Chao-li (pseud.). 'A New Upsurge of National Revolution', *Hung Ch'i*, no. 5 (1 August 1958), English translation in *PR*, no. 26 (26 August 1958).

'Imperialism Is the Sworn Enemy of Arab National Liberation', *Hung Ch'i*, no. 7 (1 April 1959), translated in *PR*, no. 14 (7 April 1959).

Yü Kuang. *Chung-tung feng-huo (The Middle East Ablaze)*. Hong Kong: Chao-yang ch'u-pan she, 1970.

Yuan Fang. 'Ya-chou jen-min fan-tui Mei-kuo p'in-ts'ou Chung-tung ch'in-lüeh chi-t'uan' ('Peoples of Asia Oppose the Rigging-Up of an Aggressive Bloc in the Middle East by the United States'), *SCCS*, no. 4 (20 February 1954), pp. 12–14.

ARABIC SOURCES

Arab sources on the PRC or on China's Middle East policy are rather meagre. This is but another evidence of the fact that the Middle East was far more important to China than China was to the Arabs. Usually, Arab interest in China grew in times of crisis, such as in the late 1950s and during the Sino-Indian conflagration in autumn 1962. In recent years there has been a growing Arab interest in China though not necessarily in its Middle

Eastern policy. As a result, several studies have been published, particularly in *al-Siyāsa al-Duwaliyya (International Politics)*, a scholarly monthly issued in Cairo. Information concerning China's relations with the Palestinians appears regularly in the annual volumes of the PLO Research Centre's *al-Yawmiyāt al-Filasṭiniyya (Palestinian Diary)*. Most useful were Arab newspapers and radio broadcasts, as well as several less known articles and books concerning China's policy in the Middle East.

Fatḥ, Ḥarakat al-Taḥrīr al-Watanī al-Filasṭīnī (Fataḥ, the Palestinian National Liberation Movement). *Dirāsāt wa Tajārib Thawriyya (Revolutionary Trials and Lessons)*, no. 4, al-Tajriba al-Ṣīniyya (The Chinese Experience). n.p.: 1967.

Hassouna, Mohamed Abdel Khalek (Ḥassūna, Muḥammad 'Abd al-Ḥāliq). *The First Asian–African Conference Held at Bandung, Indonesia (April 18–24, 1955)*, report submitted to the League of the Arab States' Council. Cairo: Imprimerie Misr, 1955.

Haykal, Muḥammad Ḥasanayn. *Aḥādīth fī Āsiyā (Dialogues in Asia)*. Beirut: Dār al-Ma'ārif, 1973.

Heikal, Mohamed (Haykal, Muḥammad). *Nasser, the Cairo Documents*. London: New English Library, 1973.

Al-Jamāl, 'Alī Ḥamdī. *Al-Nizā' bayn al-Hind wa 'l-Ṣīn (The Conflict between India and China)*. Cairo: Dār al-Qalām, 1964.

Munaẓẓamat al-Taḥrīr al-Filasṭīniyya (The Palestine Liberation Organisation). *Munaẓẓamat al-Taḥrīr al-Filasṭīniyya wa-Jumhūriyyat al-Ṣīn al-Sha'abiyya (The Palestine Liberation Organisation and the People's Republic of China)*. ?Cairo: ?1966.

Al-Nashāshībī, Nāṣir al-Dīn. *'Arabī fī 'l-Ṣīn (An Arab in China)*. Cairo: Dār al-Qalām, 1965.

Farra, Randa. 'The Chinese People's Republic and the Arab World', *Middle East Forum* (Beirut), no. 42 (Winter 1966), pp. 43–50.

Al-Ṣāḥib, Fu'ād. *'Irāqī fī 'l-Ṣīn al-Ḥamrā' (An Iraqi in Red China)*. Beirut: Dār al-Nahār li 'l-Nashar, 1969.

Salīm, Muḥammad al-Sayyid. 'Al-Ṣīn al-Sha'abiyya wa 'l-Qaḍiya al-Filasṭīniyya) ('People's China and the Palestinian Problem'), *Al-Siyāsa al-Duwaliyya (International Politics)*, vol. VIII, no. 25 (July 1971), pp. 58–83.

Sam'o, E. 'The Arab States and China's UN Representation', *Middle East Forum*, vol. XLVIII, no. 2 (Summer 1972), pp. 43–54.

Al-Shuqayrī, Aḥmad. *Min al-Qimma ilā 'l-Hazīma (From Zenith to Defeat)*. Beirut: Dār al-'Awda, 1971.

'Al-Ṣīn al-Sha'abiyya wa 'l-Qaḍiya al-Filasṭīniyya'. *Al-Hadaf* (Beirut), vol. VI, no. 271 (28 September 1974), pp. 15–18.

WESTERN AND OTHER SOURCES

Although the Middle East was for a long time considered to be of marginal importance in China's foreign policy, there is a fairly considerable amount of literature on China and the Middle East. In addition, China's Middle East policy has been dealt with indirectly in many other studies. Of the latter, only those which shed more light on China's relations with the Middle East have been included.

Adie, W. A. C. 'China and the Arabs: Applying the Maoist Formula', *Middle East International*, no. 42 (December 1974), pp. 7–9.

'China and the Bandung Genie', *Current Scene*, vol. III, no. 19 (15 May 1965).

'China and the Bandung Spirit', *Mizan*, vol. VIII, no. 1 (January–February 1966), pp. 2–14.

'China, Israel and the Arabs', *Conflict Studies*, no. 12 (May 1971), pp. 1–18.

'China, Russia and the Third World', *China Quarterly*, no. 11 (July–September 1962), pp. 200–14.

'China's Middle East Strategy', *The World Today*, vol. XXIII, no. 8 (August 1967), pp. 317–26.

'China's West Asian Strategies', in Ian Wilson (ed.), *China and the World Community*, pp. 179–99. Sydney: Angus and Robertson, 1973.

'Chou En-lai on Safari', in Roderick MacFarquhar (ed.), *China Under Mao: Politics Takes Command*, pp. 462–82. Cambridge, Mass.: MIT Press, 1966.

'The Communist Powers and the Middle East, Peking's Revised Line', *Problems of Communism*, vol. XXI, no. 5 (September–October 1972), pp. 54–68.

'The Middle East: Sino-Soviet Discords', *Survey*, no. 42 (January 1962), pp. 132–47.

Agwani, M. S. *Communism in the Arab East*. London: Asia Publishing House, 1969.

'The Reactions of West Asia and the UAR [to the Sino-Indian War]', *International Studies*, vol. V, nos. 1–2 (July–October 1963), pp. 75–9.

'The Soviet Union, China and West Asia', *International Studies*, vol. VI, no. 4 (April 1965), pp. 345–66.

Alkazaz, Aziz, and von der Decken, Klaus. 'Die Politik Chinas im Nahen und Mittleren Osten'. *Orient*, no. 1 (March 1972), pp. 11–26.

Allen, Robert Loring. *Middle Eastern Economic Relations with the Soviet Union, Eastern Europe, and Mainland China*. Charlottesville, Virginia: Woodrow Wilson Department of Foreign Affairs, University of Virginia, 1958.

Ben-Dak, J. D. 'China and Peace in the Middle East: A Proposal for Conflict Resolution', *Middle East Information Series*, vol. XVIII (April 1972), pp. 30–5.

'China in the Arab World', *Current History*, vol. LIX, no. 349 (September 1970), pp. 147–52.

Brecher, Michael. 'Israel and China: A Historic "Missed Opportunity"', in Michael Curtis and Susan A. Gitelson (eds.), *Israel and the Third World*, pp. 218–33. New Jersey: Transaction Books, 1976.

Israel, the Korean War and China: Images, Decisions and Consequences. Jerusalem: The Jerusalem Academic Press, 1974.

Carlson, Sevinc. 'China's Urgent Need for Stability in the Middle East', *New Middle East*, no. 36 (September 1971), pp. 25–31.

'The Explosion of a Myth – China, the Soviet Union and the Middle East: The Chinese Intrusion', *New Middle East*, no. 26 (December 1970), pp. 32–40.

Chen, F. T. 'Peiping and the Worsening Relations between Egypt and the Soviet Union', *Issues and Studies*, vol. IX, no. 1 (October 1972), pp. 13–16.

Chin Pao-chih. 'Mao's Plot in the Middle East', *Asian Outlook*, no. 6 (February 1971), pp. 42–6.

'China, the Arab World and Africa – A Factual Survey, 1959–1964'. *Mizan*. Special China Issue, London 1964.

'China and the Death of President Nasser'. *China News Summary*, no. 339 (1 October 1970), pp. B4–B5.

'China, the Mideast and the Oil Crisis'. *Current Scene*, vol. XII, no. 4 (April 1974), pp. 13–17.

'China and the Middle East and North Africa, July 1967–May 1970'. *China Topics*, no. 550 (16 June 1970), pp. 1–11.

'China – Opportunist Ally of the Arabs'. *China Topics*, no. 434 (29 June 1967), pp. 1–5.

'China's Middle East Overtures'. *Asian Analyst*, April 1970, pp. 14–18.

'Chinese Comment on the Middle East War'. *China Topics*, no. 436 (July 1967), pp. 1–9.

Cooley, John K. 'China and the Palestinians'. *Journal of Palestine Studies*, vol. I, no. 2 (Winter 1972), pp. 19–34.

    Green March, Black September, The Story of the Palestinian Arabs. London: Frank Cass, 1973.

Copper, John F. 'Chinese Objectives in the Middle East', *China Report*, no. 5 (January–February 1969), pp. 8–13.

Dadiani, L. 'Peking's Middle East Policy', *International Affairs* (May 1978), pp. 49–58.

Deutscher, Isaac. 'Moscow, Peking and Arab Nationalism', *Reporter*, no. 19 (4 September 1958), pp. 13–16.

Dunner, Johseph. 'Israel and the People's Republic of China', *Southeast Asian Perspectives*, no. 8 (December 1972), pp. 1–26.

Dutt, V. P. *China's Foreign Policy 1958–62.* London: Asia Publishing House, 1964.

Giniewski, P. 'La Chine et le Conflit du Moyen Orient', *International Spectator*, vol. XXVI, no. 12 (June 1972), pp. 1081–8.

Gittings, John. *Survey of the Sino-Soviet Dispute.* London: Oxford University Press, 1968.

    The World and China, 1922–1972. London: Eyre Methuen, 1974.

Gottlieb, G. 'China and the Middle East', *Middle East Information Series*, vol. XVIII (April 1972), pp. 2–10.

Gozzano, Francesco. 'China's Stand on the Middle East', *New Outlook*, vol. XV, no. 1 (1972), pp. 39–42.

Griffith, William E. (comp.). *The Sino-Soviet Rift.* Cambridge, Mass.: MIT Press, 1964.

Hacohen, David. 'Behind the Scenes of Negotiations between Israel and China'. *New Outlook*, vol. VI, no. 9 (1963), pp. 29–44.

    Yoman Burma (Burmese Diary). Tel Aviv: 'Am 'Oved, 1963 (in Hebrew).

Harris, Lilian Craig. 'China's Relations with the PLO', *Journal of Palestine Studies*, vol. VII, no. 1 (Autumn 1977), pp. 123–53.

'Heightened Chinese Interest in the Middle East'. *Middle East Economic Digest*, 30 October 1970.

Ismael, Tareq Y. 'The People's Republic of China and the Middle East', in Tareq Y. Ismael et al., *The Middle East in World Politics, A Study in Contemporary International Relations*, pp. 138–61. Syracuse, New York: Syracuse University Press, 1974.

Israeli, R. 'Sino-Arab Relations'. *Wiener Library Bulletin*, no. 22 (Autumn 1968), pp. 13–18.

Joffe, Ellis. 'China's Strategy and the Middle East', in Avigdor Levy (ed.), *The Arab–Israeli Conflict: Risks and Opportunities*, pp. 69–74. Tel Aviv: STRATIS, 1975.

Joyaux, François. 'La Politique Chinoise au Moyen Orient', *Orient*, no. 40 (4e trimestre 1966), pp. 25–46.

'Le Problème de la Palestine dans la Presse Chinoise', *Orient*, no. 38 (2e trimestre 1966), pp. 101–10.

'Les Minorités Musulmanes en Chine Populaire', *L'Afrique et l'Asie*, no. 68 (4e trimestre 1964), pp. 3–12.

'Les Musulmans de Chine et la Diplomatie de Pékin'. *L'Afrique et l'Asie*, no. 77 (1er trimestre 1967), pp. 17–24.

'Les Musulmans en Chine Populaire', *Notes et Etudes Documentaires*, no. 2915 (20 August 1962), p. 76.

Kahin, George McTurnan. *The Asian–African Conference, Bandung, Indonesia, April 1955*. Ithaca, New York: Cornell University Press, 1956.

Katz, Zeev. 'Sino-Soviet Conflict and the Arabs', *New Outlook*, vol. VII, no. 4 (1964), pp. 35–7.

Kerr, Malcolm H. 'The Middle East and China, the Scope and Limits of Convergent Interests', in A. M. Halperin (ed.), *Policies Toward China – View from Six Continents*, pp. 437–56. New York: McGraw-Hill, 1965.

Khalili, Joseph E. 'Communist China and the United Arab Republic', *Asian Survey*, vol. X, no. 4 (April 1970), pp. 309–19.

Communist China's Interaction with the Arab Nationalists Since the Bandung Conference. New York: Exposition Press, 1970.

'Sino-Arab Relations', *Asian Survey*, vol. IX, no. 8 (August 1968), pp. 678–90.

Khrushchev Remembers. With an introduction, commentary and notes by Edward Crankshaw. London: Sphere Books, 1971.

Khrushchev Remembers, the Last Testament. London: André Deutsch, 1974.

Kimche, David. *The Afro-Asian Movement, Ideology and Foreign Policy of the Third World*. Jerusalem: Israel Universities Press, 1973.

Klein, Sydney. 'China's Trade and Aid Relations with Africa and the Middle East, 1951–1966', *China Mainland Review*, vol. II, supplement (June 1967), pp. 357–68.

Kräuter, Uwe. 'Interview with the Mission of the PLO in Peking', *Eastern Horizon*, vol. XVI, no. 12 (December 1977), pp. 20–3.

Lang, Nicolas. 'Chinese Activities in the Middle East', *Est et Ouest*, 16 December 1965.

'Nasir, the U.S.S.R. and China', *Est et Ouest*, 16 November 1965.

Laqueur, Walter Z. *Communism and Nationalism in the Middle East*, 3rd edn. London: Routledge and Kegan Paul, 1961.

The Soviet Union and the Middle East. London: Routledge and Kegan Paul, 1959.

Larkin, Bruce D. *China and Africa 1949–1970*. Berkeley, California: University of California Press, 1971.

Lee, Christopher D. 'Soviet and Chinese Interest in Southern Arabia', *Mizan*, vol. XIII, no. 1 (August 1971), pp. 35–47.

Lowenthal, Richard. 'China', in Zbigniew Brzezinski (ed.), *Africa and the Communist World*, pp. 142–203. Stanford, California: Stanford University Press, 1963.

'Chinas Rolle im Nahen Osten', in Erik von Groeling and Marie-Luise Näth (eds.), *Die Aussenpolitik Chinas*, pp. 309–16. Munich: R. Oldenbourg Verlag, 1975.

'Mao Tse-Tung's Thought Taints the Middle East'. *Chinese Communist Affairs: Facts and Features*, vol. I, no. 17 (12 June 1968), pp. 5–7.

'Maoists Train Arab Units'. *Free China Weekly*, vol. XI, no. 37 (13 September 1970), p. 2.

Ma'oz, Moshe. 'Soviet and Chinese Influence on the Palestinian Guerrilla Movement', in Alvin Z. Rubinstein (ed.), *Soviet and Chinese Influence in the Third World*, pp. 109–30. New York: Praeger, 1975.

'Soviet and Chinese Relations With the Palestinian Guerrilla Organisations', *Jerusalem Papers on Peace Problems* (The Leonard Davis Institute for International Relations, the Hebrew University of Jerusalem), no. 4 (March 1974), pp. 5–34.

Masannat, G. S. 'Sino-Arab Relations', *Asian Survey*, vol. vi, no. 4 (April 1966), pp. 216–26.

Medzini, Meron. 'China and the Arab–Israeli Conflict', in Ch. Boasson (ed.), *The Changing International Community*. The Hague, 1974.

'China and the Palestinians – A Developing Relationship?', *New Middle East*, no. 32 (May 1971), pp. 34–7.

'Chinese Penetration in the Middle East', *New Outlook*, vol. vi, no. 9 (1963), pp. 16–28.

'Israel and China: A Missed Opportunity?', *Wiener Library Bulletin*, vol. xxv, nos. 20–1 (October 1971), pp. 33–42.

'Peiping and the Middle East: Ideology vs. Expediency', *Issues and Studies*, vol. vii, no. 11 (August 1971), pp. 40–52.

'Reflections on Israel's Asian Policy', in Michael Curtis and Susan A. Gitelson (eds.), *Israel and the Third World*, pp. 200–11. New Jersey: Transaction Books, 1976.

Mendès-France, Pierre. *Dialogues avec l'Asie d'Aujourd'hui*. Paris: Editions Gallimard, 1972.

'The Middle East: Soviet Anxieties', *Mizan*, vol. ix, no. 4 (July–August 1967), pp. 146–52.

Mon'im, Nasser-Eddine [Mun'im, Nāṣir al-Dīn]. *Arab–Chinese Relations (With Special Emphasis on Egyptian–Chinese Relations) 1950–1971*. Beirut: The Arab Institute for Research and Publishing, n.d.

Munthe-Kass, Harold. 'China–Middle East, No Time for Peace', *Far Eastern Economic Review*, 13 August 1970, p. 8.

Nahumi, Mordehai. 'China and Israel', *New Outlook*, vol. ix, no. 6 (1966), pp. 40–8.

'The Tactics of China's Enmity for Israel', *Israel Horizon*, vol. xiv (August–September 1966), pp. 7–10.

Namir, Mordecai. *Shliḥut be-Mosqva, Yeraḥ Dvash ve-Shnot Za'am (Israeli Mission in Moscow)*. Tel Aviv: 'Am 'Oved, 1971 (in Hebrew).

Neuhauser, Charles. *Third World Politics, China and the Afro-Asian People's Solidarity Organization*. Cambridge, Mass.: Harvard East Asian Monographs, 1968.

Nieh, Yu-hsi. 'Das Chinesische-ägyptische Militärabkommen', *China Aktuell*, vol. v, no. 5 (1976), pp. 277–80.

Ogunsanwo, Alaba. *China's Policy in Africa 1958–71*. Cambridge University Press, 1974.

Pauker, Guy J. 'The Rise and Fall of Afro-Asian Solidarity', *Asian Survey*, vol. v, no. 9 (September 1965), pp. 425–32.

'Peiping Jeopardizes Peace in the Middle East', *Issues and Studies*, vol. vii, no. 2 (November 1970), pp. 1–4.

'Peking and the Middle East', *China Reporting Service*, no. 7 (1 April 1970), pp. 1–2.

'Peking's Bid for Influence in the UAR', *China News Summary*, no. 326 (2 July 1970), pp. B1–B2.

'La Pénétration Chinoise en Syrie', *Revue Militaire Générale*, no. 4 (April 1966), pp. 541–4.

Perera, Judith. 'Chinese–Arab Relations: No Change Expected', *The Middle East*, November 1976, pp. 10–13
Raddock, D. M. 'Russia, China and the Arab–Israeli Conflict: A Study of Sino-Soviet Third World Politics'. Unpublished M.A. dissertation, Columbia University, 1970.
Rhee, T. 'The Sino-Soviet Conflict and the Middle East', *New Outlook*, vol. XIII, no. 7 (1970), pp. 20–4.
Richer, Philippe. *La Chine et le Tiers Monde*. Paris: Payot, 1971.
Robinson, Thomas W. 'Peking's Revolutionary Strategy in the Developing World: The Failures of Success', *Annals of the American Academy of Political and Social Science*, no. 386 (November 1969), pp. 64–77.
Rondot, Pierre. 'Le Petit Livre Rouge dans les Pays du Coran'. *Projet*, no. 40 (December 1969).
Roucek, J. 'Communist China's Penetration of the Middle East', *Ukrainian Quarterly*, no. 26 (Summer 1970), pp. 149–63.
Schleifer, Abdulla. 'La Percée Chinoise au Proche-Orient', *Jeune Afrique*, no. 537 (20 April 1971), pp. 40–1.
Schram, Stuart R. and d'Encausse, Hélène Carrère. *Marxism and Asia*. London: Allen Lane, The Penguin Press, 1969.
'L'U.R.S.S. et la Chine devant la Révolution Turque', *Orient*, no. 14 (1960).
Shamir, Shimon, and Confino, Michael (eds.), *The U.S.S.R. and the Middle East*. Jerusalem: Israel Universities Press, 1973.
Shichor, Yitzhak. 'The Palestinians and China's Foreign Policy', in Chün-tu Hsüeh (ed.), *Dimensions of China's Foreign Relations*, pp. 156–90. New York: Praeger, 1977.
Shimoni, Yaacov. 'Israel and the People's Republic of China', in Michael Curtis and Susan A. Gitelson (eds.), *Israel and the Third World*, pp. 212–17. New Jersey: Transaction Books, 1976.
Shub, Louis. 'China–Israel', *Jewish Affairs Background Reports* (The University of Judaism, Center for Study of Contemporary Jewish Life), vol. I, no. 3 (October 1972).
Smolansky, Bettie M. and Smolansky, Oles M. 'Soviet and Chinese Influence in the Persian Gulf', in Alvin Z. Rubinstein (ed.), *Soviet and Chinese Influence in the Third World*, pp. 131–53. New York: Praeger, 1975.
Ting Kuang-hua. 'Peiping and the Middle East', *Chinese Communist Affairs*, vol. IV, no. 6 (December 1967), pp. 23–5.
'Peiping's Infiltration of the United Arab Republic', *Chinese Communist Affairs*, vol. IV, no. 5 (October 1967), pp. 49–56.
Tretiak, Daniel. 'Is China Preparing to "Turn Out"?: Changes in Chinese Levels of Attention to the International Environment', *Asian Survey*, vol. XI, no. 3 (March 1971), pp. 219–37.
Trevelyan, Humphrey. *The Middle East in Revolution*. London: Macmillan, 1970.
Tsai Ching-lang. *Chinese Communists' Support to Palestinian Guerrilla Organizations*. Taipeh: World Anti-Communist League, February 1973.
Tsou, Tang and Halperin, Morton 'Mao Tse-tung's Revolutionary Strategy and Peking's International Behavior', *American Political Science Review*, March 1965, pp. 80–99.
US Congress, House of Representatives, Committee on Foreign Affairs, Subcommittee on the Middle East, Hearing. *A Sino-Soviet Perspective in the Middle East*. 92nd Congress, 2nd Session, 1972.
Van Ness, Peter. *Revolution and Chinese Foreign Policy*. Berkeley, California: University of California Press, 1971.

Volsky, D. 'Middle East Schemes of Peking', *New Times*, no. 3 (22 January 1969), pp. 15–16.

Watt, D. C. 'The Persian Gulf – Cradle of Conflict?', *Problems of Communism*, vol. xxi, no. 3 (May–June 1972), pp. 32–40.

Weinstein, Franklin B. 'The Second Asian–African Conference: Preliminary Bouts', *Asian Survey*, vol. v, no. 7 (July 1965), pp. 359–73.

Wheeler, G. 'Soviet and Chinese Policies in the Middle East', *The World Today*, vol. xxii, no. 2 (February 1966), pp. 64–78.

Woodman, Dorothy, 'China and the Arabs', *New Statesman*, no. 69 (23 April 1965), p. 630.

Yodfat, Aryeh. 'China and the Middle East', *International Problems*, vol. xv, no. 1–2 (Spring 1976), pp. 16–25 (in Hebrew).

'People's China, the Sino-Soviet Conflict, and the Arab Countries', *Molad*, no. 21 (August–September 1971), pp. 208–18 (in Hebrew).

Zagoria, Donald. *The Sino-Soviet Conflict 1956–61*. New York: Atheneum, 1966.

INDEX

Abbās, Ferḥat, 99
Abū ʿAmār, see Arafat, Yasser
Abū Ḥamad, Khalīl, 176
Abū Jihād, see al-Wazīr, Khalīl
Abū Luṭf, see Qaddūmī, Fārūq
Aden, 75, 117, 151–4 *passim*
Afghanistan, 18, 22, 29, 53
Africa, 99; Chinese interest, 4, 7, 12, 13, 15, 16, 76, 97, 148; and PRC's Middle East policy, xii, 2, 28, 47, 166; Soviet threat to, 5, 121, 145, 160
Afro-Asian People's Solidarity Organisation, 80, 97–8, 121, 135
Aghā, Muṣṭafā, 127–9, 239 n. 79
agreements, 87, 102; cease-fire, 149, 186; cultural, 42–4, 47, 102; dis-engagement, 169, 171; economic, 32, 74, 42–4, 47, 104, 109–10, 114, 203–4; military, 170; Paris Peace, 162; scientific and techni-cal, 82, 109–10; Sudan, 30; Suez Canal Evacuation, 31
Aḥmad, Imām, 104
aid, 60, 61, 113, 168, 205–7; Egypt, 49–50, 109–10, 114, 124, 138, 169–70, 205–6, 241 n. 124; Iraq, 102, 172; nuclear, 109, 236 n. 15; PDRY, 151–2, 172, 206, 207; PFLOAG, 154; PFLP, PDFLP, 157; PLO, 124, 141, 144, 159; Syria, 114, 124, 150–1, 171; Yemen, 82, 114, 171, 205–6, 207
Algeria, 71, 98, 111, 117, 122–3
All-China Students' Federation, 59
ʿĀmir, ʿAbd al-Ḥakīm, 46, 111, 224 n. 42
Anglo-Egyptian Treaty (1936), 14, 30
Anglo-Iranian Oil Company, 29
Arab communism, 3, 4, 31, 32, 87–8; PRC attitude towards, 8, 17,

76–8, 81, 82, 106, 126, 128, 234 n. 90; USSR criticised by, 136–7
Arab–Israeli conflict, 140–1, 144, 149, 150; Chinese attitude, (impartiality), 33–5, 36, 51–5, 57–9, (pro-Arab), 114–16, 151, 154, 170–1, (back to moderation), 180, 185–8, 247 n. 94; wars, (1948) 34–5, 225 n. 69, 227 n. 99, (1956) 38, 50, 58–9, 66, (1967) 126, 129, 132–6, (1973) 164, 167–9, 184–8; see also Israel, UN, US, USSR
Arab League, 51, 52, 76; Chinese criticism of, 34–5, 219 n. 81; recognises Taiwan, 27
Arab Socialist Union, 127, 168
Arab summit conferences, 116, 138
Arabian Peninsula, 15, 151, 152, 153, 164, 177
Arafat, Yasser, 117, 149, 158–9, 184, 237 n. 40
ʿĀrif, ʿAbd al-Salām, 111
armed struggle, 16, 17–18, 60, 125–6, 152, 180–1, 187; Palestinian, 116, 118, 119, 142, 155–6, 188
arms deals, 62; Egypt, 38, 41–2, 45–7, 61; Syria, 150, 224 n. 43; Palestinians, 159
al-Asad, Ḥāfiẓ, 151, 184
Asian–African Conference (Bandung 1955), 9, 20, 31, 35, 40–1, 74, 76, 121; Israel's exclusion, 27, 51; USSR's exclusion, 62, 68, 227 n. 112
Asian–African Conference (Algeria 1965), 107, 109, 111, 119, 124–5; Arab attitude towards, 121–2, 129; and USSR's participation, 123, 239 n. 66
Asian–African Economic Seminar, 121–2